AF544734

THE FINEST IN CONTEMPORARY INTERNATIONAL ART & ILLUSTRATION

BEYOND ILLUSTRATION

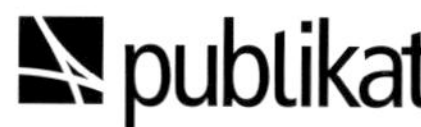

BEYOND ILLUSTRATION

THE FINEST IN CONTEMPORARY INTERNATIONAL ART & ILLUSTRATION

First published in 2009 by:
Publikat Verlags- und Handels GmbH & Co. KG
Hauptstraße 204
D - 63814 Mainaschaff
Tel: +49 (0) 60 21 / 900 40 - 0
Fax: +49 (0) 60 21 / 900 40 - 20
info@publikat.de
http://www.publikat.de

Concept Patrick Hartl I Yvonne Winkler I Michael Matthias I Daniel Schüßler
Design and Layout 2009 Patrick Hartl I Yvonne Winkler
http://www.beyond-illustration.com
http://www.castlemagazine.de

ISBN: 978-3-939566-26-7

Printed and bound in China.

» ACCORDING TO THE CLASSICAL DEFINITION ILLUSTRATION IS REGARDED AS A SERVICE. IT SERVES A CUSTOMER AND HIS TEXT. ON THE OTHER HAND IN ART THE CREATOR IS HIS OWN CUSTOMER. USING THE VARIOUS VIEWS AND POSITIONS OF INVITED ARTISTS AND ILLUSTRATORS WE WILL TRY TO DISCUSS THIS PHENOMENON.

PATRICK HARTL & YVONNE WINKLER | CASTLEMAGAZINE.DE

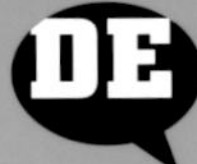

KUNST IST, EINEN PUDDING AN DIE WAND ZU NAGELN.

End of Painting

„Bang-bang-bang-bang-bang", fünf Schüsse aus einem Revolver, abgegeben von einem Westernhelden. Wir sehen ihn von hinten. Der Raum ist ziemlich leer, von rechts weht ein Stück Vorhang ins Bild. An der Wand befindet sich ein großer Spiegel, der Schütze steht davor, breitbeinig, in Duellantenpose. Gemeinsam mit ihm fokussieren wir das anvisierte Ziel. Es ist sein eigenes Spiegelbild, schwer durchlöchert. Die Anzahl der abgegebenen Schüsse lesen wir an den Treffern im Spiegel ab. Der noch in der Luft hängende Schmauch deutet an, dass sich diese Szene eben erst ereignet hat. Auf der imaginärenTonspur hallt der Knall der Feuerwaffe nach. Westernkenner wissen: Da ist noch eine Kugel im Lauf. Wie geht die Szene weiter? Ist der sechste Schuss schon gefallen, wird er nur von den Schmauchwolken verdeckt?

Das beschriebene Bild, entstanden 1984, stammt von dem amerikanischen Künstler Mark Tansey. Es hat viele Eigenschaften, die es auch als klassische Romanillustration ausweisen könnten: sehr erzählerisch gehalten, mit einer gekonnten Lichtführung, die atmosphärische Dichte erzeugt und eine reale Raumsituation nachbildet. Die Arbeit brilliert durch handwerkliches Können, erkennbar am Einsatz der malerischen Mittel zur Erzeugung illusionistischer Täuschungen. Und der „Retrolook" des Malstils erinnert an Illustrationen der 30er- und 40er-Jahre. Das Bild könnte also durchaus einem Westernroman entnommen sein. Dennoch ist es keine Illustration, sondern Kunst.

Der Titel des Werks lautet End of Painting, womit sich Tansey auf Arthur C. Dantos Thesen vom „Ende der Kunst" durch und mit Erreichen der Postmoderne bezieht, die so manchen Künstler in Verwirrung und Ratlosigkeit gestürzt hat. Tanseys Held zerschießt einen Spiegel, zerstört damit sein Spiegelbild. Nur: In Wahrheit ist es nie sein Spiegelbild gewesen. Denn dieser Cowboy existiert lediglich als Rückansicht, ist nichts als Fläche. Seine gespiegelte Vorderseite wäre nichts weiter als Leinwand. Bei genauer Betrachtung stellt man fest, dass eine kleine, aufklappbare Kinoleinwand der Malgrund ist. Wir blicken auf eine Projektionsfläche unserer Sehnsüchte – Cowboymythos –, projiziert auf eine Kinoleinwand, die eine Projektion seiner selbst (Spiegelbild) zerstört. Zu dem sich in der bildlichen Repräsentation ankündigenden Scherbenhaufen kommt es dennoch nicht, denn in Bildern steht die Zeit still. Tansey untersucht und nimmt Abbildungen sowie die Möglichkeiten und Unmöglichkeiten der Malerei auseinander, was sich durch sein gesamtes Werk zieht. Tansey betrat die Welt der Kunst zu einem Zeitpunkt, als die Moderne bereits alle Mythen der klassischen Malerei zerstört hatte und die seit Jahrhunderten tradierte illusionistische Malerei obsolet erscheinen ließ. Das Vorfinden der Tradition als Trümmerhaufen muss für viele Künstler der letzten 50 Jahre irritierend gewesen sein und machte neue Strategien für den Umgang mit der Kunst erforderlich. Mark Tansey genießt das Anfertigen von Bildern, und die Freude an der gegenständlichen

Abbildung spricht aus seinen Arbeiten. Die Erfahrung, dass die mimetische Repräsentation in der Kunst wertlos geworden, ja dass selbst das Ringen um Schönheit der Kunstwelt suspekt ist, muss für einen naturalistisch arbeitenden Künstler wie ihn schmerzlich sein. Tanseys Antwort darauf sind Bilder, die mit eigentlich als überholt geltenden, illustrativ anmutenden Mitteln der Malerei alle aktuellen Theorien der Ästhetik und Semiotik hinterfragen. Er zählt damit zu den Künstlern, die sich im Zuge einer Vorwärtsverteidigung mit der „Malerei über Malerei" auseinandersetzen.

End of Illustration – die wollen doch nur spielen

Diese Lust an der Erstellung von Bildern unter Rückgriff auf den Abbildungscharakter der illusionistischen Zeichnerei und Malerei ist sicherlich allen Illustratoren gemein, wobei die hier versammelte Riege junger Bilderzeuger keine Ausnahme ist. Aber ihre Generation trägt heute an der Last einer breiten medialen Bilderflut, wie sie der Kunstwelt noch nie zuvor zur Verfügung gestanden hat – ein Fundus, der verarbeitet, verhackstückt, gesampelt und neu zusammengesetzt werden will. Beim Durchblättern des vorliegenden Buchs und beim Lesen der Statements ahnt man, dass in der Welt der Illustration seit einiger Zeit eine ähnliche Verunsicherung herrscht wie vor Jahrzehnten in der Kunst. Die hier gezeigten Arbeiten sind überwiegend ohne Auftragsdruck entstanden, erfreuen den Betrachter durch ein hohes Maß an Einfallsreichtum, stilistischer Vielfalt, formaler Qualität und verspielter Leichtigkeit – und dennoch lösen sie scheinbar kleine Sinnkrisen in ihren ambitionierten Machern aus. Künstler fragen sich seit Anbruch der Postmoderne, was und wie sie überhaupt noch malen können. Diese Frage war für den Illustrator bisher nicht relevant, wurde ihm das Was und das Wie doch stets vorgegeben. Die Verunsicherung geht darauf zurück, dass diese Zeichner und Maler ihre Bilderlust nun auch ohne Auftrag ausleben. Aber ist ein Bild ohne Auftrag und ohne inhaltlichen Bezug zu einem Text überhaupt noch eine Illustration? Oder wird ein Werk durch die Loslösung von äußeren Zwängen nicht automatisch zu Kunst? Sind wir nun am „Ende der Illustration"? Sicher nicht. Aber die Frage ist vertrackt, führt sie doch direkt zur Mutter aller Fragen: Was ist Kunst? Seit mehr als 2.000 Jahren haben Philosophen und Künstler dieses Thema diskutiert und eine Vielzahl ästhetischer Theorien entwickelt. Nun setzen sich auch Illustratoren mit der Frage auseinander.

Eine umfassende Antwort haben sie noch nicht gefunden, ihre Lust am Spiel mit Bildern ist aber zu erkennen. Was fehlt ist Selbstreflexion. Gebetsmühlenartig wird wiederholt, dass auch in der Renaissance jede Kunst Auftragskunst war, woraus sie folgern, dass jeder Illustrator wohl auch Künstler ist. Übersehen wird dabei, dass in den vergangen 500 Jahren diverse radikale Umbrüche vollzogen wurden. Eine künstlerische Position benötigt zunächst Orientierung, die eine Standortortbestimmung erst ermöglicht. Daraus kann dann ein eigener künstlerischer Ansatz entstehen – einer, der den ganzen medialen Bilderschrott, der uns täglich zu erdrücken droht, nicht nur gefällig arrangiert, sondern so bearbeitet, dass sich dem Betrachter neue Erkenntnismöglichkeiten eröffnen. Es könnten Bilder entstehen, die ein geschlossenes und schlüssiges Zeichensystem bilden und eine neue Sprache sprechen; Bilder, die sich dem Verstehen entziehen – und das nicht, weil es nichts zu verstehen gibt, sondern weil das Verstehen Reifezeit erfordert; Bilder, die hinter der schicken Form noch Gedanken und Ideen enthüllen. Wenn uns die Bilder selbst etwas erzählen und uns nicht übersättigt, sondern satt zurücklassen, haben die Illustratoren die Grenze zur Kunst zumindest touchiert.

Prof. Mike Loos, Januar 2009

Mike Loos, Jahrgang 1964, ist Professor für visuelle Kommunikation an der Hochschule Augsburg | Fakultät für Gestaltung.

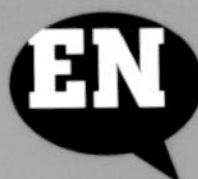

ART IS NAILING THE PUDDING TO THE WALL.

End of Painting

»Bang-bang-bang-bang-bang« -- five revolver shots, fired by the hero of a Western. We see him from behind. The room is almost empty; on the right, part of a curtain blows into the frame. There's a large mirror on the wall, the gunman stands right in front of it, wide-legged, posing for a duel. We zoom in on the focused target with him. It is his own mirror image, already perforated. We can count the number of shots from the holes in the mirror. From the smoke hanging in the air, we know it happened just moments ago.If the picture had an audio track, we could probably still hear the echo of the shots Experts know: there is always one more bullet in the barrel. Will the scene keep going? Or has the sixth shot already been fired, and we just don't see it because of all the smoke?
This image was created in 1984 by the American artist Mark Tansey. It displays many of the features that could characterize it as a classic novel illustration: it tells a story; it purposefully uses light and shadows to create atmospheric intensity; it recreates a realistic spatial setting. The work indulges in the brilliance of its own craftsmanship, using it to create its trompe-l'oeil. The painting's "retro" style is reminiscent of illustrations from 1930s and 40s – the image could have been taken from a Western novel. And yet, it is not an illustration – it is art. The title of the work is "End of Painting." Tansey thus refers to Arthur C. Danto's thesis that art history has ended with postmodernism, which results in many artists being confused and disorientated about the status of their work. Tansey's hero shoots the mirror to pieces, destroying – in the process – his own mirror image. But it is worth noting that it has never been his mirror image. Because this cowboy exists only as someone painted from behind – he is nothing but surface, and his front side, which should have been the object of reflection, is nothing but canvas Careful examination reveals that the color has been applied onto a small, folding projection screen. In fact, we are looking at the image of our own dreams and desires – the myth of the cowboy – projected onto a movie screen which destroys a projection of itself (its mirror image). Nevertheless, the ensuing ruin of pictorial representation will not come to its end; Because pictures stand outside of time. Tansey examines and dissects representation and the possibilities and paradoxes of painting, a thread that runs through his entire oeuvre. Tansey entered the art world at a time when modernity had already destroyed every myth of classical painting and had made centuries-old illusionistic painting obsolete. It must have been a disconcerting experience over the past fifty years for artists to encounter the rubble of tradition which called for new artistic strategies. Mark Tansey relishes the creation of images. His enjoyment of representational art speaks through his works. The realization that mimetic representation in the arts has become worthless – that even wrestling with beauty has become suspect in the art world – must be painful for someone who intrinsically wants to "present" things in illusionistic manner and must be all the more painful for someone who is adequately talented to realize this artistic vision. Tansey

responds by painting images that call into question all those recent aesthetic and semiotic theories precisely by employing purportedly obsolete, seemingly illustrative means of painting. He belongs to the group of artists who engage in forward defense by exploring the possibilities of "painting about painting."

End of Illustration – They Just Want to Have Fun

This enjoyment of producing images by taking recourse to the representational qualities of illusionistic painting and drawing is shared by all illustrators – the young image producers assembled here are no exception. But their generation carries the burden of a pervasive flood of images never before available to the world of art – an archive to be sampled, digested, and recombined; an archive to be reckoned with. While looking at this book and reading the various statements, you will notice that the world of illustration today has been rattled in the same way as was the world of art in previous decades. Most of the works showcased here were not commissions; they excite the viewer with their inventiveness, the scope of their styles, their formal accomplishment and their playfulness; and yet, they incite in their creators only crises of identity and meaning. Ever since the advent of postmodernity, artists wonder what is left for them to paint, and how (Gerhard Richter). Thus far, illustrators were sheltered from this anxiety as both the What and the How were decided for them. Their anxiety comes from the fact that these illustrators and painters realize their creative energies without commissions. But can an unsolicited image that does not refer to a textual source even be called an illustration? Doesn't a work automatically become art when it gains its independence from external constraints? Have we reached the "end of illustration"? Surely not. But the question may be more complex than it seems, and it leads to the mother of all questions: what is art? For more than 2,000 years, philosophers and artists have discussed this matter and developed a plethora of aesthetic theories. They are now joined by illustrators posing similar questions.

Their own answers are still in the making, but the pleasure they derive from toying with images is apparent. What is lacking is self-reflection. In their statements, the contention is repeated time and again that even in the Renaissance, art was always solicited and that every illustrator is thus an artist. This does not take into account that over the past 500 years several major breaks have occurred. Every artistic position is in need of a frame of reference that allows for its own coordinates to be determined. Only then can a genuine artistic approach emerge – an approach that will not only pleasurably arrange the rubble of images that the media delivers on a daily basis, but an approach that engages with it in a way that opens up new epistemic avenues to the viewer. This can engender images that form their own coherent and convincing sign system and speak their own language; images that will never be fully understood – not because there is nothing to understand, but because interpretation needs time to mature; images that reveal true thoughts and ideas. If these images themselves have something to tell us, and do not leave us bloated but satisfied, then illustrators have at least touched the border to art.

Prof. Mike Loos, January 2009

Mike Loos, year 1964, is professor for visual communication at the University of Applied Science Augsburg | Design Department.

BEYOND ILLUSTRATION

FEATURED ARTISTS:

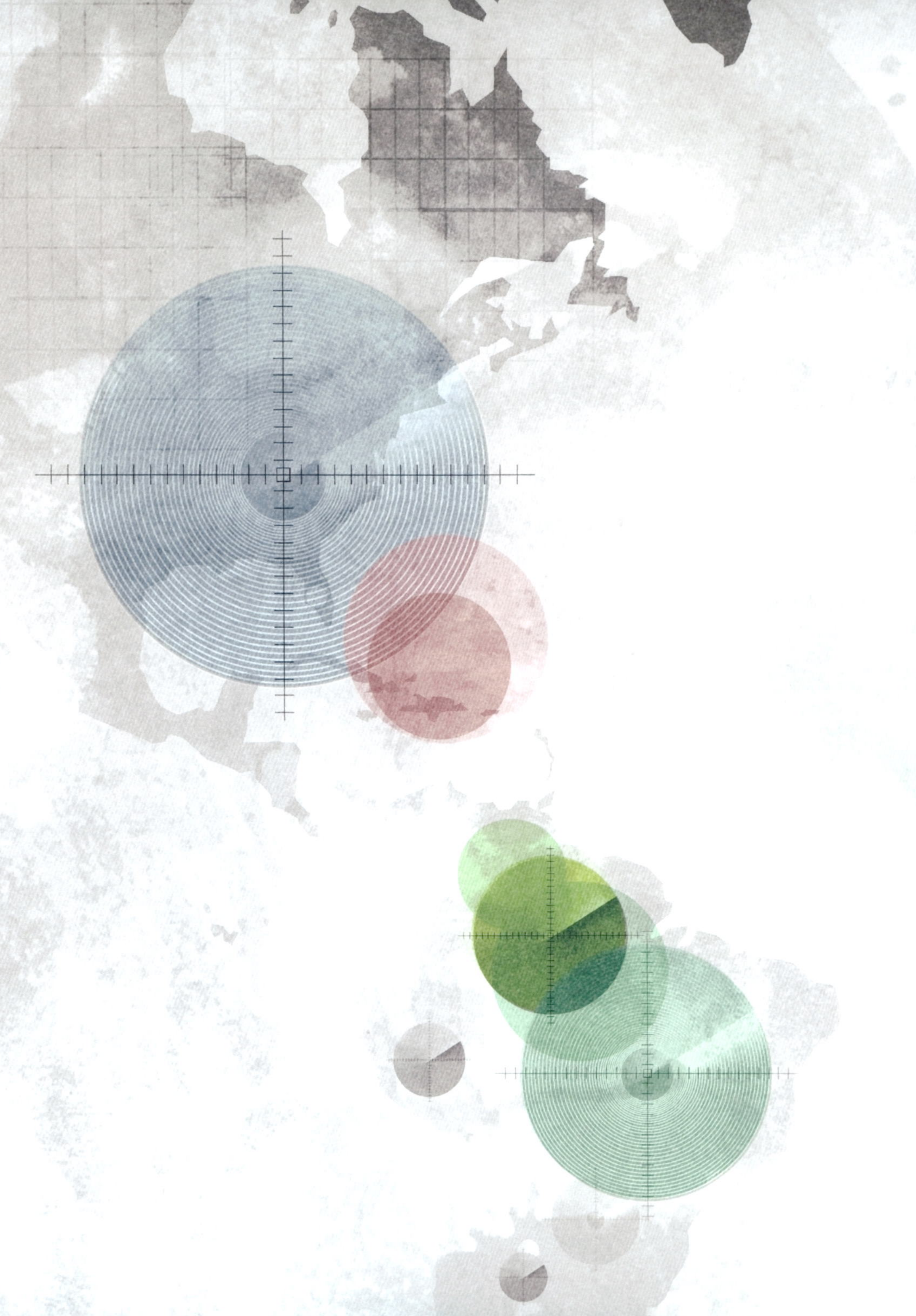

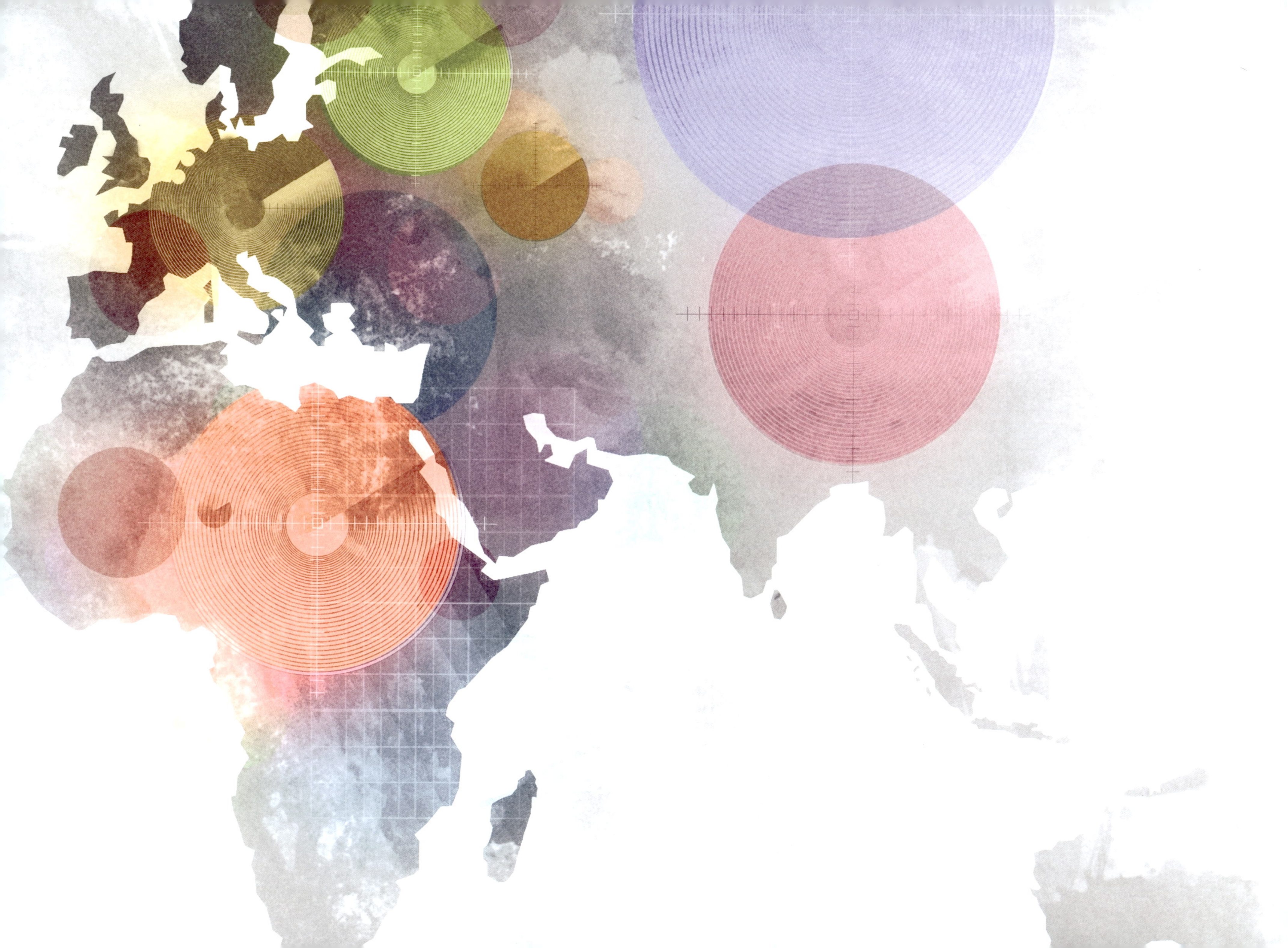

ANDREW HEM

NATIONALITY:	CAMBODIAN
LOCATION:	WORKING IN VENICE BEACH | LIVING IN CULVER CITY
PUBLICATIONS:	SOCIETY OF ILLUSTRATORS 48 | 49 | 50 PRINT REGIONAL DESIGN 2006 | 3x3 MAGAZINE AMERICAN ILLUSTRATION 26 | SWALLOW 4
REFERENCES:	ADIDAS | LUCKY BRAND | LOS ANGELES TIMES SONY PICTURES | CHICAGO TIME OUT
EXHIBITIONS:	THINKSPACE GALLERY | RECIEVER GALLERY COMPOUND GALLERY | COREY HELFORD 111 MINNA GALLERY
CONTACT:	WWW.ANDREWHEM.COM 310.904.8137 (U.S.A.)
TECHNIQUE:	MAINLY GOUACHE
BORN:	1981

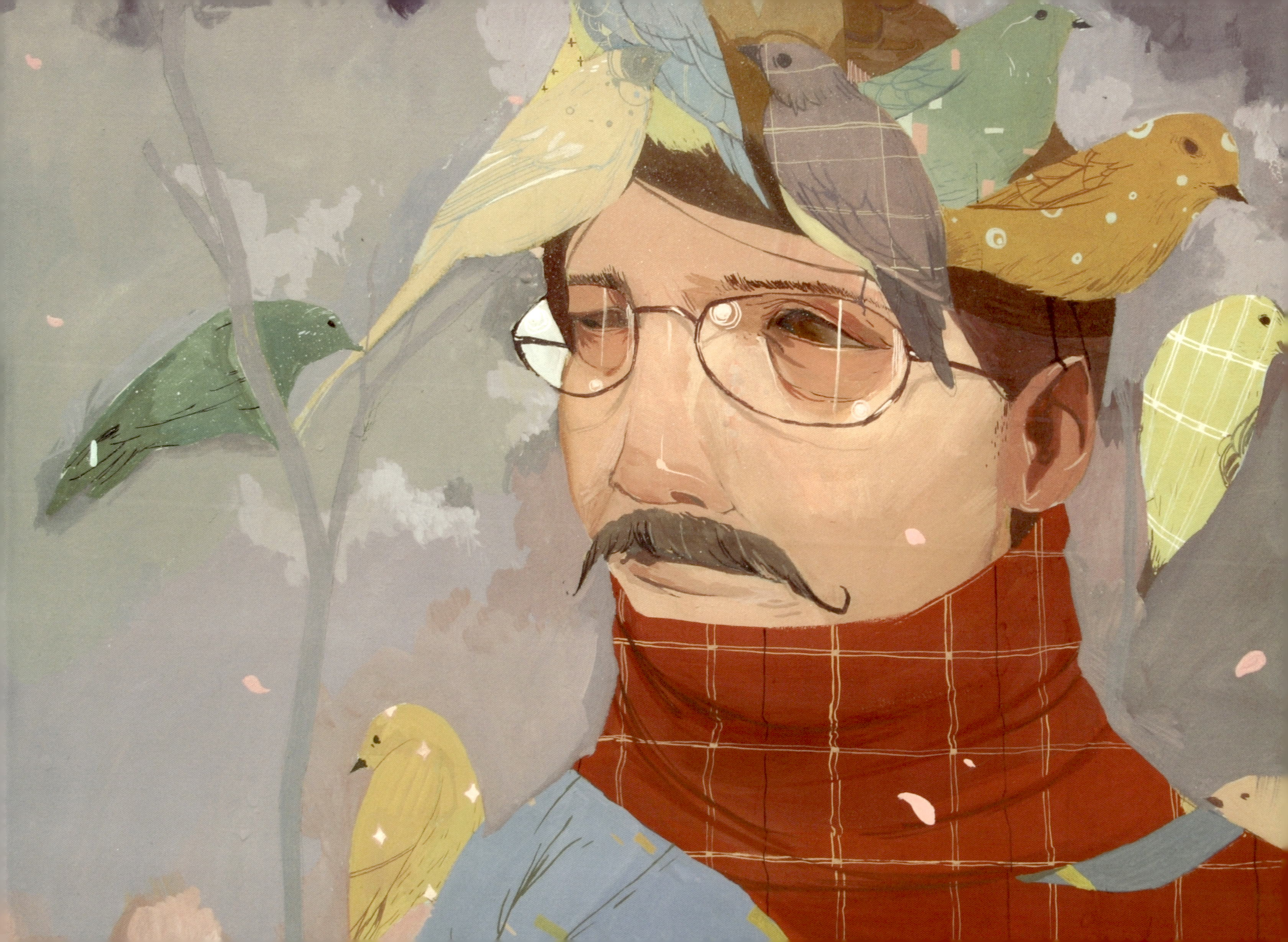

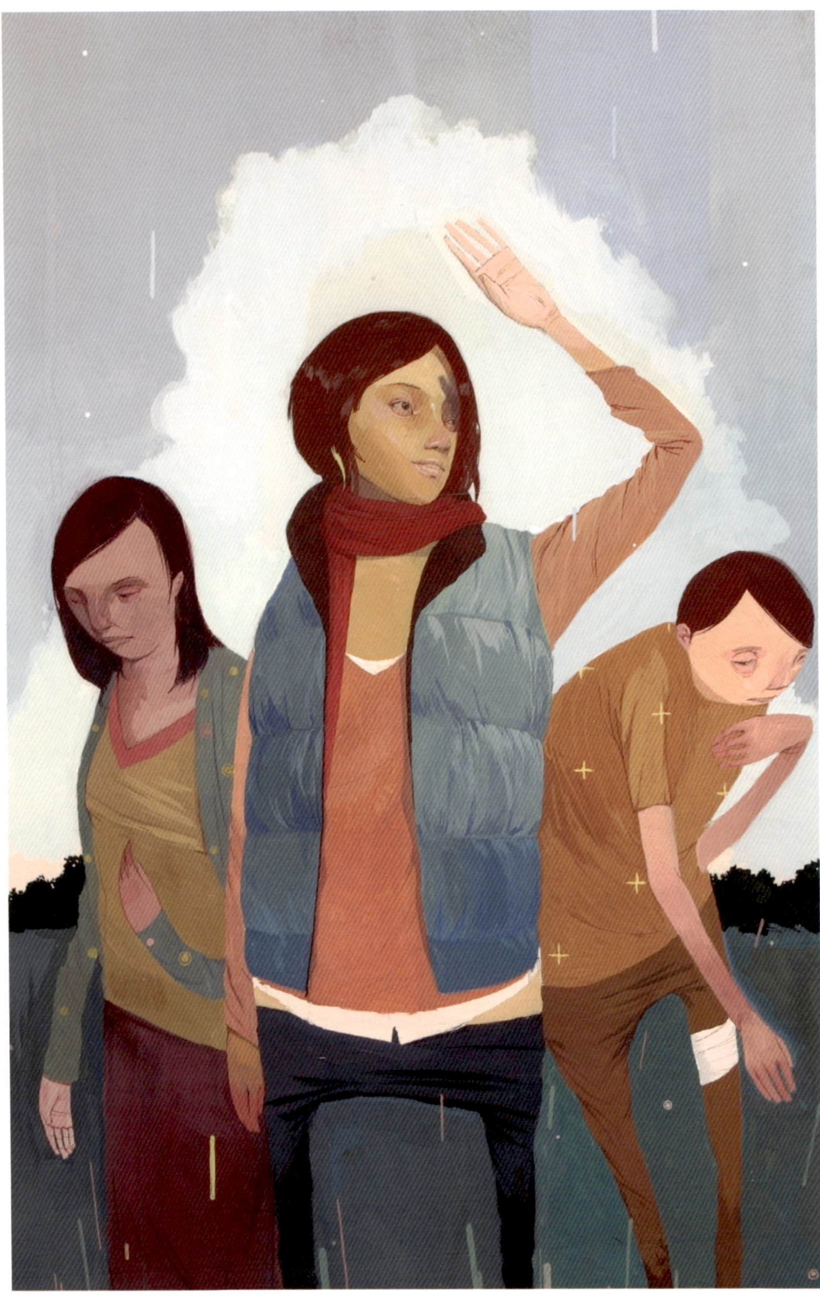

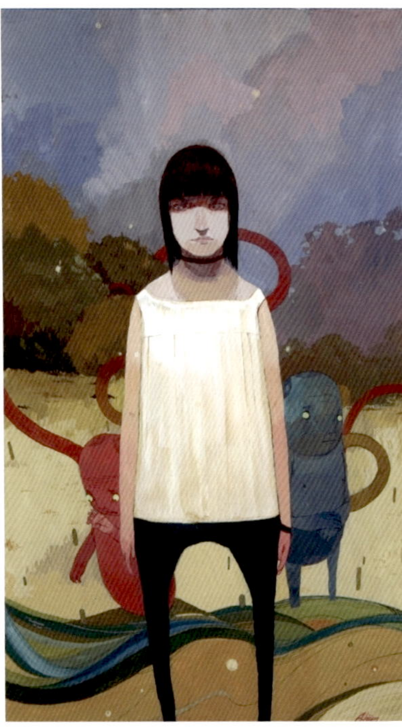

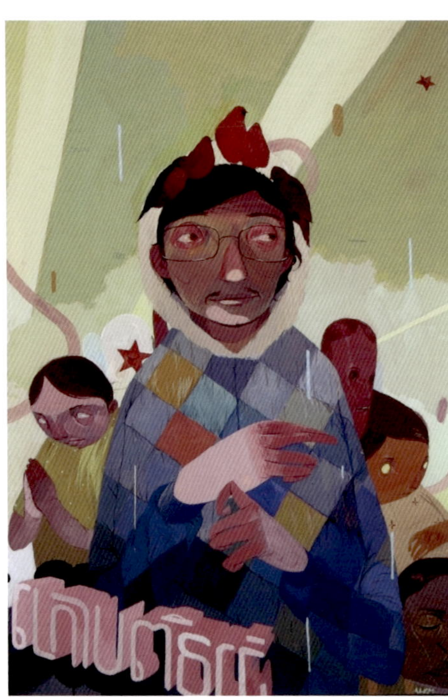

INTRODUCTION: ghettobird
LEFT PAGE:
LEFT: moving foward
MIDDLE: yukoe
RIGHT: wait for it
RIGHT PAGE:
RIGHT: daved

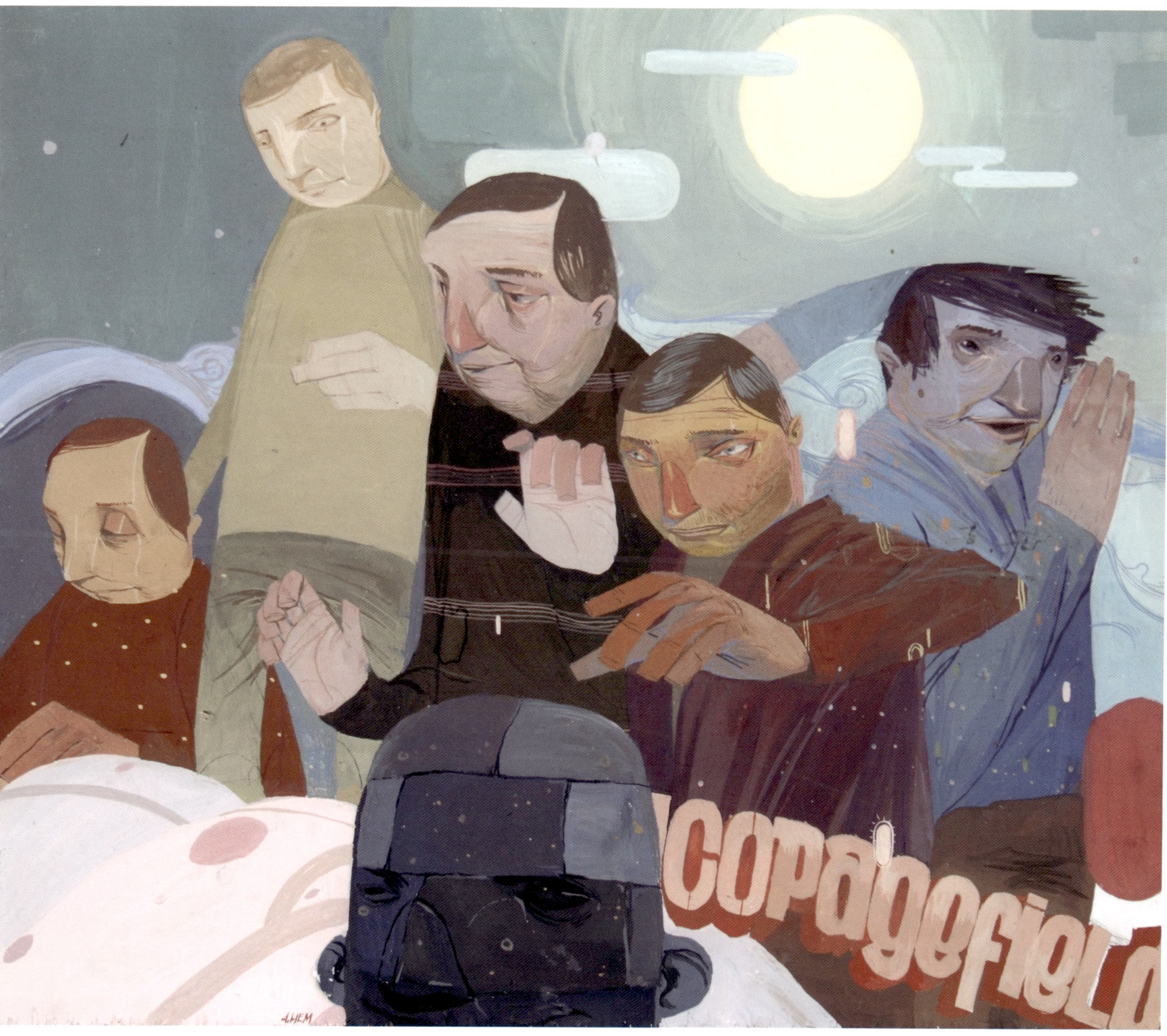

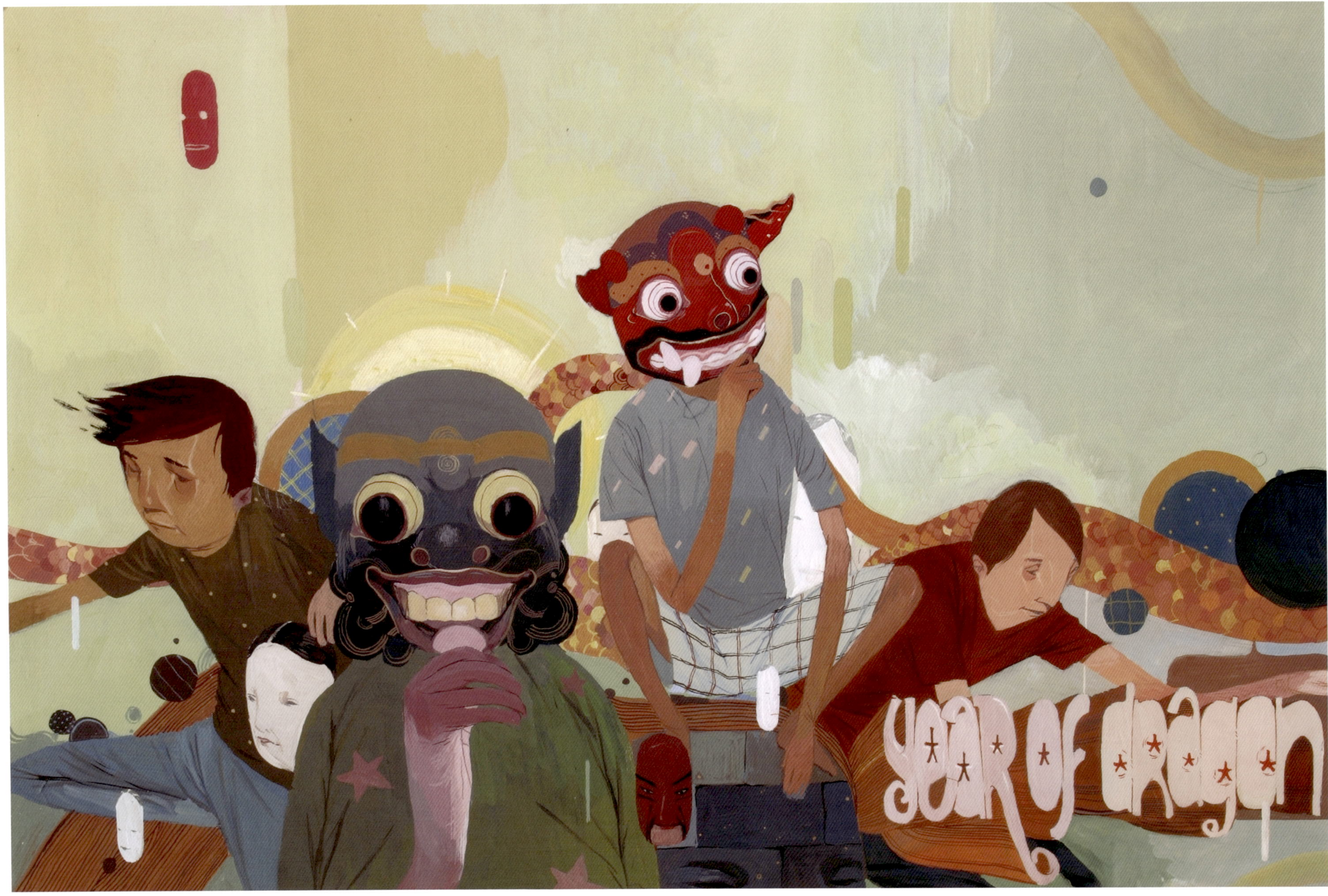
year of dragon

DE Für mich sind meine Illustrationen im Grunde vergleichbar mit meiner persönlichen Arbeit. Tendenziell sind sie ein wenig erzählerischer und stehen unter der Regie eines Artdirectors, aber ansonsten gibt es keinen Unterschied. Generell halte ich die klassische Definition von Illustration für zutreffend, lässt man allerdings den Text beispielsweise eines werbenden Unternehmens weg, handelt es sich im Wesentlichen um Kunst. Illustratoren werden wegen ihrer Fähigkeit, eine bestimmte Aufgabenstellung zu lösen, eingesetzt. Sie erbringen also eine Dienstleistung für einen Kunden. Gibt es aber keinen zu bebildernden Artikel oder eine ähnliche Aufgabe, so ist es Kunst, die gekauft wird. Ich kenne viele Illustratoren, die ihre kommerziellen Illustrationen in einer Galerie anbieten und umgekehrt. Jedes Bild macht sich also doppelt bezahlt. Und dass ihre Bilder in beiden Bereichen Verwendung finden, beweist, dass diese zu einem verschmelzen können. Ich glaube, dass immer mehr Galerien beginnen, nach Illustratoren Ausschau zu halten, und Werbeagenturen sehen sich vermehrt nach Künstlern um. Früher konnte ich nur am Medium selbst feststellen, ob ein Werk als Illustration oder Kunst gedacht ist. War es in Photoshop ausgeführt worden, wusste ich automatisch, dass es für ein Unternehmen angefertigt worden ist. Früher waren Computerdrucke in Galerien einfach nicht vertreten. Inzwischen aber arbeiten in der Kunstszene massenweise Leute mit nichts anderem als Photoshop und diese Werke sind überall präsent. Für mich nähern sich diese beiden Bereiche mit jedem Tag weiter einander an. Werde ich um eine Illustration gebeten, bringe ich gern einen persönlichen Aspekt in das Bild ein. Als Folge dessen fragen Artdirectors immer häufiger, warum beispielsweise ein Kreis zum Text passe. Und das ist der Hauptunterschied zwischen Illustration und Kunst: Bei ersterer bekommt man etwas vorgegeben, Dinge, mit denen man arbeiten muss, und somit ist alles an einem Bild vorherbestimmt. Deine Aufgabe ist es dann, die Illustration so zu gestalten, dass sie sich dem Betrachter offenbart, er sie versteht. Als was ich mich selbst verstehe, ob als Illustrator, Künstler oder beides? Ich bin Künstler – aber zurzeit fällt ja alles unter Kunst. Egal, ob du Koch oder Tänzerin bist, du wirst als Künstler angesehen. Man ragt aus der Kategorie Künstler nur dann heraus, wenn man angibt, Illustrator oder Maler zu sein. Von daher verstehe ich mich als beides.

LEFT PAGE: my year
RIGHT PAGE: sho

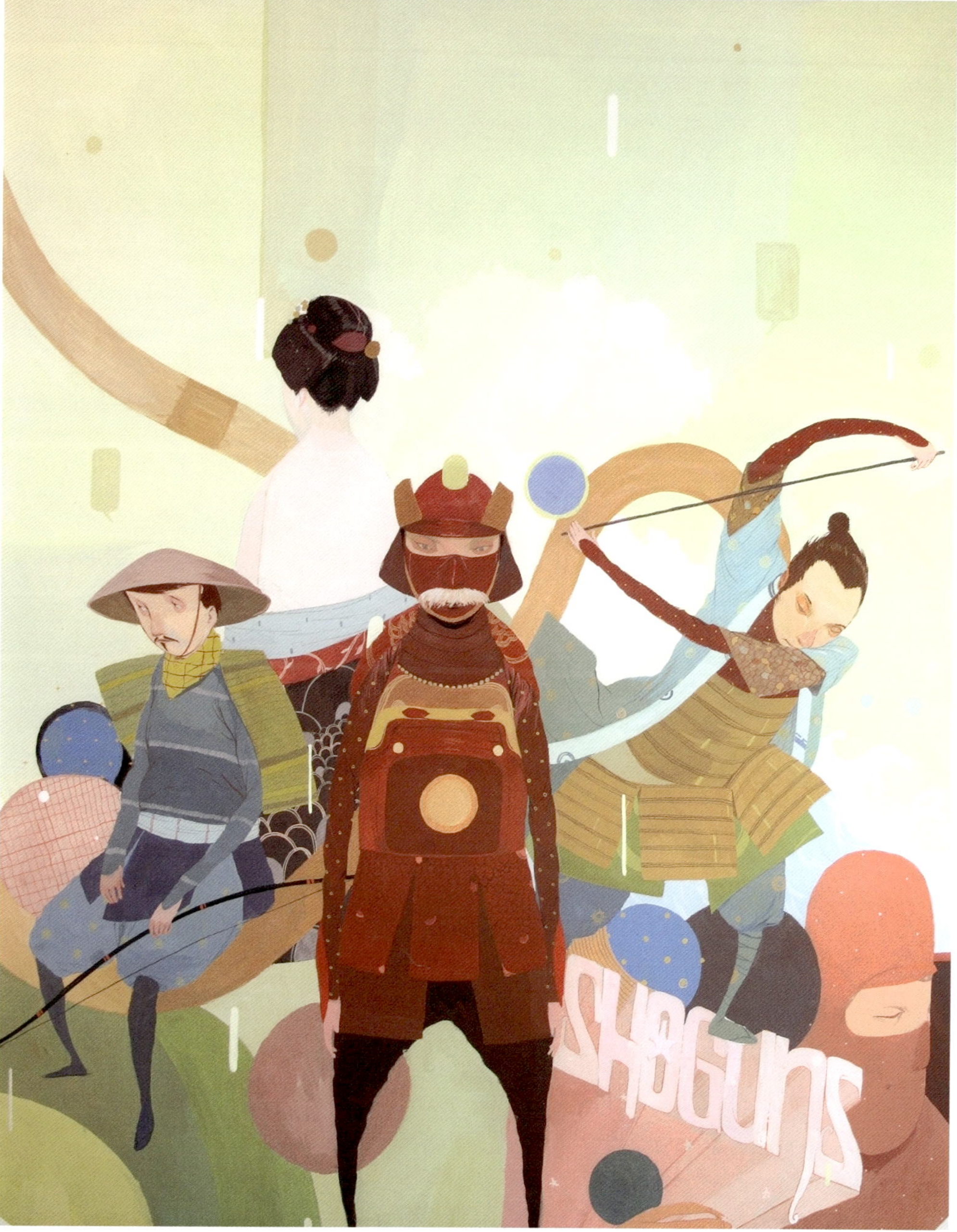

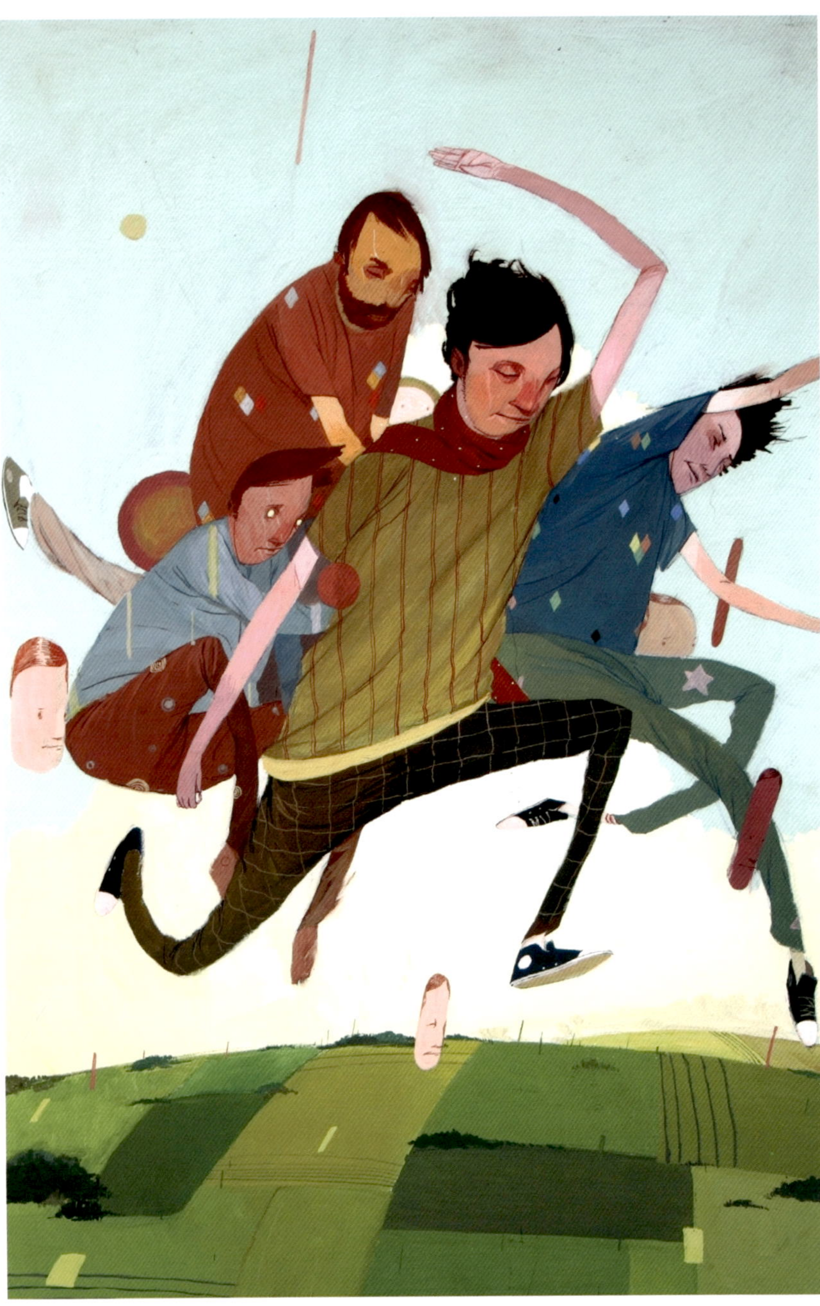

EN To me, my illustrations are really the same as my personal work. My illustrations tend to be a bit more narrative, and a bit more art-directed, but other than that there is not much of a different between the two. Generally I think the classical definition of illustration is right, but if you take away from the piece, say, the company's text , then it's basically art. Illustrators are used for their problem solving skills; they provide a service to a customer. If there was no article to be illustrated and no problem to be solved, then it wouldn't be a service to a customer, it would just be art for a buyer. I know a lot of illustrators who exhibit their commercial illustrations at a gallery and vice versa. So the pay is double for each image. The fact that they are using the same image in both fields proves that the two can become one. I think more and more galleries are beginning to look for illustrators, and agencies are opening their eyes to visual artists. Some time ago, the only way for me to tell if a piece was an illustration was to look at the medium. If it was done in photoshop, I knew automatically that it was done for a company. You never saw computer prints in a gallery. But now there are tons of artists in the fine art scene that work with nothing but photoshop, and their work is shown all over the place. To me the two fields are becoming more and more unified with each day that passes. When I get asked to do an illustration, I like to include some personal aspect in the work. As a result it happens more and more often that I get asked by an art director how, for instance, this or that circle fits in with the text. That is the main difference between illustration and art; in illustration, you are given objects to work with, everything about the work is pre-determined. Your job is to execute the illustration in a way that is accessible and comprehensible to the viewer. How do I see myself: as an illustrator, as an artist or as both? I see myself as an artist. But right now everything is called art, whether you are a chef or a dancer, you are considered an artist. Saying you are an illustrator or a painter is the only way to stand out from the artist category. In that sense I see myself as both.

LEFT PAGE: team2
RIGHT PAGE:
TOP LEFT: new forest
BOTTOM LEFT: shino
BOTTOM RIGHT:
white snow
RIGHT: yet again

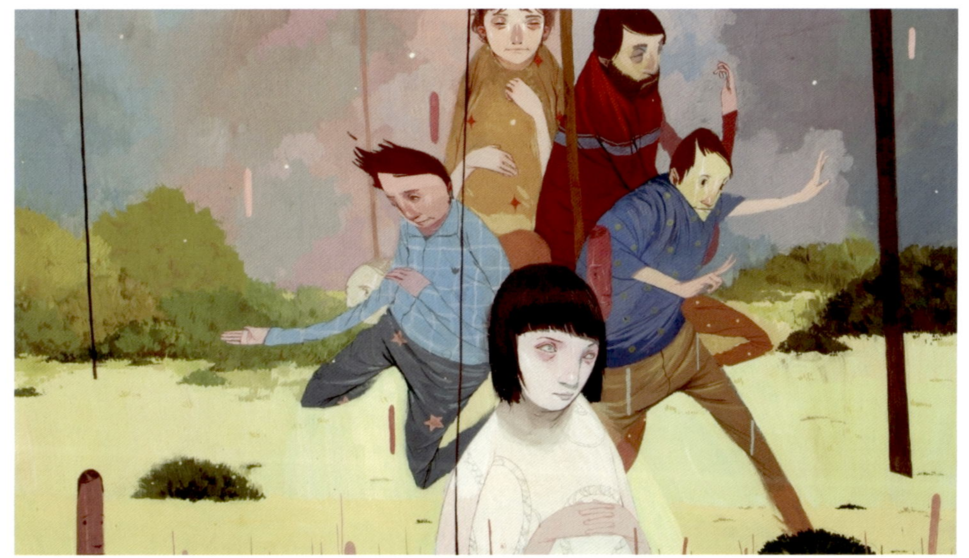

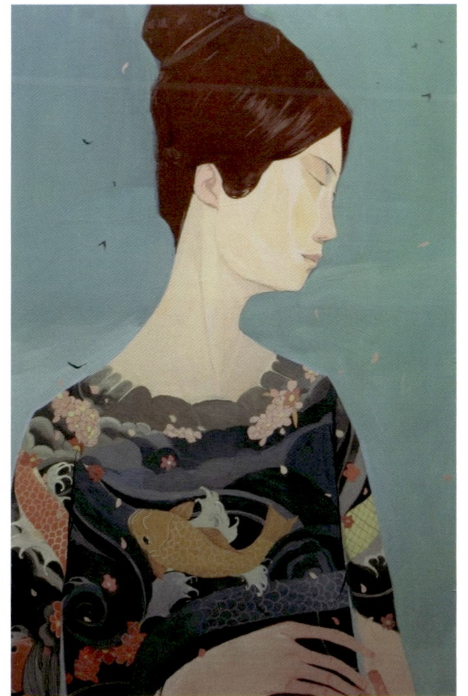

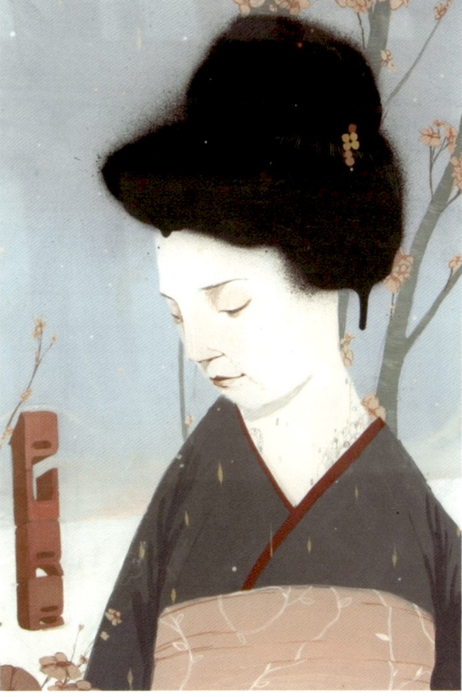

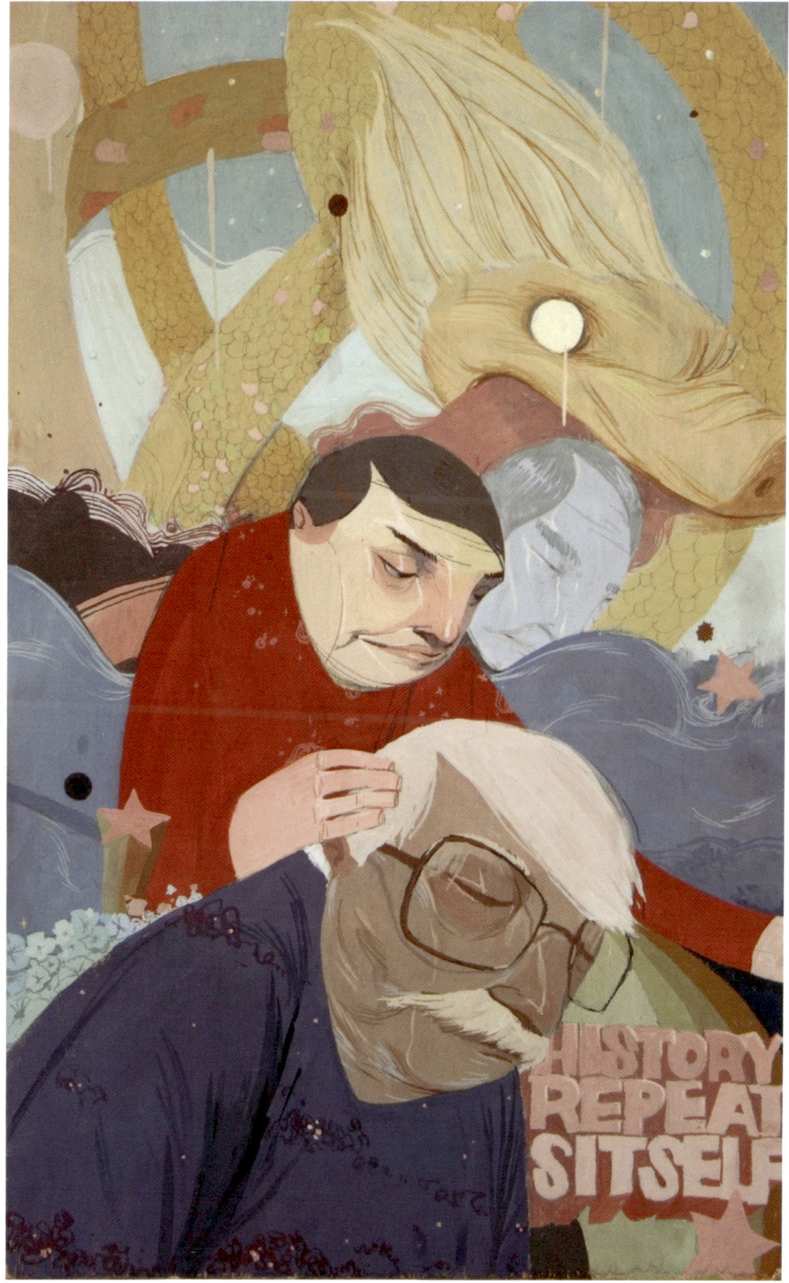
HISTORY
REPEAT
SITSELF

»DICE TSUTSUMI

NATIONALITY:	JAPANESE
LOCATION:	SAN FRANCISCO | CA
PUBLICATIONS:	OUT OF PICTURE – RANDOM HOUSE
CONTACT:	WWW.SIMPLESTROKE.COM DICE@SIMPLESTROKE.COM
TECHNIQUE:	OIL | DIGITAL | WATERCOLOR
BORN:	1974

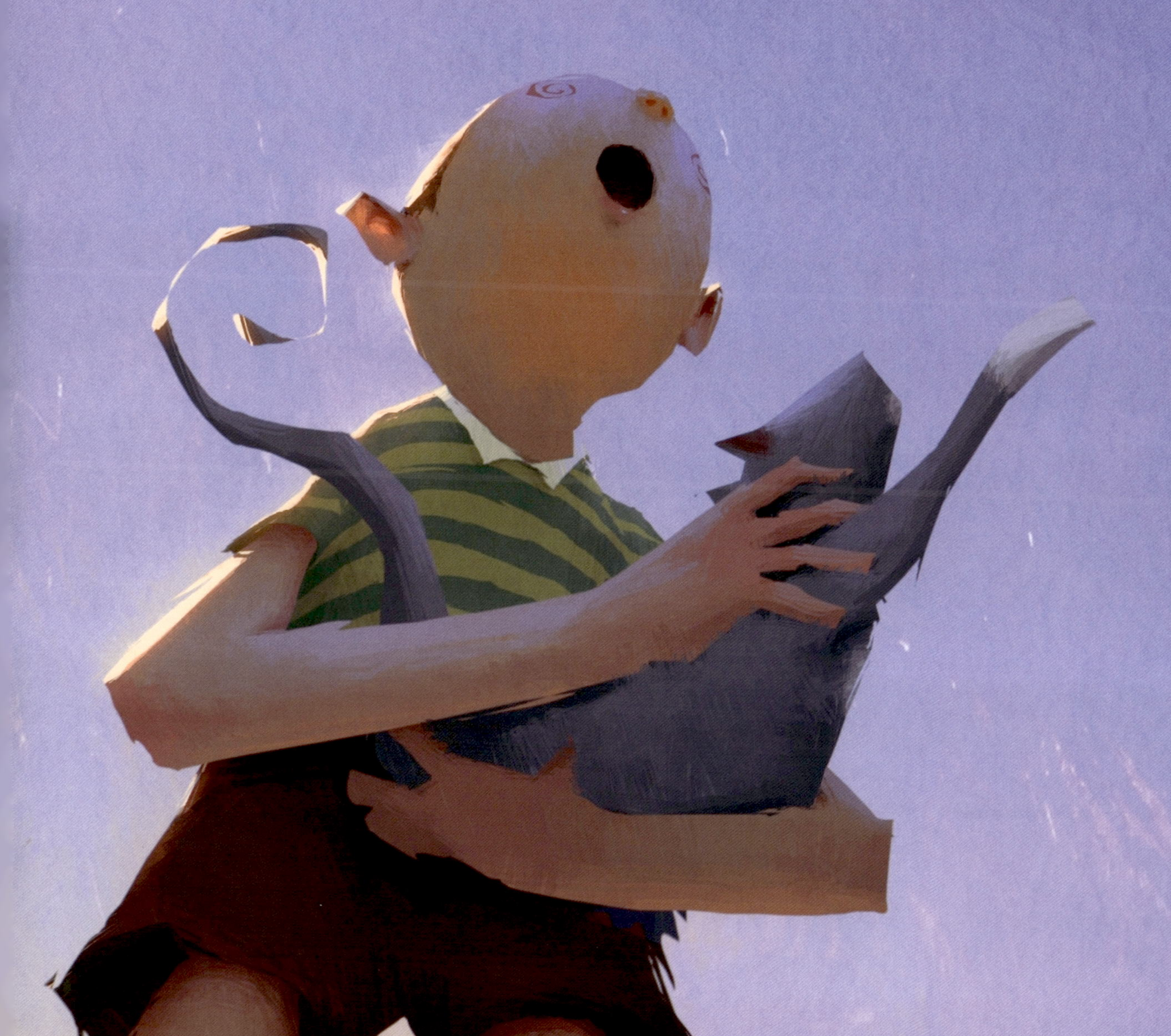
DICE
TSUT
SUMI

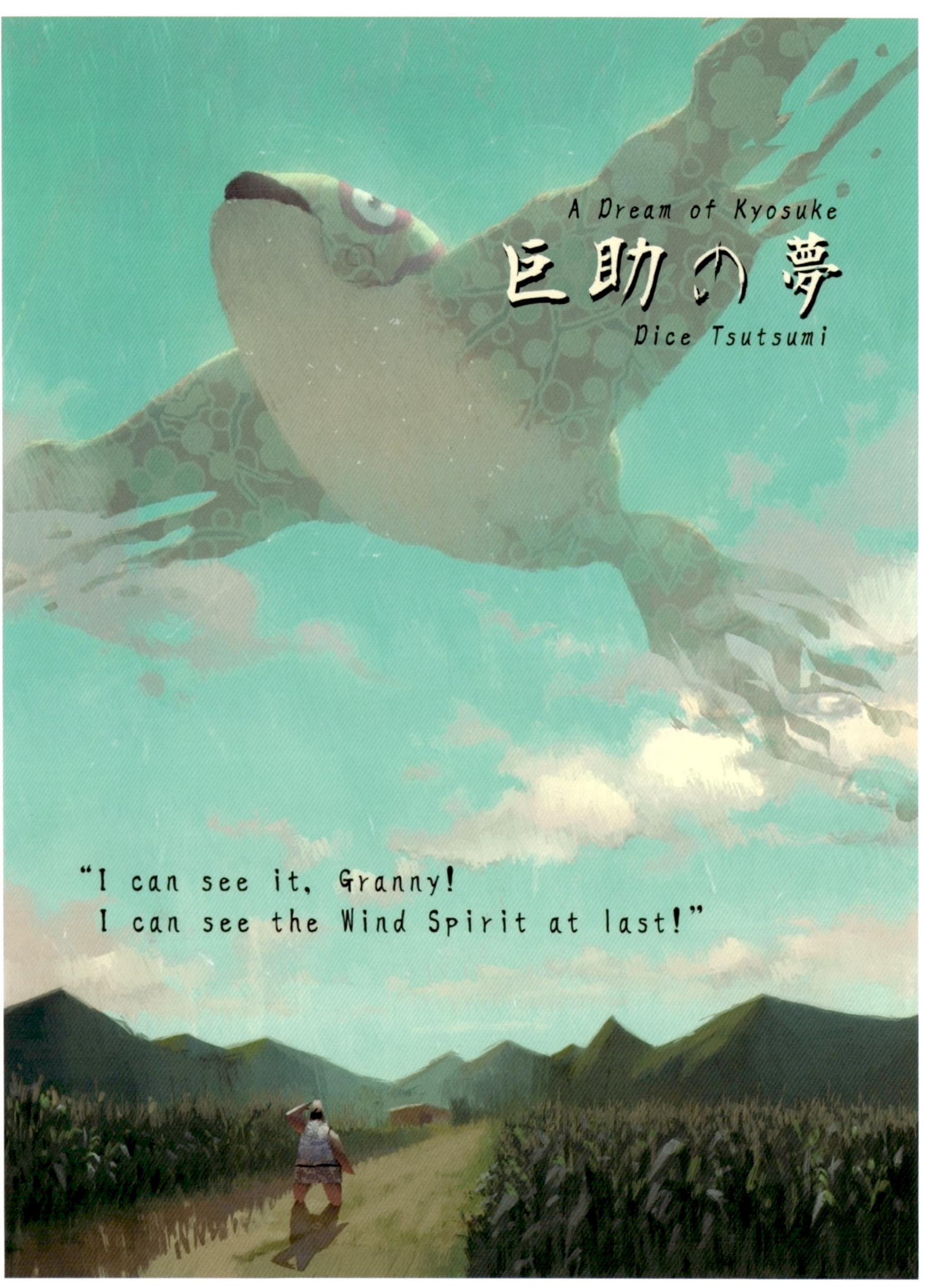

DE Für mich ist Illustration eine Form von Kunst und Kunst ist das Werk eines Künstlers. Somit kann man ein Bild für einen Kunden erstellen oder es in Galerien verkaufen oder einfach zum Spaß am Wochenende malen. Alles lässt sich gleichermaßen unter dem Begriff Kunst zusammenfassen. Ich glaube, meine Definition von Kunst unterscheidet sich von der klassischen Definition von Illustration, denn Kunst und Illustration gehören für mich zusammen. Es gibt eine Hand voll Maler, die in Galerien ausstellen und dem Wunsch ihrer Kunden entsprechen, während eine Reihe von Illustratoren quasi für sich selbst etwas schafft. Michelangelo hat die Sixtinische Kapelle für die katholische Kirche „illustriert". Niemand hat sein Meisterwerk jemals Illustration genannt oder behauptet, es sei weniger künstlerisch als irgendeine andere Art von Kunst. Ob eine Abgrenzung zwischen Illustration und Kunst existiert, notwendig oder hinfällig ist, so glaube ich, dass sie ein Muss ist. Norman Rockwell hingegen fertigte seine Illustrationen an, weil sie seine wahre Leidenschaft waren, auch wenn diese für Zeitschriftentitel bestimmt waren. Ich will damit sagen, dass man immer versuchen sollte, seine Kunst in erster Linie für sich selbst zu machen – egal, ob sie für Kunden aus der Werbung, eine Galerie oder deine Großmutter vorgesehen ist. Sehe ich mich selbst als Künstler, Illustrator oder beides? Ich sage immer, dass ich Illustrator bin, weil ich damit meinen Lebensunterhalt verdiene. Und jeder Illustrator ist ebenso Künstler wie ein Fotograf, Filmemacher, Schauspieler, Tänzer oder ähnliches.

INTRODUCTION: birds
LEFT PAGE: kyosuke titlepage
RIGHT PAGE:
TOP: battle
BOTTOM: budda

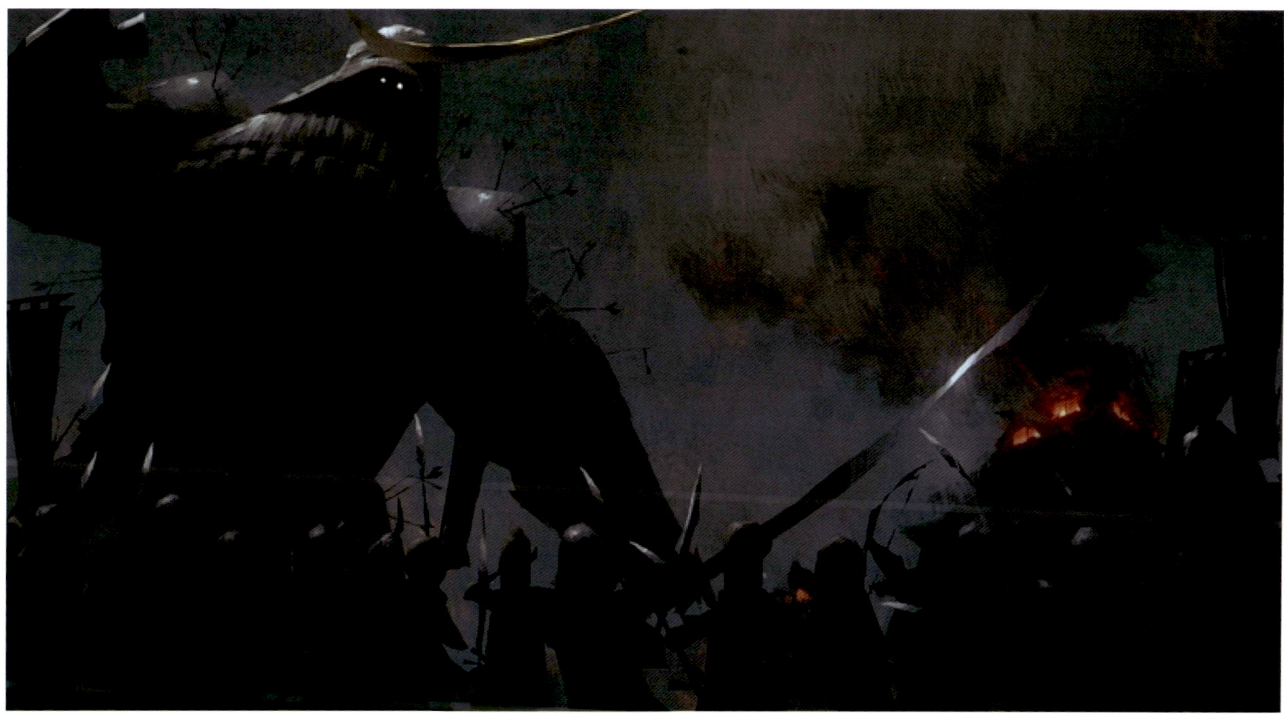

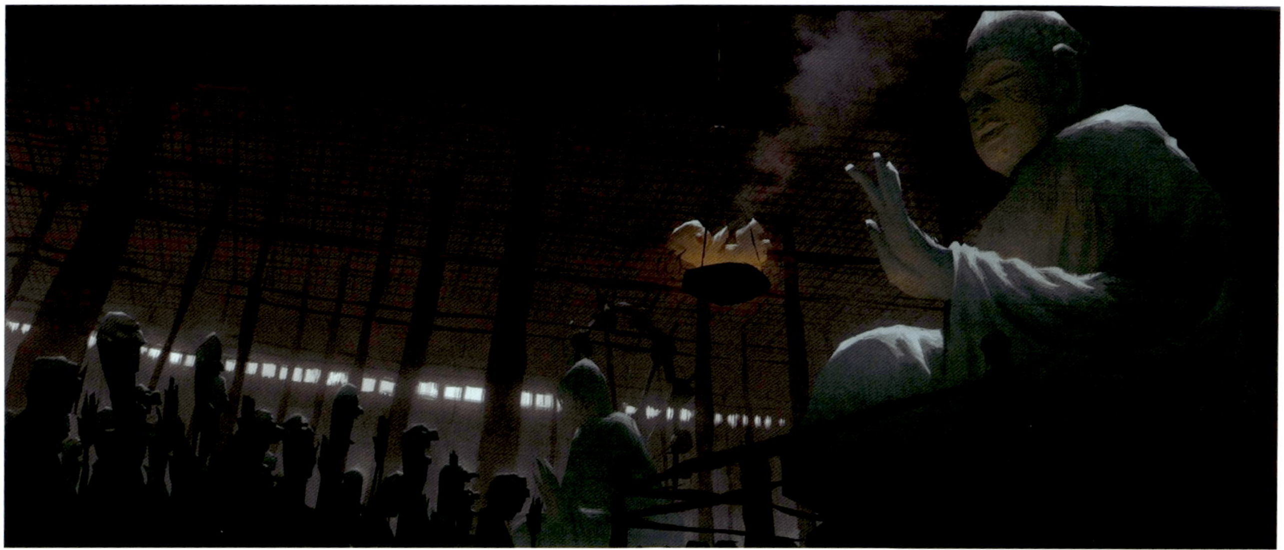

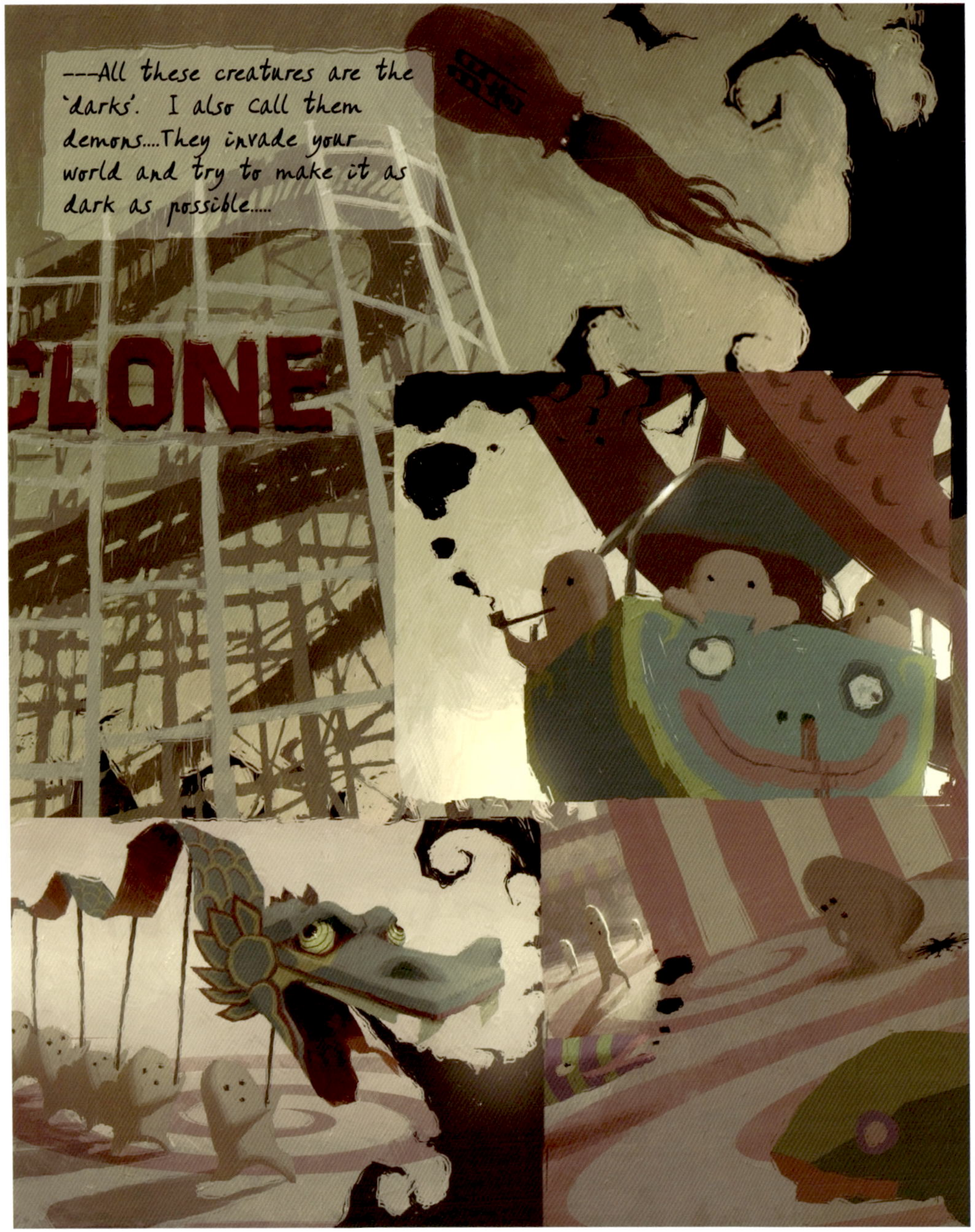

---All these creatures are the 'darks'. I also call them demons....They invade your world and try to make it as dark as possible.....

CLONE

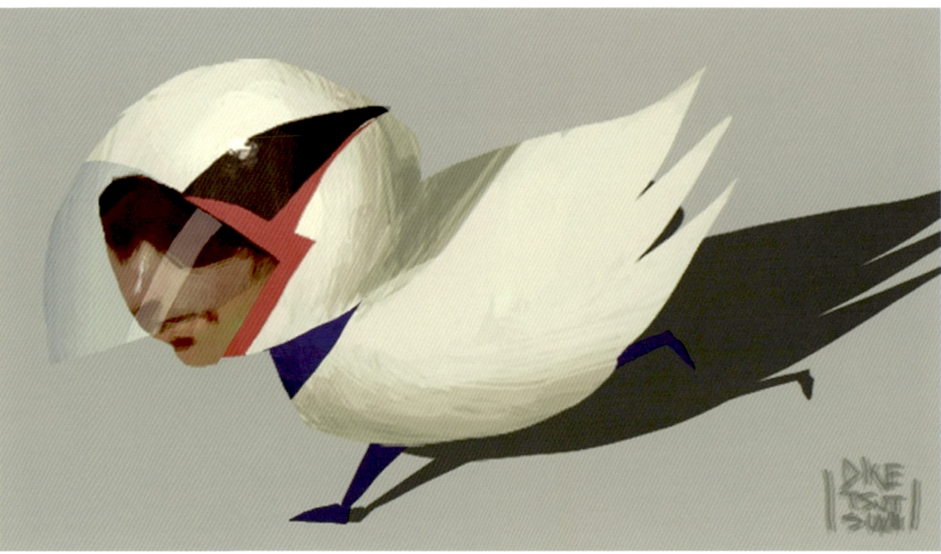

LEFT PAGE:

LEFT: oop_2

RIGHT: lunchtime sketch2

RIGHT PAGE:

LEFT: batman

RIGHT: lunchtime sketch

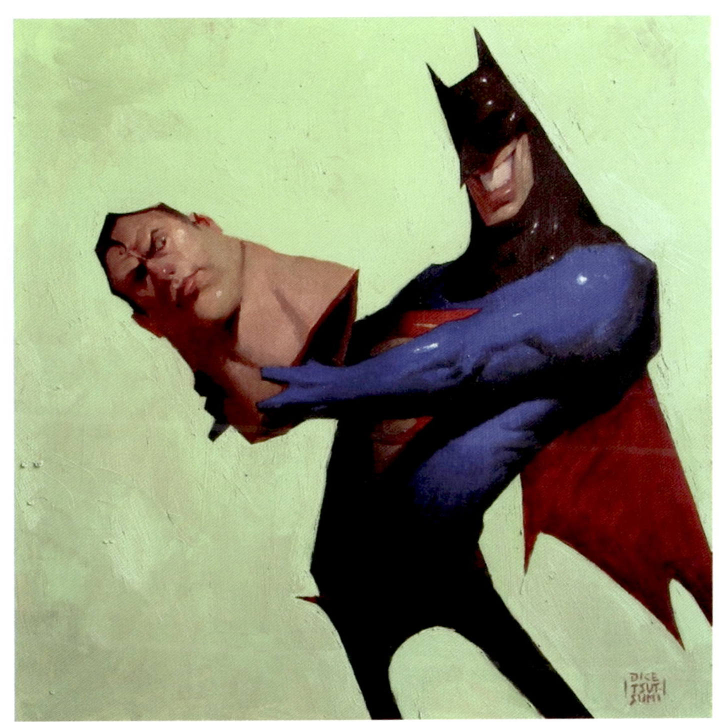
DICE
TSUT-
SUMI

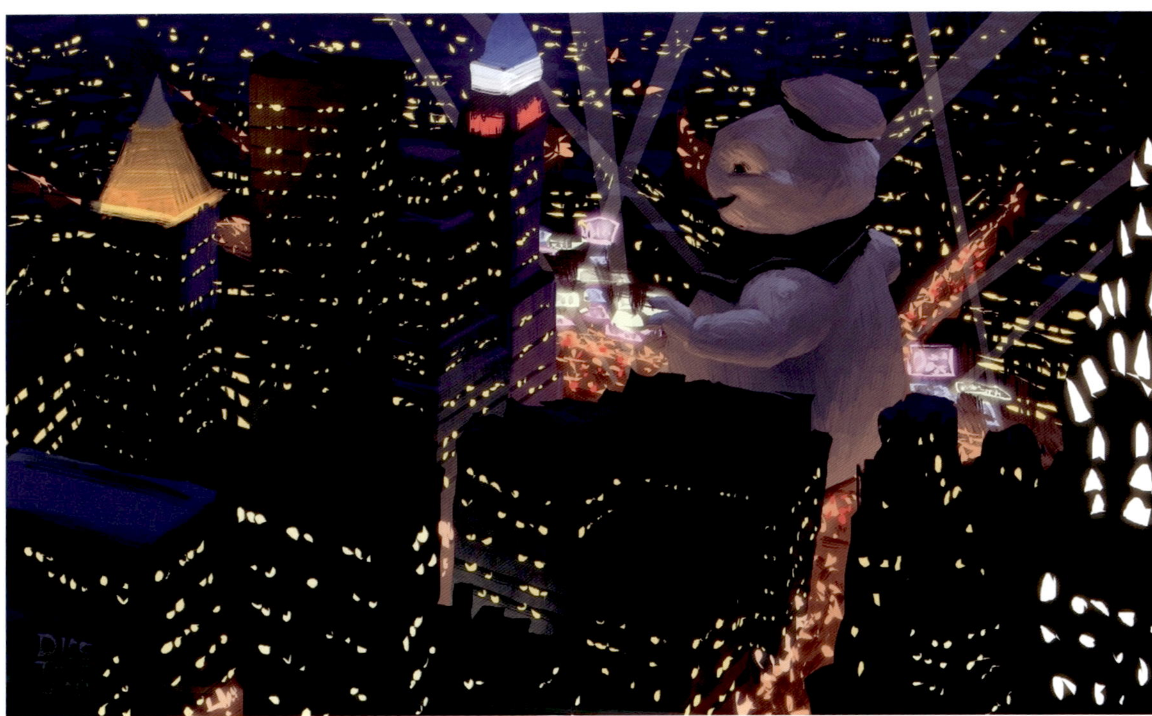

EN For me, illustration is an art form and art is created by an artist. You can produce an image for a commercial client, sell it at galleries or simply create one just for fun on the weekend. They can all be categorized as art. I feel my definition of art is different from the classical definition of illustration because for me art and illustration belong together. There are a handful of painters who exhibit their work in galleries and who fulfill the wishes of their customers, while a number of illustrators produce their work for its own sake, as it were. Michelangelo "illustrated" the Sistine Chapel for the Church. No one has ever called his masterwork an illustration or argued it was any less art than other works. As to the question whether or not there is a difference between illustration and art, whether it is necessary or obsolete, I do think it is a "must" But Norman Rockwell produced his illustrations in order to realize his true passion even though they were solicited for magazine covers. My point is that you should always try to create art for yourself, regardless if it is ultimately made for commercial clients, galleries, or your grandma. Do I see myself as an artist, as an illustrator or as both? I always say I'm an illustrator because that's what I do for a living. And any illustrator is as much of an artist as a photographer, a film maker, an actor, a dancer etc.

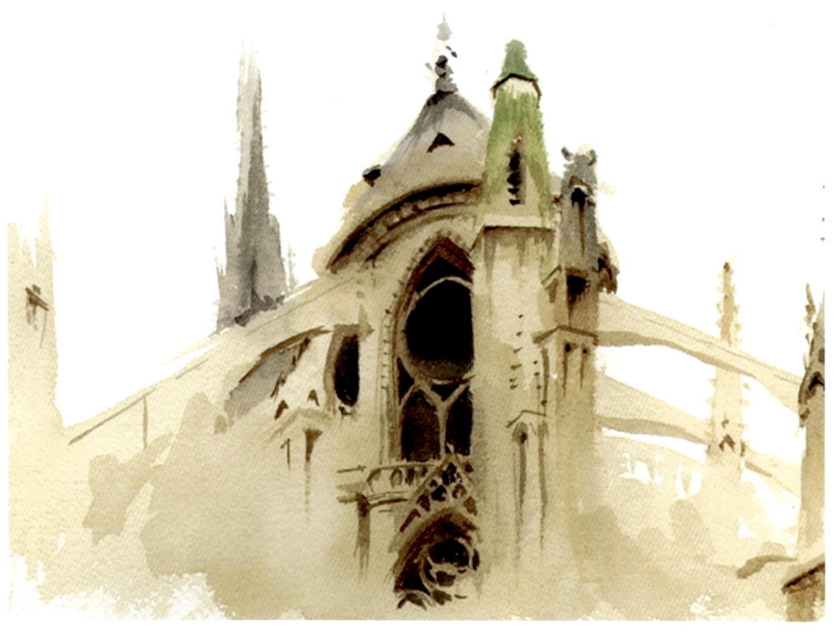

LEFT PAGE: lifepainting2
RIGHT PAGE:
LEFT: lifepainting1
RIGHT: lifepainting3

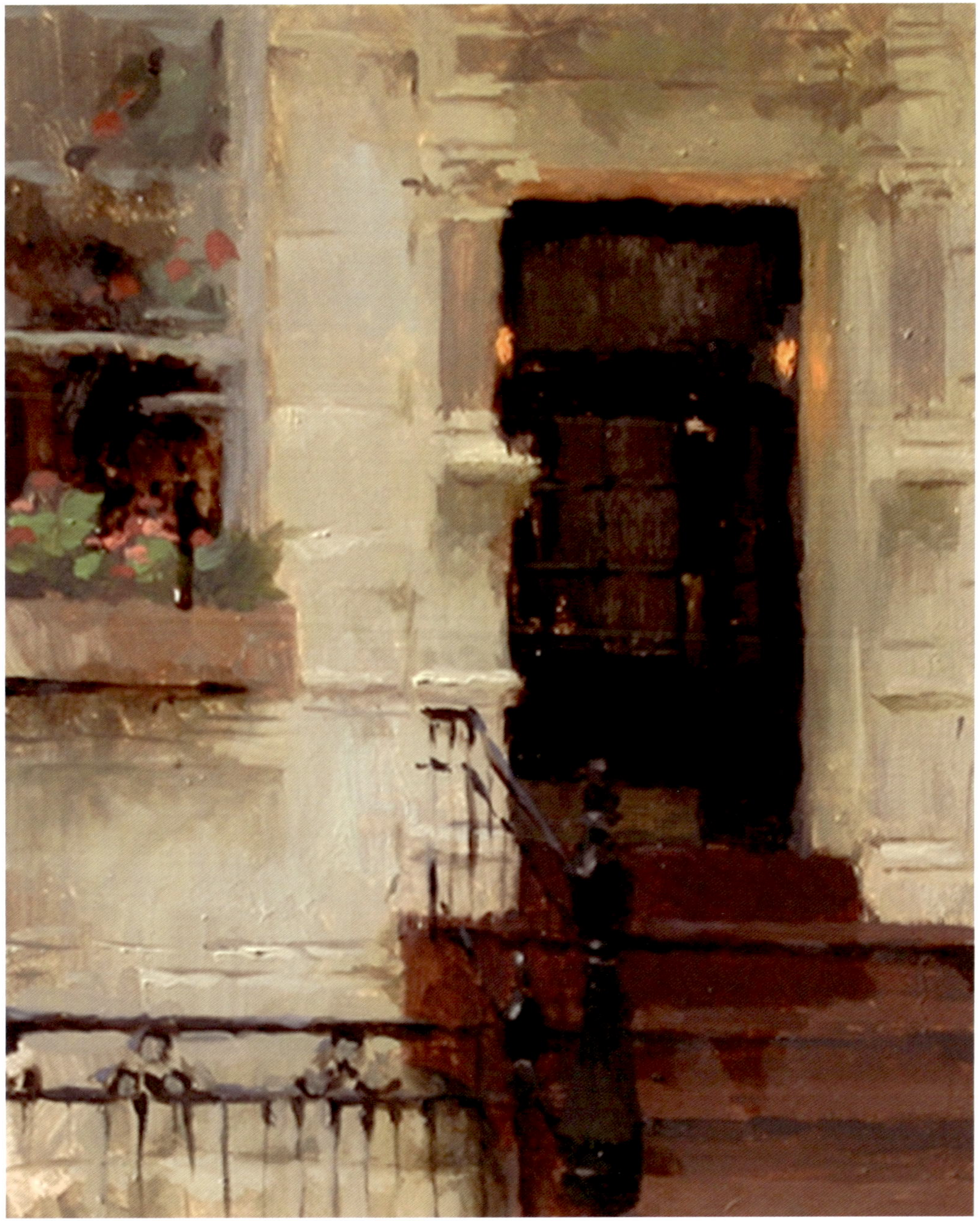

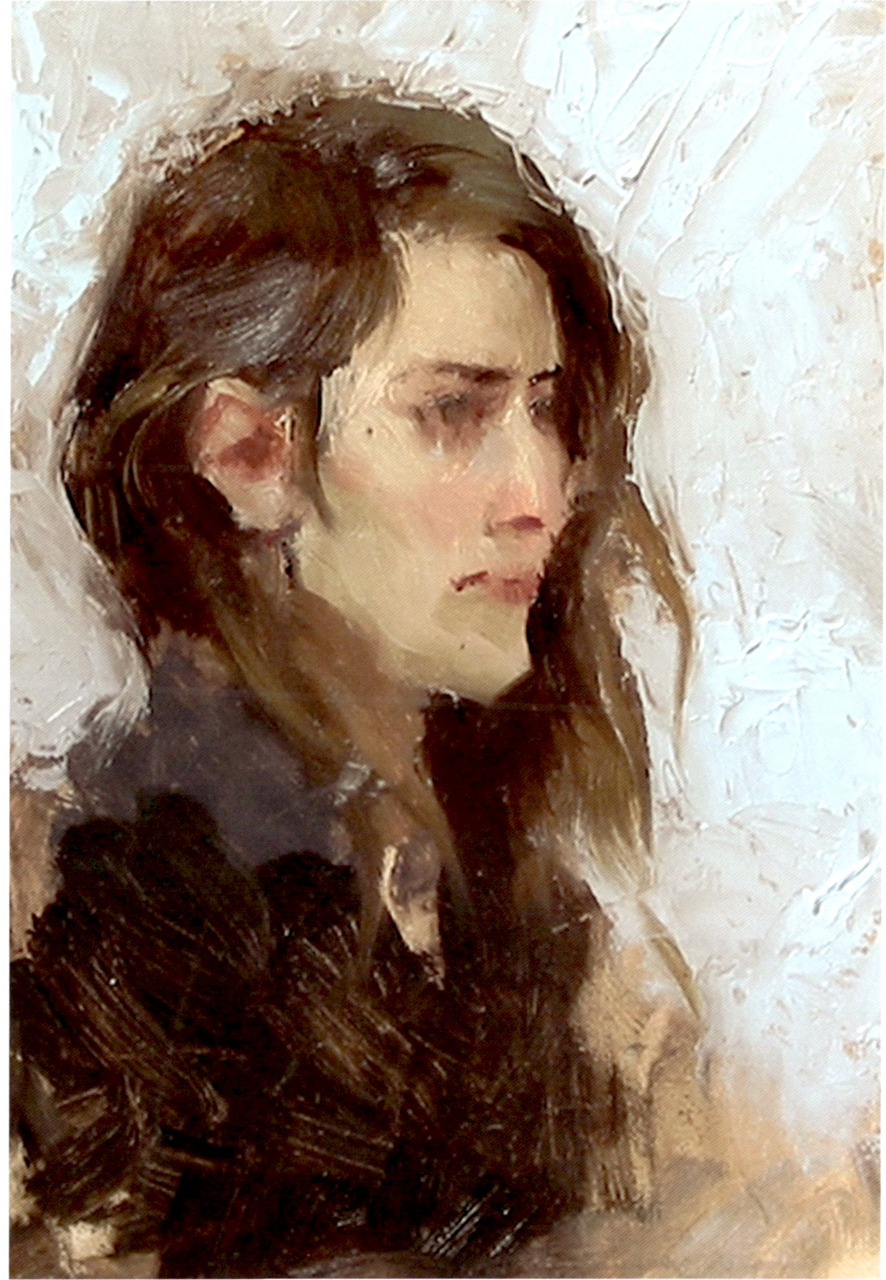

»IMA ONE

NATIONALITY:	JAPANESE
LOCATION:	TOKYO
PUBLICATIONS:	UNDERCOVER MAGAZINE (UK) SB SKATEBOARD JOURNAL (JP) GRAPHOTISM (UK) DAYDREAM MAGAZINE (UK) KAZE MAGAZINE (JP) | RACKGAKI (UK) SCRATCH ON THE WALL (JP) INDOLE DIFFERENT SIGNS (IT) GRAFFITI JAPAN (US) | STICKER BOMB (UK)
EXHIBITIONS:	ART FROM THE RABBIT HOLE COMPOUND GALLERY – PORTLAND QUINTESENTIAL GRENADE ART GALLERY – LONDON THE WORLD OF URBAN ART INTOXICATED DEMONS GALLERY – BERLIN
REPRESENTIVES:	GRENADE ART GALLERY (UK)
CONTACT:	WWW.IMAONE.COM
TECHNIQUE:	VARIOUS
BORN:	1980

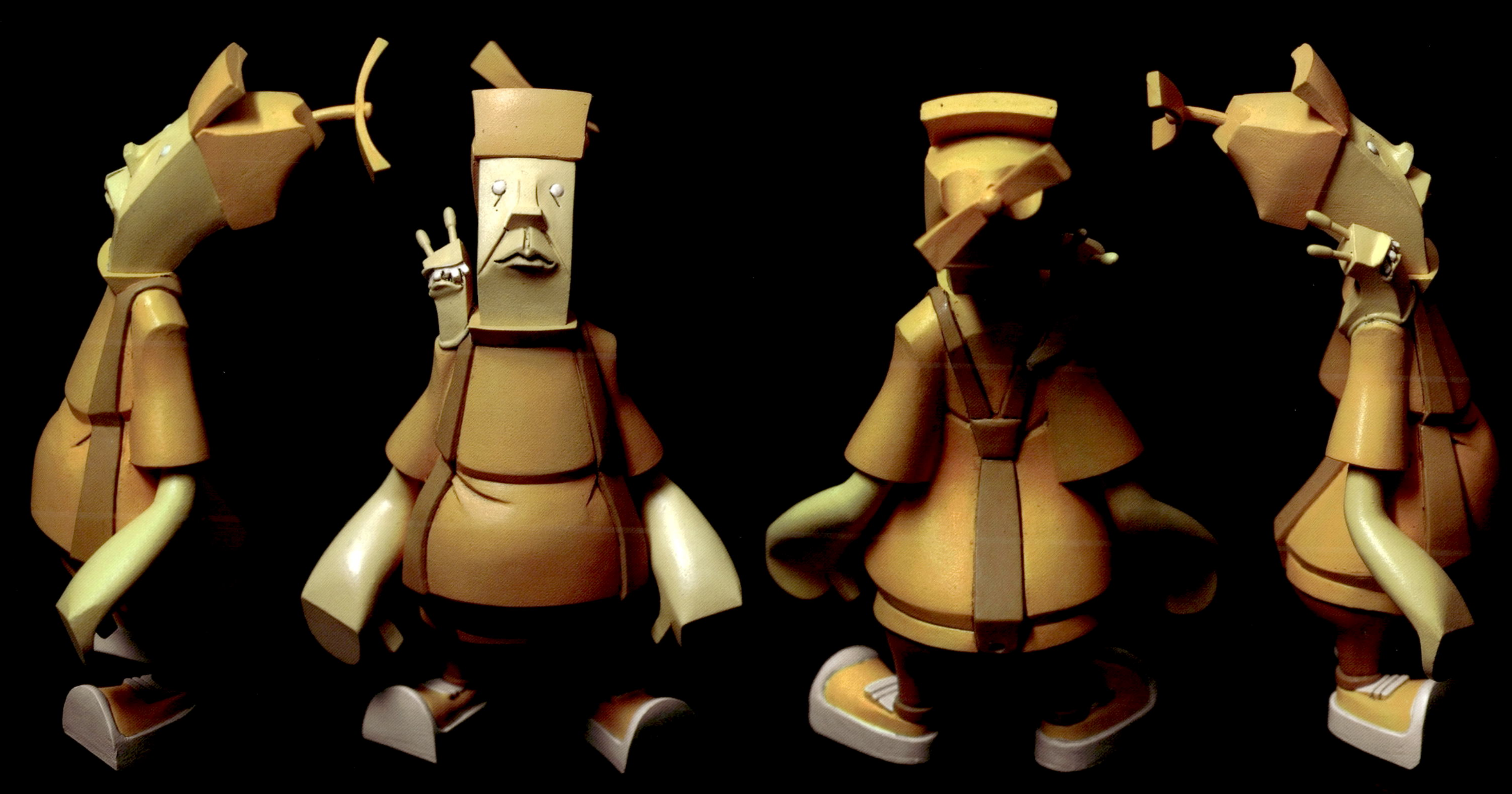

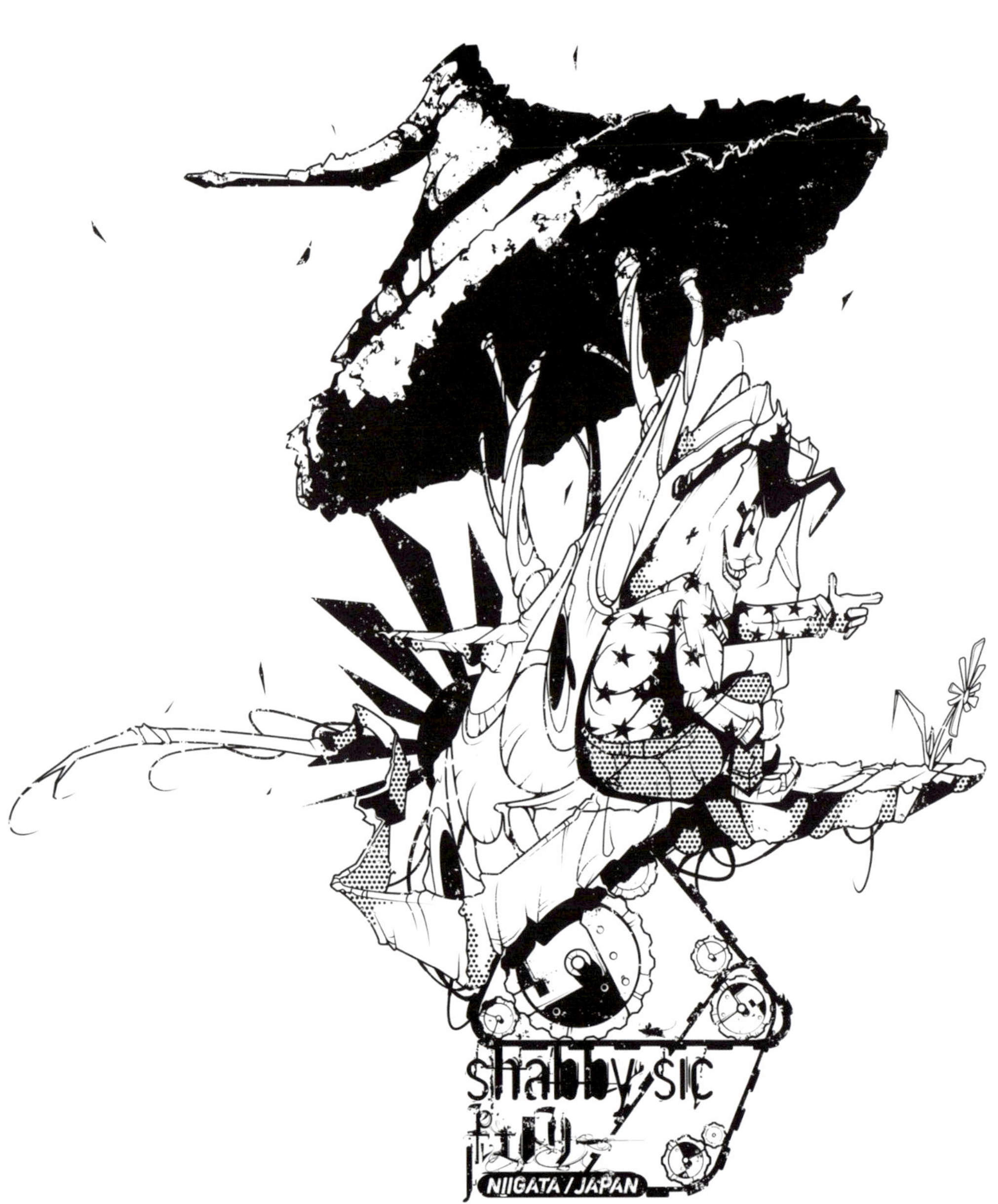

DE Dass Illustration nur eine Dienstleistung sein soll, hört sich schrecklich an. Natürlich möchte ich vermeiden, Arbeiten zu schaffen, denen es an Originalität fehlt, die oberflächlich und dementsprechend schlecht sind. Wenn ich aber eine gute Beziehung zu meinem Auftraggeber habe, sollten und werden normalerweise meine eigene Vorstellung und mein persönlicher Geschmack das Endprodukt prägen, wobei es letzten Endes vor allem den Erwartungen des Kunden entsprechen muss. Wichtig ist, dass alle zufrieden sind, oder nicht? Das ist es, was mich interessiert, und das ist der Weg, der uns zum Ziel führt. „Der Künstler ist sein eigener Mäzen." hört sich vielleicht gut an, aber Sätze wie dieser und Künstler, die an sie glauben, erscheinen mir zeitweise arrogant. Definitionen sind langweilig und ich würde gern daran glauben, dass wir es sind, die sie widerlegen und missachten – wenngleich es nicht das ist, wofür ich mich ins Zeug legen würde. Für mich sind hingegen „Atmosphäre" und „Timing" die Schlüsselwörter, von denen alles abhängt. Somit sind die Unterschiede zwischen Illustration und Kunst nicht allzu wichtig. Beides, die Illustration sowie die Kunst, ändern ihre Form und ihren Ausdruck in Abhängigkeit von der Stimmung, in der sie entstehen, und der Wahl des richtigen Zeitpunkts. Auf meiner Visitenkarte steht „Design / Illustration / Wandgestaltung". Als ich sie gemacht habe, war das zutreffend – wie leicht die Leute doch zu beeindrucken sind.

INTRODUCTION: night head / feat.U
LEFT PAGE: shabby sic poetry
RIGHT PAGE:
LEFT: march01
RIGHT: march02

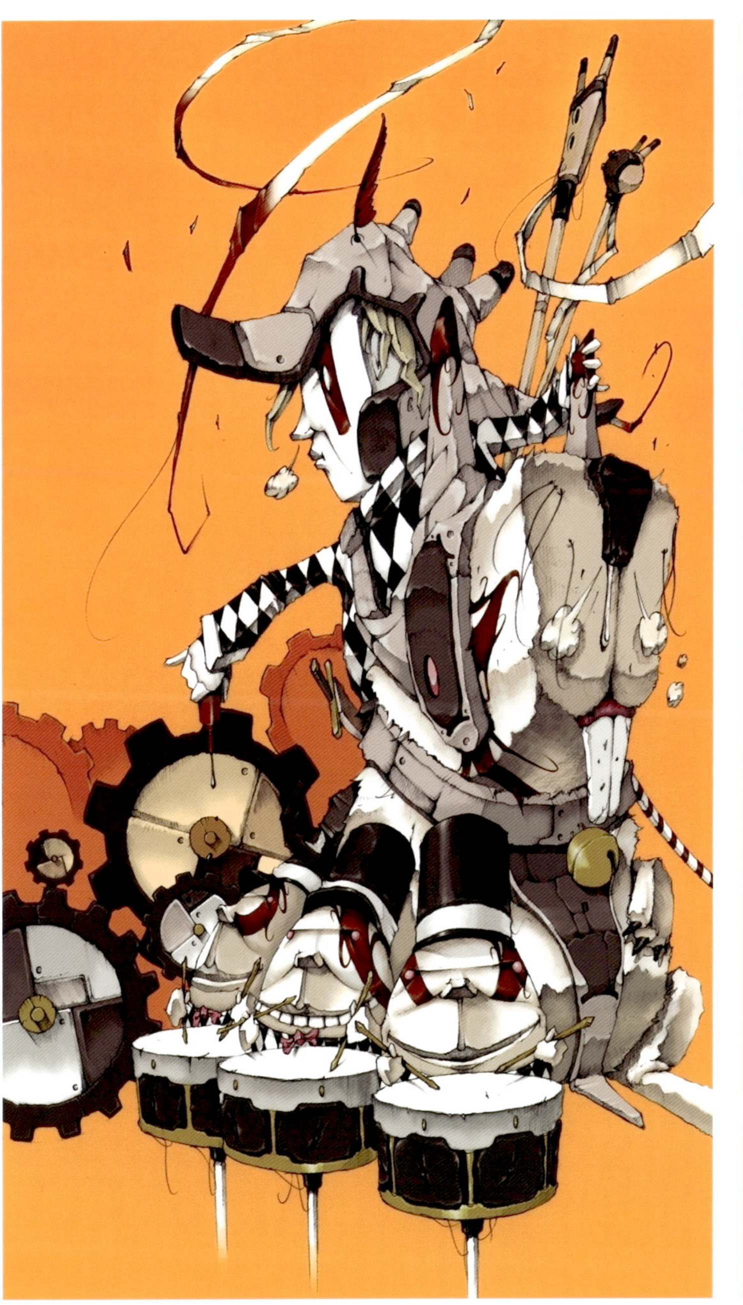

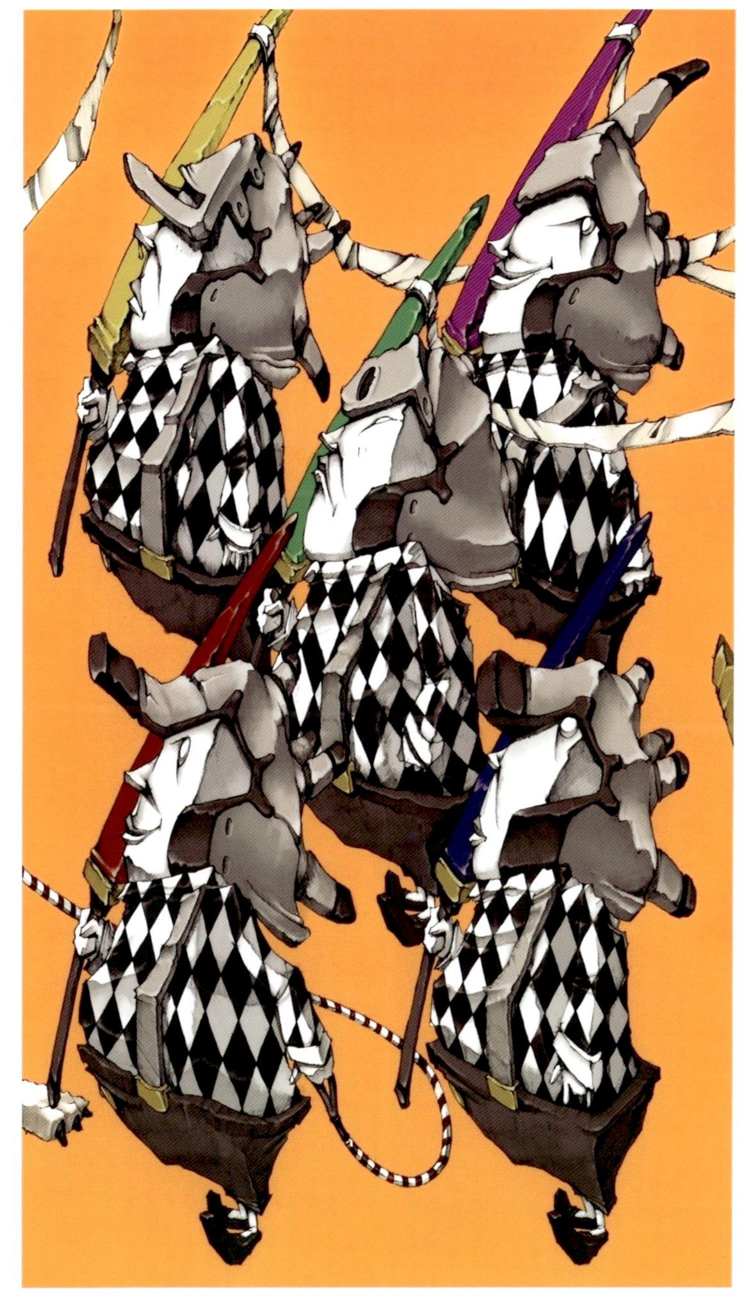

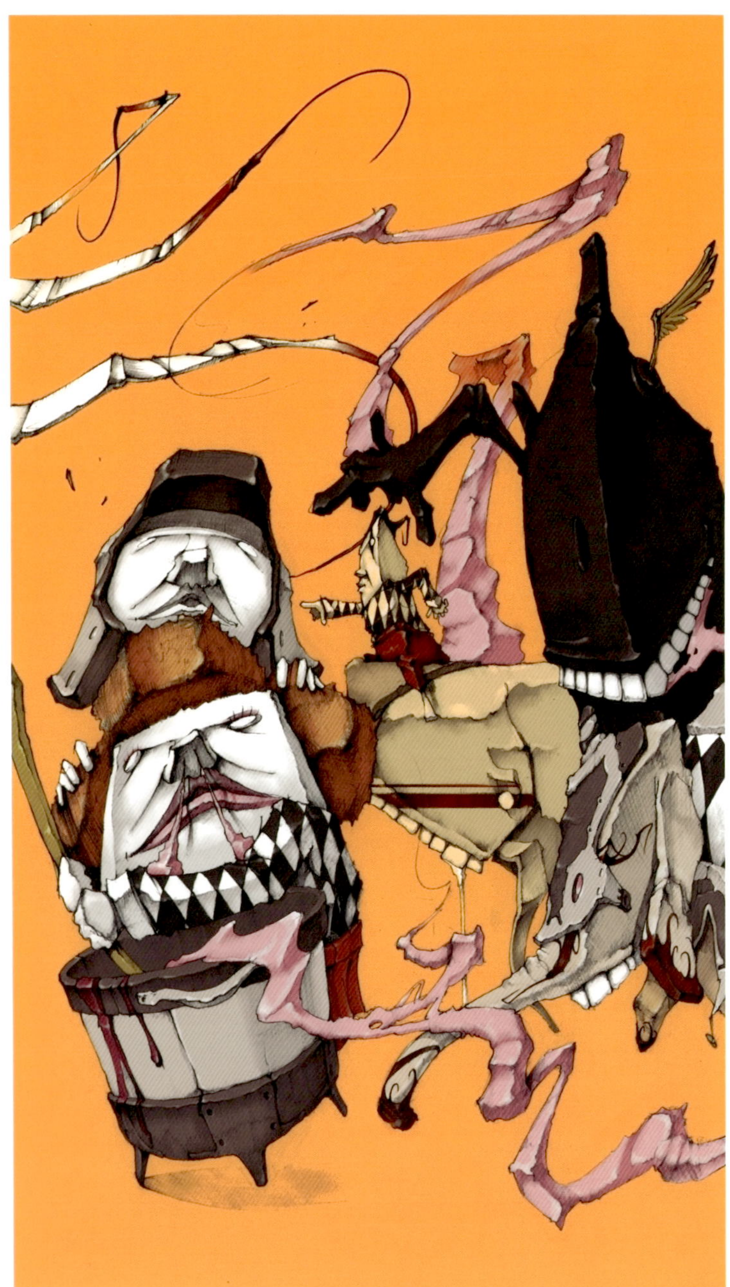

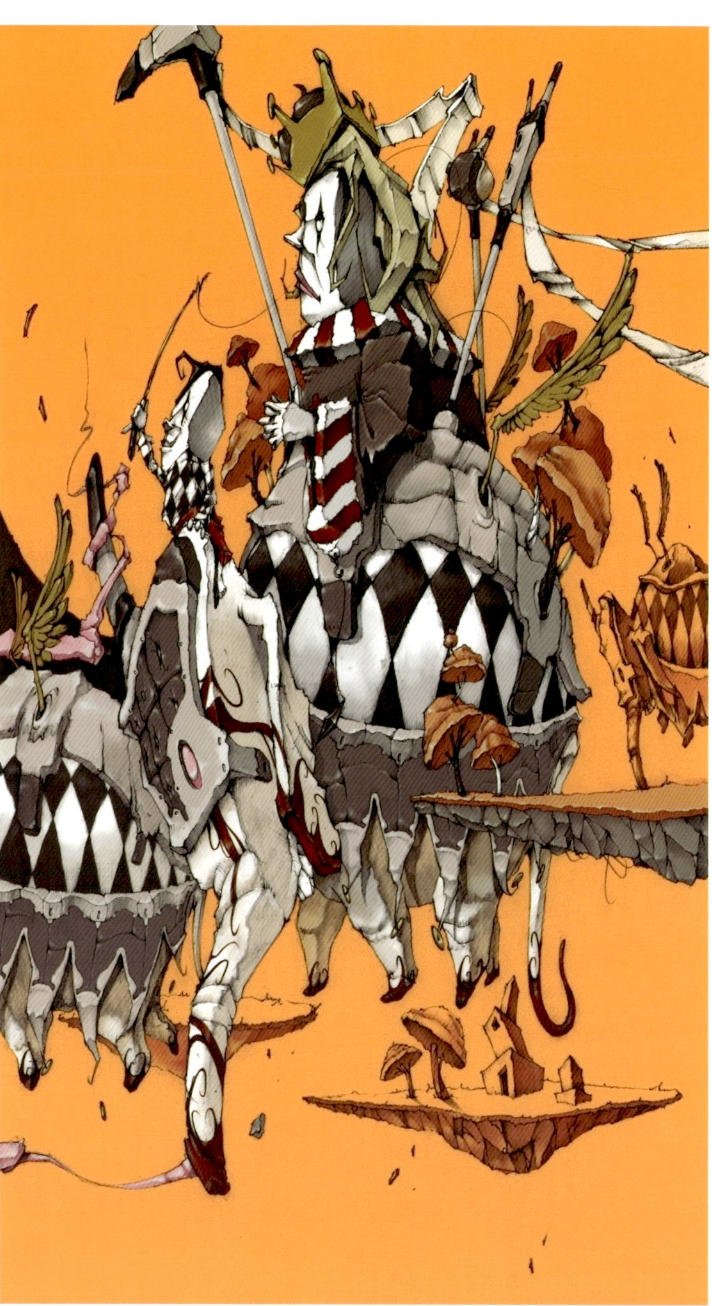

LEFT: march03
RIGHT: march04

LEFT: march05
RIGHT: march06

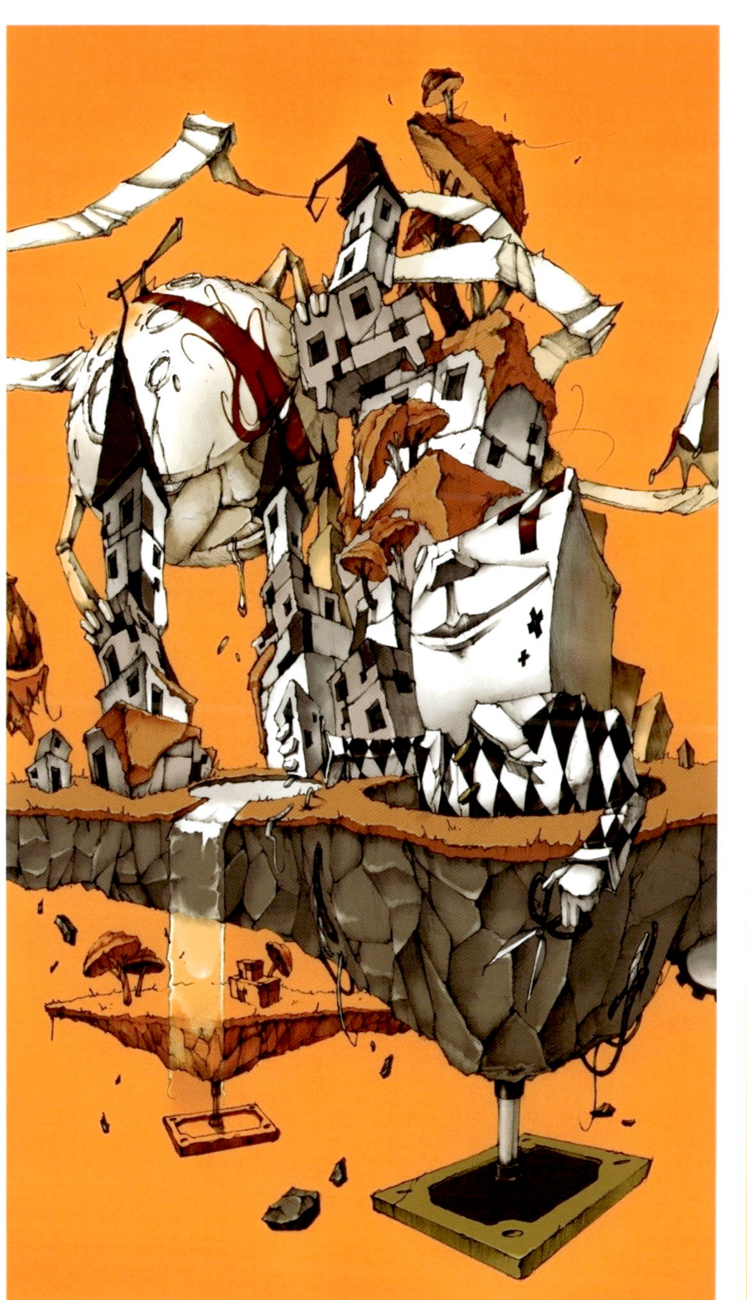

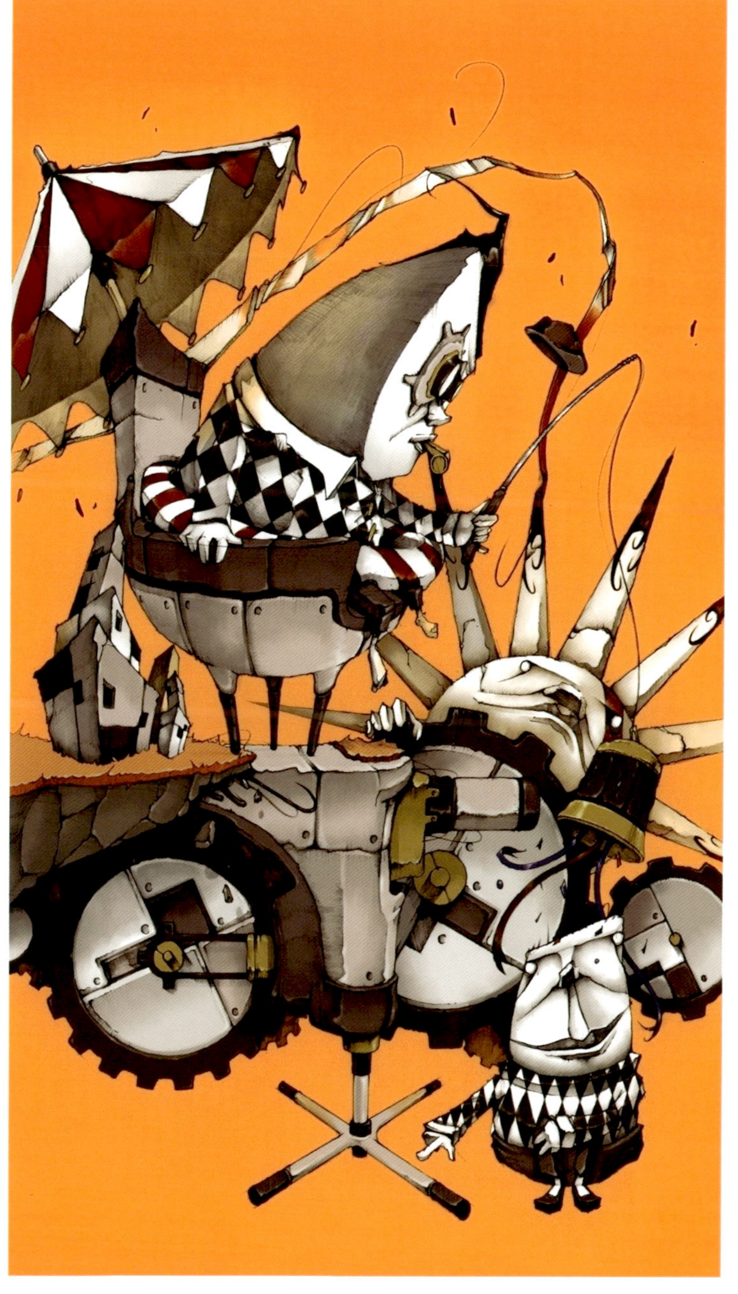

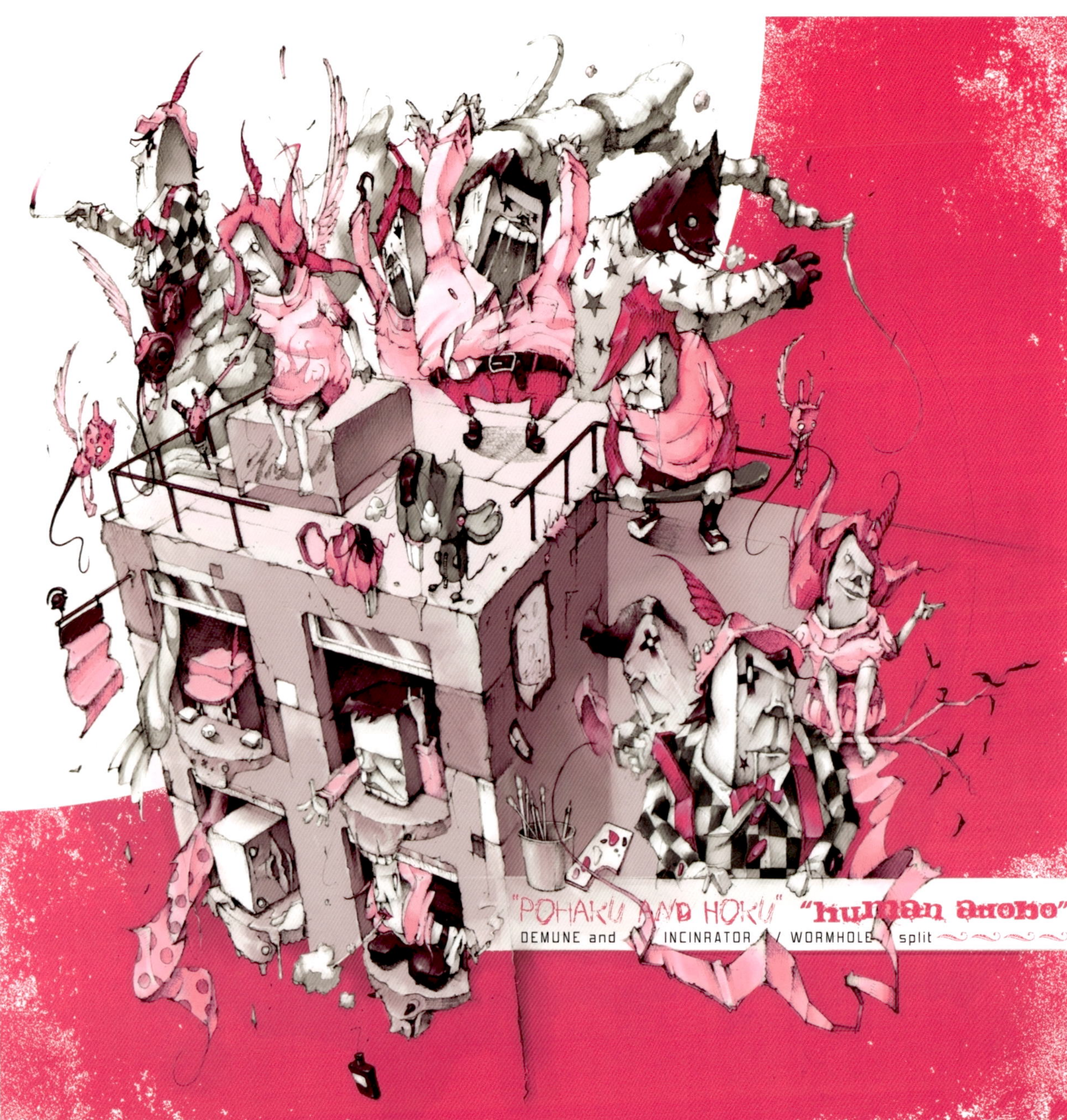

LEFT PAGE: pohaku and hoku

RIGHT PAGE: moon struck moles

EN

It sounds terrible that illustration should just be a service. Of course, I try to avoid creating anything that lacks originality and is superficial and hence bad. But if I have a good relationship with my client, the final product will always reflect my own taste and my own ideas, even if, at the end of the day, it has to satisfy the client's needs. What's important is that everyone is happy, isn't it? That's what I'm interested in and that's the way forward. "The artist is his own patron" may sound good, but sometimes I can't help but find statements like this and artists who believe in them arrogant. Definitions are boring and I would like to think it's us who can disprove and ignore them. However, that's not something I would work hard at. Keywords for me are "vibes" and "timing." Everything depends on them. Hence, the differences between illustration and art don't matter a great deal. Both illustration and art change their shape and expression in relation to the mood and the moment in which they are conceived. My business card says, "design / illustration / mural." It sounded right at the time I printed them. Aren't people easy to impress?

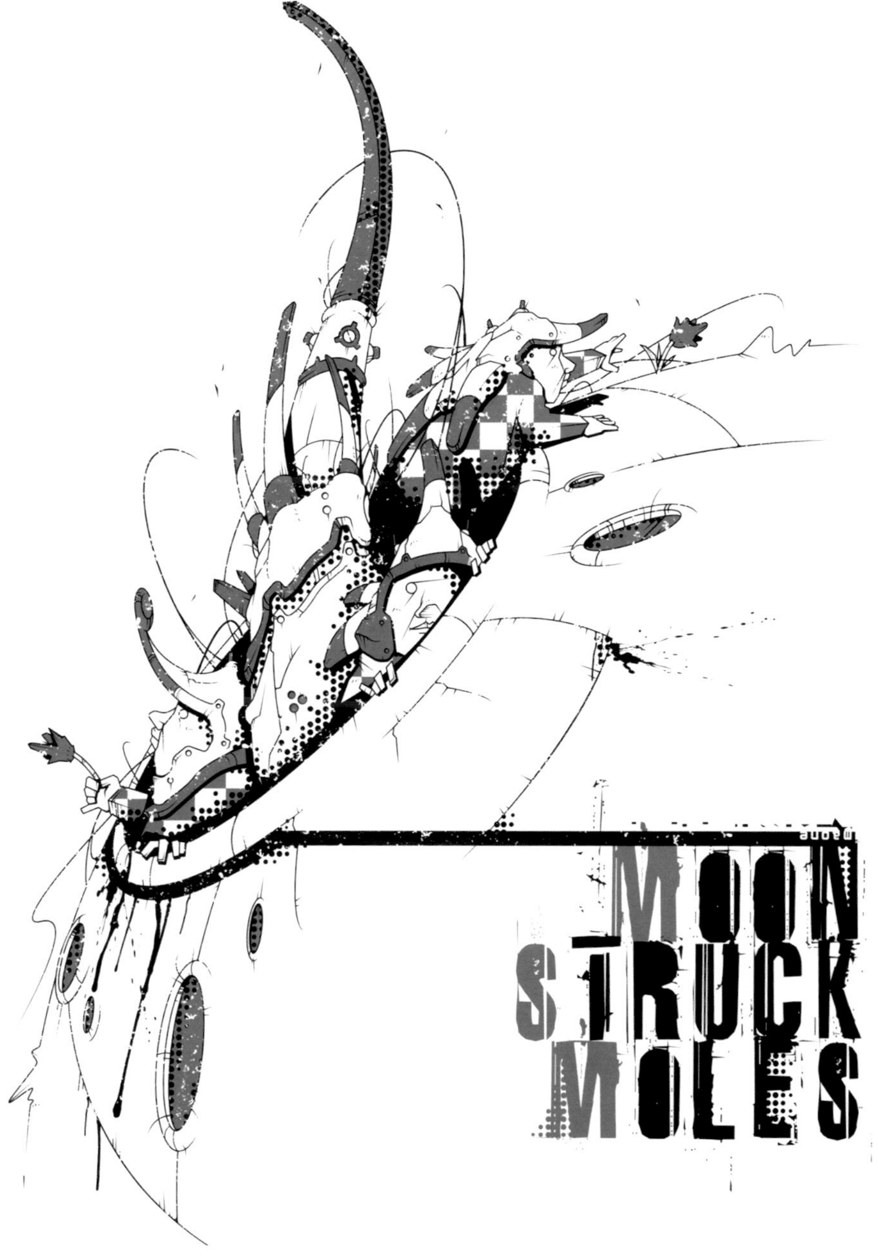

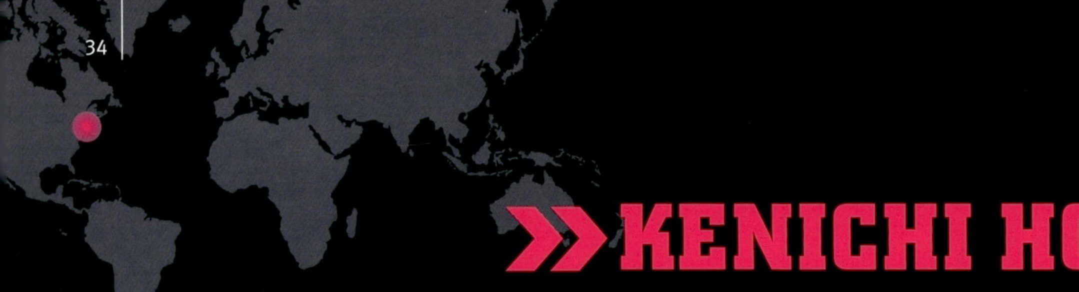

KENICHI HOSHINE

NATIONALITY: JAPANESE

LOCATION: NEW YORK CITY

CONTACT: WWW.KENICHIHOSHINE.COM

TECHNIQUE: PAINTING AND DRAWING

BORN: 1977

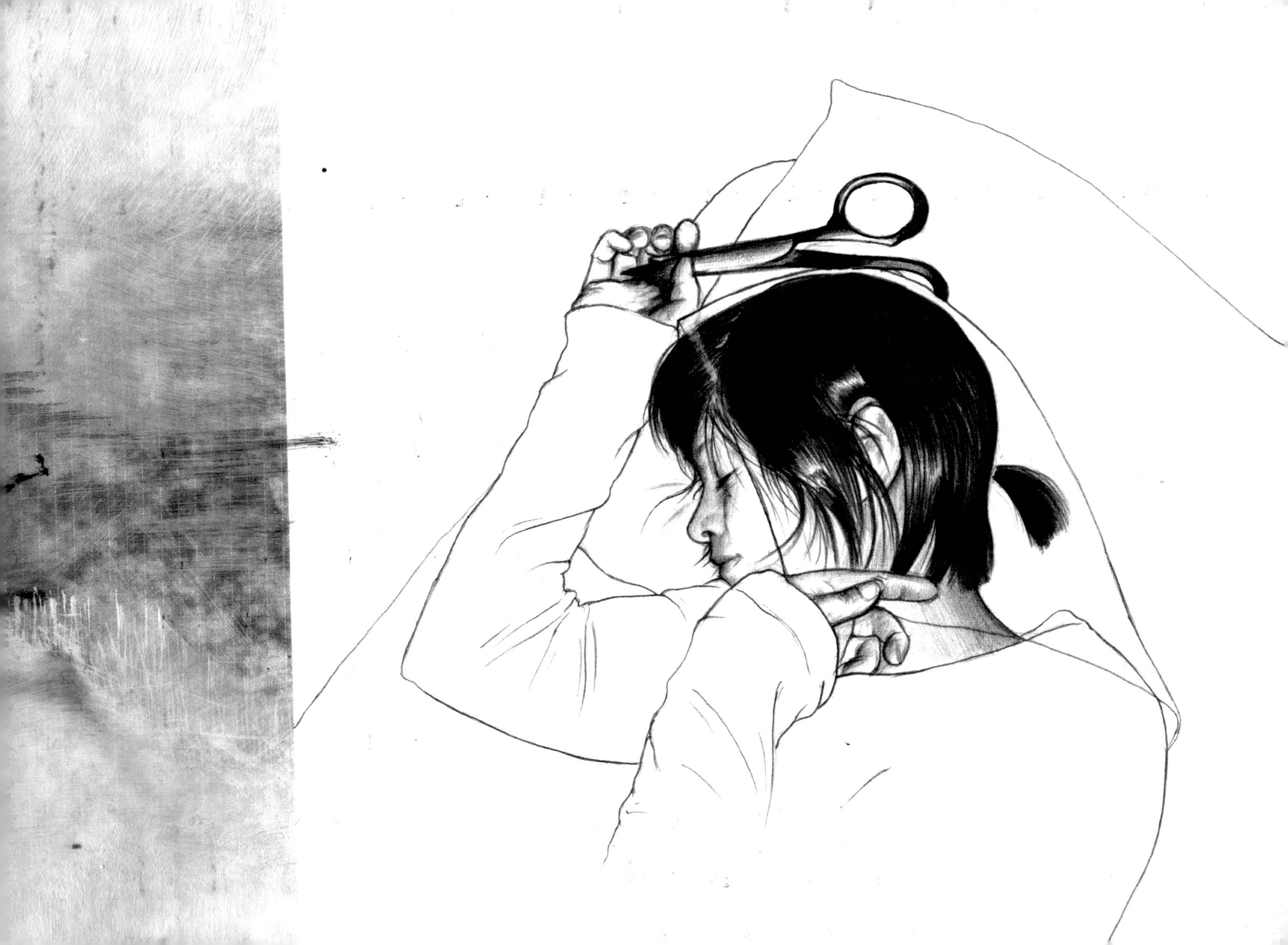

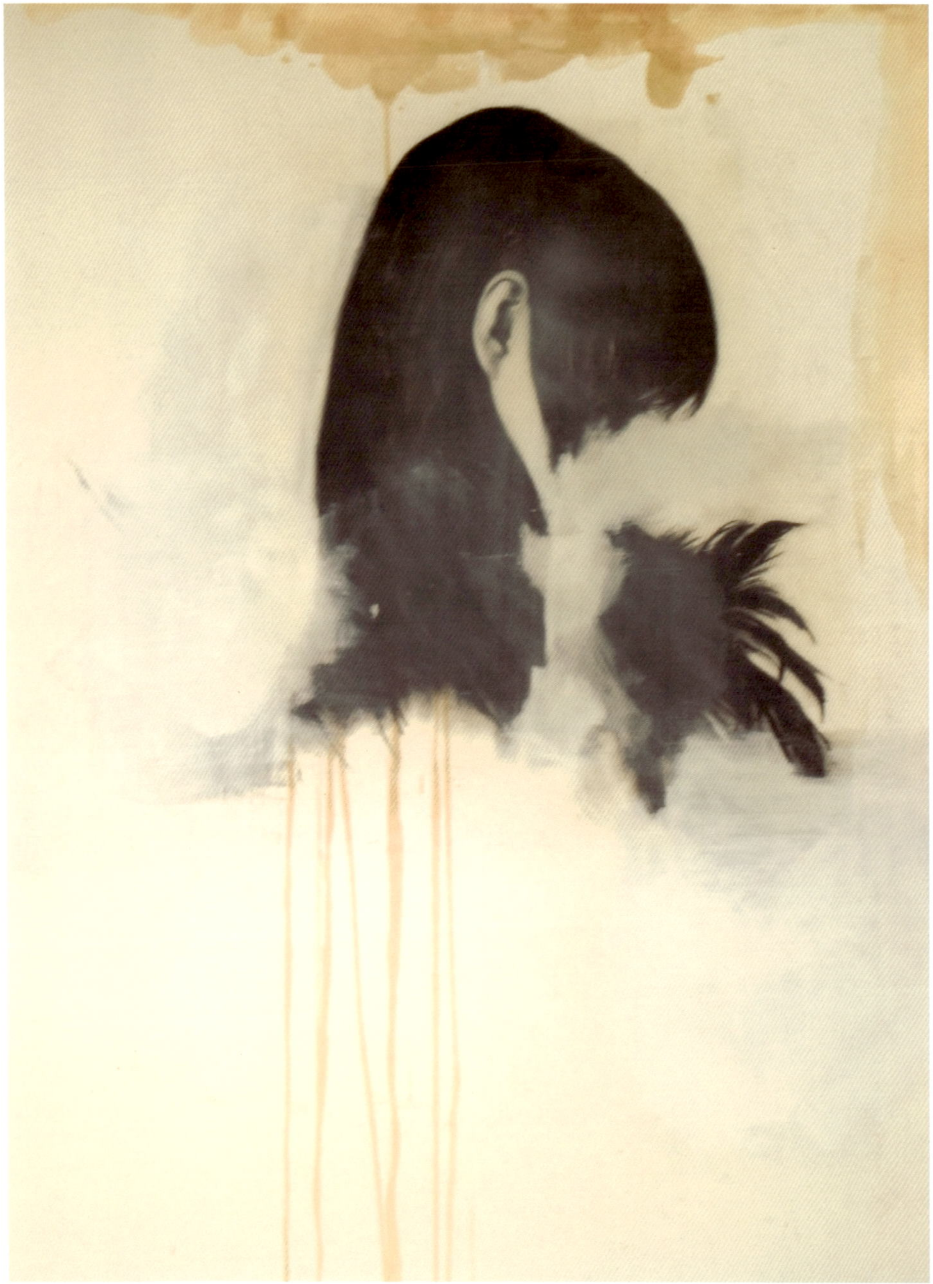

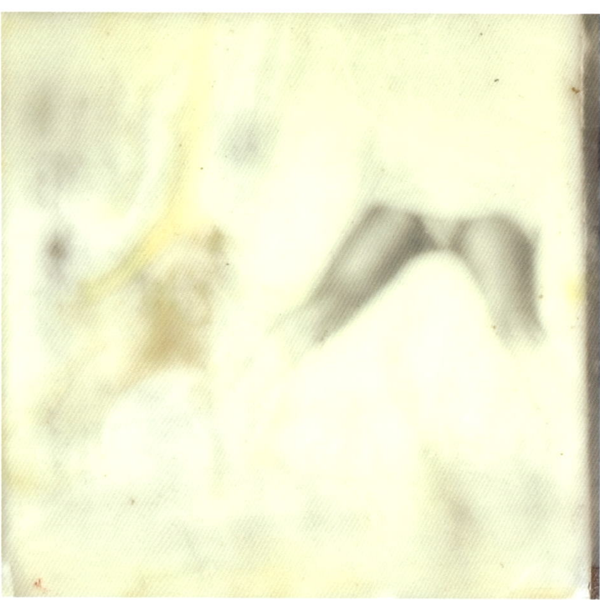

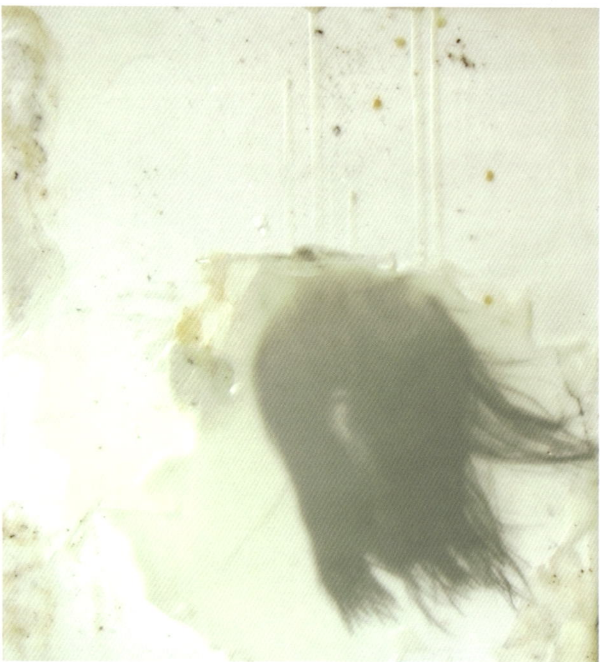

DE Heutzutage verschwimmen die Grenzen zwischen Illustration und Kunst zunehmend. Einen „illustrativen“ Stil in einer Kunstgalerie zu entdecken ist heute nichts Ungewöhnliches mehr. Ebenso erlebt man immer häufiger, dass Illustratoren erfolgreicher in Galerien sind als auf dem Gebiet der kommerziellen Illustration, wo sie sich normalerweise bewegen. Ich persönlich finde es wunderbar, dass sich die Grenzen allmählich auflösen, denn der Werdegang eines Künstlers oder das, als was dieser bezeichnet wird, sollten bei der Betrachtung von Kunst keine Rolle spielen. Werke sollten stattdessen für sich sprechen. Ich selbst verstehe mich als Maler beziehungsweise Künstler, weil ich eigentlich keine kommerziellen Illustrationen mache. Aber ein kleiner Teil von mir ist definitiv Illustrator, nachdem ich während meines Kunststudiums einige Illustrationskurse belegt und dabei wertvolle Dinge gelernt habe.

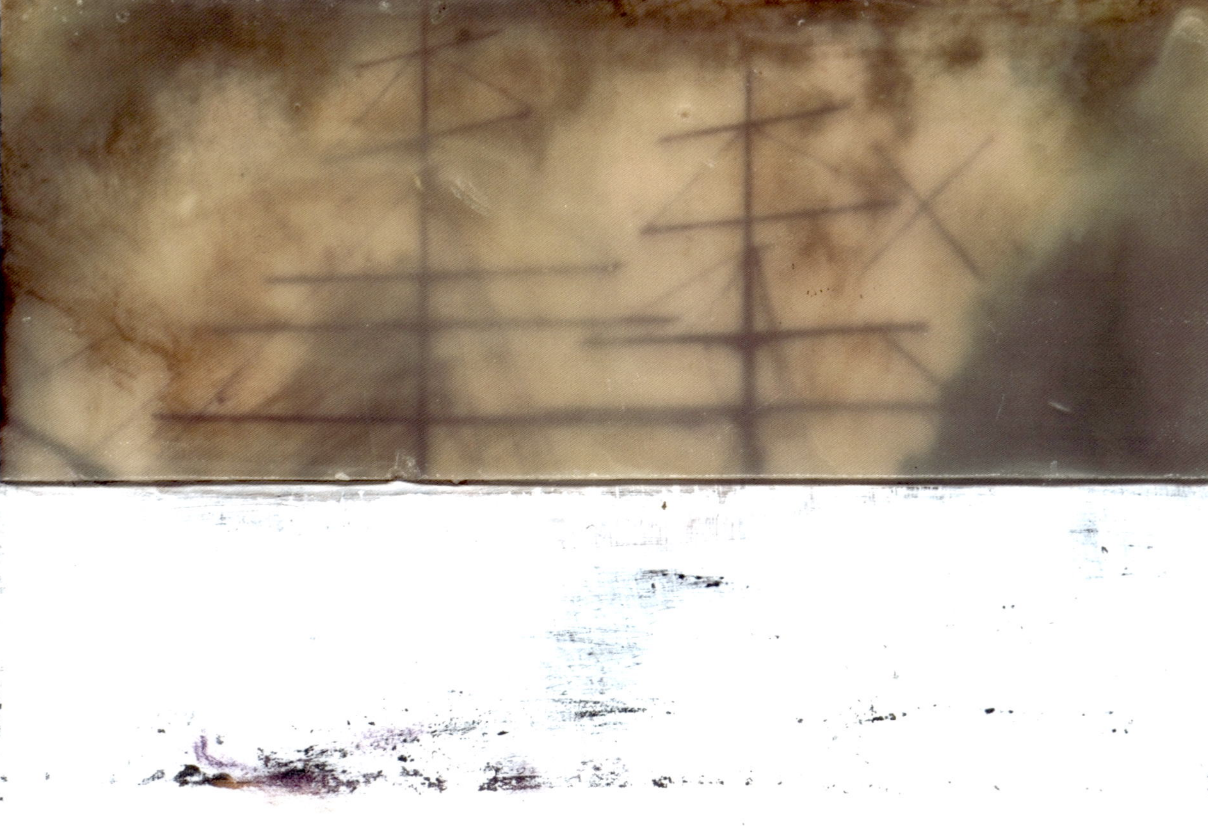

INTRODUCTION:
poison control vol.1
book project illustration
LEFT PAGE:
LEFT: untitled
TOP RIGHT: politewinter #039
DOWN RIGHT: untitled
RIGHT PAGE: politewinter #003

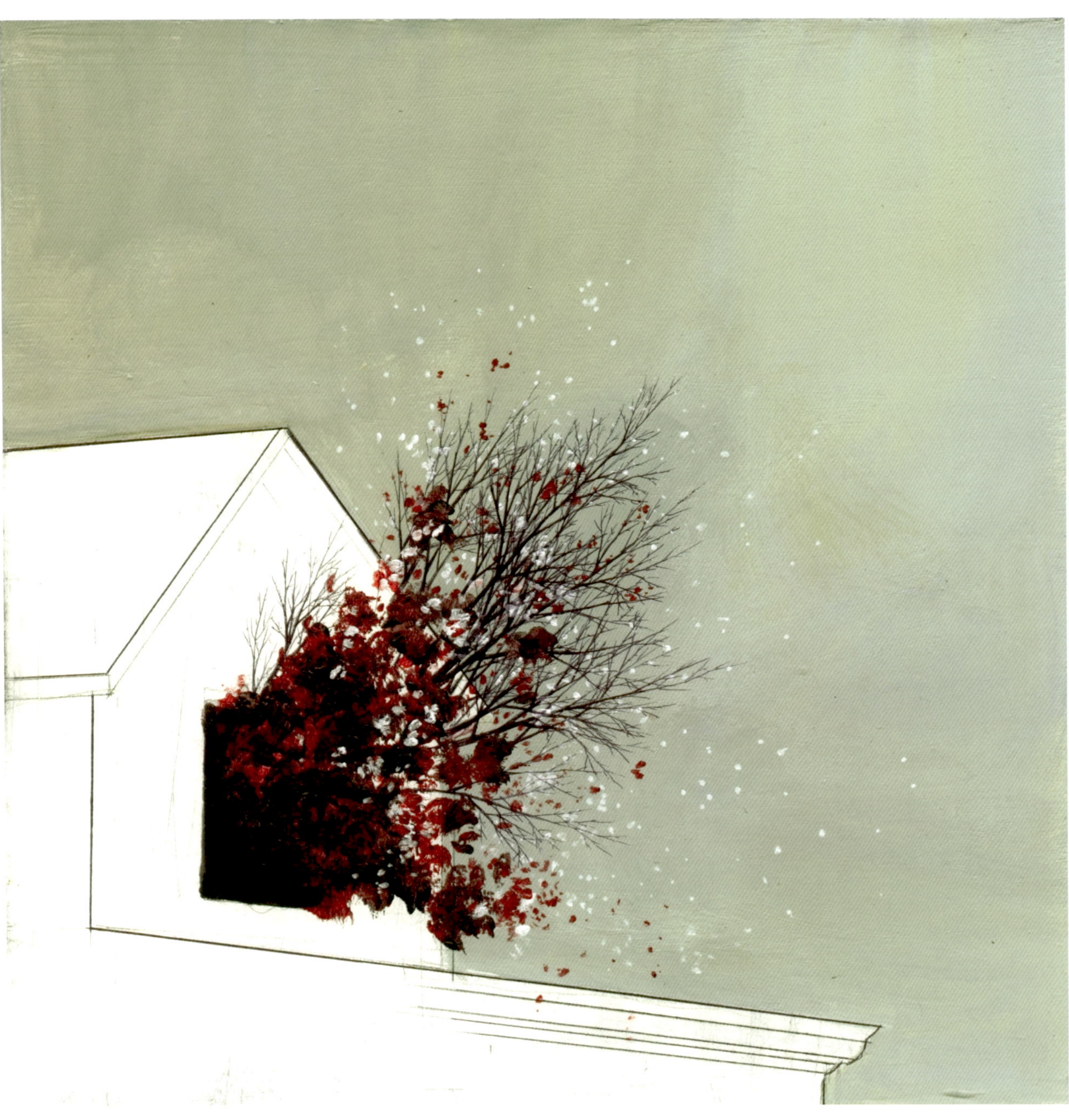

LEFT PAGE: politewinter #021
RIGHT PAGE:
LEFT: untitled
RIGHT: untitled

EN These days the line that separates the illustration world and the fine art world is being blurred more and more. It's nothing unusual for an "illustrative" style to be showcased in a fine art gallery. Equally, it is happening more and more often that illustrators are more successful in galleries than in the commercial illustration world that they would usually find themselves. Personally, I think it is wonderful that boundaries disappear because the career path and the label of an artist shouldn't matter when one looks at their art. Works should speak for themselves. I see myself as a painter, or a fine artist, because I don't really do commercial illustrations. But there definitely is a small part of me that is an illustrator since I took illustration classes at my art school that taught me some valuable lessons.

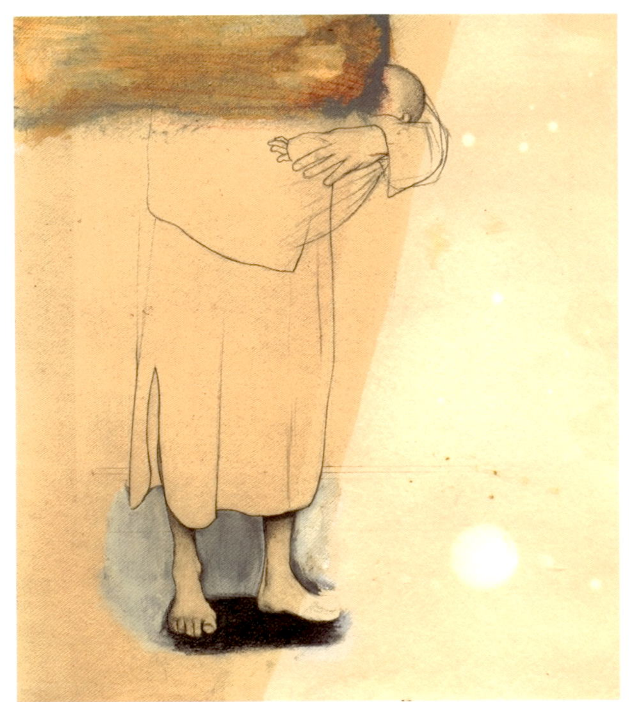

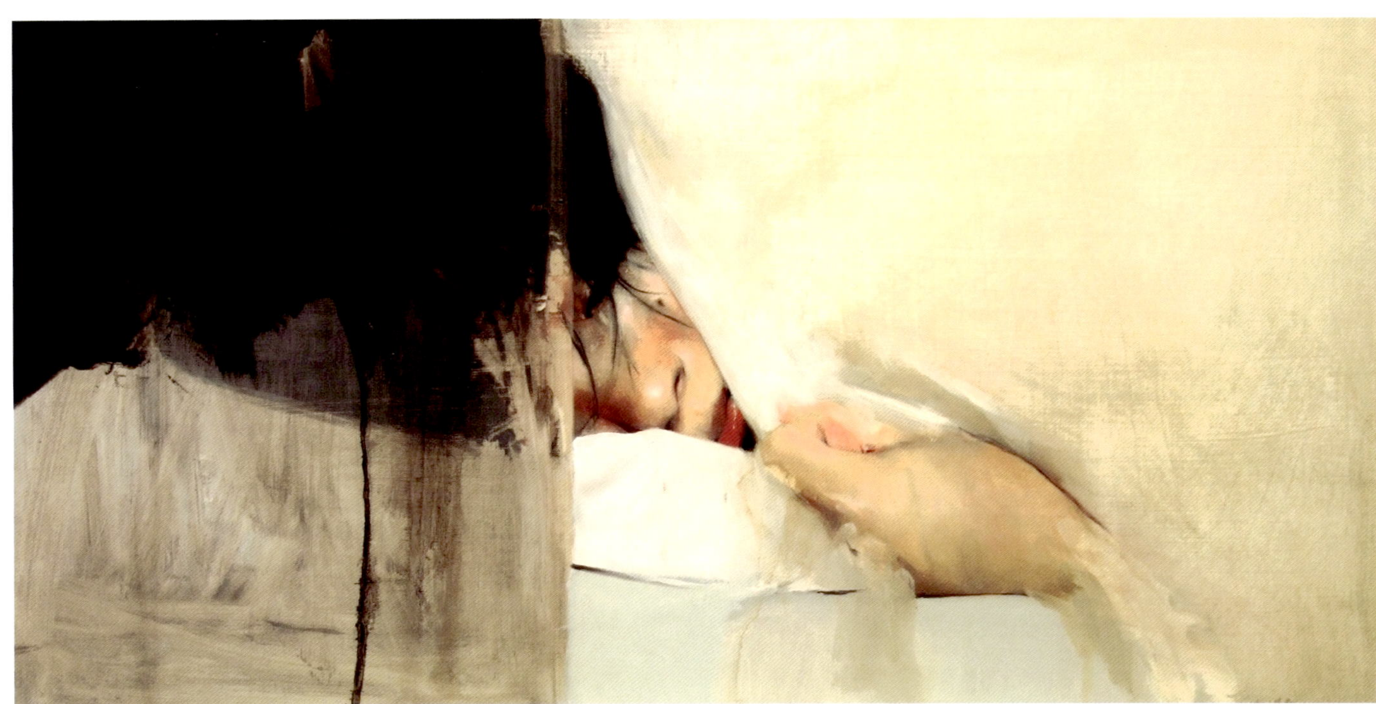

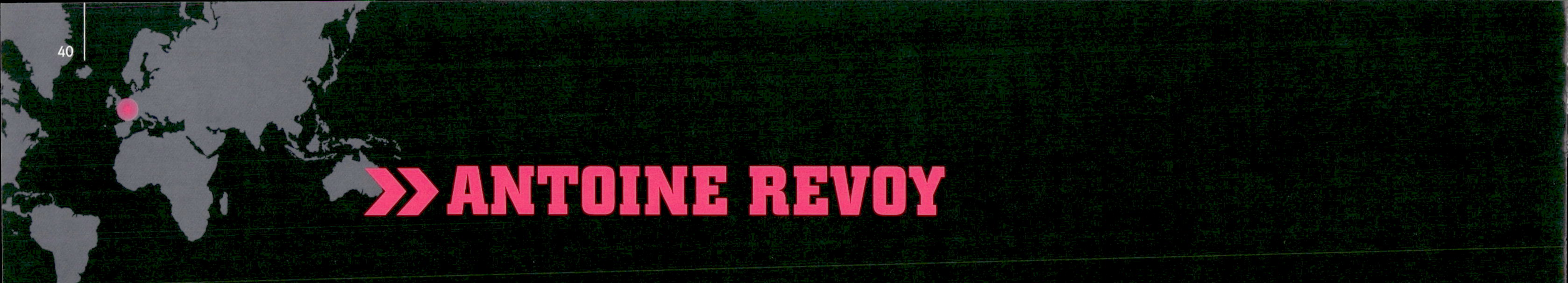

» ANTOINE REVOY

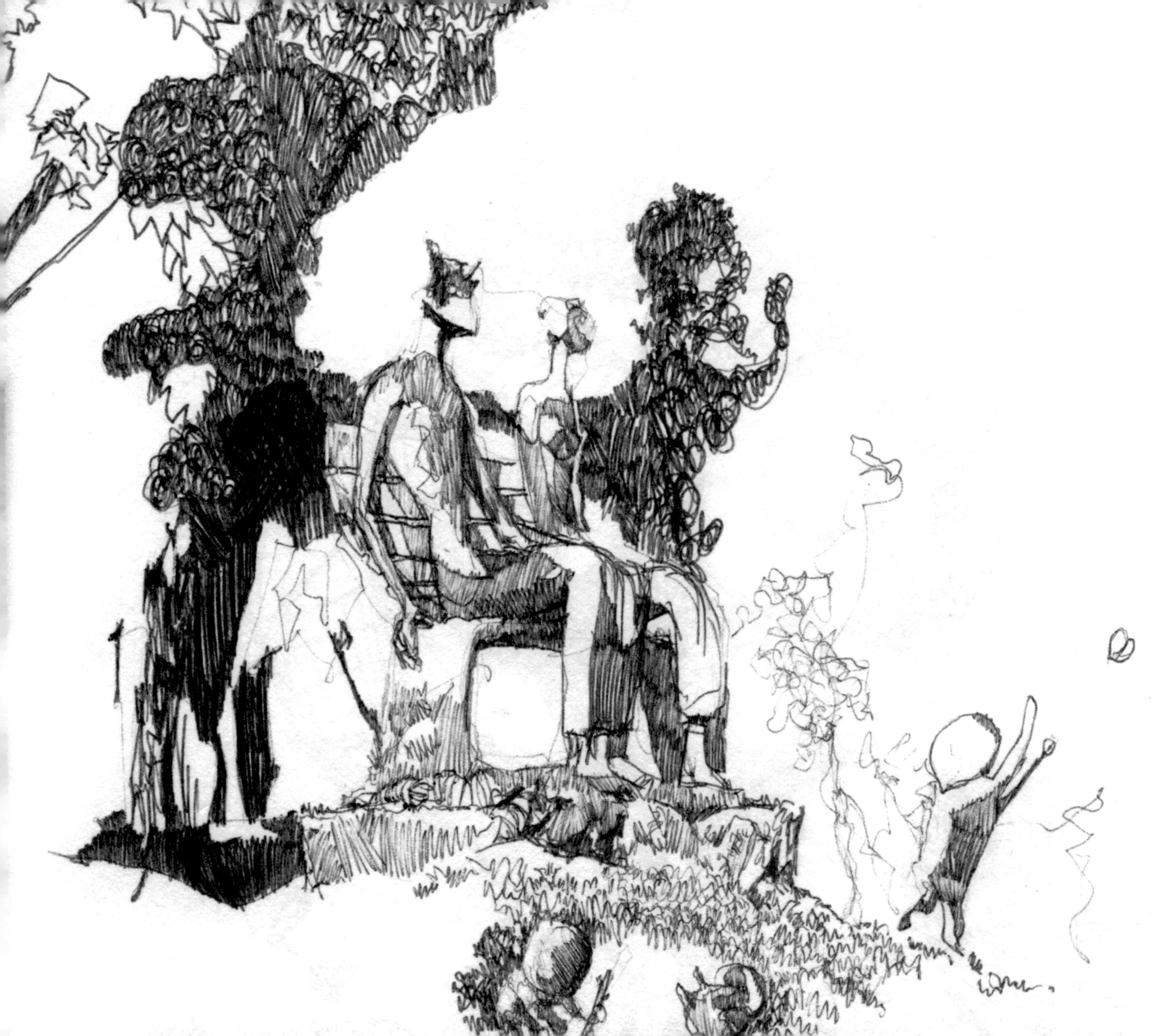

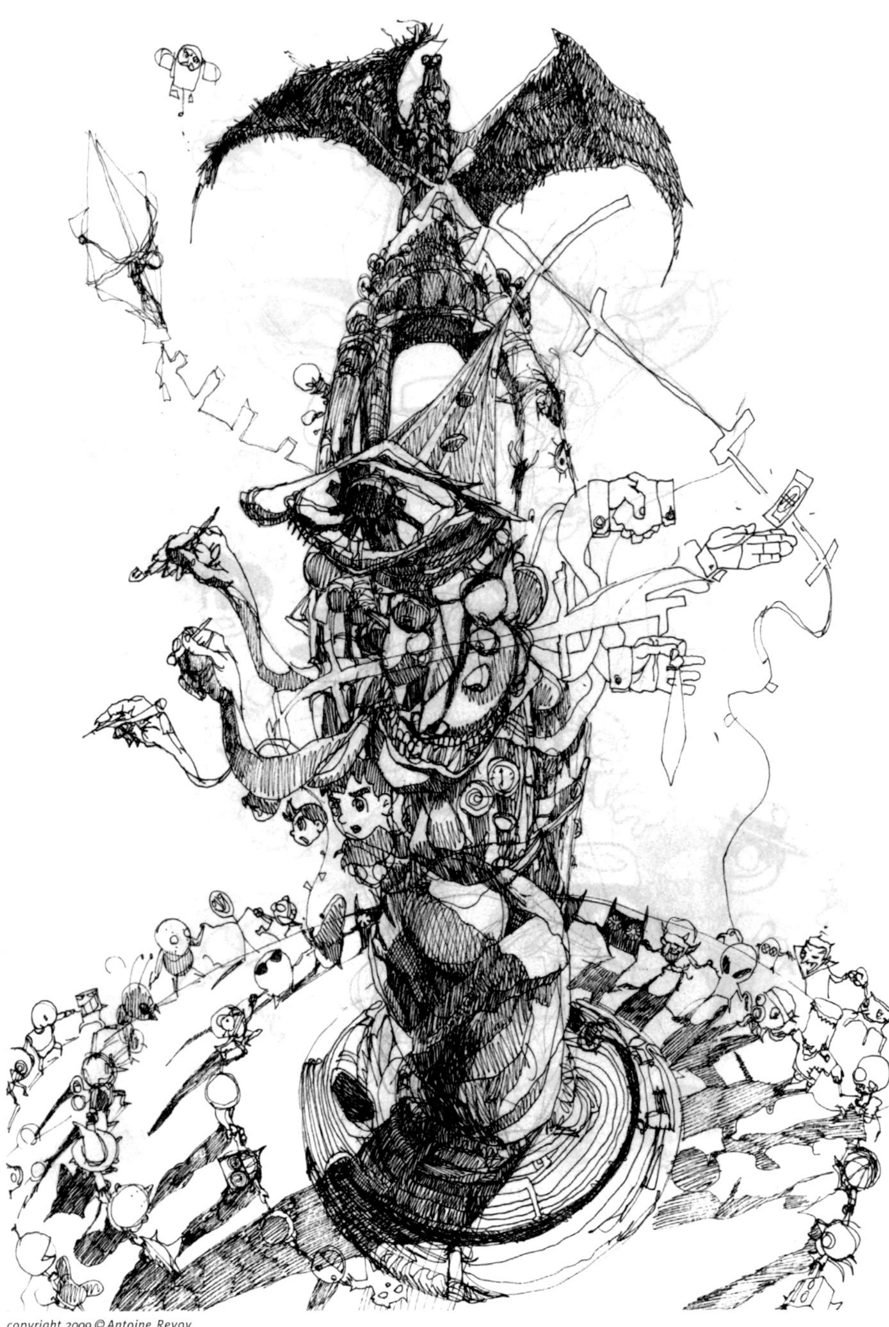

copyright 2009 © Antoine Revoy

copyright 2009 © Antoine Revoy

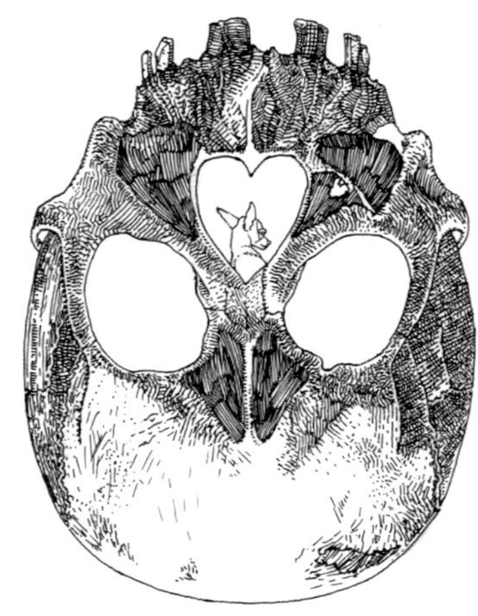

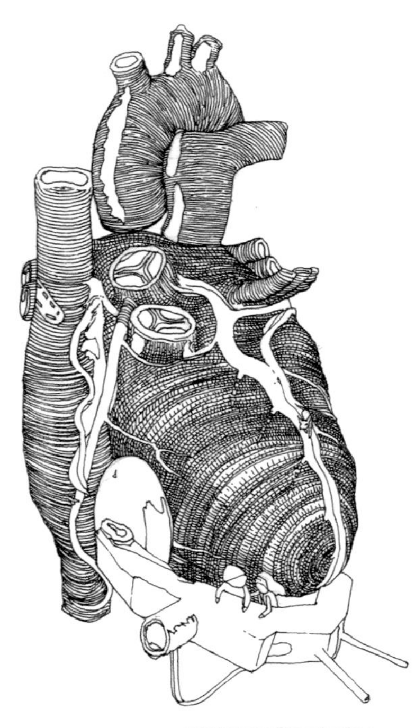

copyright 2009 © Antoine Revoy

DE Die Beziehung zwischen Illustration und Kunst ist Gegenstand der Auseinandersetzung und Debatte unter Kunstgeschichtlern und Kritikern und basiert auf dem kommerziellen Prinzip, da ihr Denken auf dieselbe Art und Weise fixiert ist, wie künstlerische Werke durch bestimmte Faktoren – nämlich den Endkunden – beeinflusst werden. Ich würde zunächst einmal stark bezweifeln, dass man Kunst, die deren Urteil nach um der Kunst willen produziert wird, von Notwendigkeiten wie zum Beispiel einem Einkommen trennen kann – wie direkt oder indirekt es auch sein mag – oder von Bedingungen, die eine von außen kommende Klientel vorgibt. Es ist kein Zufall, dass Renaissancekünstler religiöse und politische Bilder schufen, oder dass moderne abstrakte Künstler Serien entwickelten, die für Galerien bestimmt sind. In kreativer Hinsicht ist Illustration als Produktion visuellen, bewegten oder

INTRODUCTION:
butterfly chaser | 1998
LEFT PAGE:
LEFT: totem pole | 1998
MIDDLE: skull | 2006
RIGHT: clamp | 2006
RIGHT PAGE: playjinx | 2001

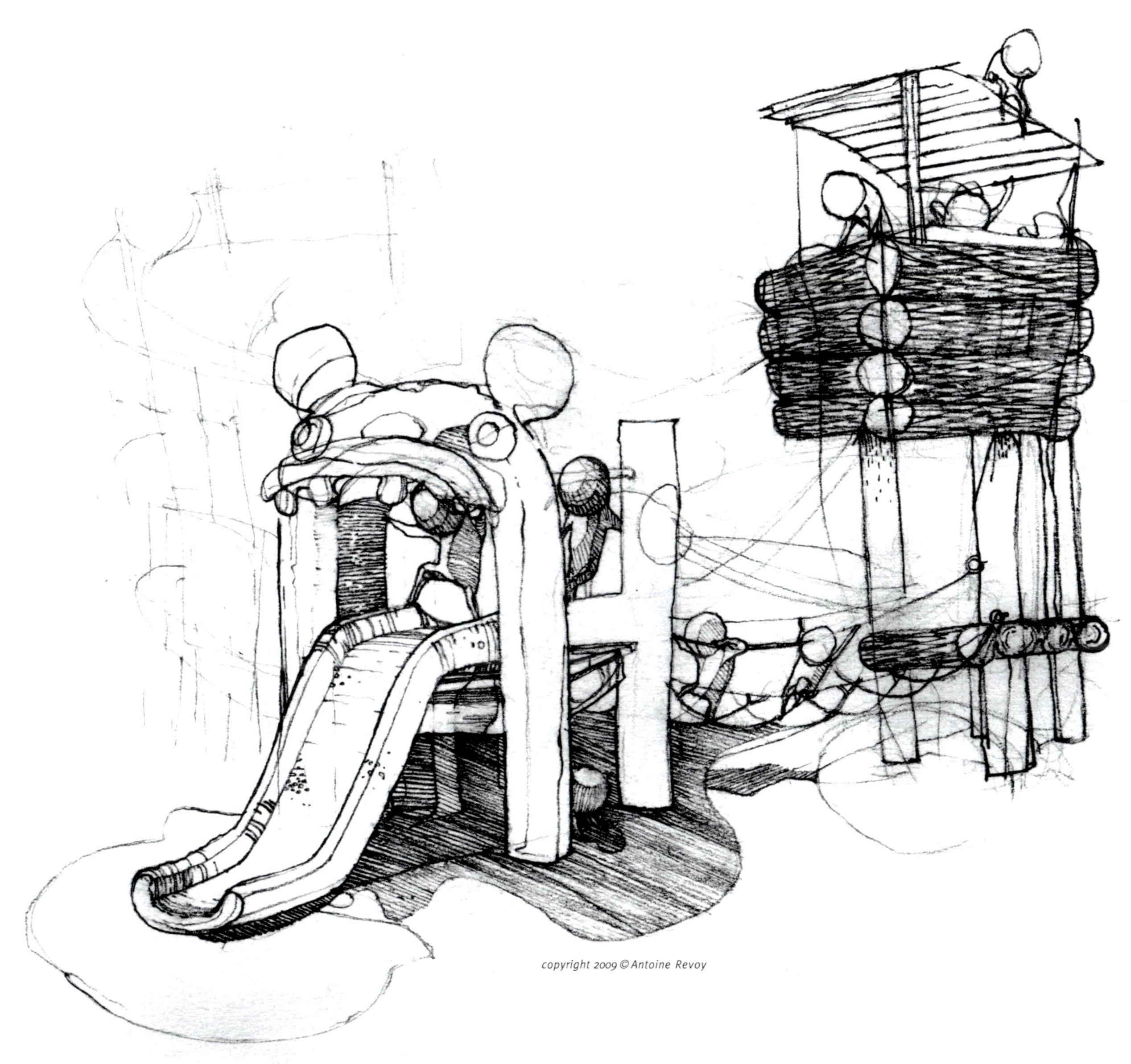

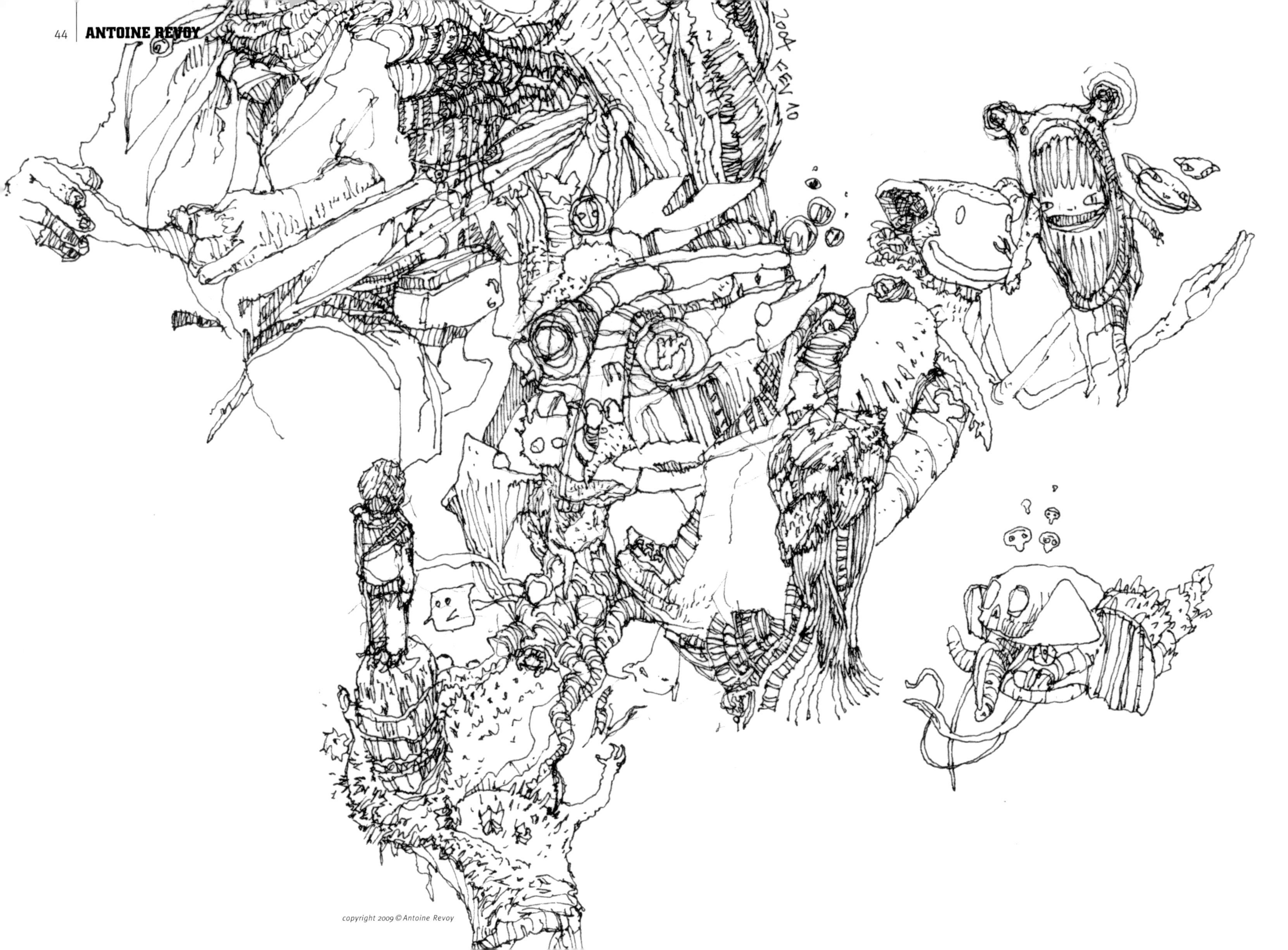
2004 FEV 10

hörbaren Inhalts ihrem Ursprung nach ein künstlerisches Streben par excellence. Von der vom Kunden verlangten Dienstleistung abgesehen bietet Illustration mir Gelegenheit, die schlichte Freude am Zeichnen zu erleben – ein spielerischer Prozess, dessen Natur von meinen frühesten Werken bis zur Tätigkeit als professioneller Illustrator unverändert geblieben ist. Lange nachdem die Illustration ihren kommerziellen Zweck erfüllt hat und die entsprechenden Einzelheiten vergessen sind, ist es die Kunst im eigentlichen Sinn, die übrig bleibt und in der der Betrachter neue, unabhängige Bedeutungen entdecken kann.

LEFT PAGE: cactus | 2004
RIGHT PAGE:
LEFT: satellite card-game | 2000
RIGHT: pumpkin | 2005

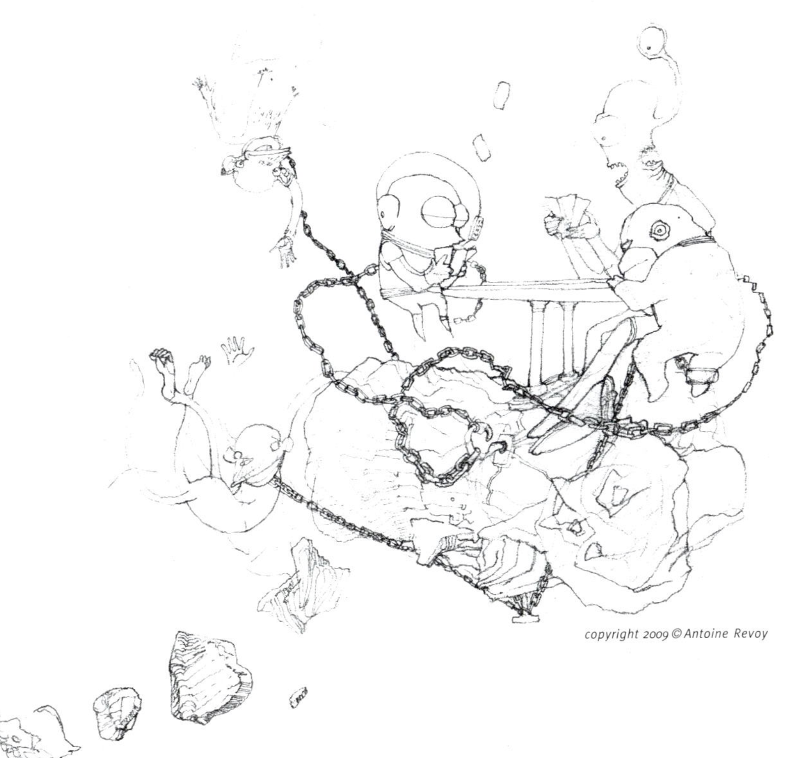

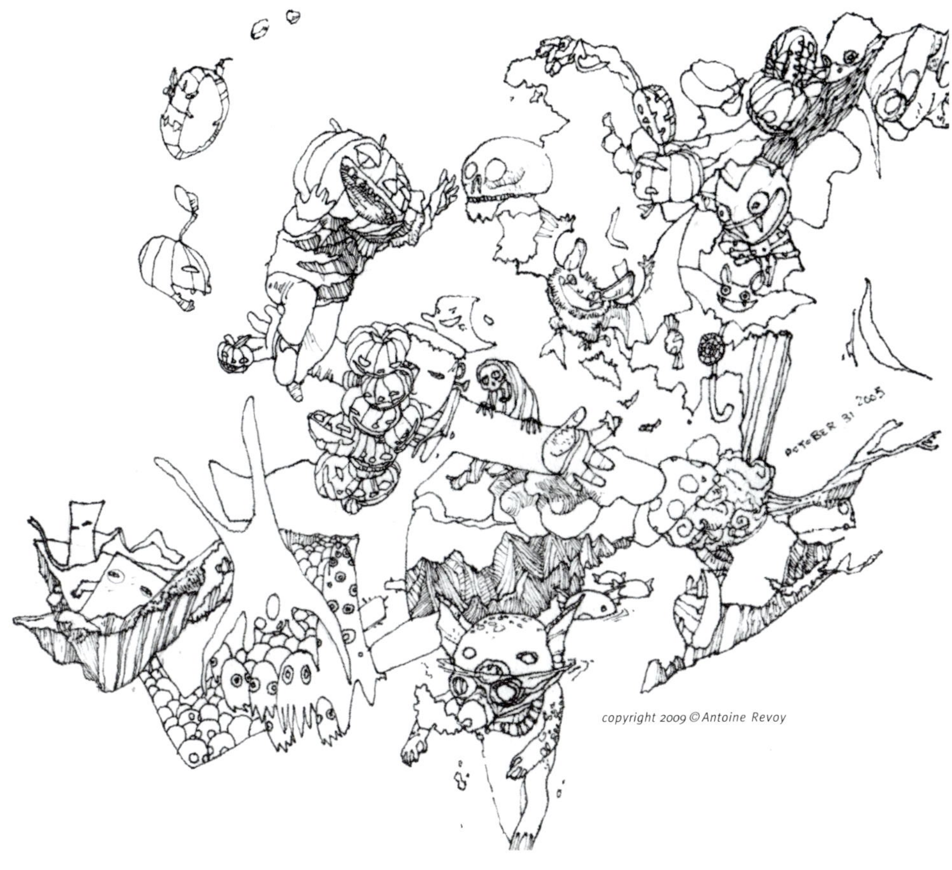

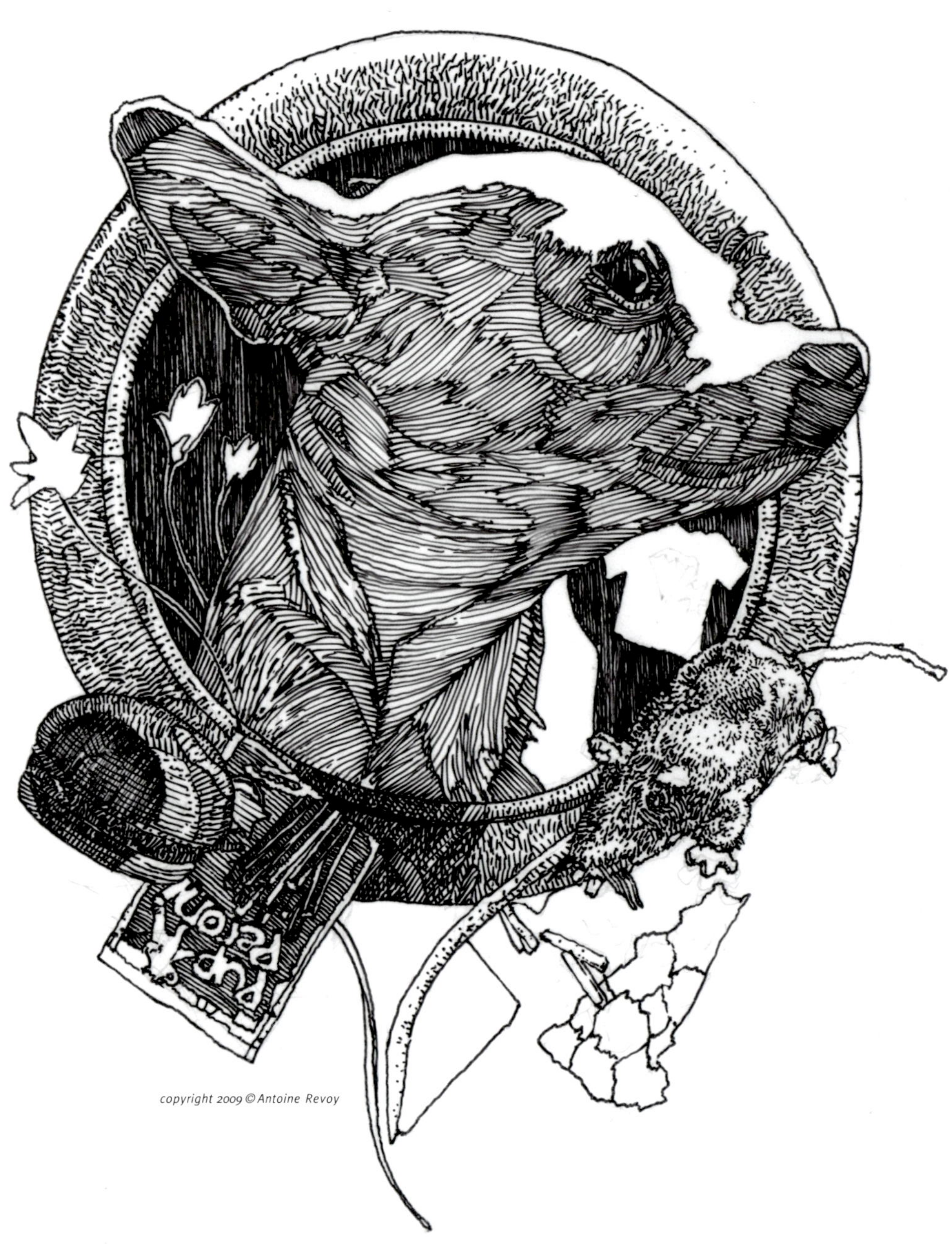

EN The relationship between illustration and fine art is a subject of analysis and debate among art historians and critics following a commercial premise, because their thoughts are fixated on the manner in which artistic creation is affected by the presence of a particular component, the client. First of all, I doubt that the kind of art which they deem to have been produced for art's sake is or could ever be fully independent from factors of necessity such as income, as direct or indirect as they may be, or from any constraints established by external clients. It is no accident that Renaissance artists depicted religious and political motifs or that modern abstract artists developed series for galleries. In creative terms, illustration as production of visual, moving or audio content is an artistic endeavor par excellence. Beyond the service requested by a client, an illustration is an opportunity for me to experience the simple pleasure of drawing, a playful process – the nature of which has remained unchanged from my earliest creations down to my work as a professional illustrator. Long after the commercial purpose of the illustration has been achieved and its contextual details have been forgotten, it is art in the strictest sense that remains, and the viewer can interpret it in a new and unconstrained way.

LEFT PAGE: lily | 2006
RIGHT PAGE:
LEFT: rabbits sawing tree | 2006
RIGHT: mouse planet | 1998

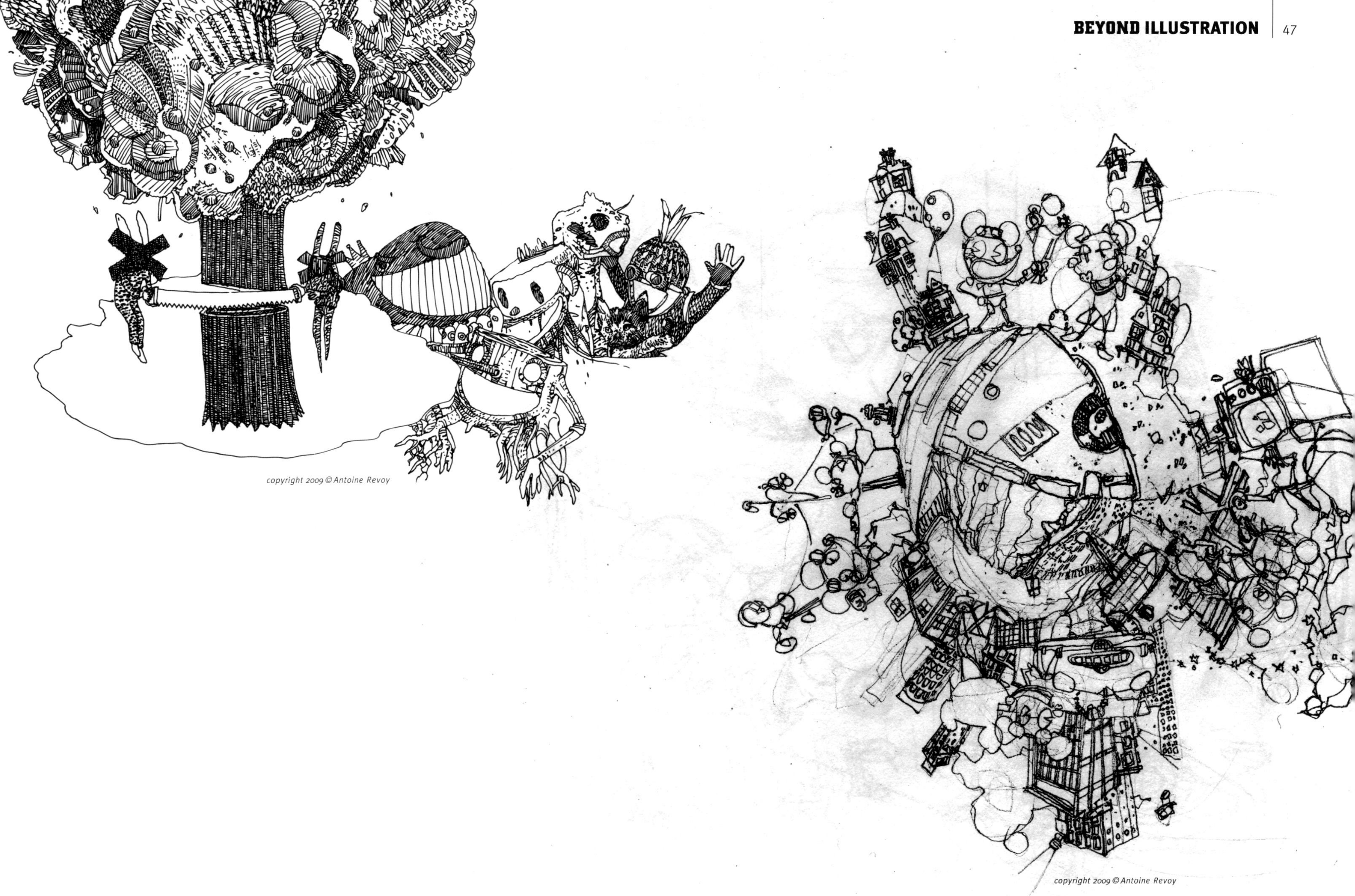

»CITYABYSS [BEATA SZCZECINSKA]

NATIONALITY:	POLISH
LOCATION:	WORLWIDE | POLAND
PUBLICATIONS:	ILLUSIVE 2 BY DIE GESTALTEN VERLAG WEB DESIGN INDEX 7 | INSTANT GRAPHICS BY ROTOVISION KATALOGUE XXL | BLACK BOOK RAW INTERNATIONAL DESIGN YEARBOOK 2 BY CHINA MADISON ORGANIZATION (FORTHCOMING) SOURCE BOOK OF ILLUSTRATION BY MAOMAO (FORTHCOMING)
REFERENCES:	COMPUTER ARTS MAGAZINE | VAROOM MAGAZINE DEDICATE MAGAZINE | CARPAL TUNELL MAGAZINE SUKCES MAGAZINE | MOLOKO+ MAGAZINE | EXKLUSIV MAG TWOJ STYL MAGAZINE | ZWIERCIADLO MAGAZINE GOSZCZDESIGN AND T&G (FORTHCOMING)
EXHIBITIONS:	CATALOG LAUNCH EXHIBITION TRAFALGAR HOTEL – LONDON – OCTOBER 2007 OSCAR NIEMEYER MUSEUM – BRAZIL CATALOG EXHIBITION MOHO GALLERY – KRAKOW (FORTHCOMING)
REPRESENTIVES:	ALABAMA | ART BUYING AND PRODUCTION HOUSE
CONTACT:	WWW.CITYABYSS.COM INFO@CITYABYSS.COM
TECHNIQUE:	HANDMADE GRAPHICS | TRADITIONAL DRAWINGS DIGITALLY PROCESSED
BORN:	1978

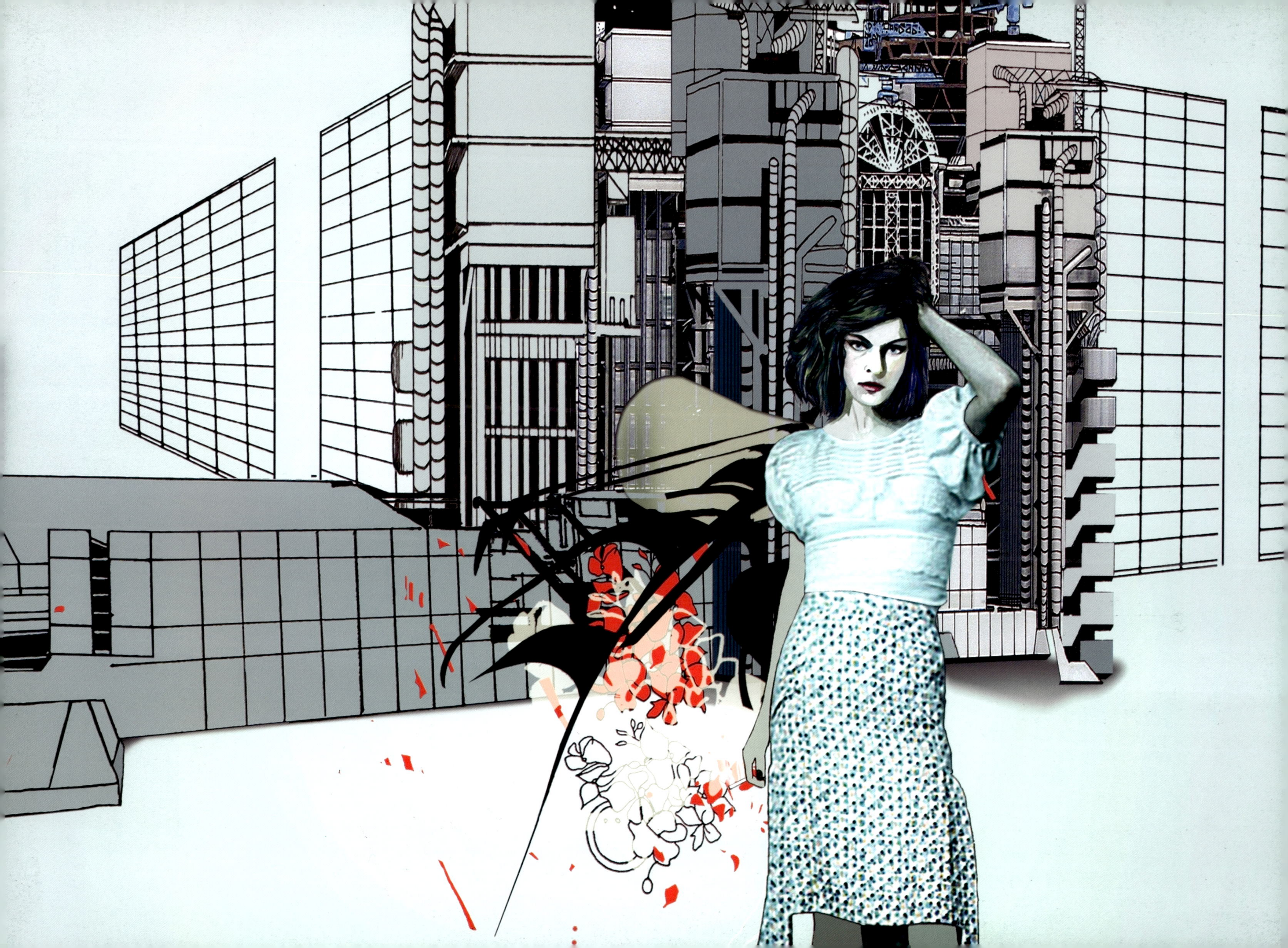

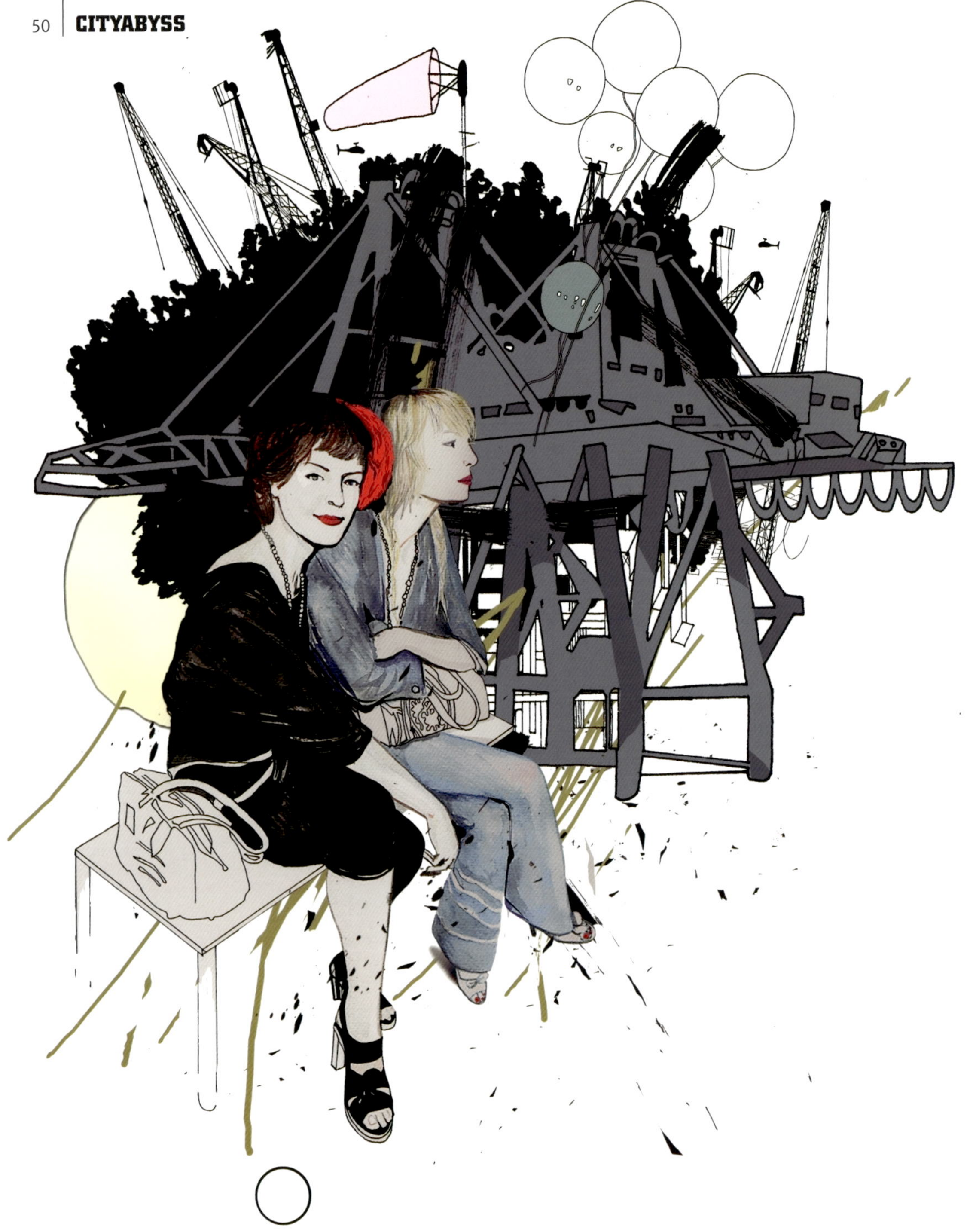

DE Die Frage, ob es eine Grenze zwischen Kunst und Illustration gibt, ist zweifellos ein aktuelles Thema. Auch heute ist die Illustration immer noch darum bemüht, auf sich aufmerksam zu machen und ihre Rolle auf dem Gebiet der Kunst gegenüber anderen Disziplinen zu verteidigen. Die Entwicklungen in der Kunst sind zahlreich, enorm viele Künstler haben den unterschiedlichen Denkweisen eine neue Richtung gegeben. Meine eigene Ausbildung basiert auf traditionellen Formen der Kunst wie Malerei, Zeichnen und Grafik. Das sind meine Schwerpunkte. Ich war schon immer ein Fan traditioneller Techniken und wollte mit diesen etwas Neues schaffen. Bei der Illustration habe ich gleich zu Beginn Text nicht einfach nur visualisiert – ganz im Gegenteil, ich wollte Arbeiten mit Inhalt zeigen, ernsthafte Werke, nicht nur hübsche Bilder. Ich ging an technische Aspekte in derselben Weise heran, wie ich Zeichnungen und Grafiken gestaltete. Generell denke ich, dass wir eines ernstzunehmenden grafischen Anspruchs bedürfen, um solche Werke zu schaffen. Dieses Bestreben wurde früher im Bereich Illustration nicht akzeptiert. Illustrationen dienten der Veranschaulichung einer Geschichte und sollten visuell das anreichern, was im Text beschrieben wurde. Illustratoren wurden in der Welt der bildenden Kunst nicht als Künstler betrachtet und Illustration war nicht als eigene Kunstform anerkannt. Heute kämpft sie um Originalität, wächst dabei rasant und als Illustrator tätig zu sein ist eine Herausforderung. Heute haben wir andere Probleme, wie zum Beispiel die Vergütung, denn für seine Arbeit bezahlt zu werden ändert eine Menge. Zum Glück gibt es immer noch Künstler, die sich davon nicht allzu sehr beeinflussen lassen. Illustration hat heute viel mit Werbung und Design zu tun – und sie hat ihren Platz in der Verkaufsförderung. Die Aufgabe guter zeitgenössischer Illustration ist gegenwärtig schwieriger denn je. Für mich persönlich sollte Illustration nicht vordergründig und banal sein, sie sollte subtile Botschaften in aufregender Form transportieren.

INTRODUCTION: milla
LEFT PAGE: rig
RIGHT PAGE: black&white

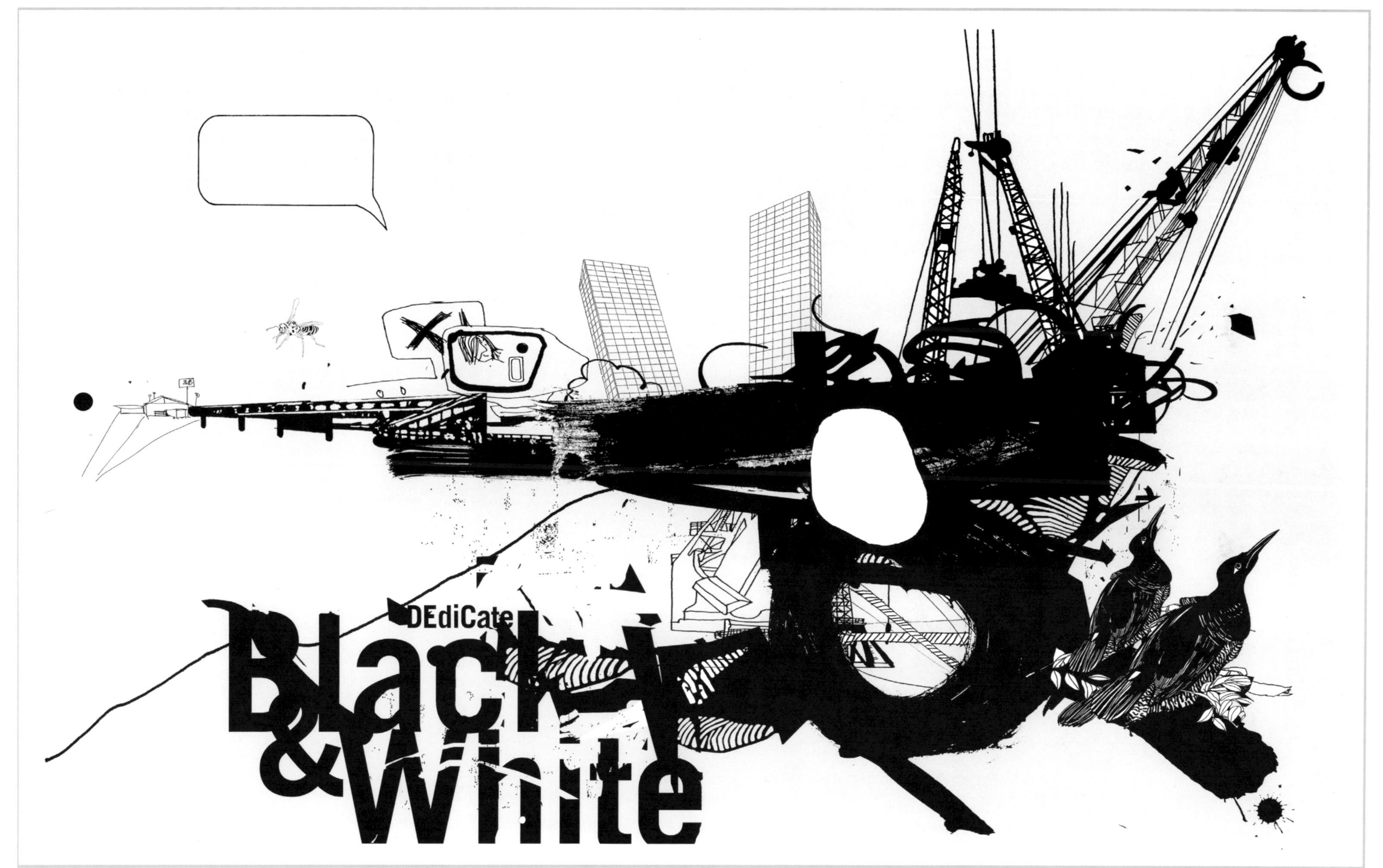
DEdiCate
Black
&White

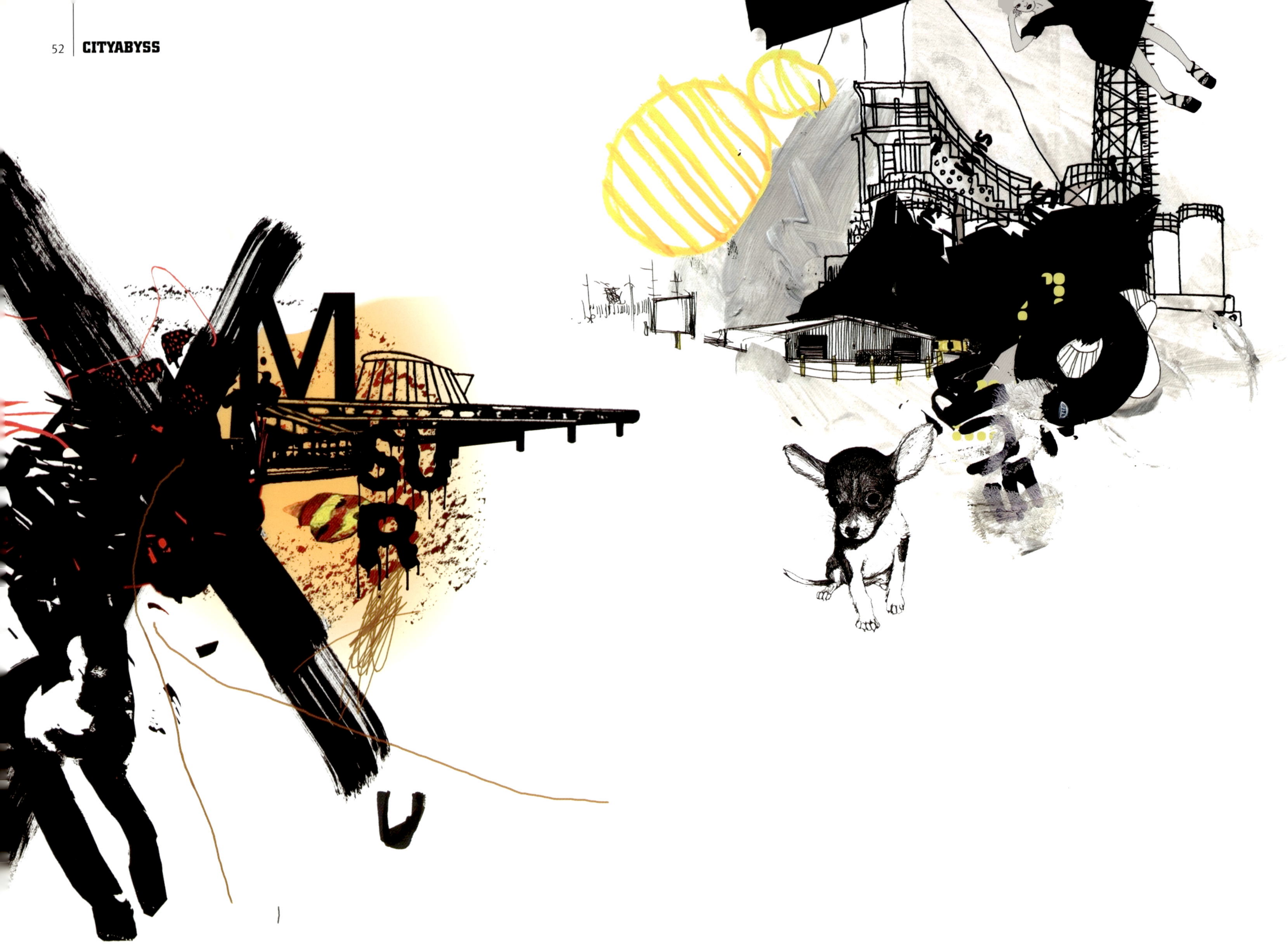

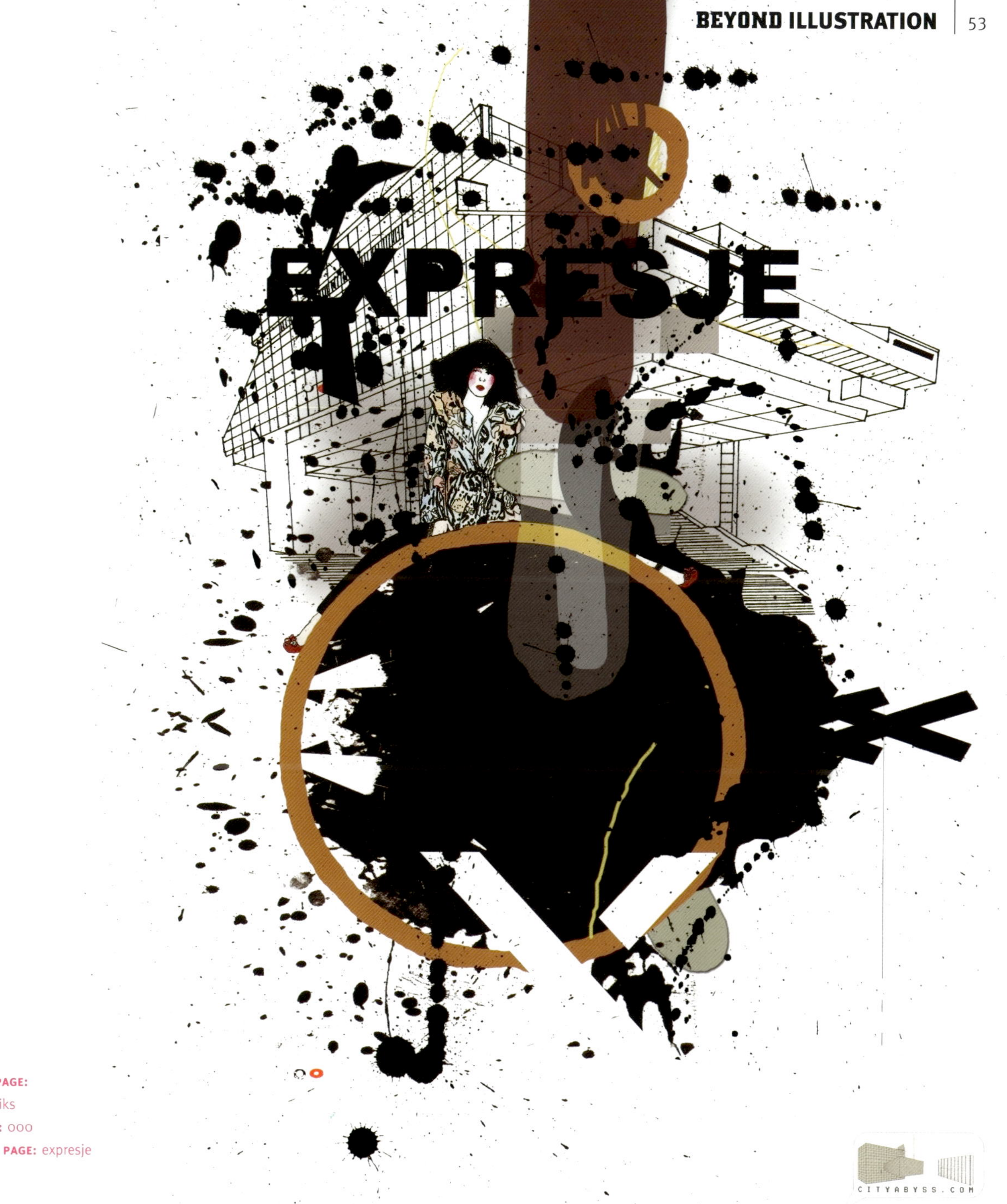

LEFT PAGE:
LEFT: iks
RIGHT: ooo
RIGHT PAGE: expresje

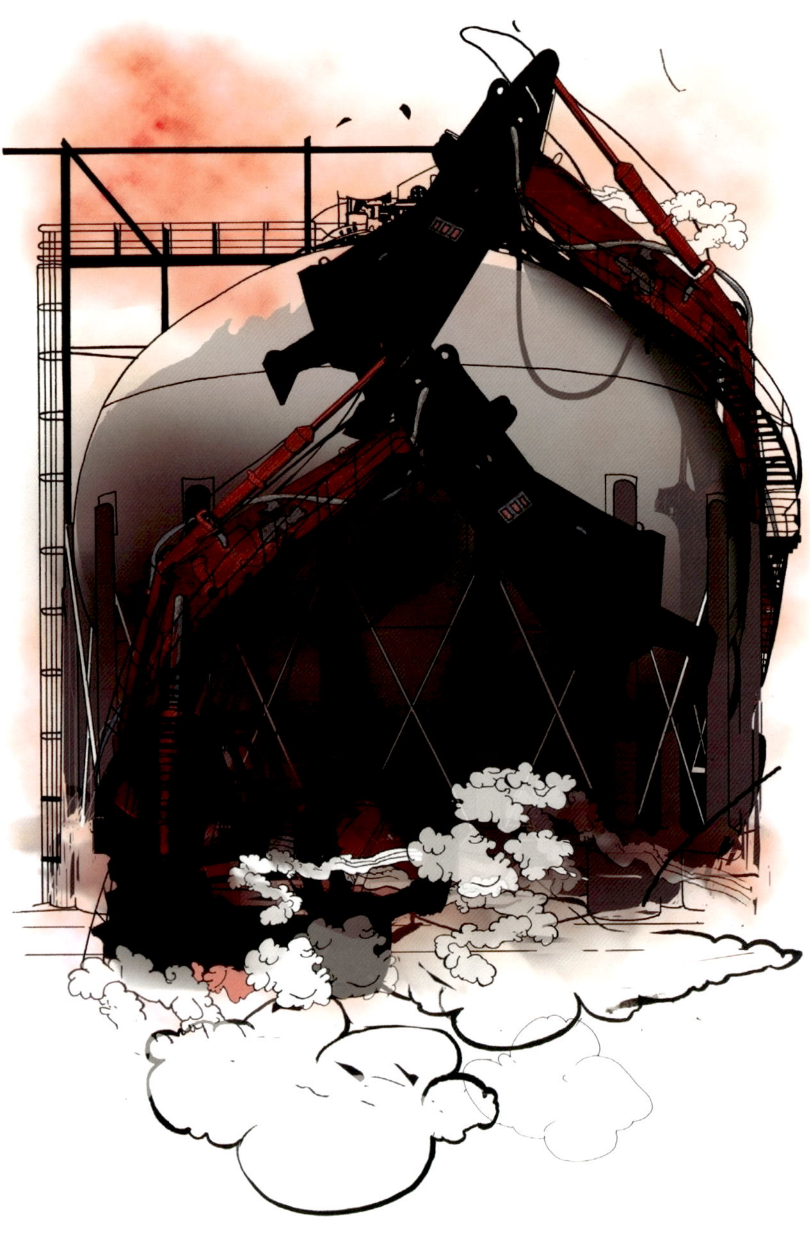

EN The question if there is a border between illustration and art is a pressing one. Illustration is still trying to attract attention and to defend its role as distinct from other disciplines. The art world abounds with new developments, and many artists have realized new concepts and ideas. My training was based on traditional art such as painting, drawing, and graphics. These are my media. I have always been a fan of traditional techniques and of using them in new ways. In illustration, I never wanted to simply visualize a text; on the contrary, I wanted to create serious, substantial works, not just pretty pictures. I approached technical questions in the same way as I used to design drawings and graphics. Generally I think we need high visual standards if we want to produce such works. In the past, that was not acceptable in illustration. Illustration was used to visualize a story, basically to add visual information to the descriptions of a text. In the world of visual arts illustrators weren't considered artists, and illustration was not seen as a legitimate discipline. Today, illustration strives for originality. The discipline is growing fast, and to work within it is a challenge. There are new problems today, for instance remuneration. Getting paid for your work changes a lot. Luckily, there are still some artists who maintain their independence. Today, illustration has a lot to do with advertising and design – it has its place in marketing. The challenges good contemporary illustration faces are more difficult than ever. For me an illustration should not be superficial and banal, it should deliver a subtile message in an exciting form.

LEFT PAGE: extra large
RIGHT PAGE:
LEFT: one
RIGHT: grid

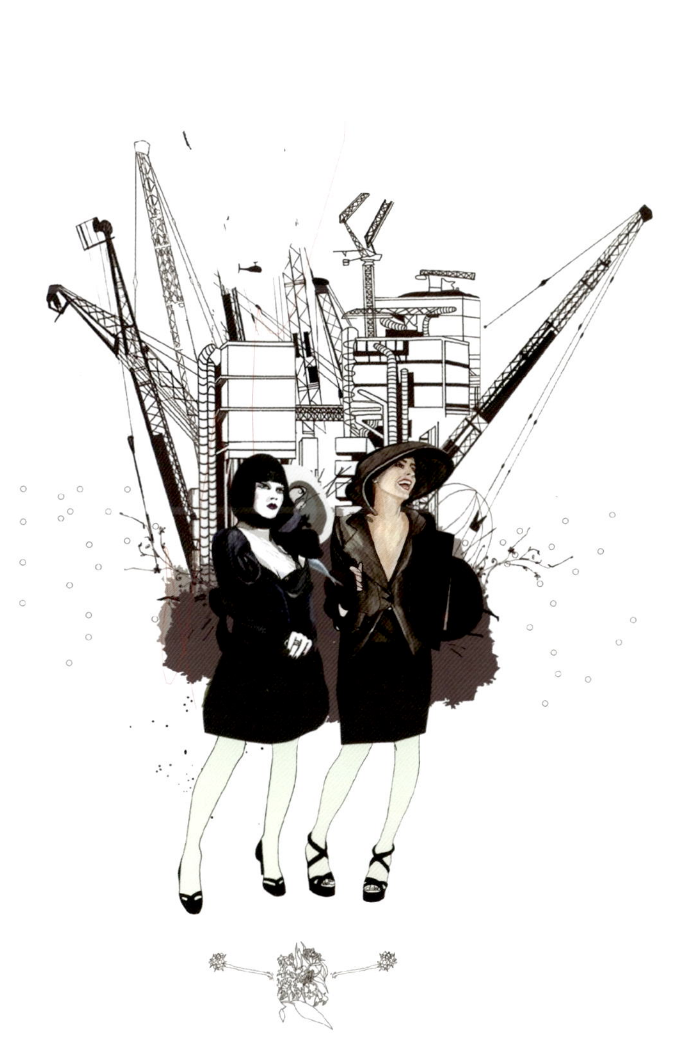

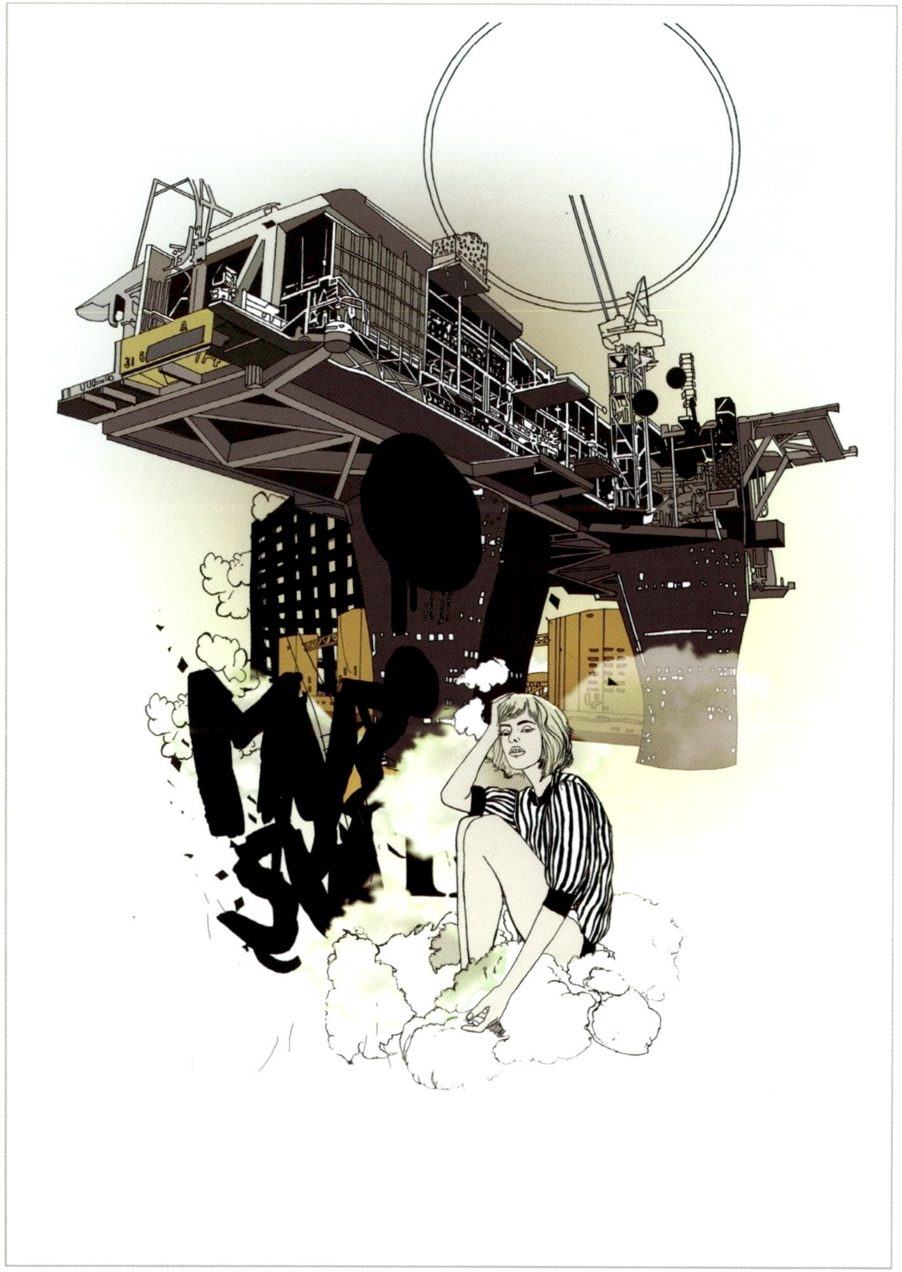

»VIERFARBRAUM [YVONNE WINKLER]

NATIONALITY:	GERMAN
LOCATION:	MUNICH
PUBLICATIONS:	FREISTIL 3 NOVUM MAGAZIN JITTER MAGAZIN
REFERENCES:	RATPACK FILMPRODUCTION JÖRG HEITSCH GALLERY SIEMENS AG
EXHIBITIONS:	GÖRRES 10 – MUNICH DIE FÄRBEREI – MUNICH GALERIE EDWARDS – AUGSBURG
CONTACT:	WWW.VIERFARBRAUM.DE INFO@VIERFARBRAUM.DE
TECHNIQUE:	DIGITAL ART | MIXED MEDIA
BORN:	1978

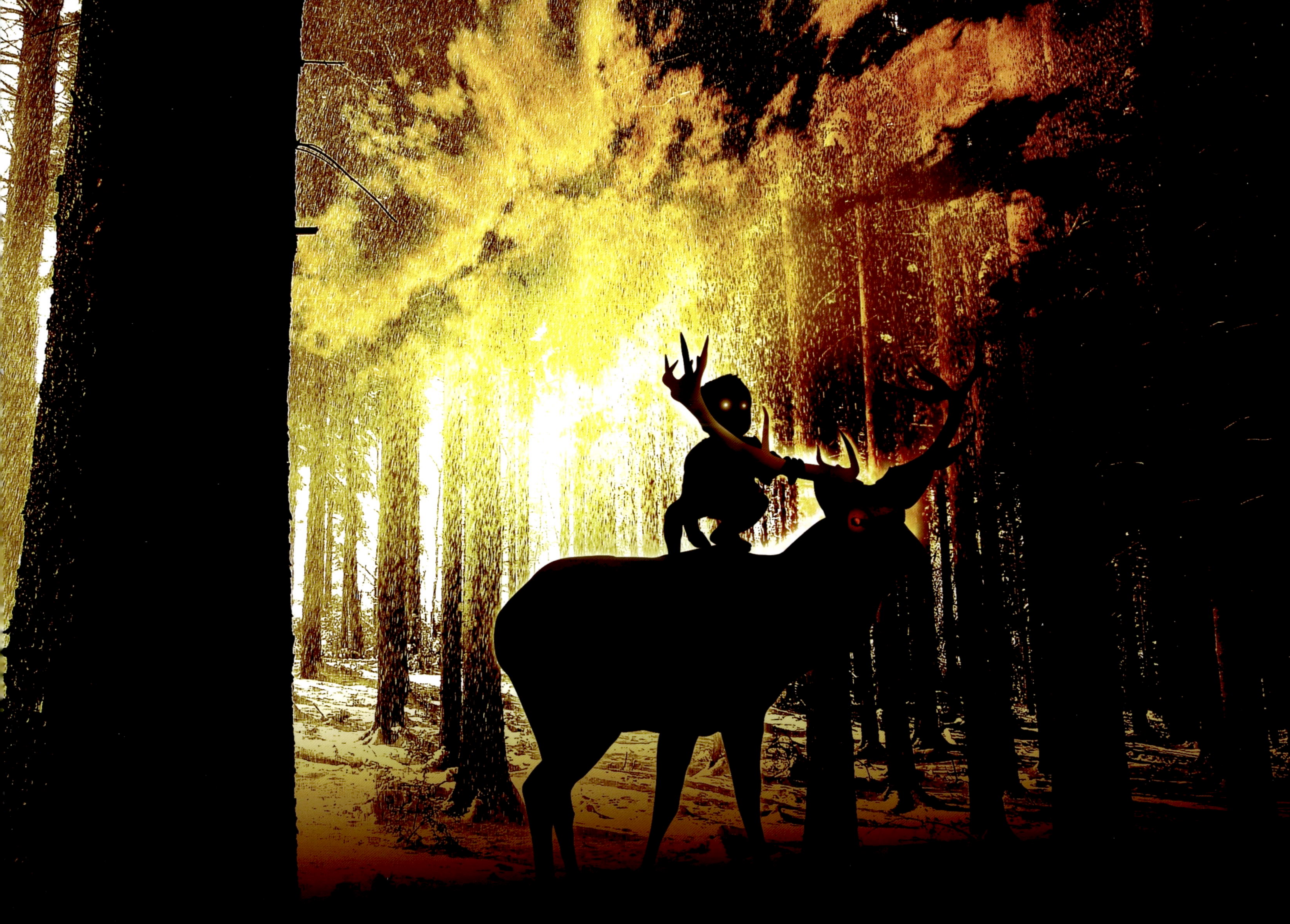

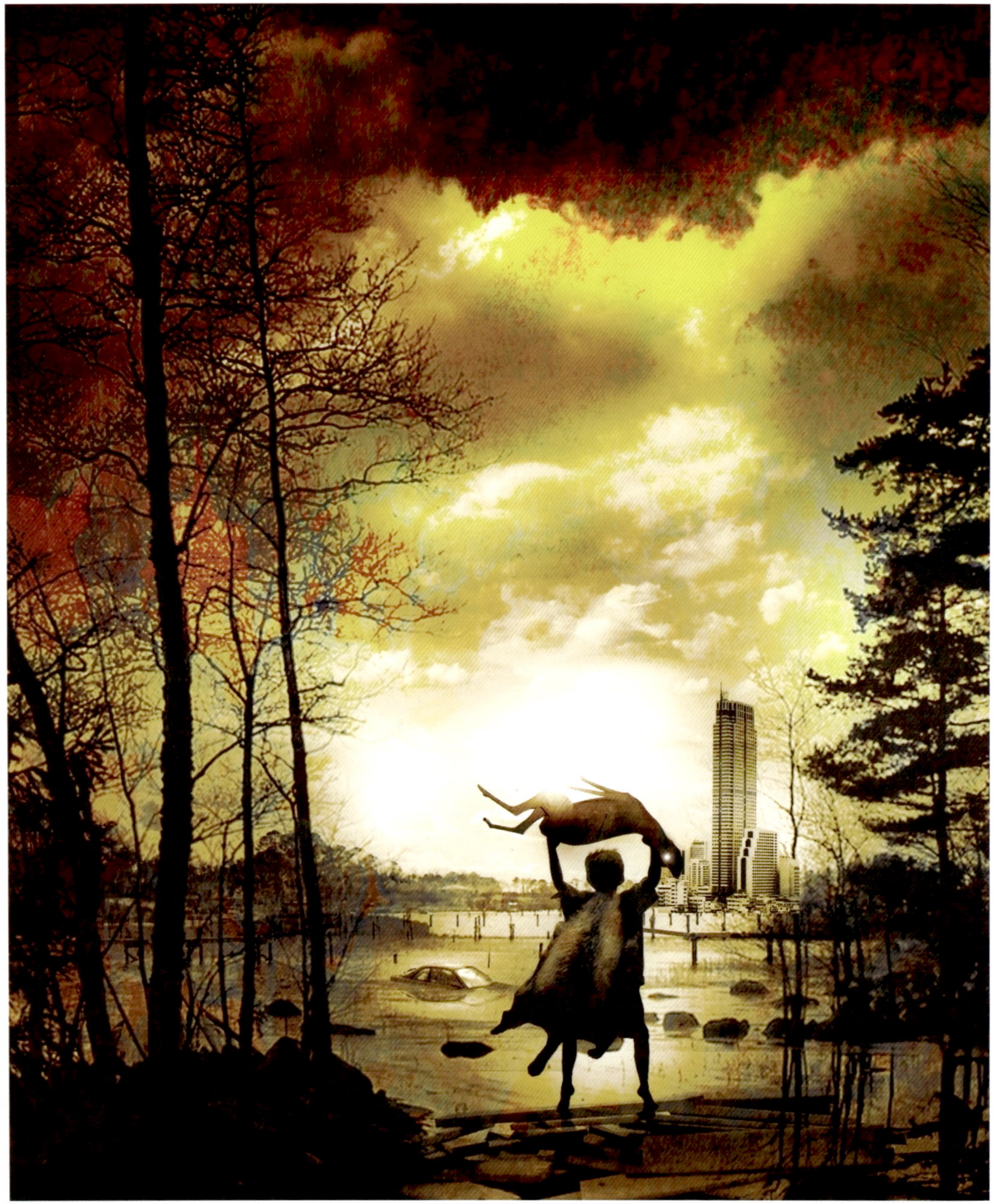

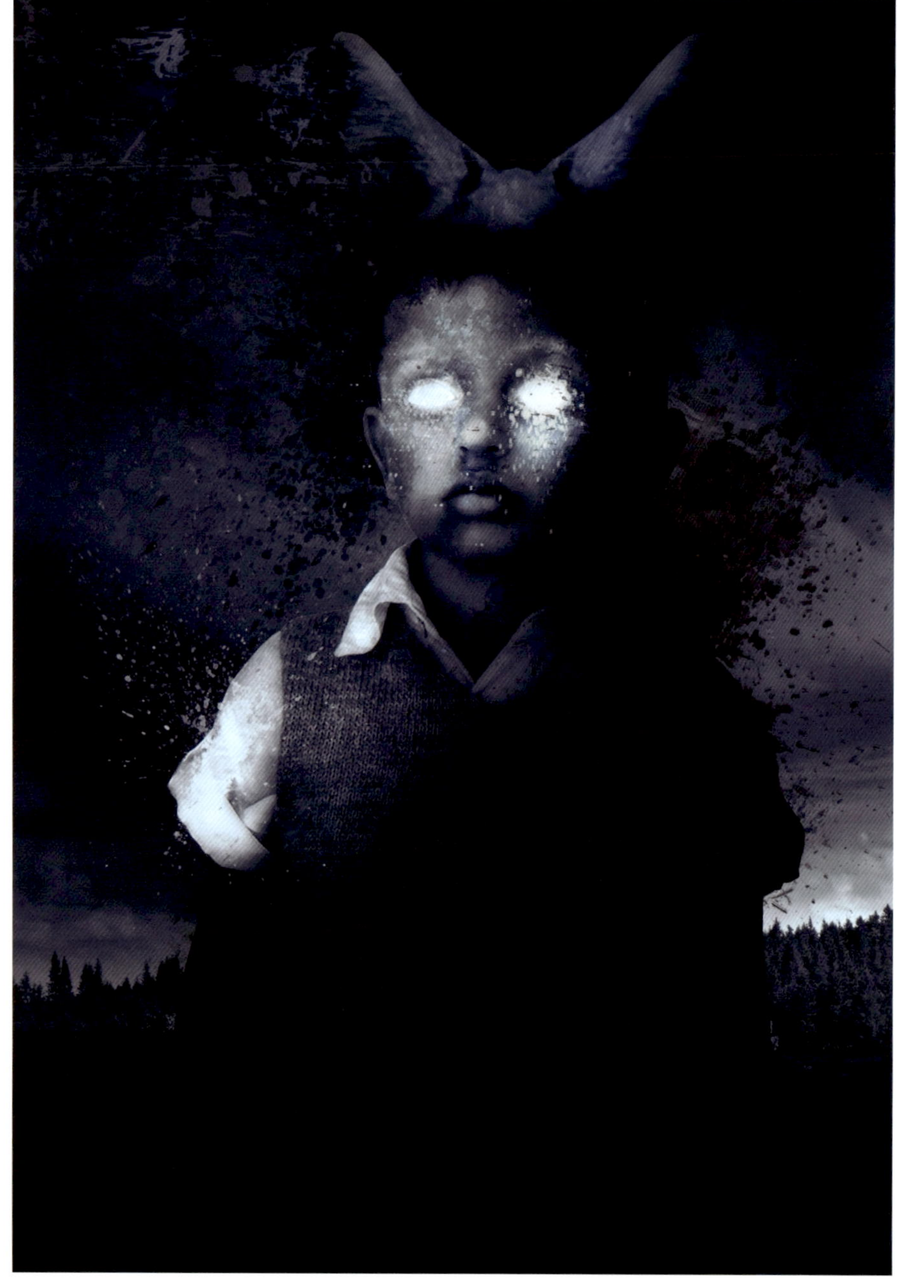

DE Nicht das Medium oder Stilmittel macht aus einer Arbeit Kunst, sondern die Intention, aus der heraus sie entstanden ist. Infolgedessen würde ich generell sagen, dass es sich bei einer reinen Auftragsarbeit in den seltensten Fällen um Kunst handelt – ich würde diese ganz profan als „Kunsthandwerk“ bezeichnen: Der Künstler setzt das von ihm Gewünschte bildlich um, zeigt sein Können und wird dafür bezahlt – nicht mehr und nicht weniger. Ich denke aber durchaus, dass ein Illustrator gleichzeitig Künstler sein kann und ein Künstler gleichermaßen Illustrator, auch wenn Letzteres wahrscheinlich seltener der Fall ist. Die meisten bildenden Künstler distanzieren sich ganz bewusst von jeglicher Form kommerzieller Gestaltung, da dies meist den faden Beigeschmack von Massenkompatibilität und künstlerischem Ausverkauf in sich birgt. Illustration aus künstlerischer Sicht aber generell zu verteufeln halte ich für falsch, denn wie ich eingangs schon sagte, steht immer die Intention im Vordergrund und nicht das Stilmittel selbst. Es gibt viele namhafte Künstler, die vordergründig allesamt illustrativ arbeiten, auf den zweiten Blick aber wegen ihrer eindringlichen Bildsprache und der tiefergehenden Thematik, die den Kunstwerken zugrunde liegt, ganz selbstverständlich als Künstler wahrgenommen werden. Illustration, also die bildliche Ausarbeitung einer Thematik – oder vielleicht sogar besser Kunsthandwerk –, hat es immer schon gegeben, sie ist auch die Wurzel dessen, was wir heutzutage als „Kunst“ bezeichnen. Alles begann mit Auftragsarbeiten für Kirche und Adel, die nach bestimmten Vorgaben, Vorstellungen und nicht selten dem Geschmack des Kunden angefertigt wurden. Das Einzige, was sich wirklich verändert hat, ist der Begriff Kunst im Allgemeinen. Heute können wir uns den Luxus erlauben, Kunstwerke ohne augenscheinliche Zweckbestimmung zu schaffen, dafür aber mit einer tiefergehenden Bedeutung, die einzig die Haltung des Künstlers widerspiegelt. Ich selbst finde es äußerst schwierig, eine passende Definition für mich und meine Arbeiten zu finden. Wo ordnet man jemanden ein, der einerseits einfach nur sehen möchte, wie eine weiße Fläche zu leben beginnt, andererseits aber auch einem hübschen Sümmchen Geld auf dem Bankkonto nicht abgeneigt ist? Vielleicht bin ich ja eine Teilzeitkünstlerin? Wer weiß, das müssen diejenigen entscheiden, die davon mehr Ahnung haben als ich.

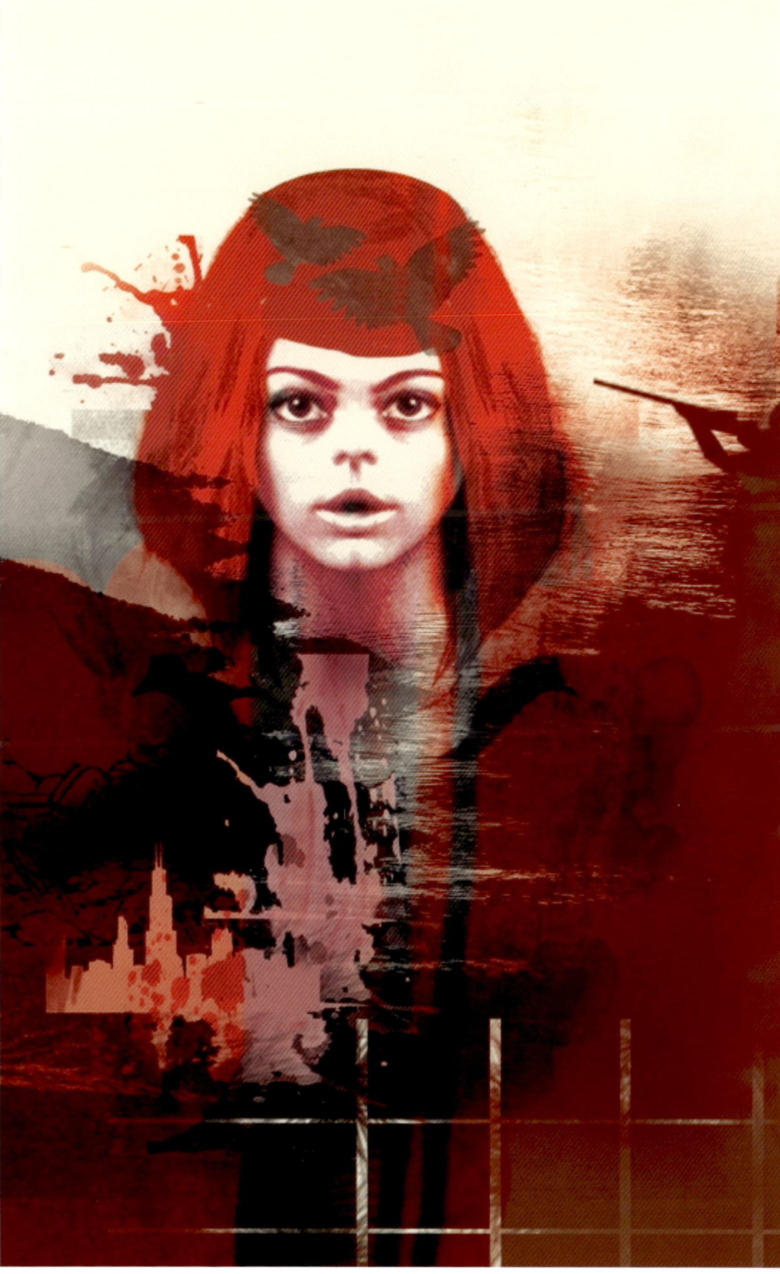

INTRODUCTION: timberland
LEFT PAGE:
LEFT: liftup
RIGHT: untitled
RIGHT PAGE: sixgun city no.1

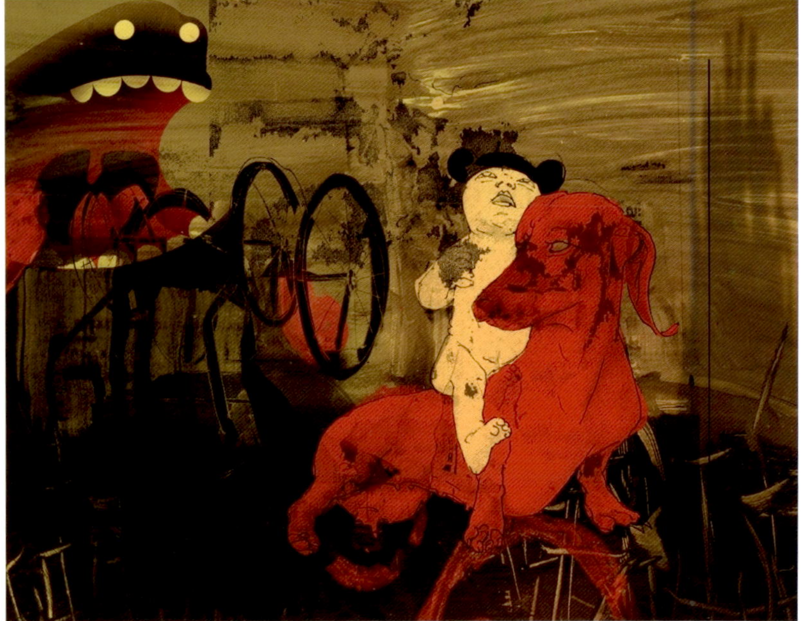

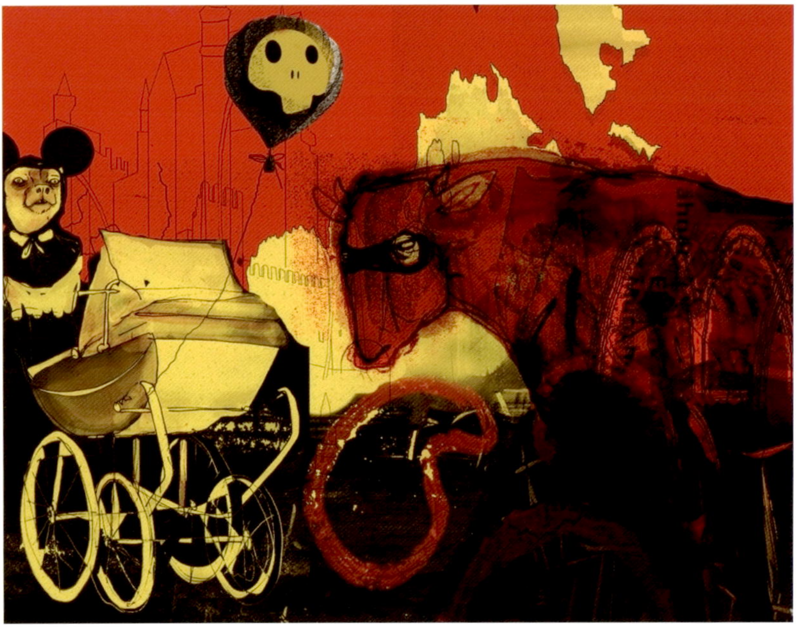

EN It is neither the media nor the style that transform a work into an artwork, but the intention out of which it was created. Hence, it is very rare for commissioned works to be art. In my view, they are products of a craftsman. He produces a visual translation of a text, thereby employing and showing his skills, and he gets paid for his work – nothing more, nothing less. However, I absolutely think that an illustrator can be an artist and an artist can be an illustrator, although the second case is probably rarer. Most visual artists distance themselves quite explicitly from all forms of commercial work, because it is associated with bland conformity to the taste of the masses and with the betrayal of one's ideals. Nevertheless, there is no reason to dismiss illustration outright from an artistic point of view, because, as I said earlier, it is always the intention that matters, rather than the medium or style. Many distinguished artists produce works that may at first appear to be illustrative; given their due attention, they reveal themselves, in both their intense visual idiom and their profound themes, as legitimate works of art. Illustration, i.e., the visualization of a given theme – or, more precisely, craftsmanship, has always existed, and it was the root of what we call "art" today. It all started with works commissioned by the Church and the aristocracy, realized according to explicit standards and specifications and often also the personal taste of the client. The only thing that has really changed is the term "art" as such. Today we can afford the luxury of producing art without any obvious purpose, but with a deeper meaning which expresses nothing but the personality of the artist. I find it extremely difficult to define myself and my works. How do you categorize someone who, on the one hand, simply wants to see a white surface coming to life, and who, on the other hand, does not say no to a little more money in their banking account? Am I a part-time artist? Who knows, that is for those to decide who know better than I do.

LEFT PAGE:
TOP LEFT: klan2-westwärts
DOWN LEFT: nanny-westwärts
RIGHT PAGE:
klan1-westwärts

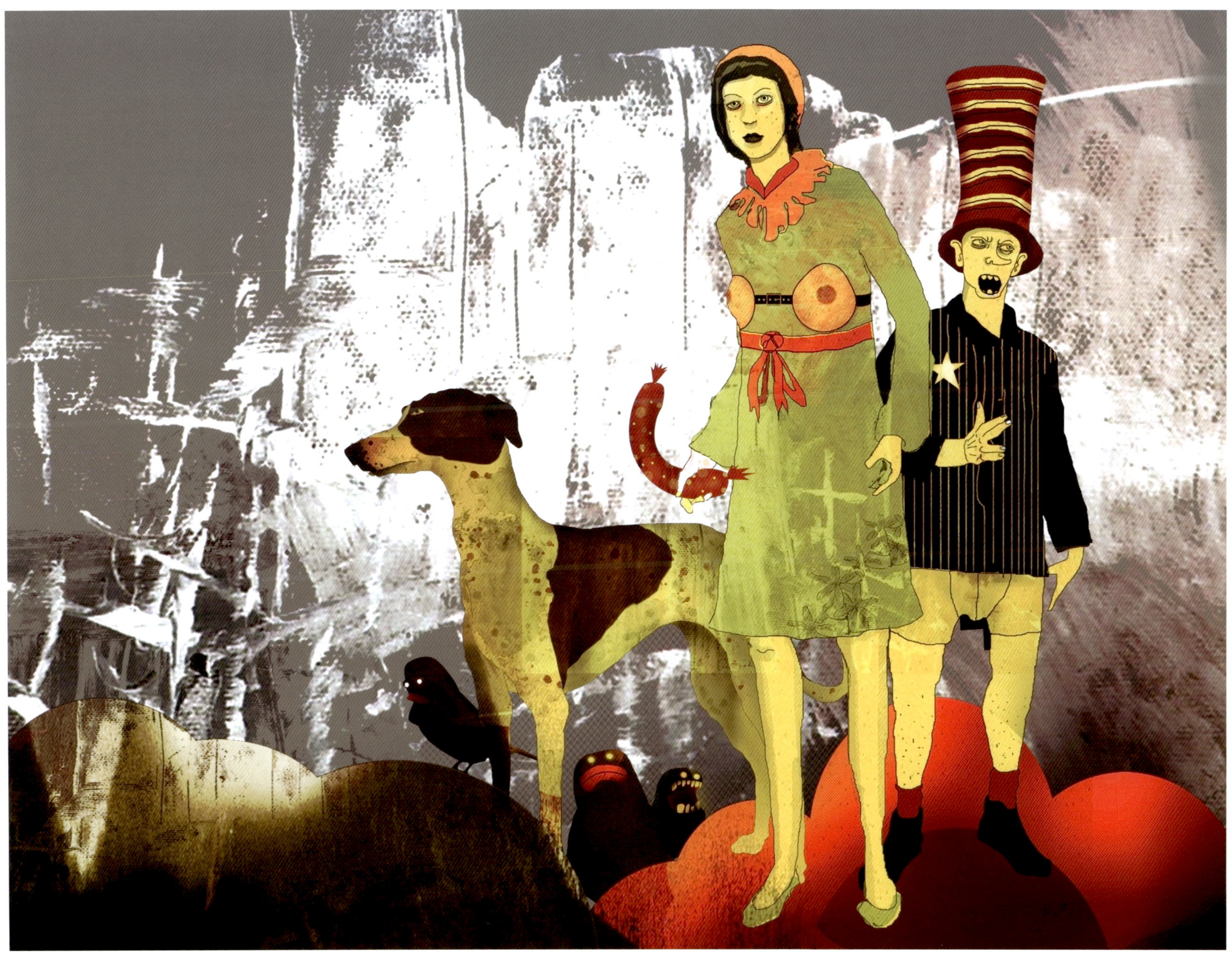

LEFT PAGE:

LEFT: rodeo-westwärts

RIGHT: freakshow no.2

RIGHT PAGE:

facing forward-westwärts

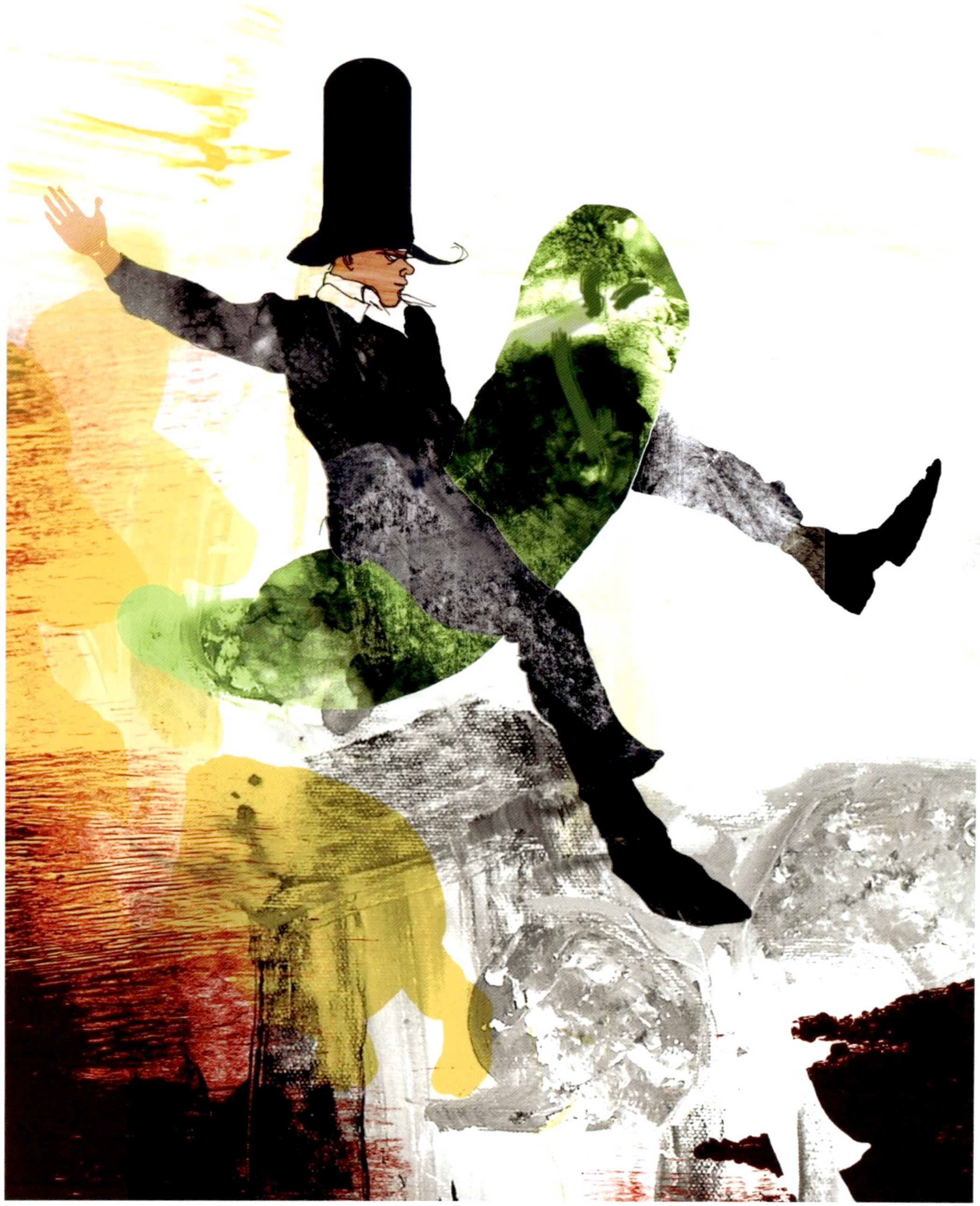

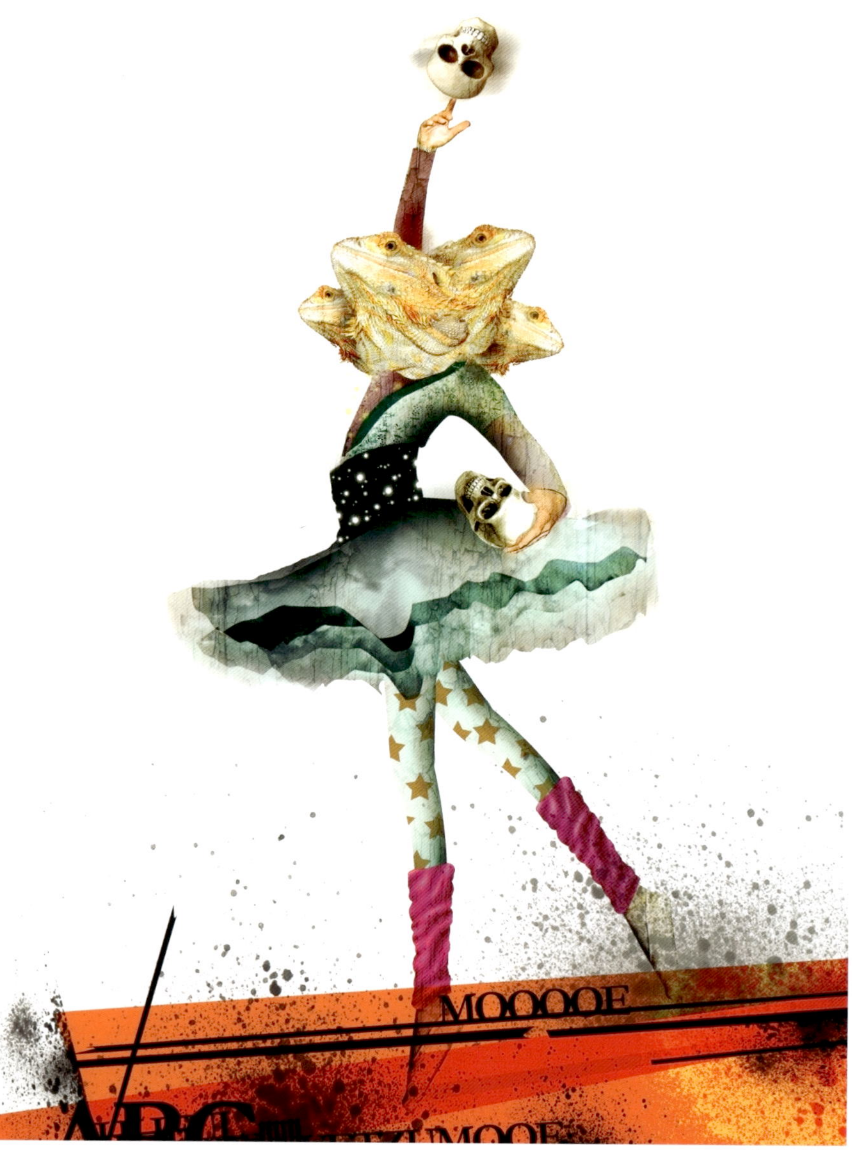

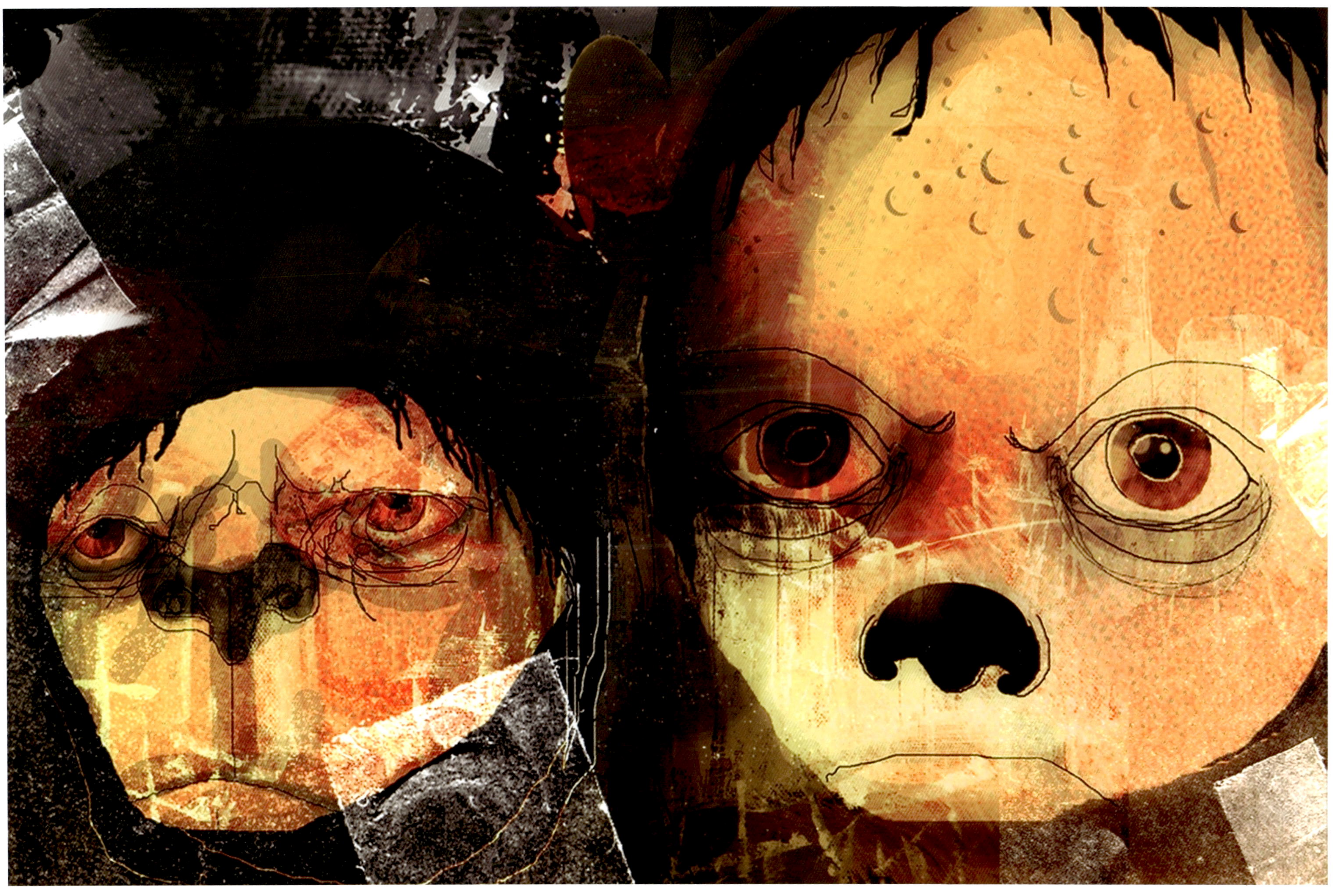

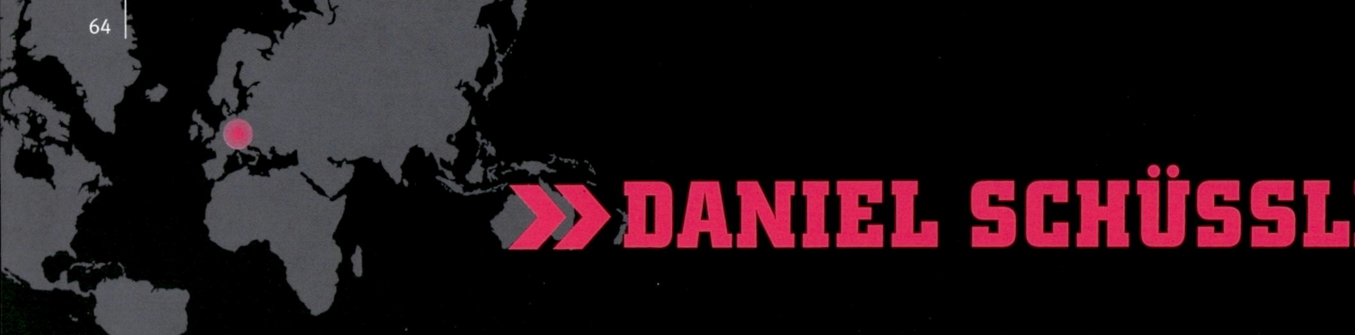

»DANIEL SCHÜSSLER

NATIONALITY:	GERMAN
LOCATION:	MUNICH
PUBLICATIONS:	JITTER – MAGAZIN FÜR BILDGESTALTUNG (ISSUE 01/07) CASTLE MAGAZINE – ONLINE PDF-MAGAZINE TERRAIN VAGUE – ARTIST-MAGAZINE (ISSUE APRIL 2005)
EXHIBITIONS:	2007 ARTFAIR 21 – MESSE FÜR AKTUELLE KUNST EXPO XXI – COLOGNE 2007 / 2008 DISCORDIA (ZWEI) GALERIE LICHTPUNKT – MUNICH 2008 SCOPE HAMPTONS ARTFAIR – WAINSCOTT I N.Y. ATTENDANCE WITH GALERIE ANDREAS BINDER – MUNICH 2008 WELTPARK GALERIE WAGNER+MARKS – FRANKFURT/MAIN 2008 SCOPE MIAMI – ARTFAIR ATTENDANCE WITH GALERIE ANDREAS BINDER – MUNICH
REPRESENTIVES:	GALERIE LICHTPUNKT – MUNICH GALERIE WAGNER+MARKS – FRANKFURT AM MAIN
CONTACT:	WWW.GALERIELICHTPUNKT.DE WWW.DANIELSCHUESSLER.BLOGSPOT.COM DANIEL.SCHUESSLER@GMX.DE
TECHNIQUE:	COLLAGE ON CANVAS ACRYLIC I C-PRINTS I OILSTICK I CRAYON I UV-FINISH
BORN:	1976

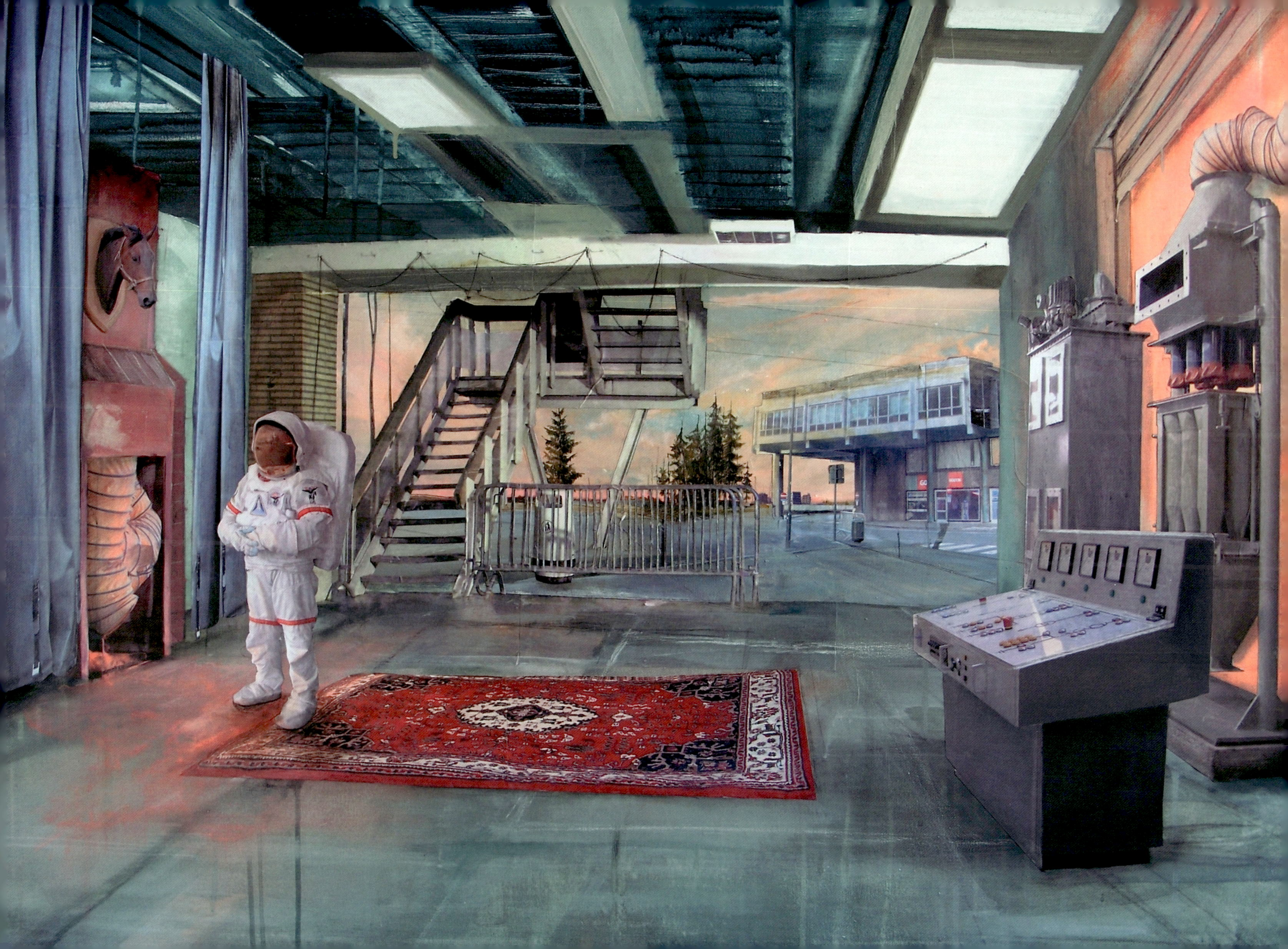

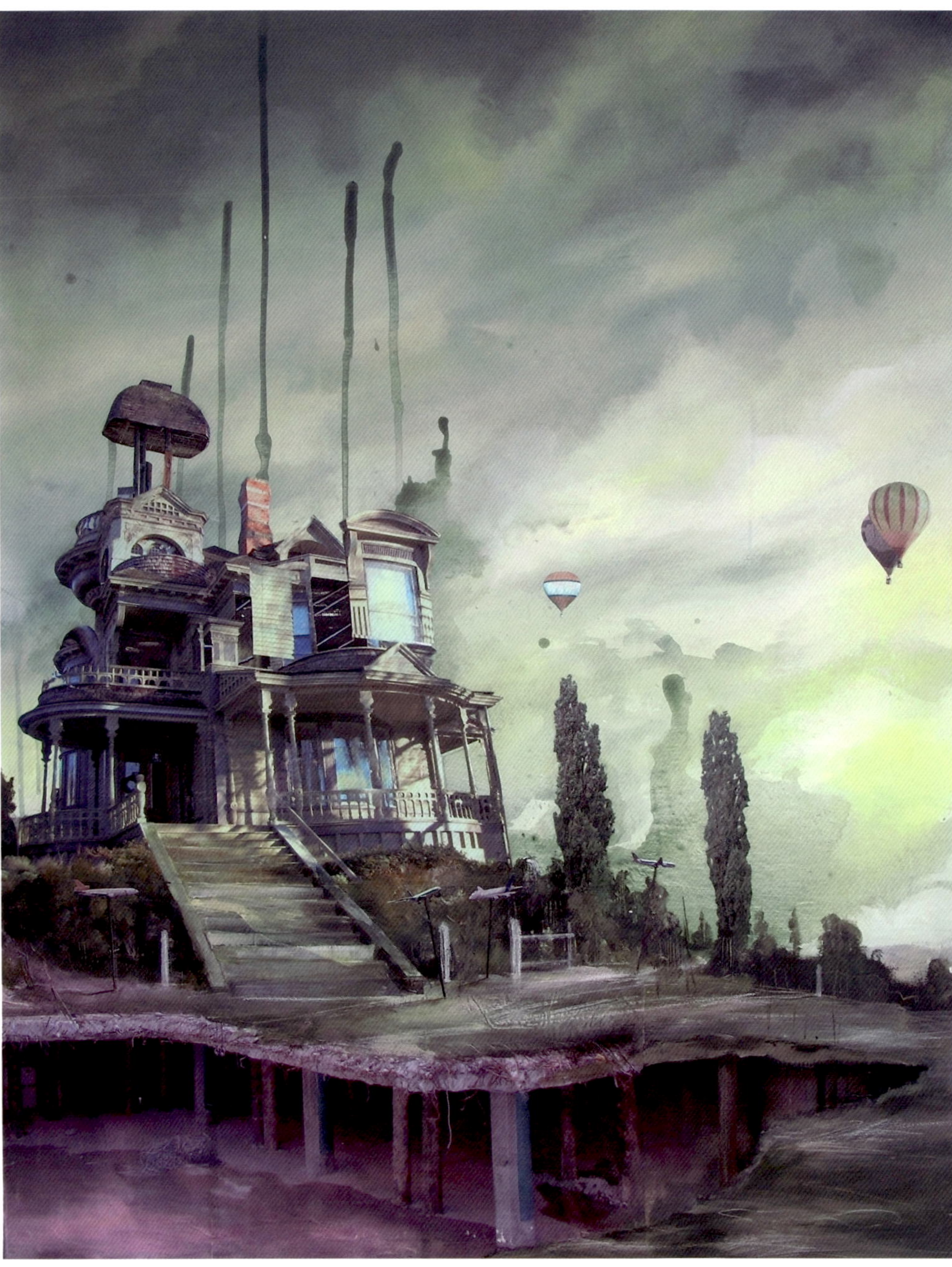

DE Da ich mich selbst als bildenden Künstler verstehe und per Definition als Schaffender selbst mein Auftraggeber bin, würde ich auch genau hier eine Grenze ziehen. Künstler ist derjenige, der aus einem inneren Antrieb heraus ein Werk erschafft, sich eine eigenständige Position erarbeitet und unabhängig von einer Zweckbindung arbeitet. Werke, die einem Text oder einem Produkt als bildnerischer Zusatz unterliegen beziehungsweise kommerziellen oder pragmatischen Kunstaspekten folgen, ordne ich klar als Illustration im klassischen Kontext ein. Allerdings beobachte ich auch, dass sich das herkömmliche Verständnis, das ein Illustrator seinem Berufsbild entsprechend hat oder nicht hat, in den letzten Jahren gravierend gewandelt hat. Damit meine ich Illustratoren, die keine Dienstleistung erbringen, sondern ihrer eigenen künstlerischen Position entsprechend arbeiten und persönliche Werke schaffen, trotzdem aber hin und wieder Aufträge und zweckgebundene Arbeiten anfertigen. Und es gibt jene, die aus der Illustrationsszene kommen, und deren Werke mittlerweile auch gern auf Messen für zeitgenössische Kunst und in Galerien gezeigt werden. Hier entsteht im Moment eine Mischform der beiden Berufsbilder, die ich noch nicht klar genug einschätzen kann, um sie zu benennen. In dieser neuen „Grauzone“ wird es mit Sicherheit noch viele ungeahnte Überraschungen geben. Was ist Kunst, was ist Illustration? Meiner Meinung nach ist diese Frage nicht allgemein gültig zu beantworten. Jeder Künstler, Illustrator, Rezipient, Sammler oder Kunde muss sie für sich selbst beantworten. Für mich ist es wichtig, mit Herz und Kopf zu arbeiten.

INTRODUCTION: zwischenstation
LEFT PAGE: wochenend villa
RIGHT PAGE: festwoche

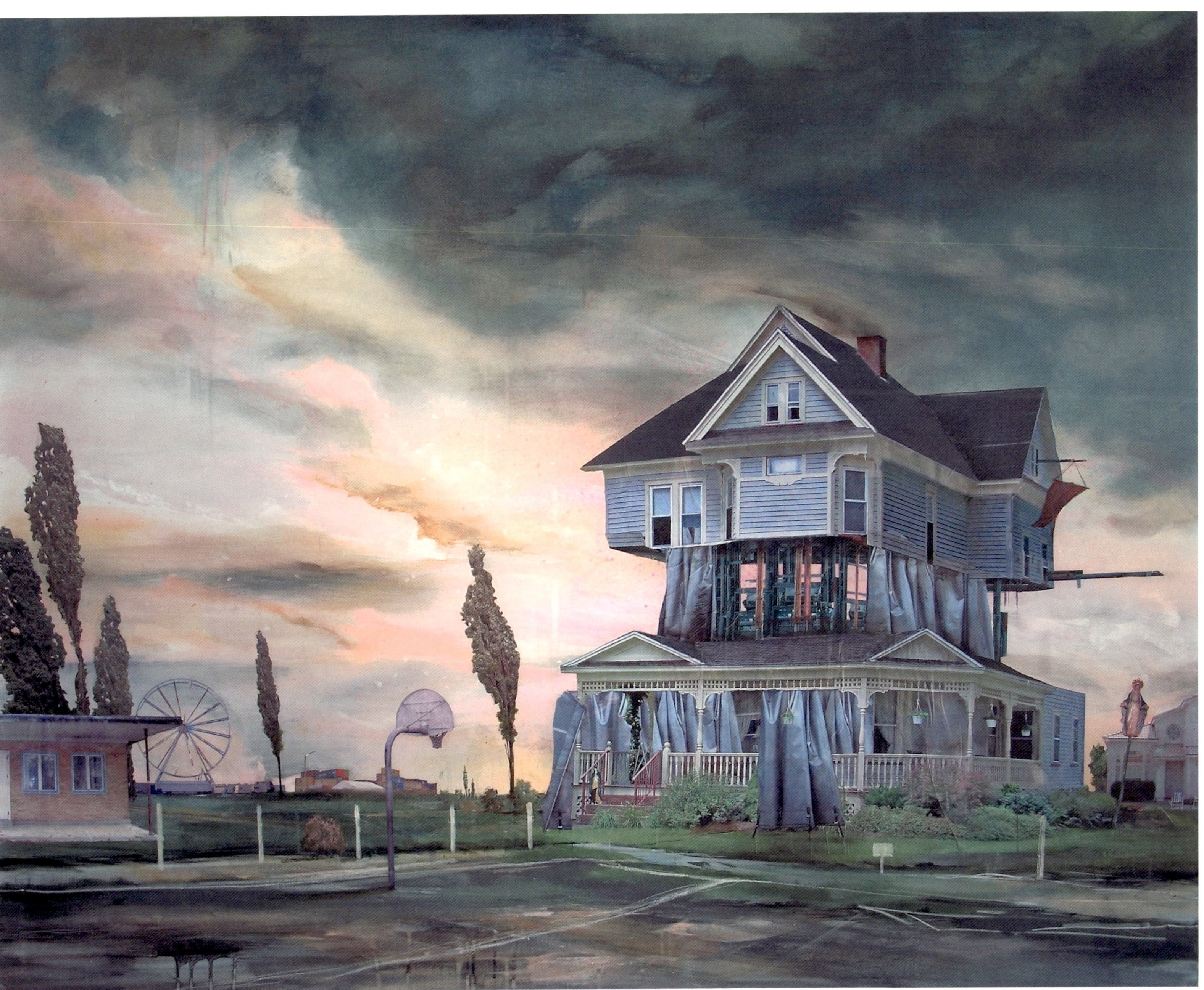

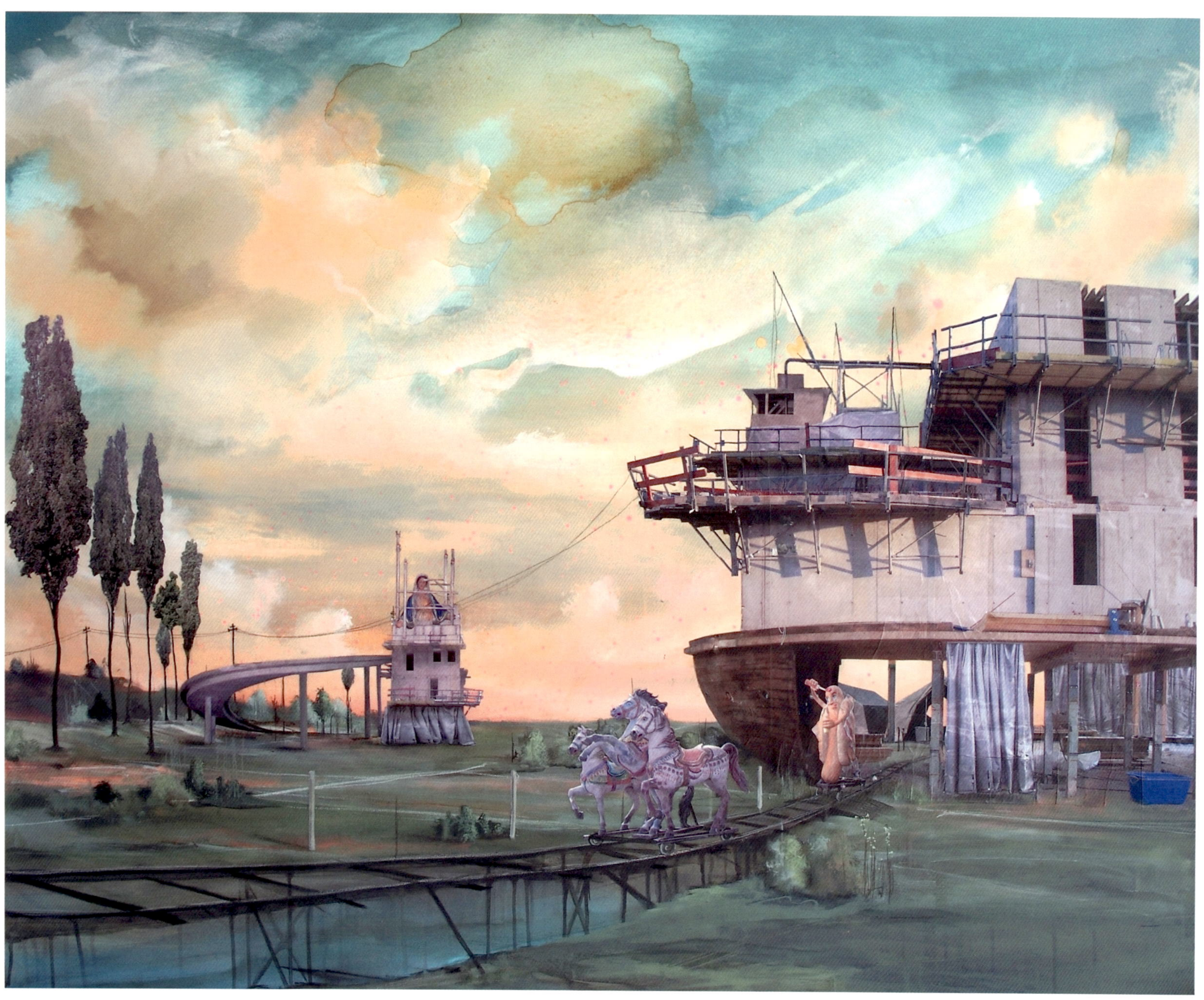

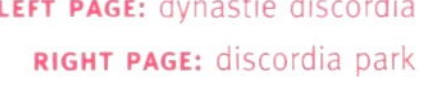

LEFT PAGE: dynastie discordia
RIGHT PAGE: discordia park

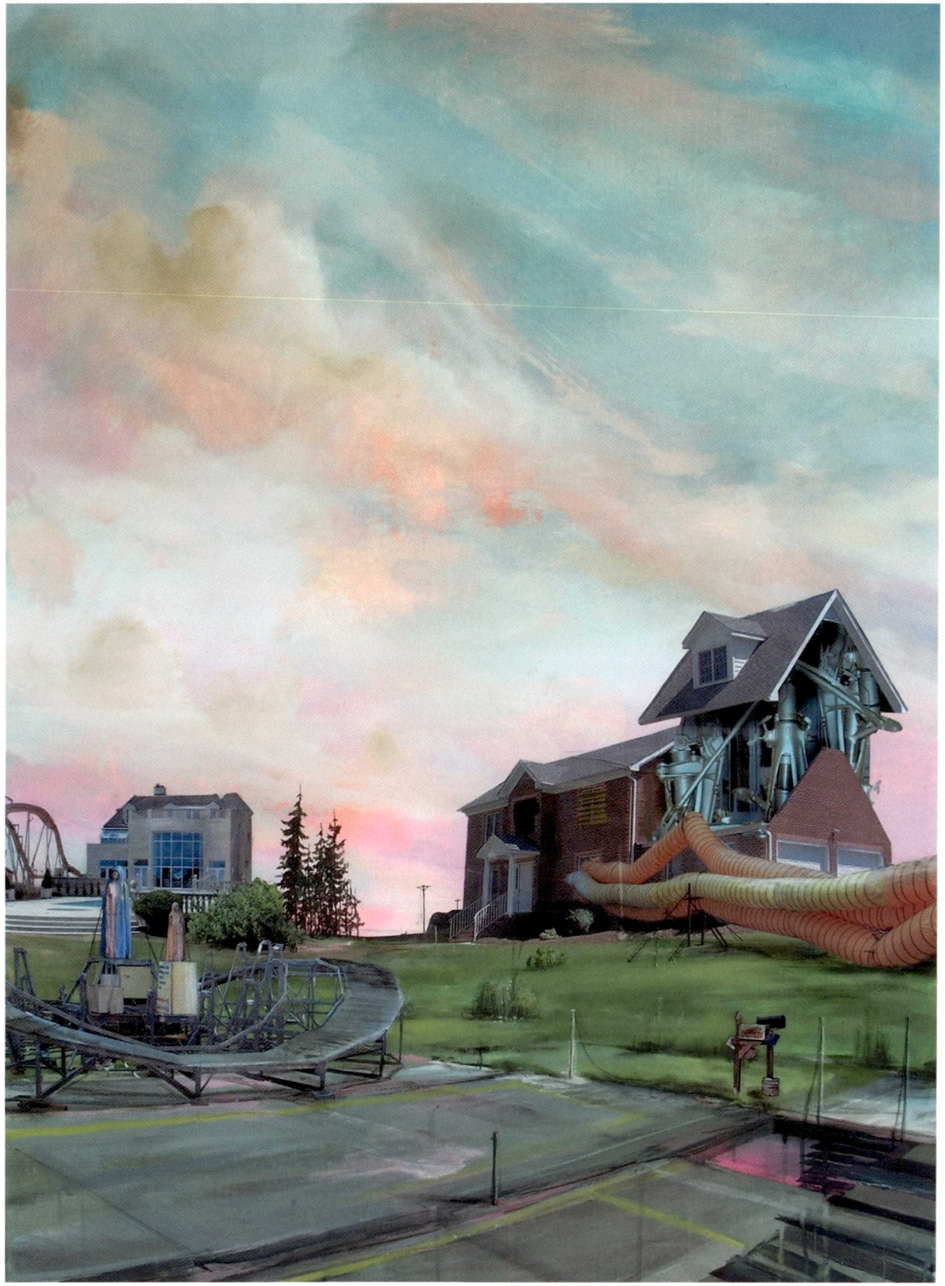

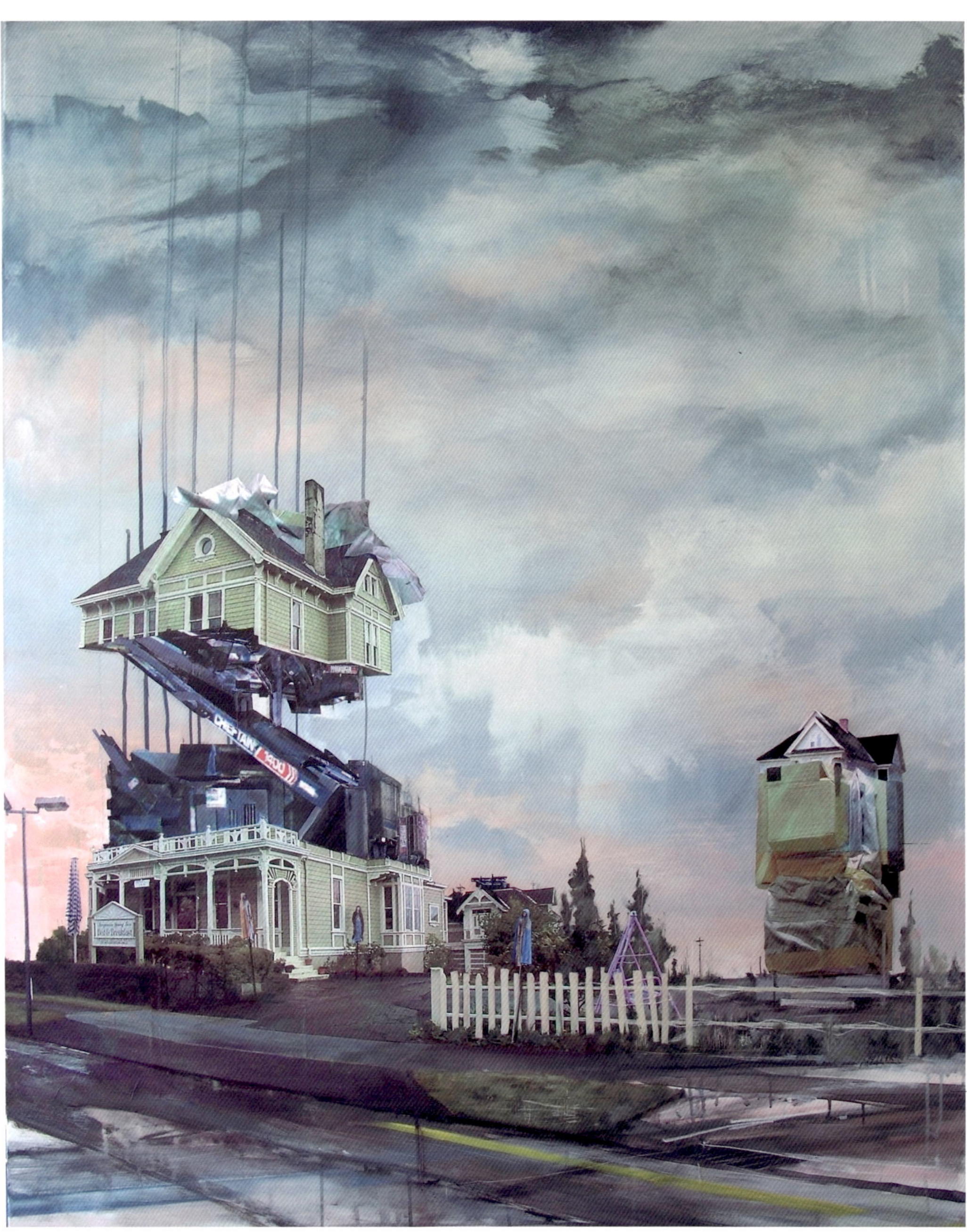

LEFT PAGE:
LEFT: der letzte sommer war sehr schön
RIGHT: silbersommer
RIGHT PAGE: räumungszentrale

EN I see myself as a visual artist who, as a creative person, is employed by himself, and this is where I would draw the line. A visual artist is someone who feels compelled to create a work, who defines his own position and whose works do not address any external needs. Works that accompany a text or product and that follow commercial or pragmatic aspects of art should be classified as illustration in its classical sense. However, I also notice that the conventional definition of what an illustrator does has been changing dramatically over the past few years. I am referring specifically to those illustrators who do not provide a service but who work according to their own artistic position and produce original works, while still occasionally working to order. There are others who are coming out of the illustration scene and whose works are regularly shown at contemporary art fairs and in galleries. The result is a mixture of both job profiles, and I cannot quite give it a name yet. I am sure this new "twilight zone" will provide us with many an unexpected surprise in the future. What is art, what is illustration? I think there is no universal answer. Every visual artist, illustrator, viewer, collector or customer has to answer this question for himself. For me it's important to work with both my heart and my head.

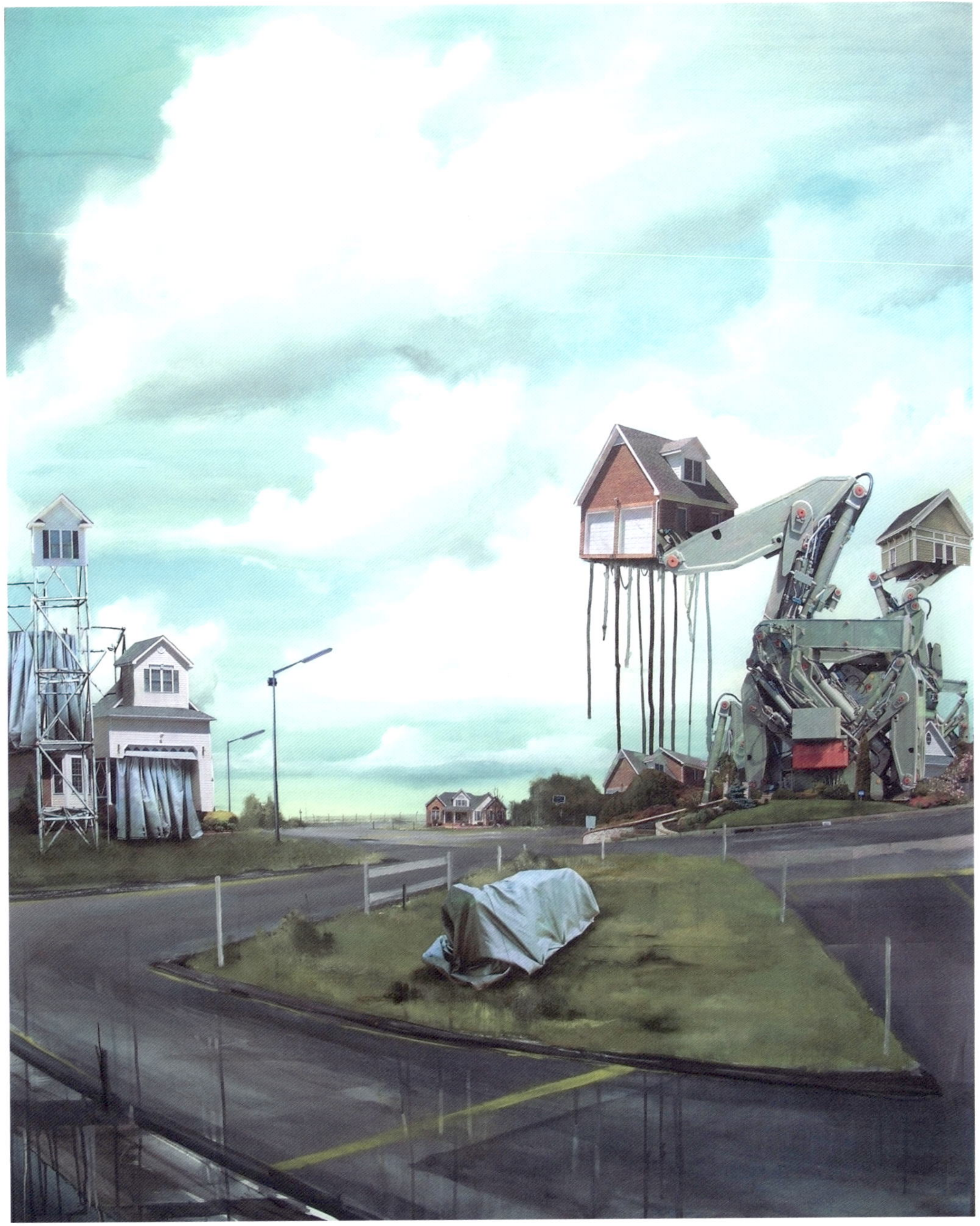

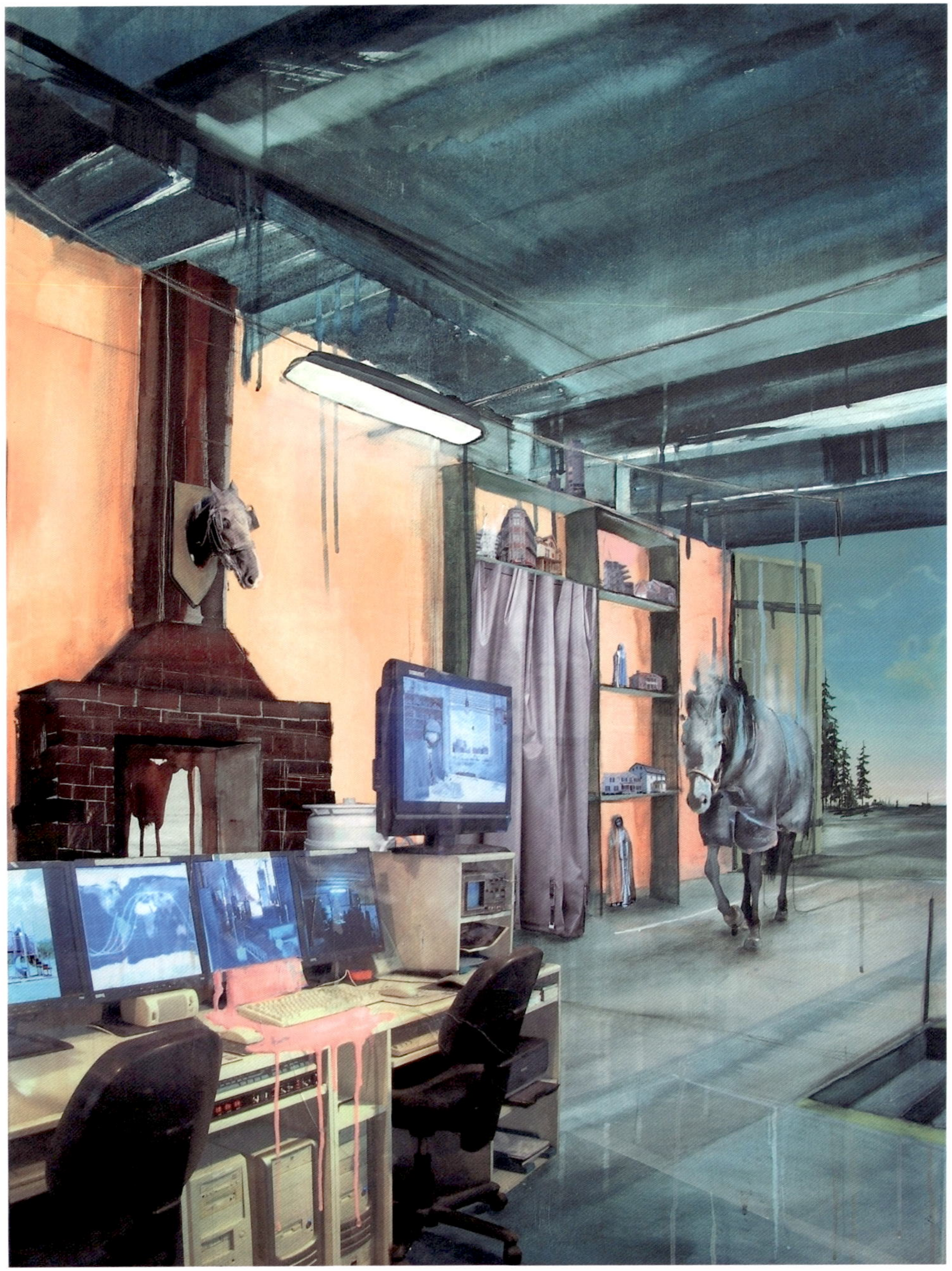

»NICHOLAS DI GENOVA

NATIONALITY:	CANADIAN
LOCATION:	TORONTO
REPRESENTIVES:	LE. GALLERY – TORONTO FREDERICKS & FREISER GALLERY – NYC GALERIE DUKAN & HOURDEQUIN – MARSEILLE
CONTACT:	WWW.MEDIUMPHOBIC.COM MEDIUMPHOBIC@GMAIL.COM
TECHNIQUE:	ANIMATION PAINT ON MYLAR | PEN AND INK ON PAPER
BORN:	1981

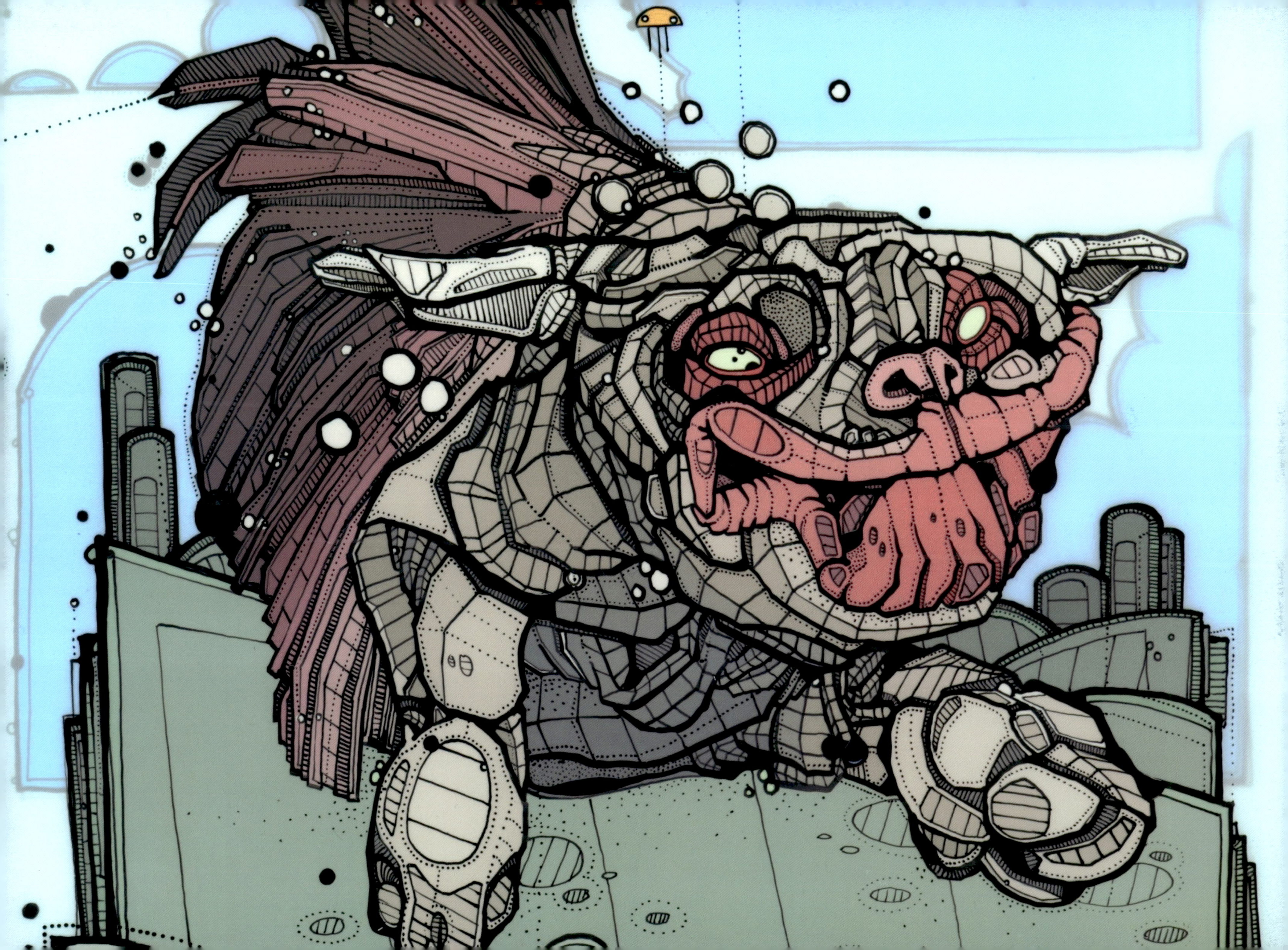

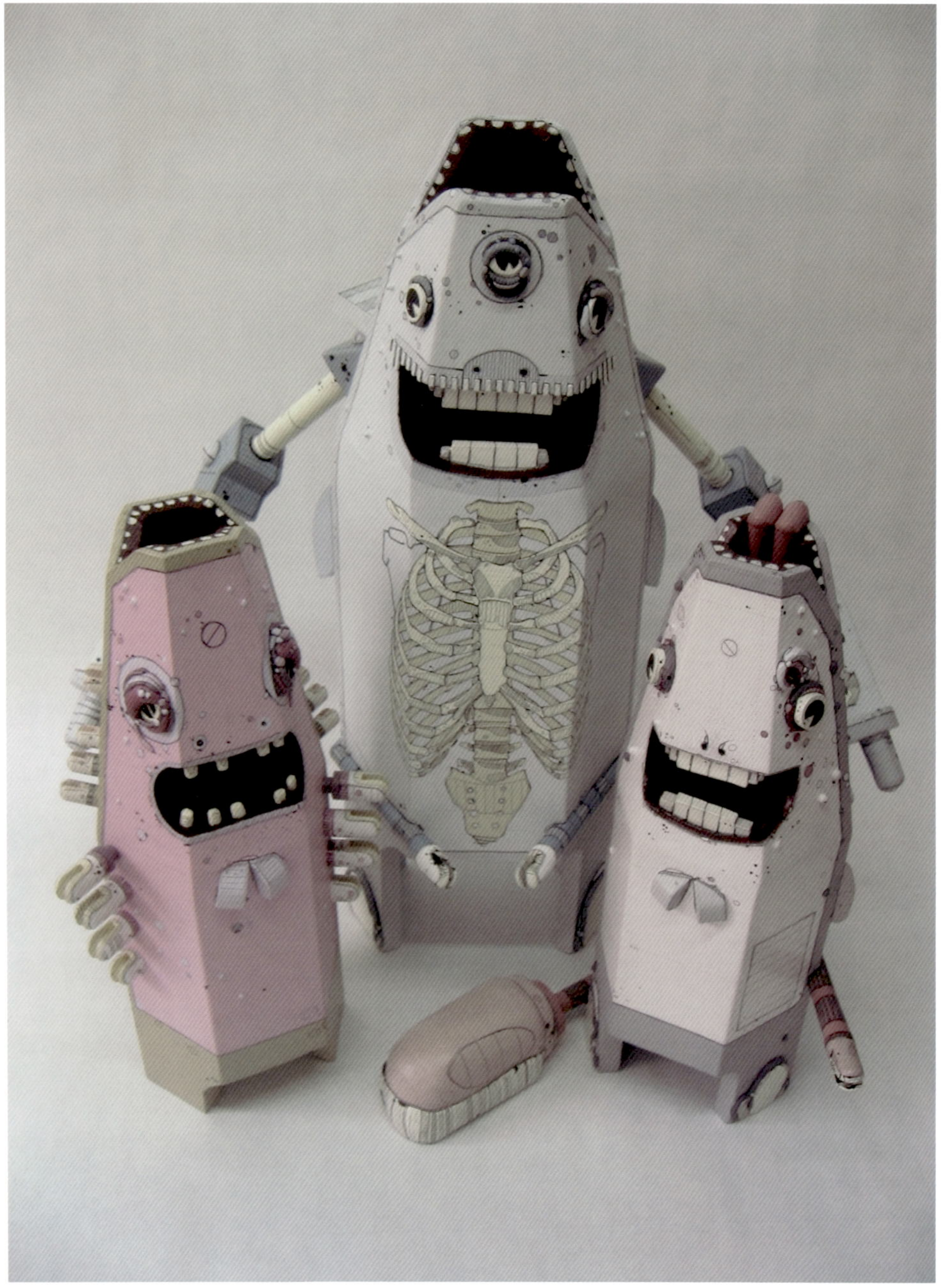

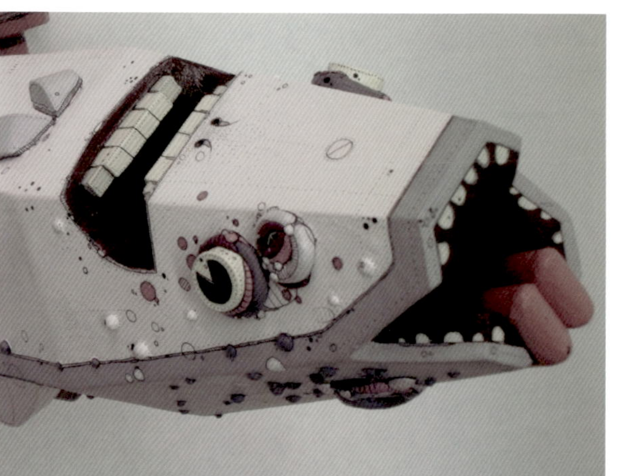

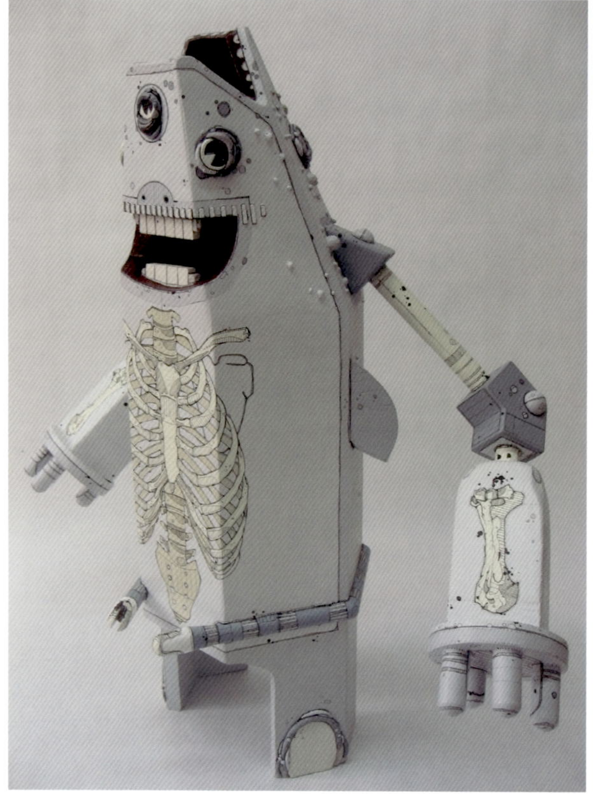

DE Ich verstehe Illustration als etwas, das im Allgemeinen nur gemeinsam mit etwas anderem funktioniert ... eine Zeichnung, die einen Text begleitet, sei es in einer Anzeige, einer Zeitschrift oder was auch immer. Kunst ist für mich etwas, das eher in der Lage ist, für sich zu stehen, ohne fremde Unterstützung ... Ich weiß, dass dies keine Definition ist, und es ist im Einzelnen auch nicht korrekt – aber es ist das, was mir in den Sinn kommt, wenn ich über die Unterschiede zwischen Illustration und Kunst nachdenke ... Eigentlich mache ich mir aber nicht viele Gedanken darüber ... Mich selbst verstehe ich wohl als Künstler, denn erfahrungsgemäß liegt mir der Umgang mit Kunden nicht so sehr.

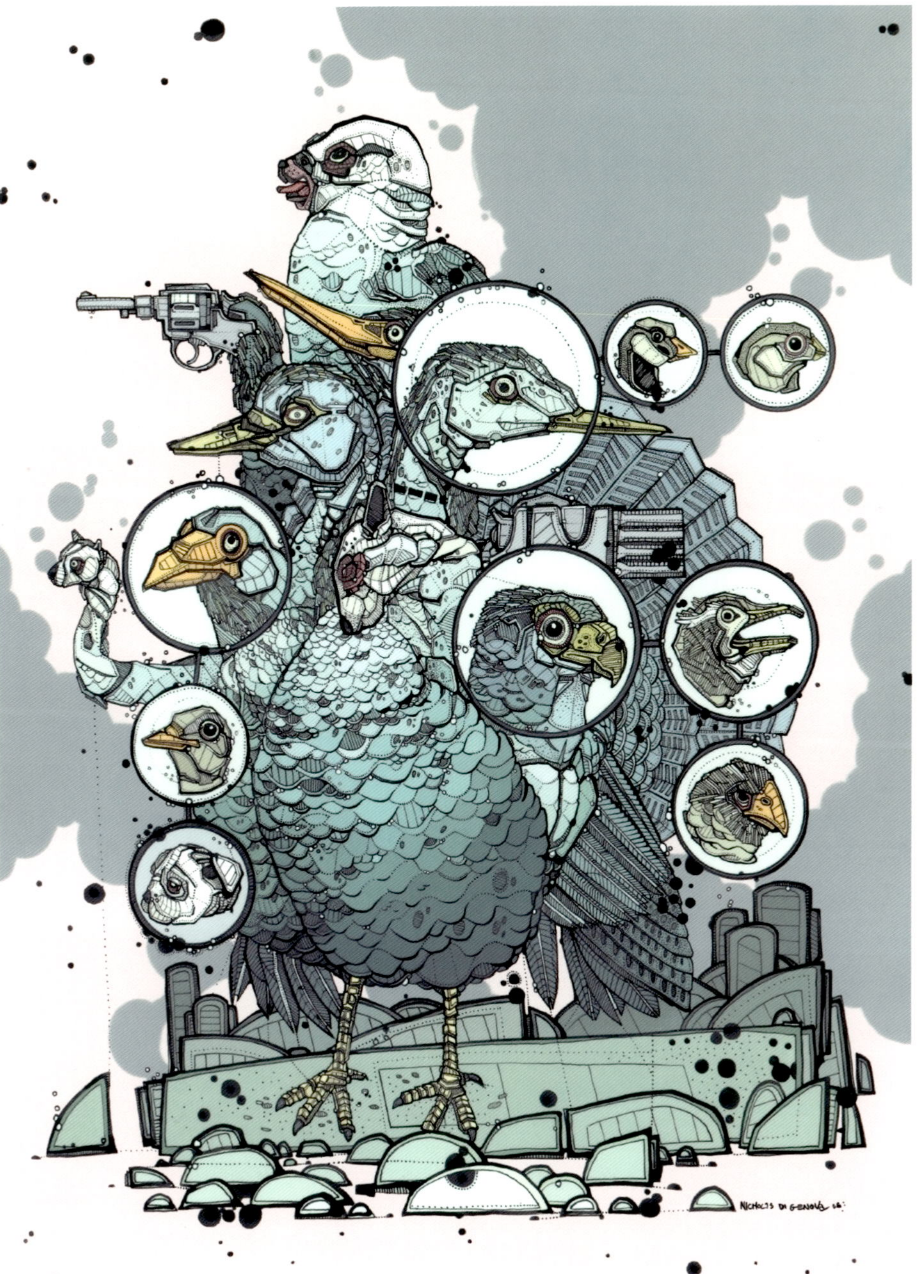

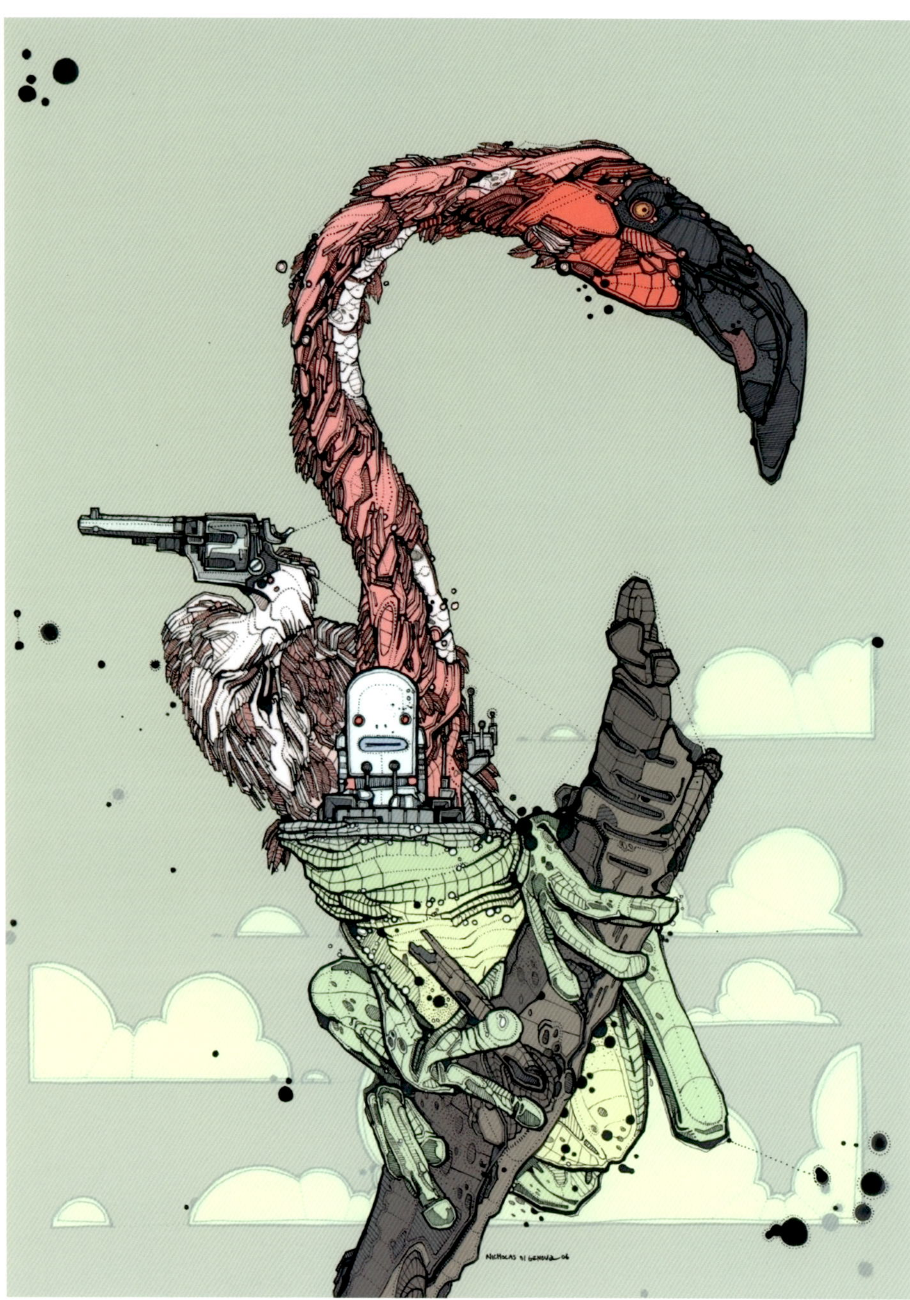

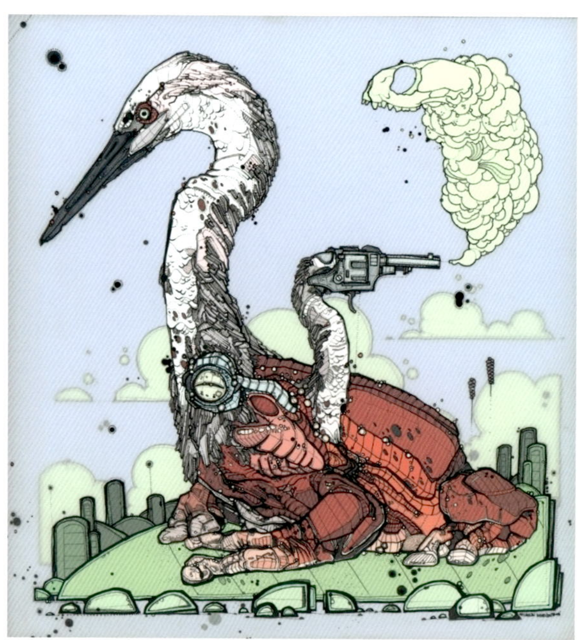

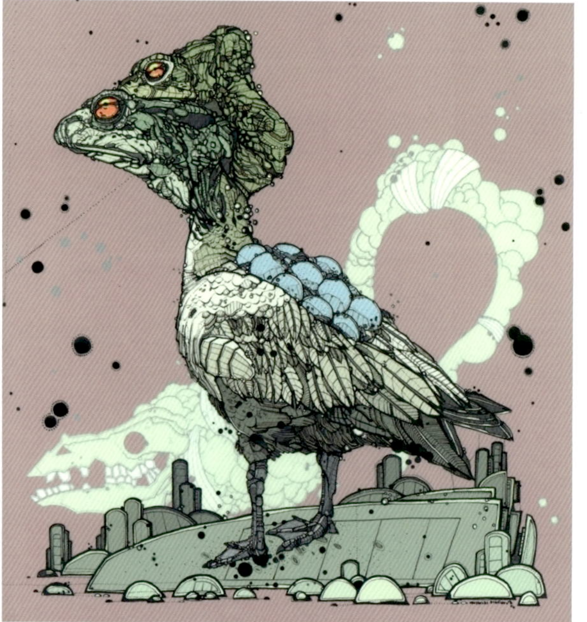

EN I think of illustration as something that generally refers to something else ... a drawing to accompany a text, be it in an ad, a magazine or whatever else. Art, for me, is something that can exist by itself without that type of support behind it ... I know this isn't a proper definition, and it is contradicted by many individual examples, but that is what comes to my mind when I consider the differences between the two ... but I really don't think about it that much ... I guess I see myself as an artist, as I'm not generally very good at working with clients.

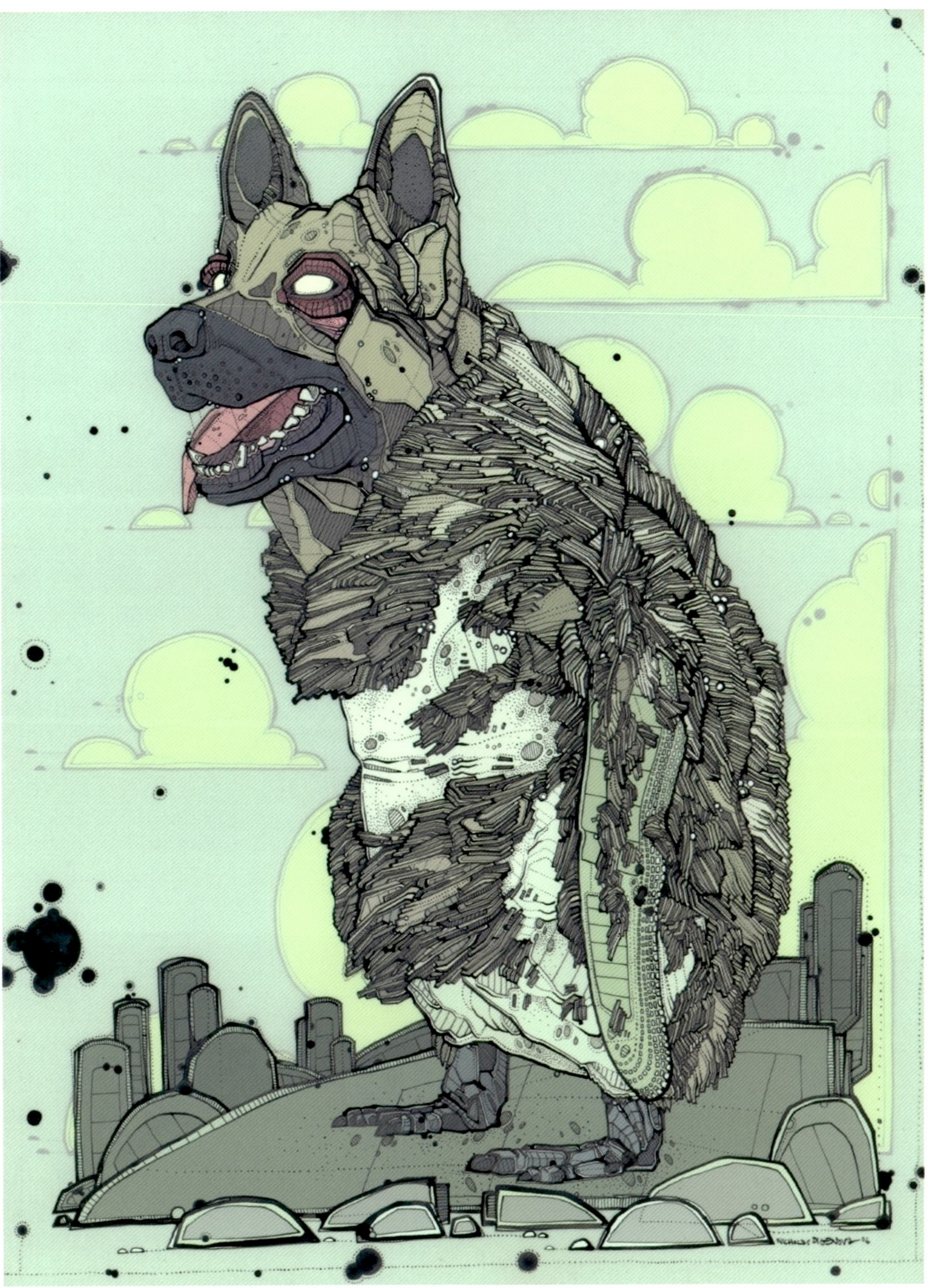

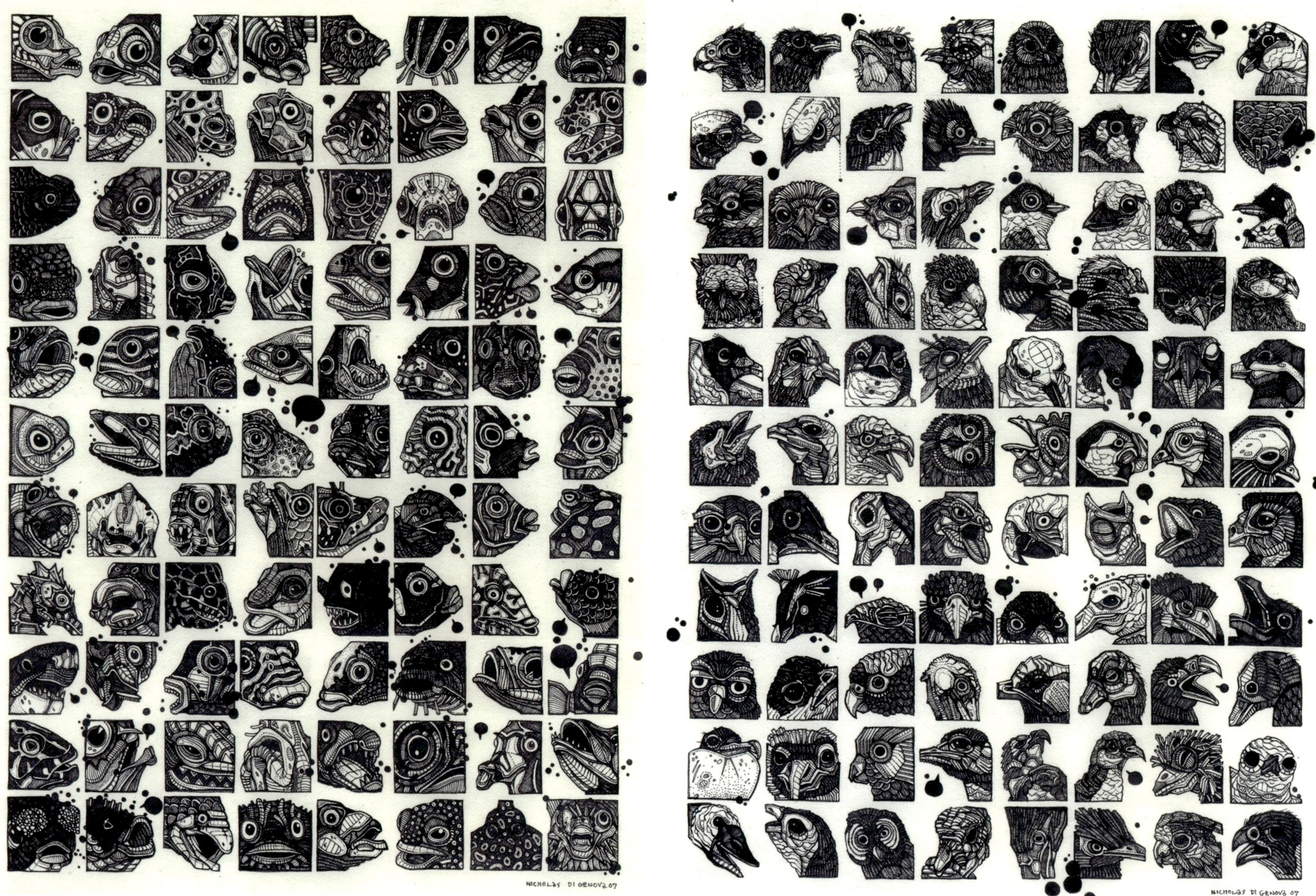
NICHOLAS DI GENOVA 07
NICHOLAS DI GENOVA 07

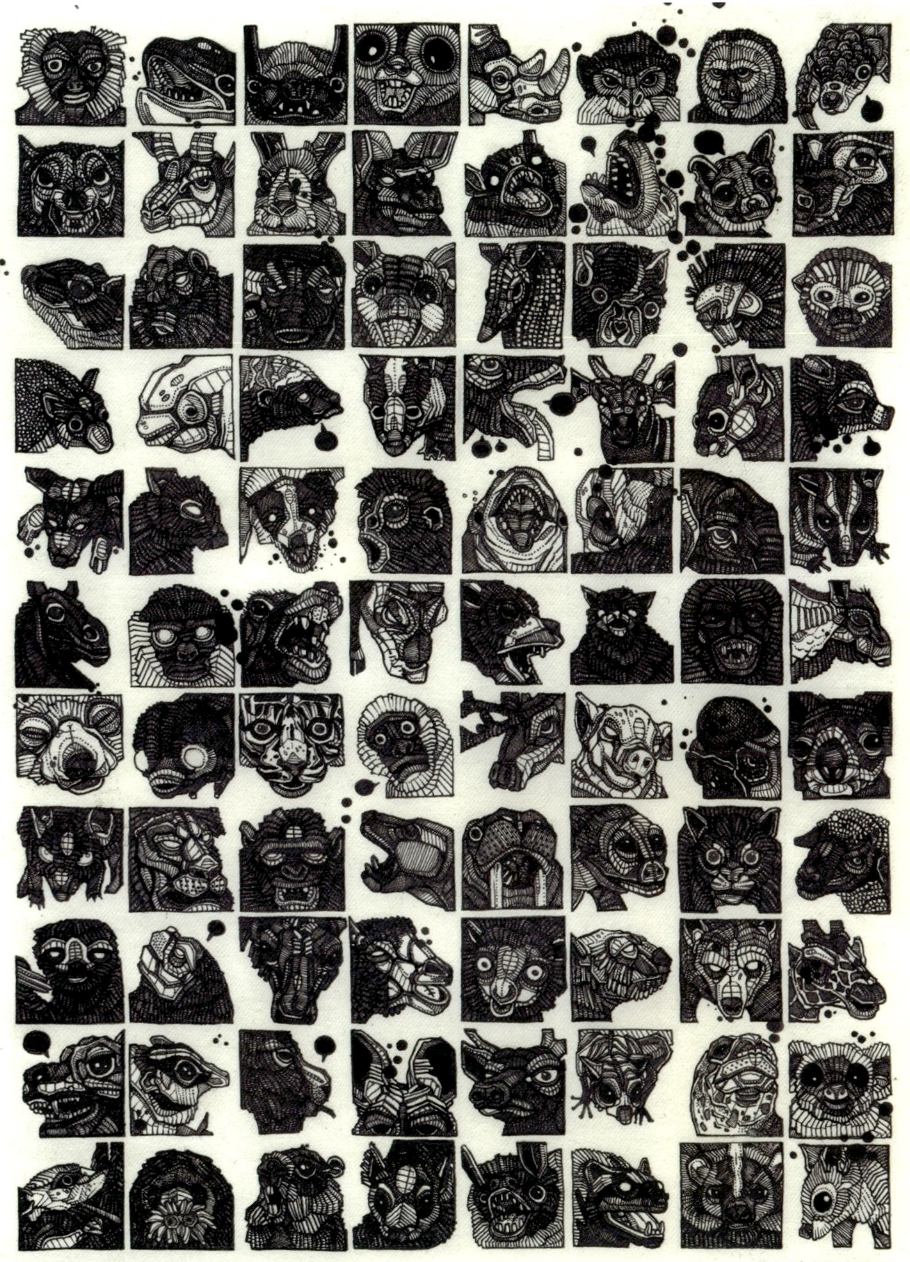
NICHOLAS DI GENOVA 07

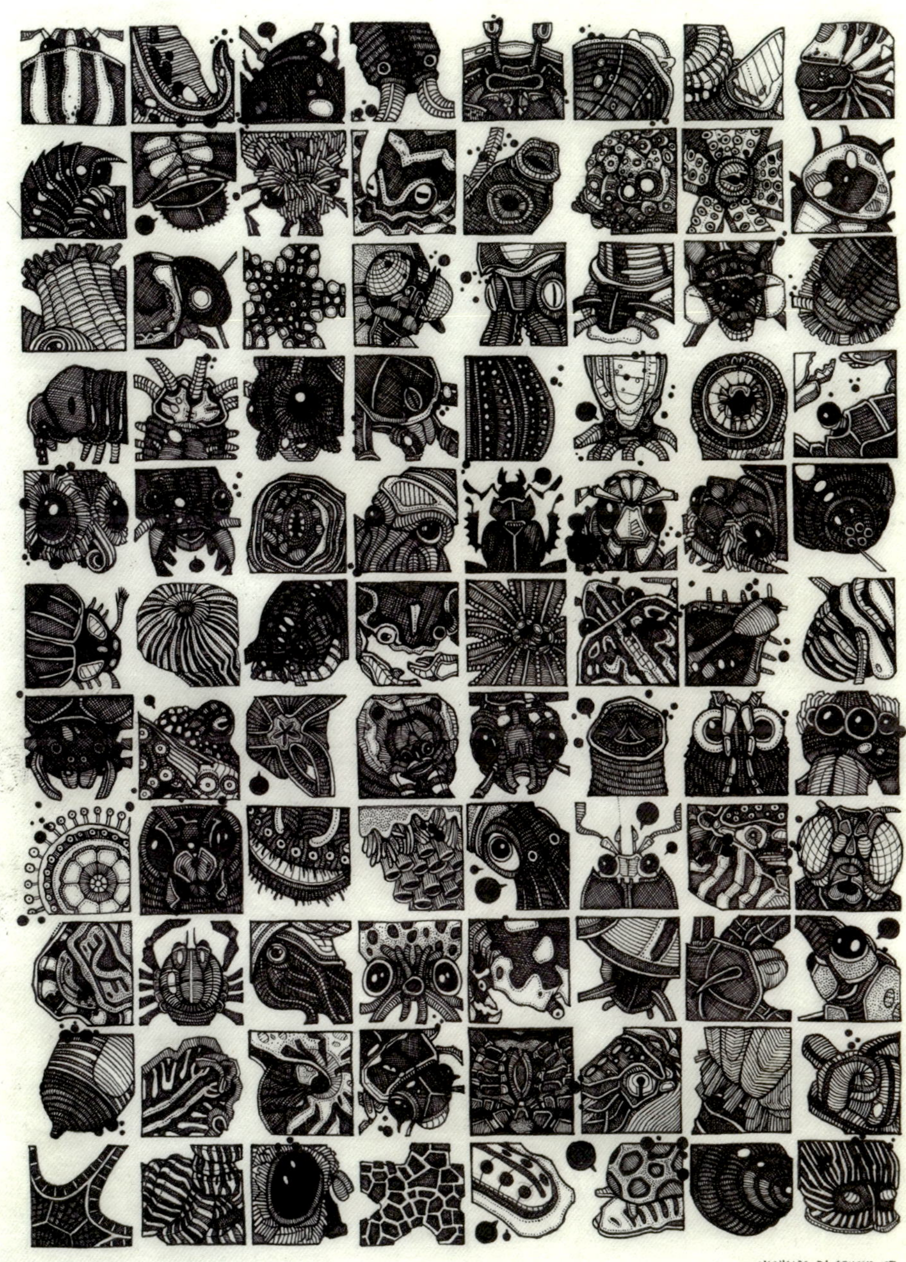
NICHOLAS DI GENOVA 07

»ERIC JOYNER

NATIONALITY: UNITED STATES

LOCATION: SAN FRANCISCO | CA

PUBLICATIONS: SPECTRUM 10-14 | ILLUSTRATORS 45 & 46
ART OF N... CALIFORNIA 03/08
AMERICAN ILLUSTRATION 22
ROBOTS & DONUTS | THE ART OF ERIC JOYNER
JUXTAPOZ MAGAZINE

REFERENCES: TECHNOLOGY REVIEW | REVENUE MAG | E SERVER MAG
ROLAND CORP. | SAN FRANCOSCO CHRONICLE

EXHIBITIONS: FORBIDDEN ADVENTURES | TANGLE IN TIN WORLD
CINE'DELERIO | MALFUNCTION

REPRESENTIVES: COREY HELFORD GALLERY | THE SHOOTING GALLERY
THE MILLER GALLERY | WIND-UP GALLERY

CONTACT: WWW.ERICJOYNER.COM
415.305.3992 OR 415.074.0708 (U.S.A.)

TECHNIQUE: OIL ON WOOD PANEL

BORN: 1960

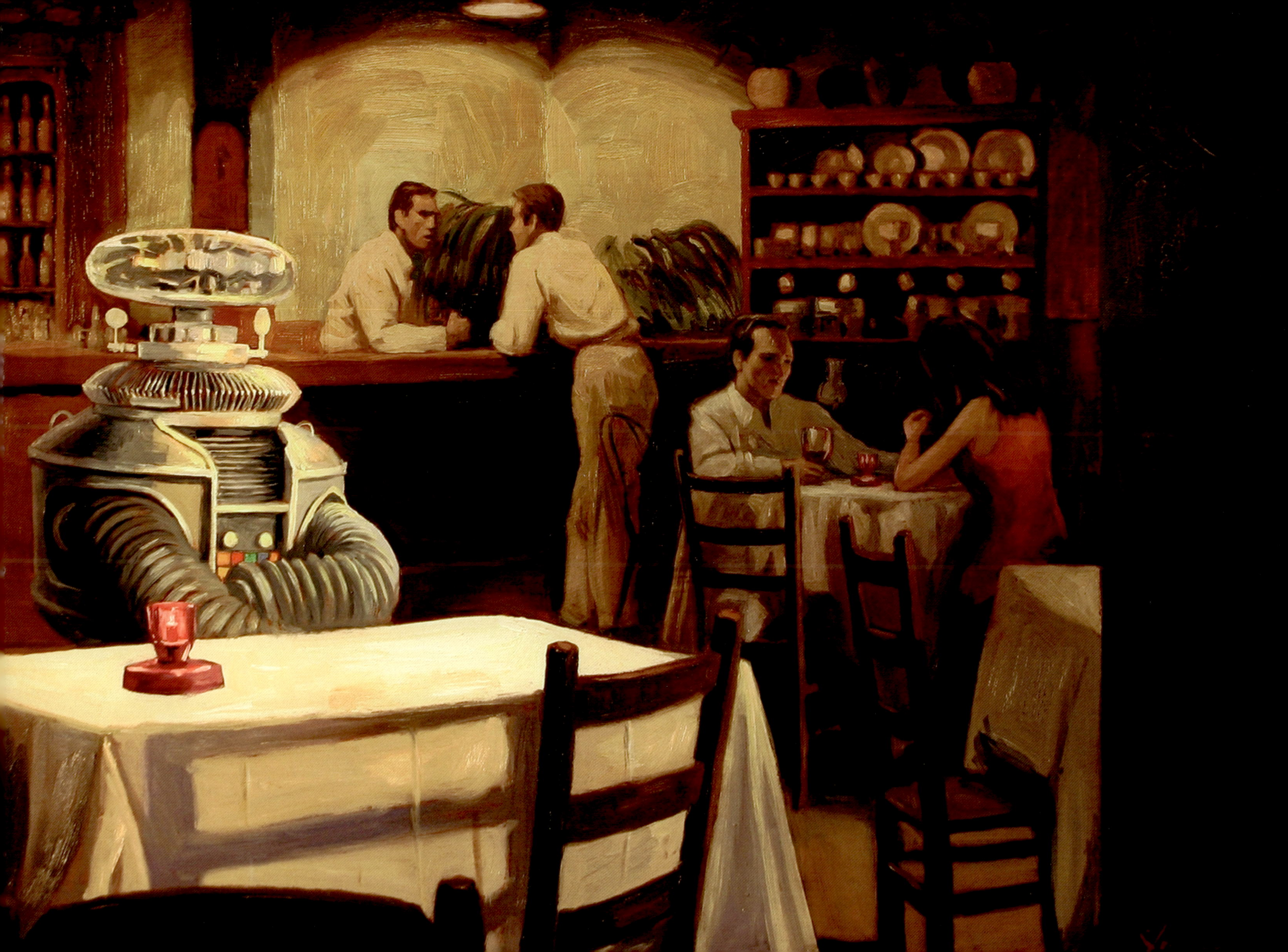

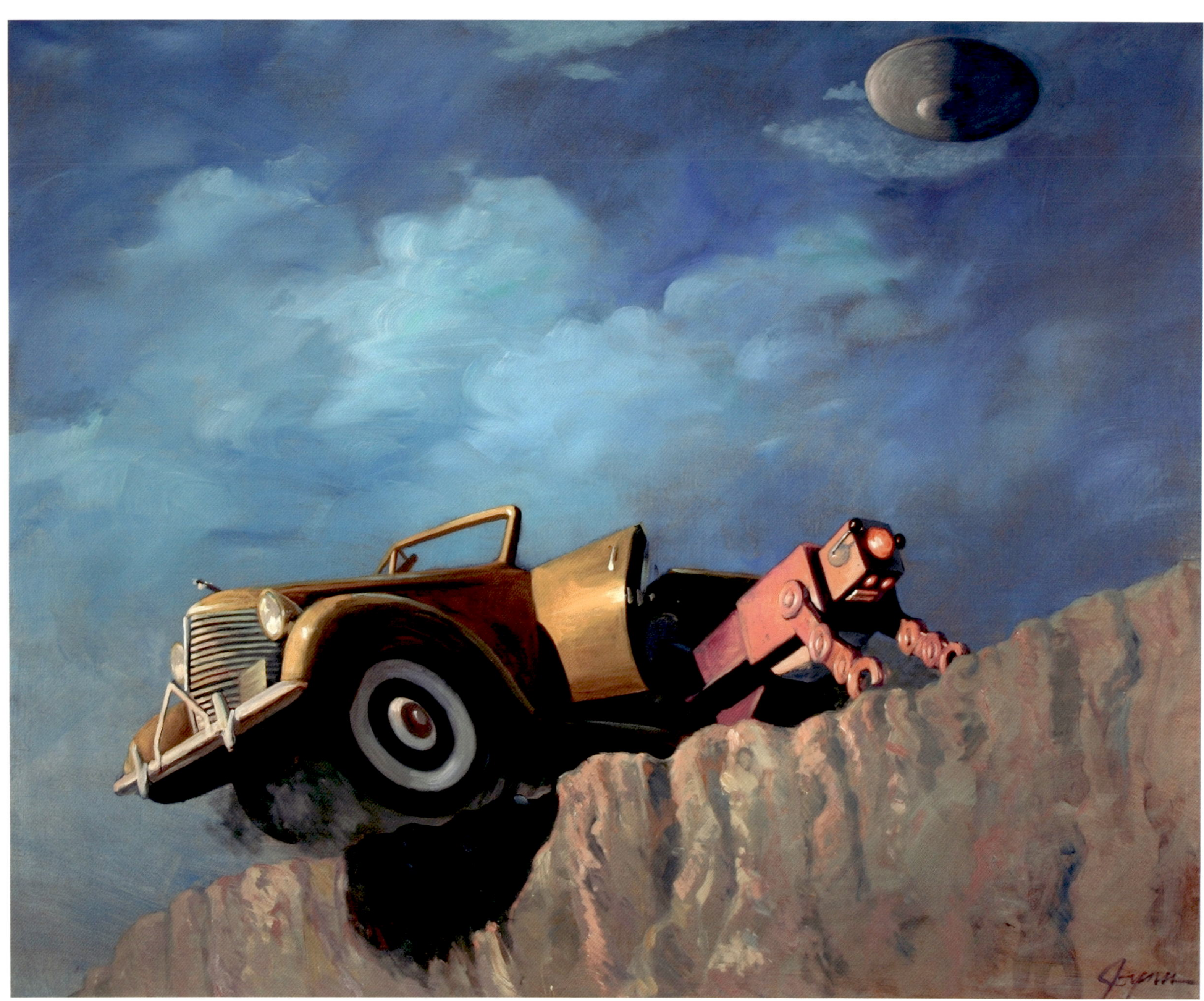

INTRODUCTION: cantina blue final
LEFT PAGE: close call2
RIGHT PAGE:
TOP RIGHT: wake 20x10 prt
DOWN RIGHT: crashtest

DE Meine Erfahrung als Illustrator hat sich im Lauf der letzten zwanzig Jahre ziemlich verändert. Ich fing in der Werbung an als gewöhnlicher, realistisch malender Illustrator. In der Regel bat man mich nicht, konzeptionelle Ideen zur Lösung einer bestimmten Aufgabe beizusteuern. Obwohl meine Arbeiten inzwischen in Galerien hängen, nehme ich weiterhin Aufträge an, aber immer häufiger wollen Artdirectors, dass ich ihre Aufgabe mithilfe der Themen umsetzte, die in meinen künstlerischen Malereien Verwendung finden: Roboter und / oder Donuts. Das ist eine schöne Sache und erhöht die Chance, dass sowohl der Kunde als auch ich selbst mit dem Ergebnis zufrieden sind. Wenn ich einverstanden bin mit dem, woran ich arbeite, sieht man es der Arbeit an. Auch wenn ich gelegentlich immer noch Aufträge annehme, die sich von meiner künstlerischen Tätigkeit vollkommen unterscheiden, verschwimmt die Grenze zwischen Illustration und Kunst eindeutig. Und sind Künstler mit ihrer Kunst schließlich erfolgreich, entwickeln sie vermutlich eine Abneigung gegen Aufträge aus der Werbung und nehmen schließlich überhaupt keine mehr an.

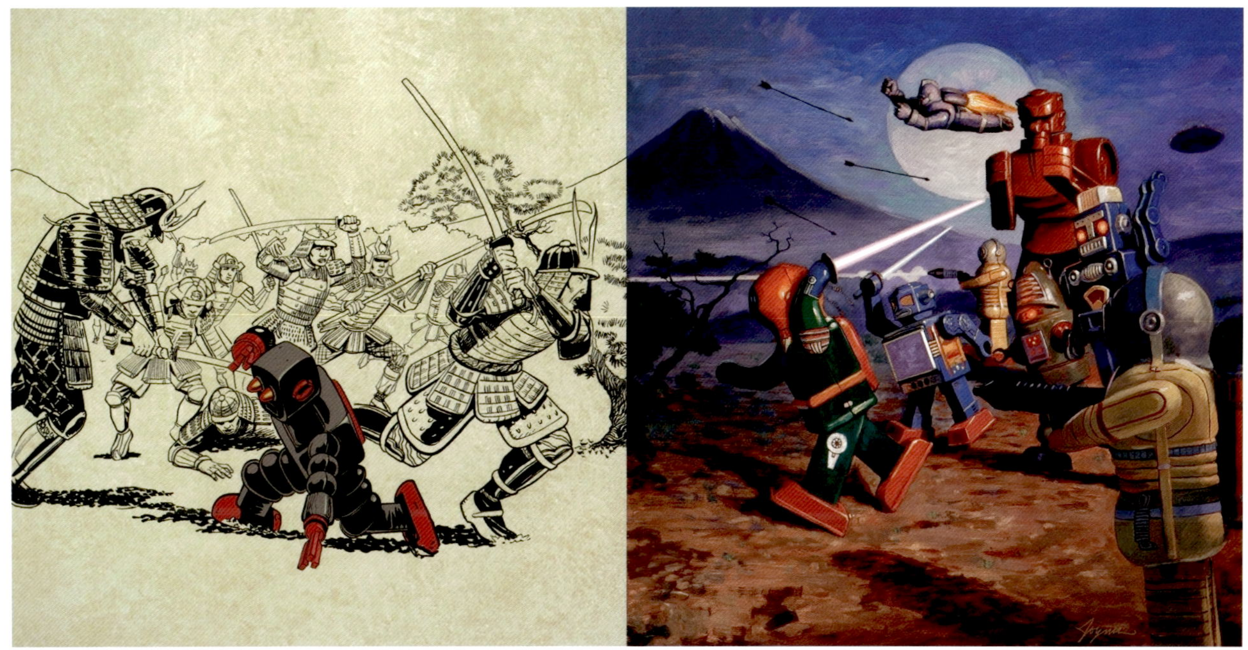

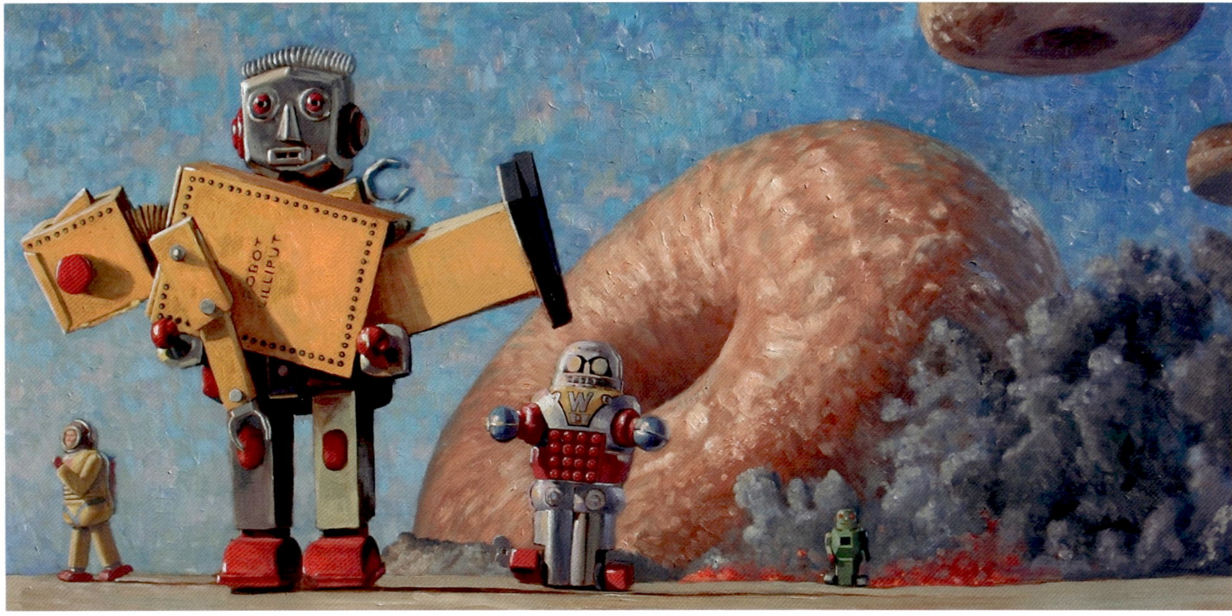

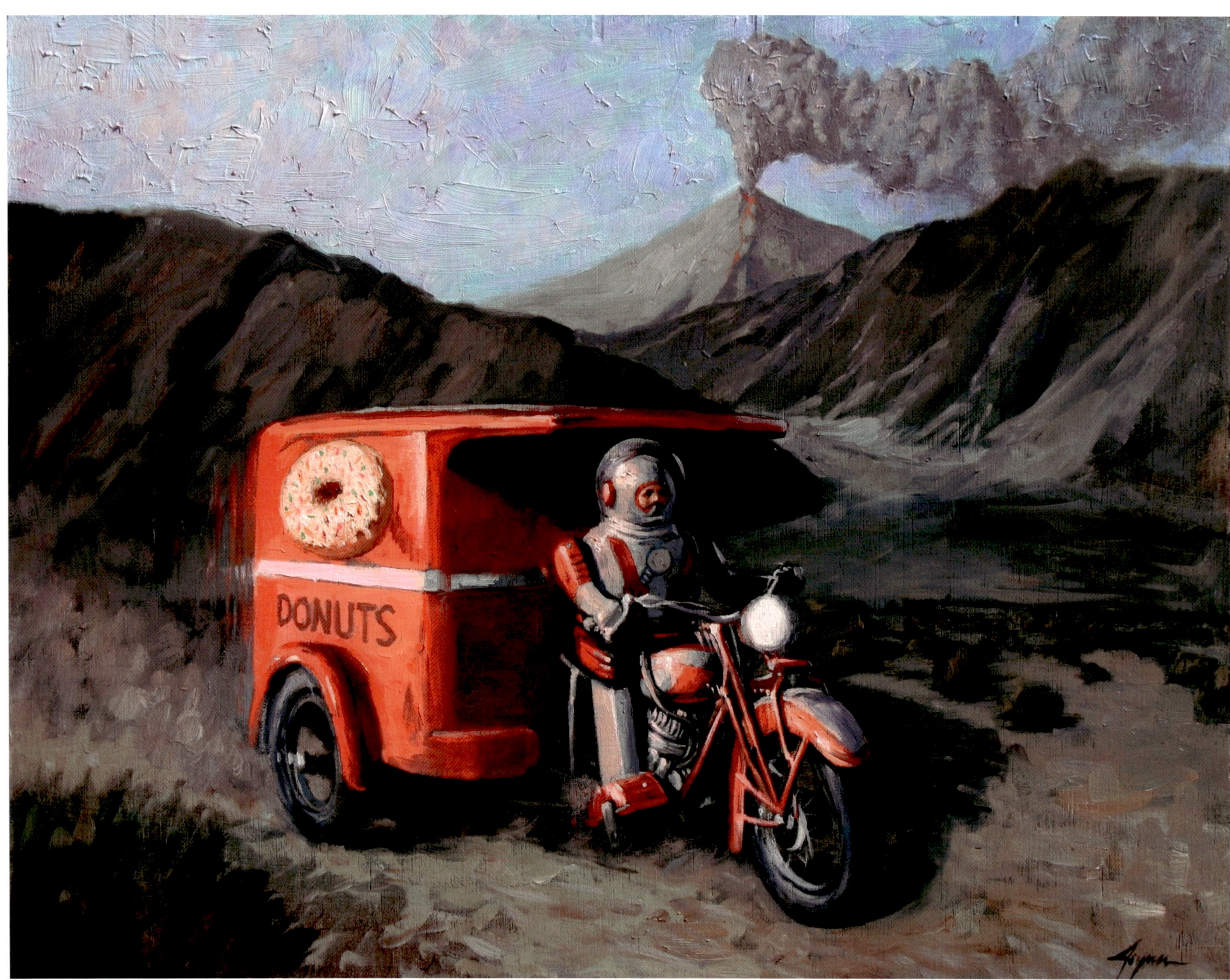

LEFT PAGE: the long journey
RIGHT PAGE: this is this

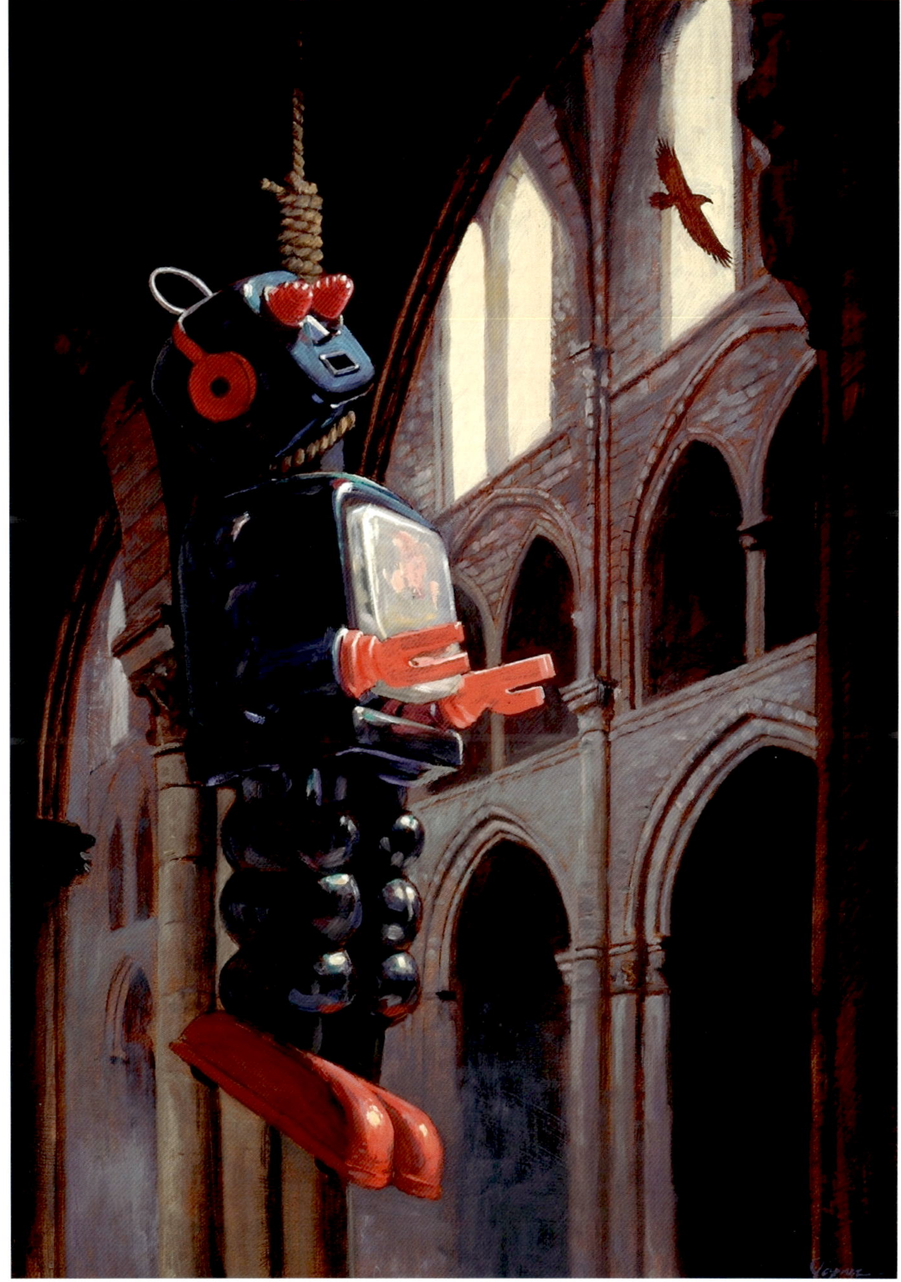

EN Working as an illustrator has changed quite a bit over the last 20 years. I started out as a generic, realistic illustrator, doing commercials. For the most part, I was never asked to give any conceptual input for a particular problem. As I have moved into gallery work, I continue to take assignments, but more and more, art directors want me to solve their problems using the subject matter that I use for my fine art paintings: robots and/or donuts. This is a good thing, increasing the chances that both the client and I are happy with the end result. When I'm happy or approve of whatever it is I'm working on, it shows in the work. Though I still on occasion take an assignment that is completely different from my fine art, the line between illustration and fine art is definitely blurring. I suppose as an artist becomes more successful doing fine art, he or she may develop distaste for commercial assignments, and eventually stop accepting them altogether.

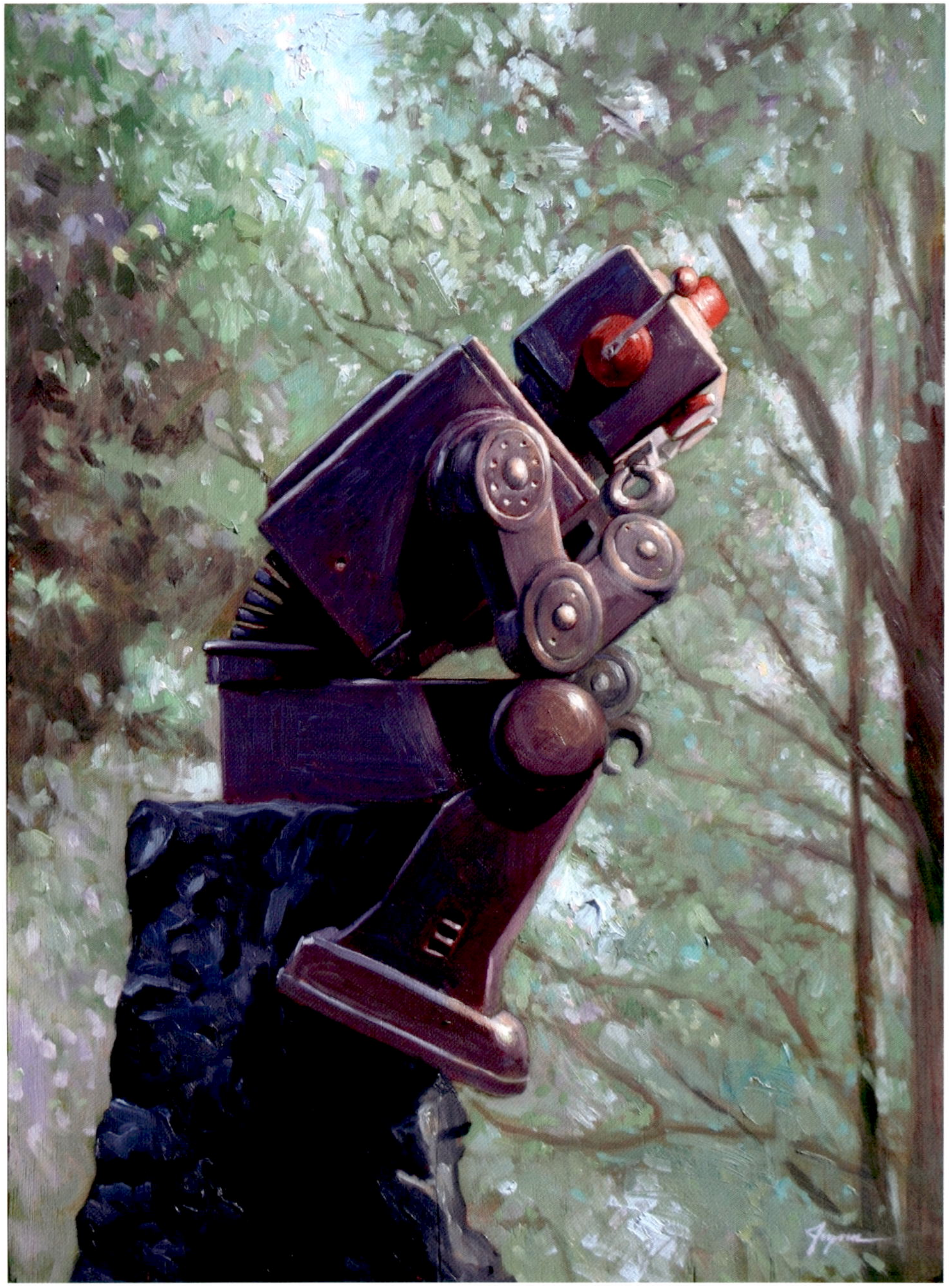

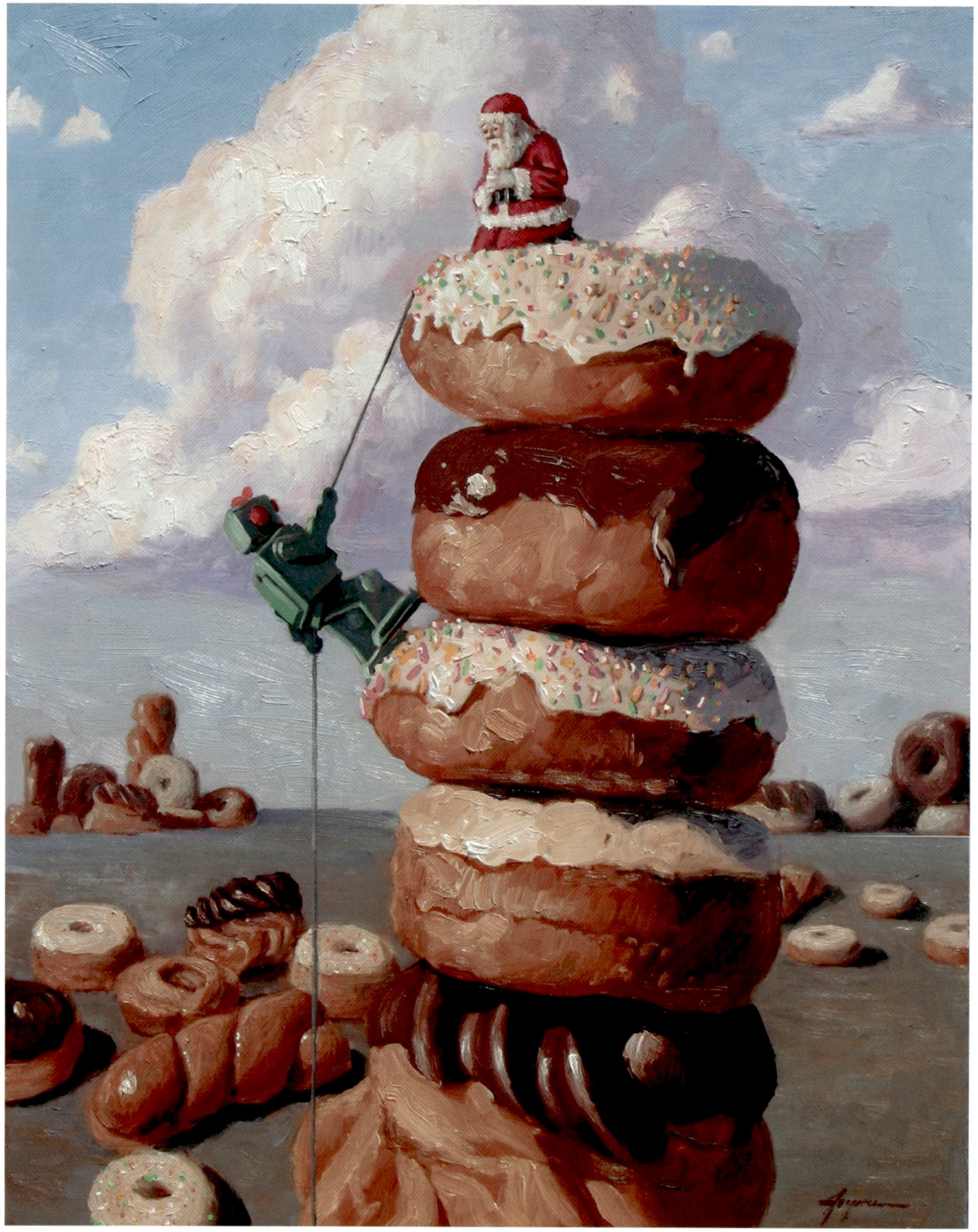

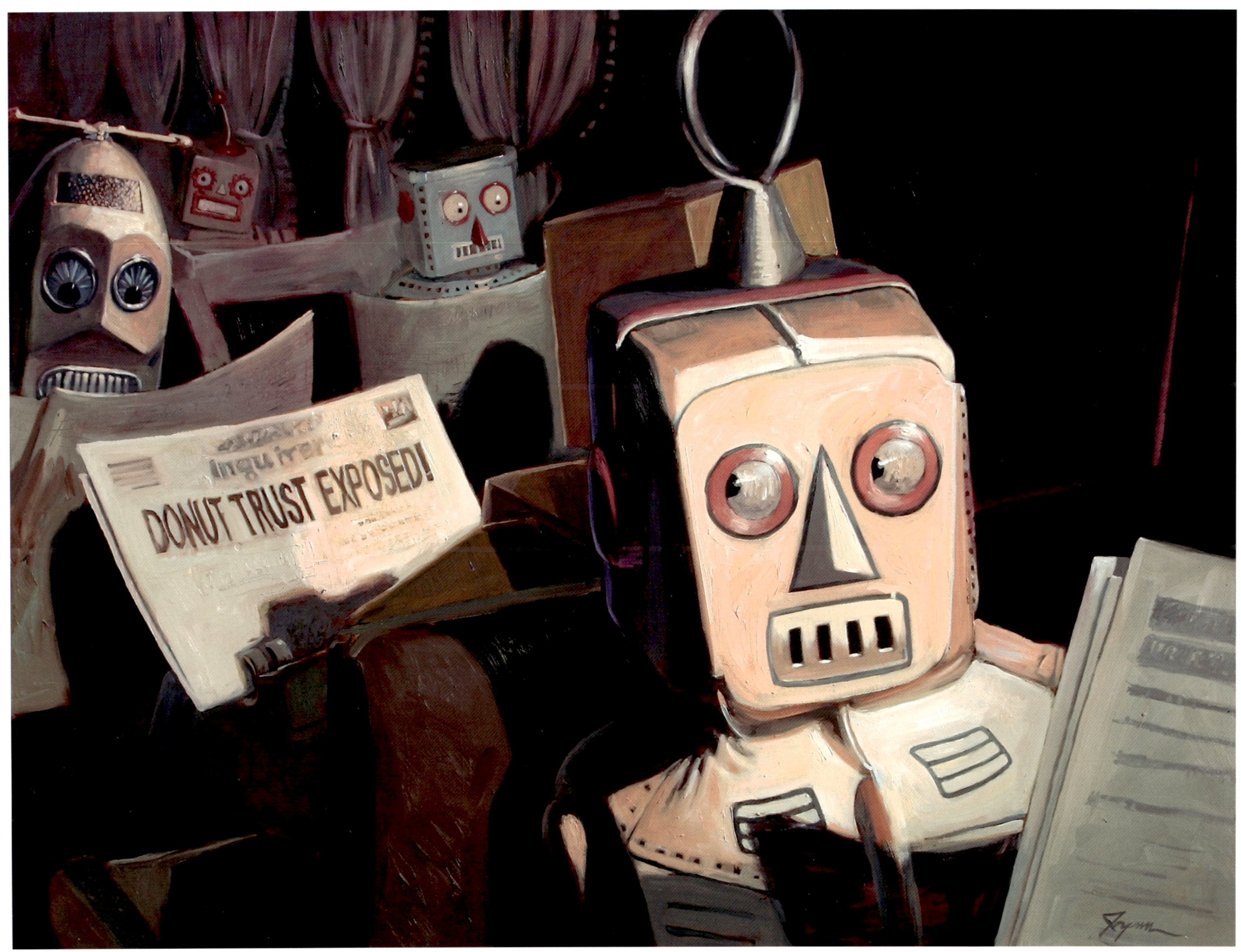

LEFT PAGE:
LEFT: collator
RIGHT: the adventurers bg
RIGHT PAGE: the headline

» STYLEFIGHTING [PATRICK HARTL]

NATIONALITY:	GERMAN
LOCATION:	MUNICH
PUBLICATIONS:	FREISTIL 3 (HERMANN SCHMIDT VERLAG) WEB DESIGN INDEX 7 (PEPIN PRESS) NOVUM MAGAZIN | PAGE | MAX MAGAZINE JITTER MAGAZIN | JUICE MAGAZINE STYLEFILE-BLACKBOOK.SESSION (PUBLIKAT VERLAG) GRAFFITI ART 2 (SCHWARZKOPF&SCHWARZKOPF VERLAG)
REFERENCES:	SONY PICTURES | CONSTANTIN FILM ORTLIEB WATERPROOF | KULTURREFERAT MÜNCHEN DEUTSCHE KINDER UND JUGENDSTIFTUNG
EXHIBITIONS:	ARTI ET AMICITAE GALLERY – AMSTERDAM VELVET DA VINCI GALLERY – SAN FRANCISCO CA CANESSA GALLERY – SAN FRANCISCO CA FRESNO ART MUSEUM – FRESNO CA CULTURE CENTRE – KATOWICE – POLAND KLINGSPOR MUSEUM – OFFENBACH GUTLEUT15 – FRANKFURT GALERIE AM GRABEN – AUGSBURG GÖRRES10 & DIE FÄRBEREI – MUNICH
CONTACT:	WWW.STYLEFIGHTING.DE HARTL@STYLEFIGHTING.DE
TECHNIQUE:	MIXED MEDIA
BORN:	1976

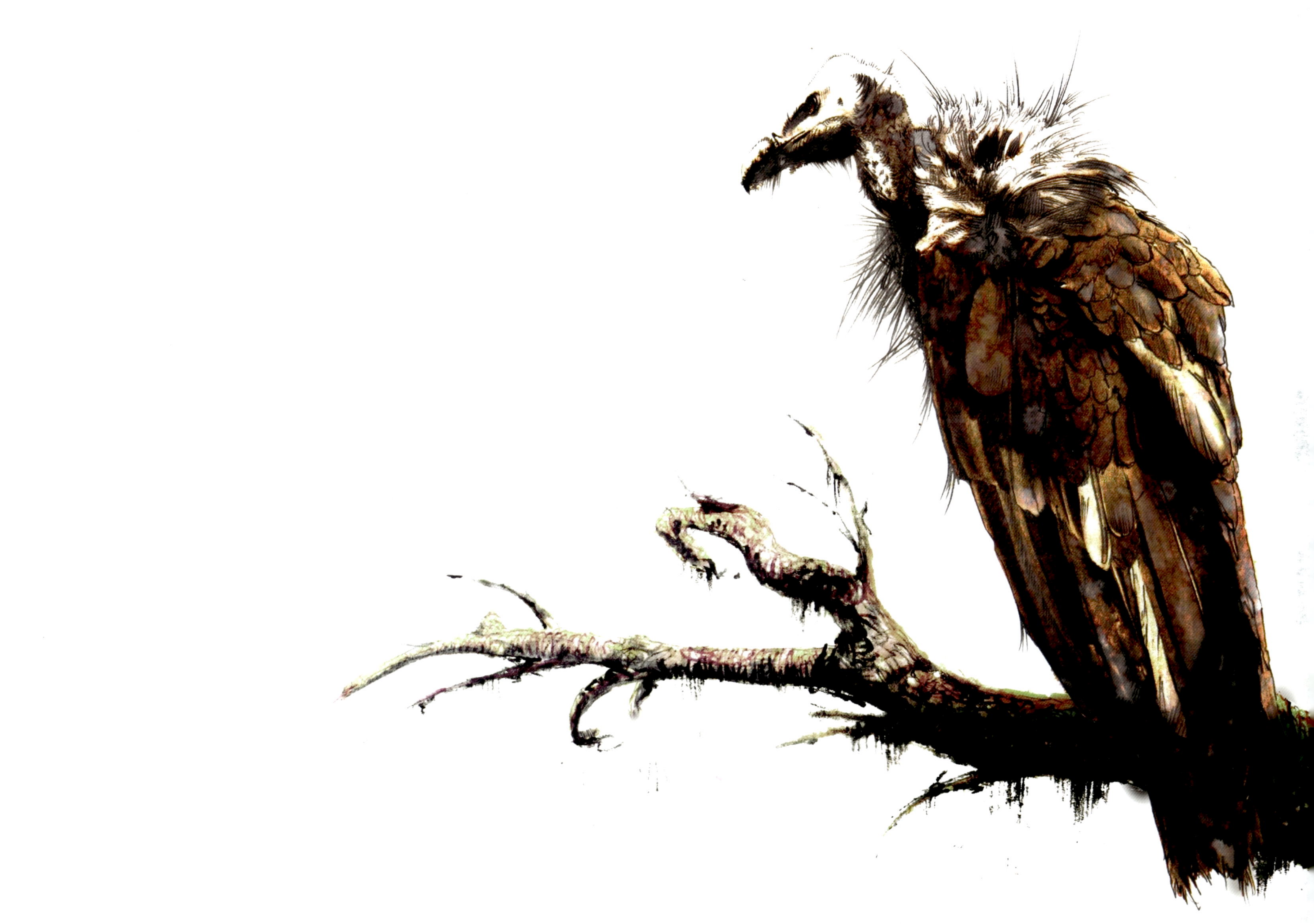

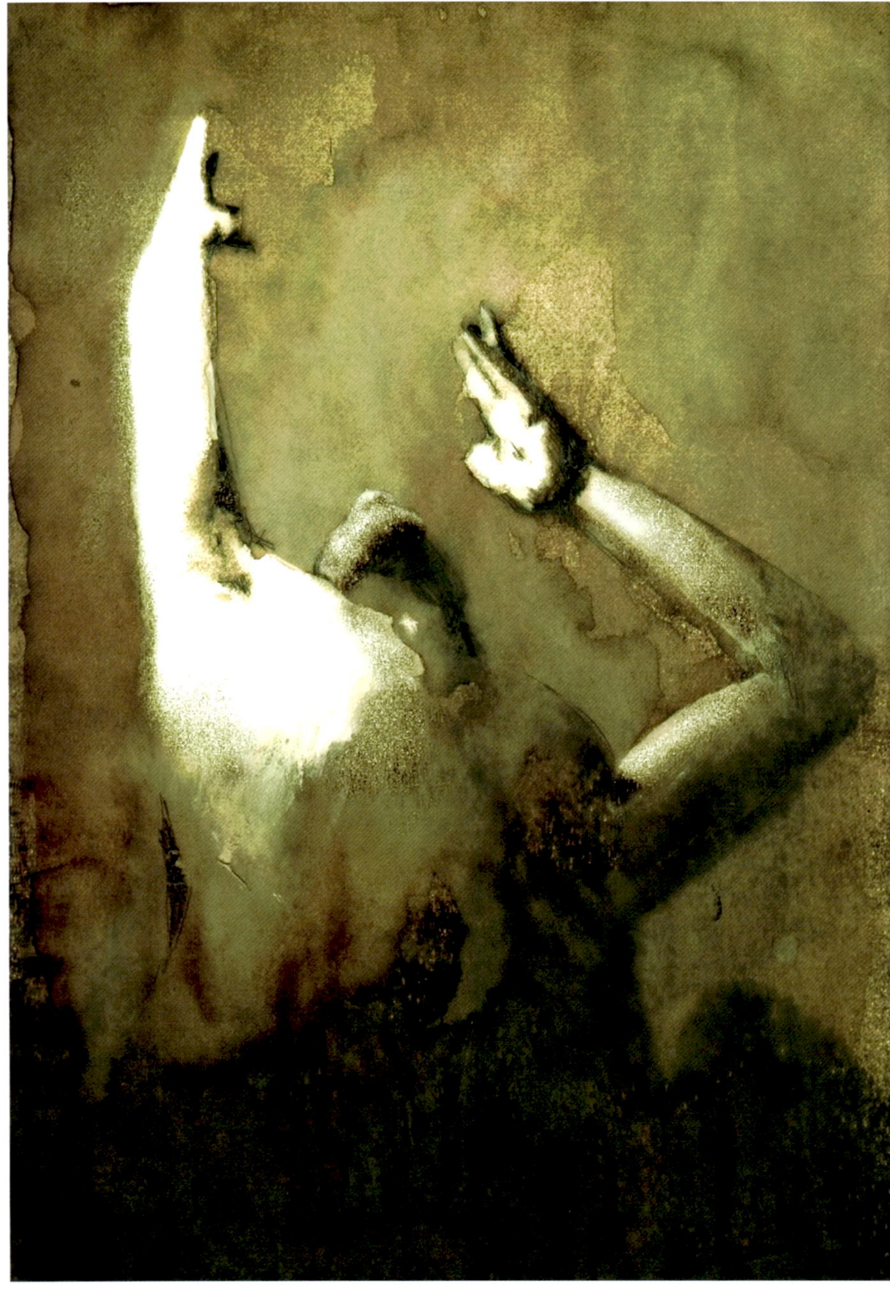

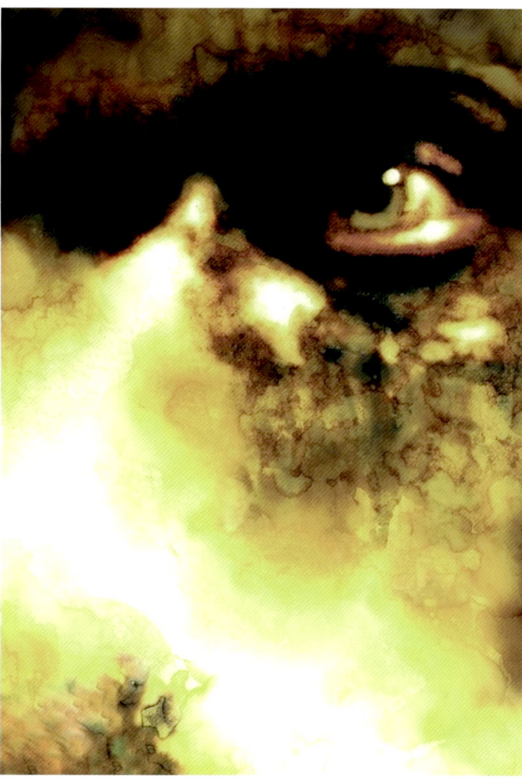

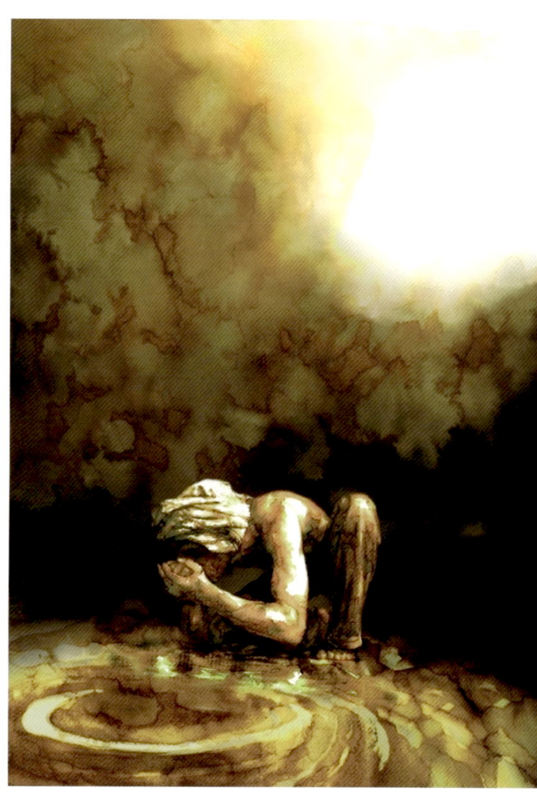

INTRODUCTION: vulture
LEFT PAGE:
LEFT: joshua gebietet
der sonne stillzustehen
MIDDLE: schöpfung
RIGHT: gideons auswahl der krieger
RIGHT PAGE:
LEFT: die vertreibung aus dem paradies
RIGHT: turmbau zu babel

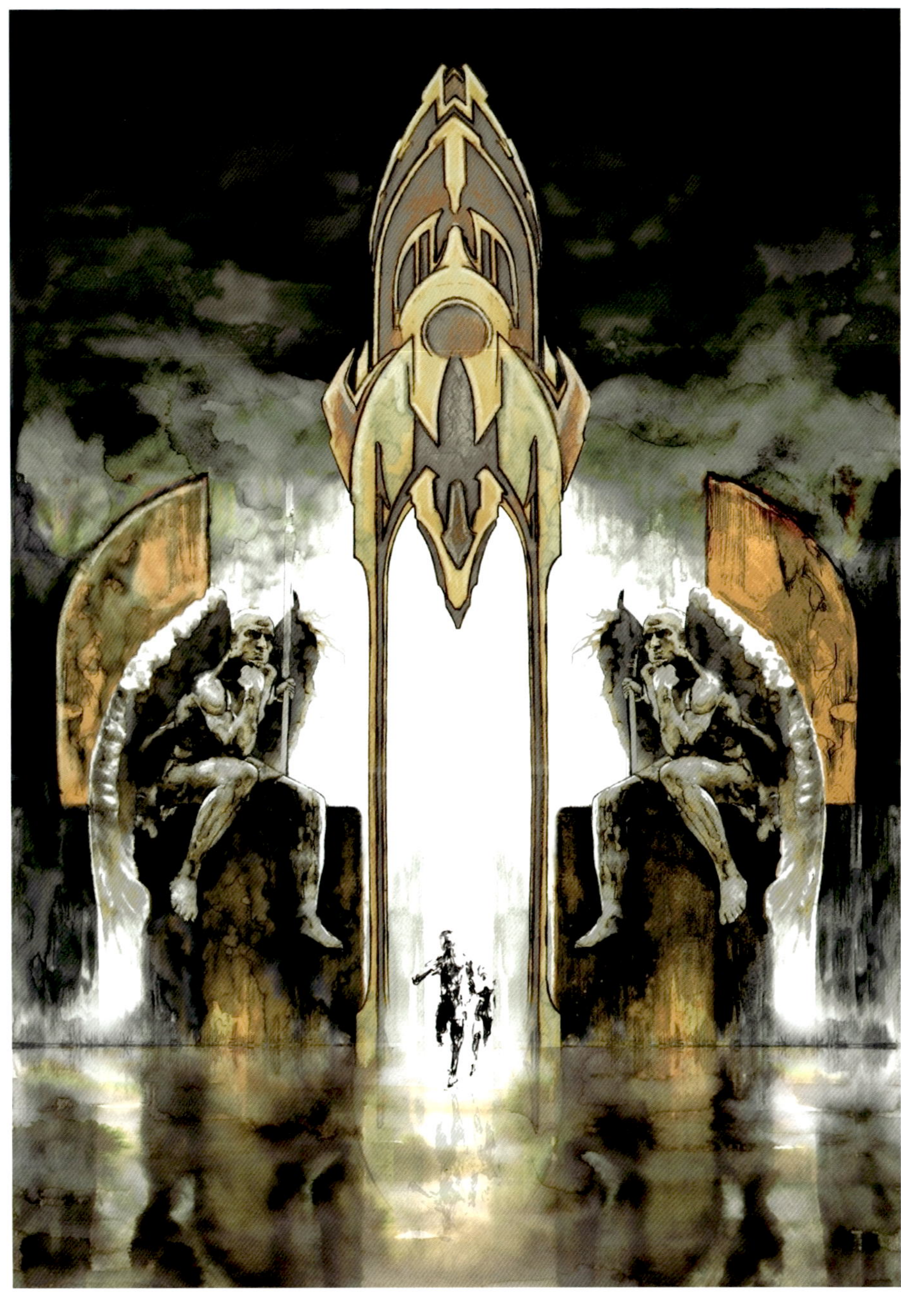

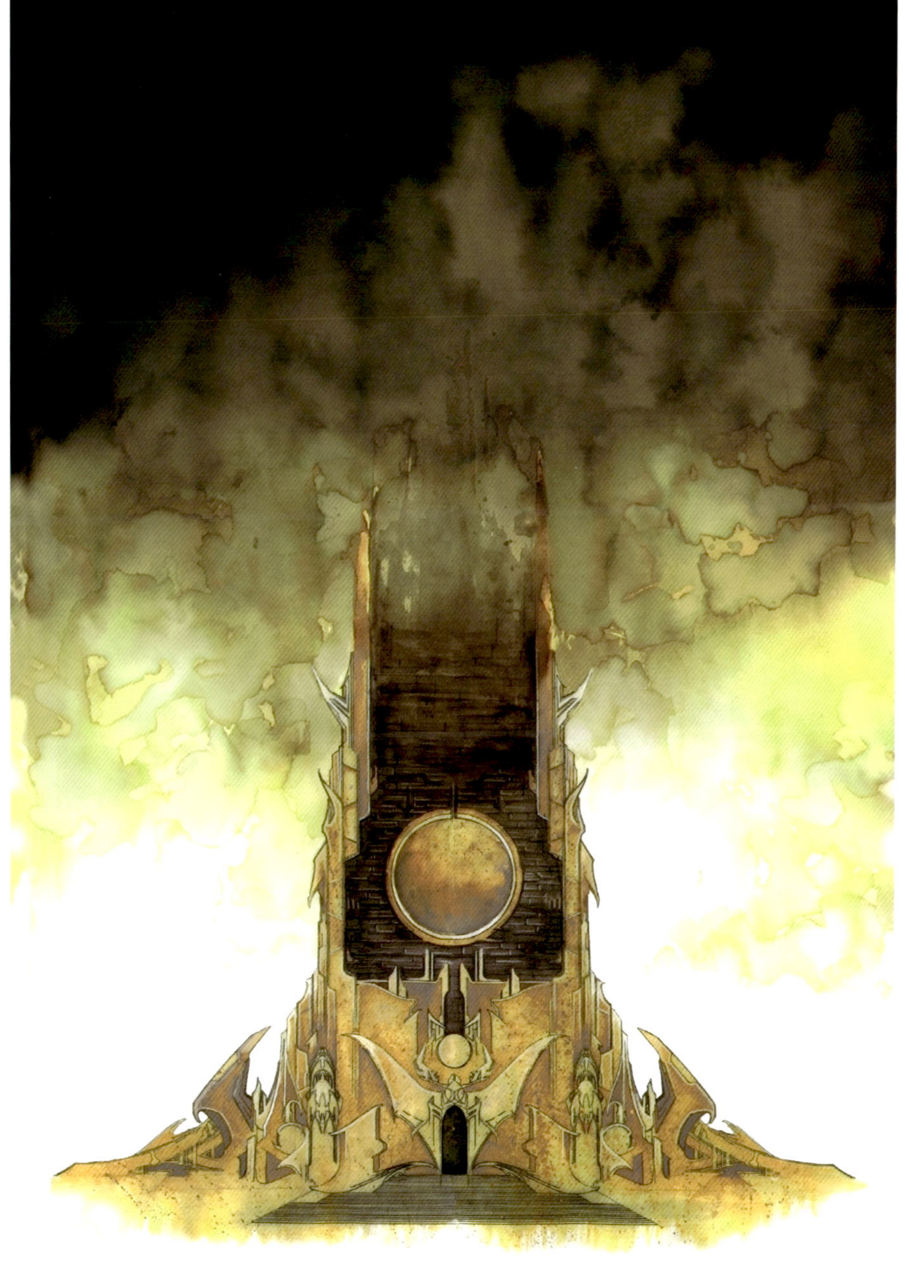

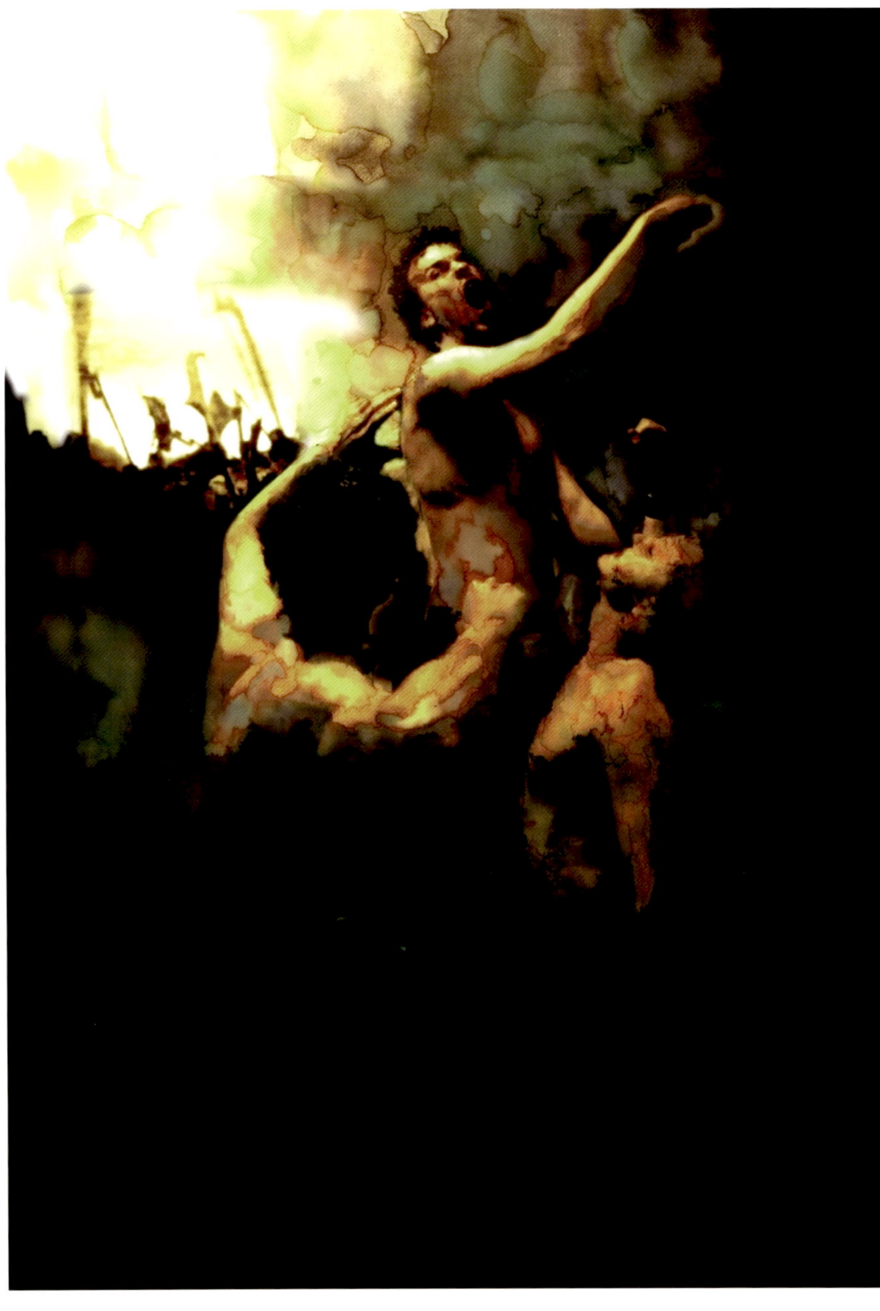

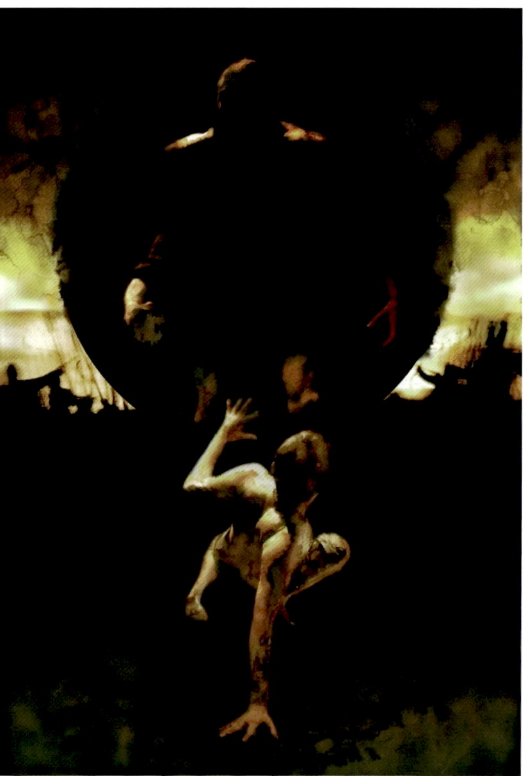

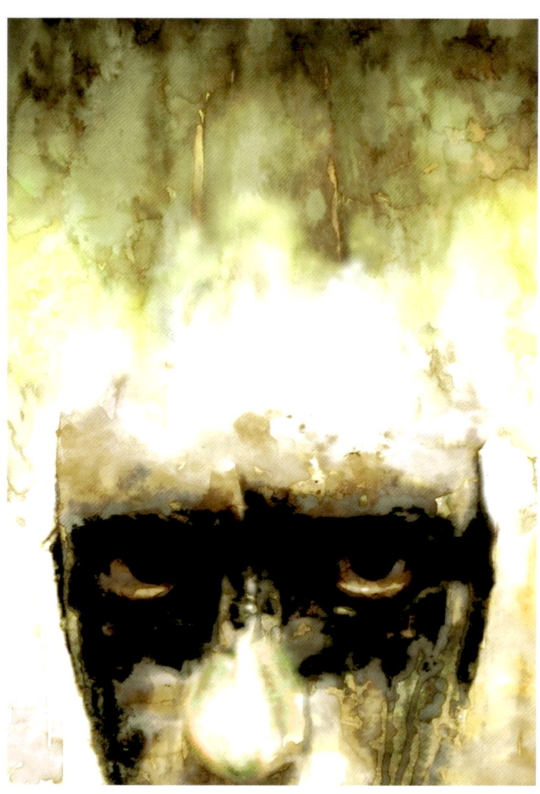

DE Ich muss zugeben, dass mir diese ganze Sache um die Definition von Illustration und Kunst nicht wirklich wichtig ist. Meine kreative Laufbahn begann als Graffiti Writer, studiert habe ich dann Design mit dem Schwerpunkt Kalligrafie und meine Diplomarbeit wiederum war zum Thema Illustrationen zum Alten Testament. Heute verdiene ich meinen Lebensunterhalt hauptsächlich mit der Gestaltung von Plakaten. Ich mache beides – Auftragsarbeiten für Kunden sowie meine eigenen, freien Arbeiten, die ich auch in Ausstellungen zeige. Was bin ich also – Graffiti Writer, Designer, Künstler, Illustrator, Kalligraf??? In eine Schublade bin ich wohl nicht leicht zu stecken – und trifft ähnliches auf andere Künstler ebenso zu, ist mir das sympathisch. Ich ziehe es vor, Dinge miteinander zu verbinden anstatt sie strikt voneinander zu trennen und bin damit wohl auch nicht der Einzige. Natürlich nehmen viele Künstler diese

Trennung nach wie vor sehr ernst und eine gewisse Abgrenzung zwischen den beiden Bereichen ist vielleicht auch nicht ganz unwichtig. Meinem Empfinden nach verschmelzen beide Disziplinen aber ohnehin immer mehr. Ich für meinen Teil empfinde die Auflösung von Grenzen als etwas durchweg Positives. Grundsätzlich ist es so, dass mich eine Arbeit entweder anspricht oder nicht – der Hintergrund, aus dem heraus diese entstanden ist, ändert daran nichts. Schlussendlich müssen sowohl Illustratoren als auch freie Künstler meist Kompromisse eingehen: Der eine ist auf seinen Kunden und die Aufgabenstellung des jeweiligen Projekts festgelegt und der andere auf seinen Galeristen und einen bestimmten Stil, den die Käufer von ihm gewohnt sind. Aber um zur ursprünglichen Frage zurückzukommen: Gibt es eine Grenze zwischen Illustration und Kunst? Was ist Kunst? Ich kann das nicht beantworten und ich will diese Frage auch gar nicht beantworten. Ist meine Arbeit eines der wichtigsten Dinge in meinem Leben? Ja. Für mich ist das ausreichend.

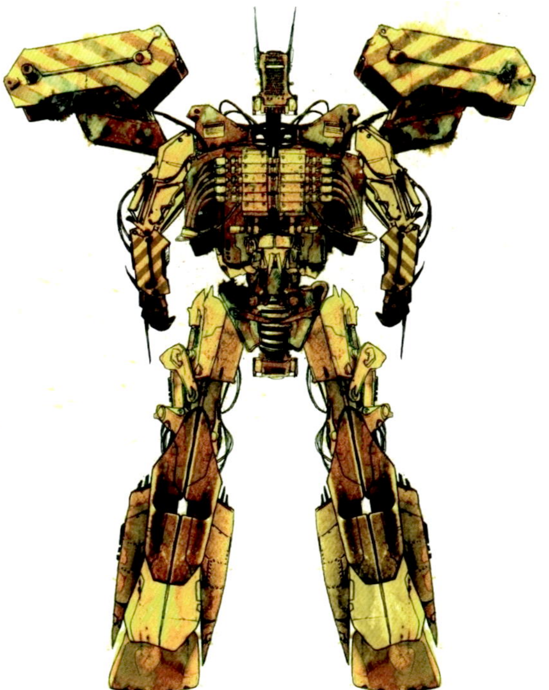

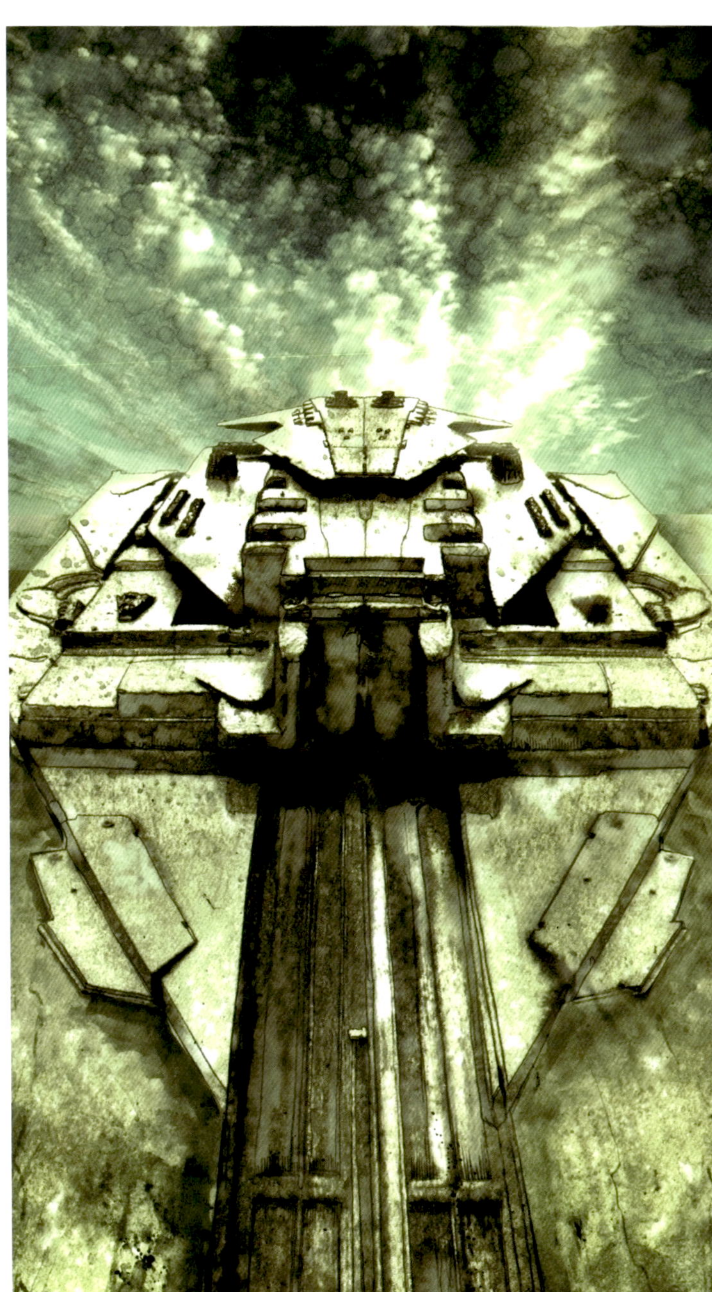

LEFT PAGE:
LEFT: simsons sieg über die philister
MIDDLE: david gegen goliat
RIGHT: der mensch
RIGHT PAGE:
LEFT: model htl-76
RIGHT: dark tower

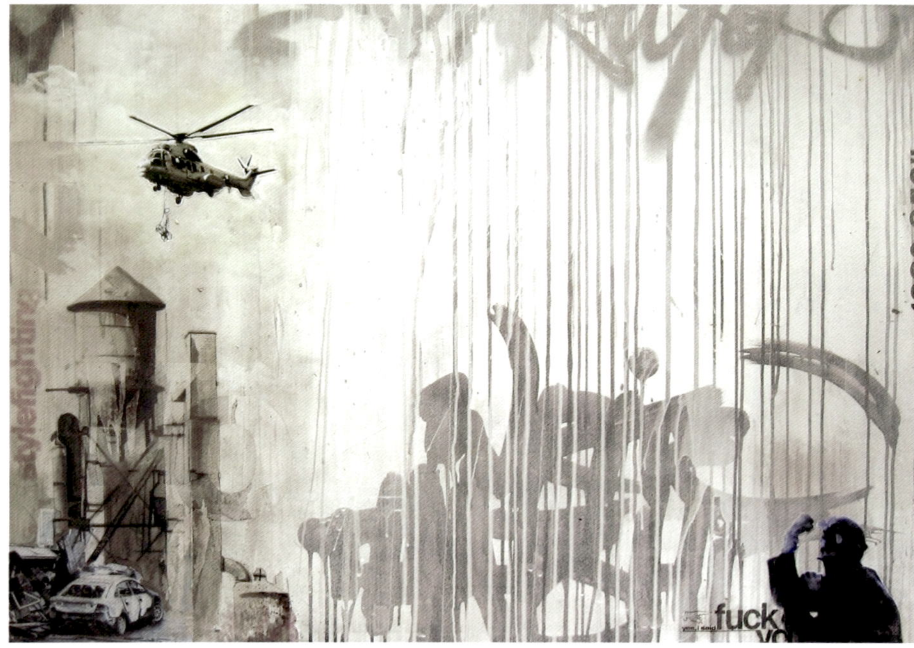

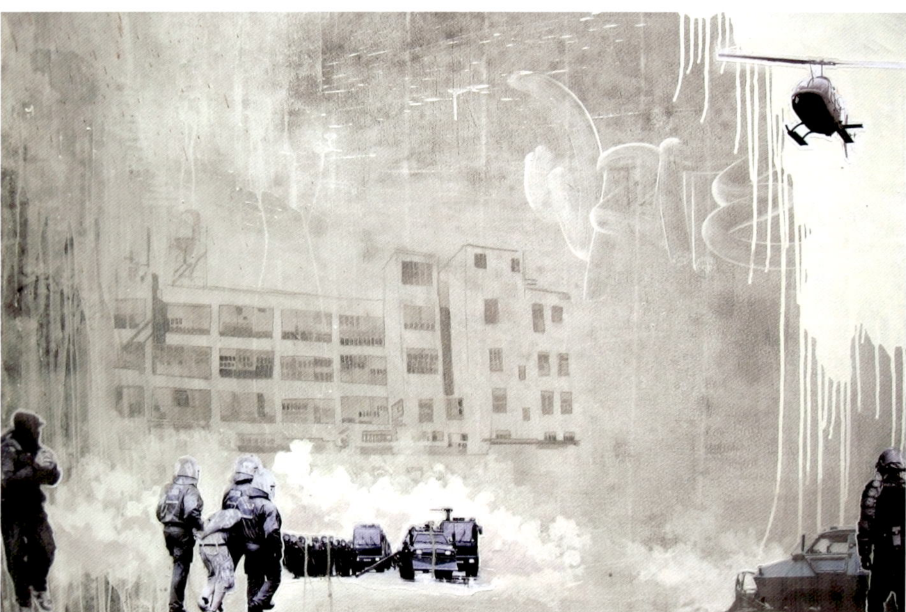

TOP LEFT: streetfighting 1
DOWN RIGHT: streetfighting 2

EN To be honest, I am not terribly interested in the whole discussion about the definitions of art and illustration. I began my creative career as a graffiti-writer, I then studied design with a focus on calligraphy, and my diploma thesis dealt with illustrations to the Old Testament. Today I earn my money mainly with poster design. I do both: I work for clients, and I produce my own, unsolicited works, which I also show in exhibitions. So what am I – graffiti writer, designer, artist, illustrator, calligrapher??? Apparently I can't be pigeonholed that easily, and I always like it if other artists experience the same. I prefer combining things to rigidly separating them, and I think I'm not the only one here. Needless to say that many artists still take this separation very seriously, and maybe some sort of differentiation isn't altogether unimportant. In my view, both disciplines are merging anyway, and I see it as something totally positive when boundaries disappear. A work is either appealing to me or not – the motivation out of which the work has been created is of no great concern. In the end, illustrators as well as artists have to compromise: the one is restricted by his clients and the specifications of a particular job, the other by his gallery owner and by the style that buyers expect from him. But going back to the initial question: is there a difference between illustration and art? What is art? I can't answer this question, and I don't even want to answer it. Is my work one of the most important things in my life? Yes. For me that's enough.

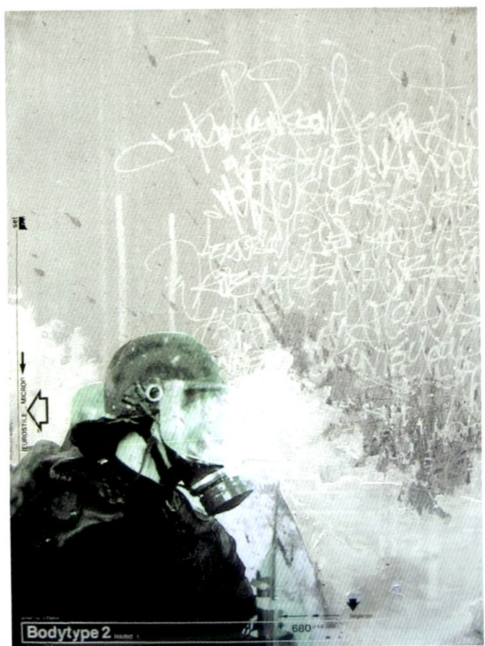

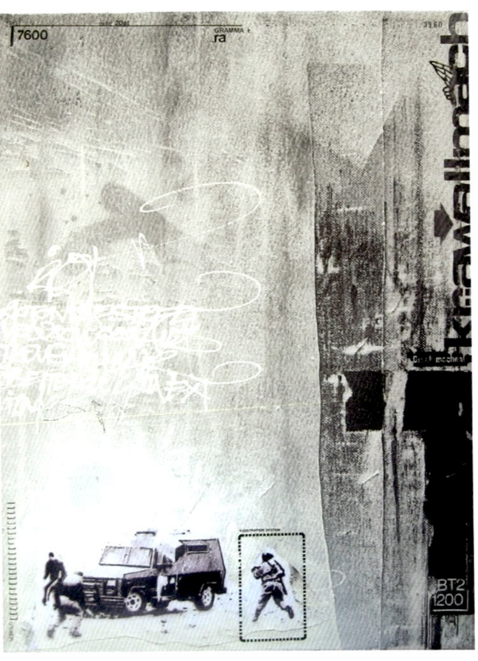

LEFT: streetfighting 3
MIDDLE: streetfighting 4
RIGHT: streetfighting 5

»FLIN

NATIONALITY:	GERMAN
LOCATION:	SOMEWHERE IN WEST GERMANY
PUBLICATIONS:	SÜDDEUTSCHE ZEITUNG A.M.
REFERENCES:	ANIMATION STUDIOS & ADVERDTISING AGENCIES
EXHIBITIONS:	WATCH OUT FOR THE THIRD RAIL CENTRAL STATION – MUNICH DER ZUG IST ABGEFAHREN CENTRAL STATION – MUNICH URBAN DISCIPLINE – HAMBURG AUFSTAND DER ZEICHEN TOSKANISCHE SÄULENHALLE – AUGSGBURG A TRIBUTE TO STYLE KALLMANN MUSEUM – ISMANING GOING OVER GALERIE HEITSCH – MUNICH
CONTACT:	FLINSKY@WEB.DE
TECHNIQUE:	VARIOUS
BORN:	BABYLONIAN

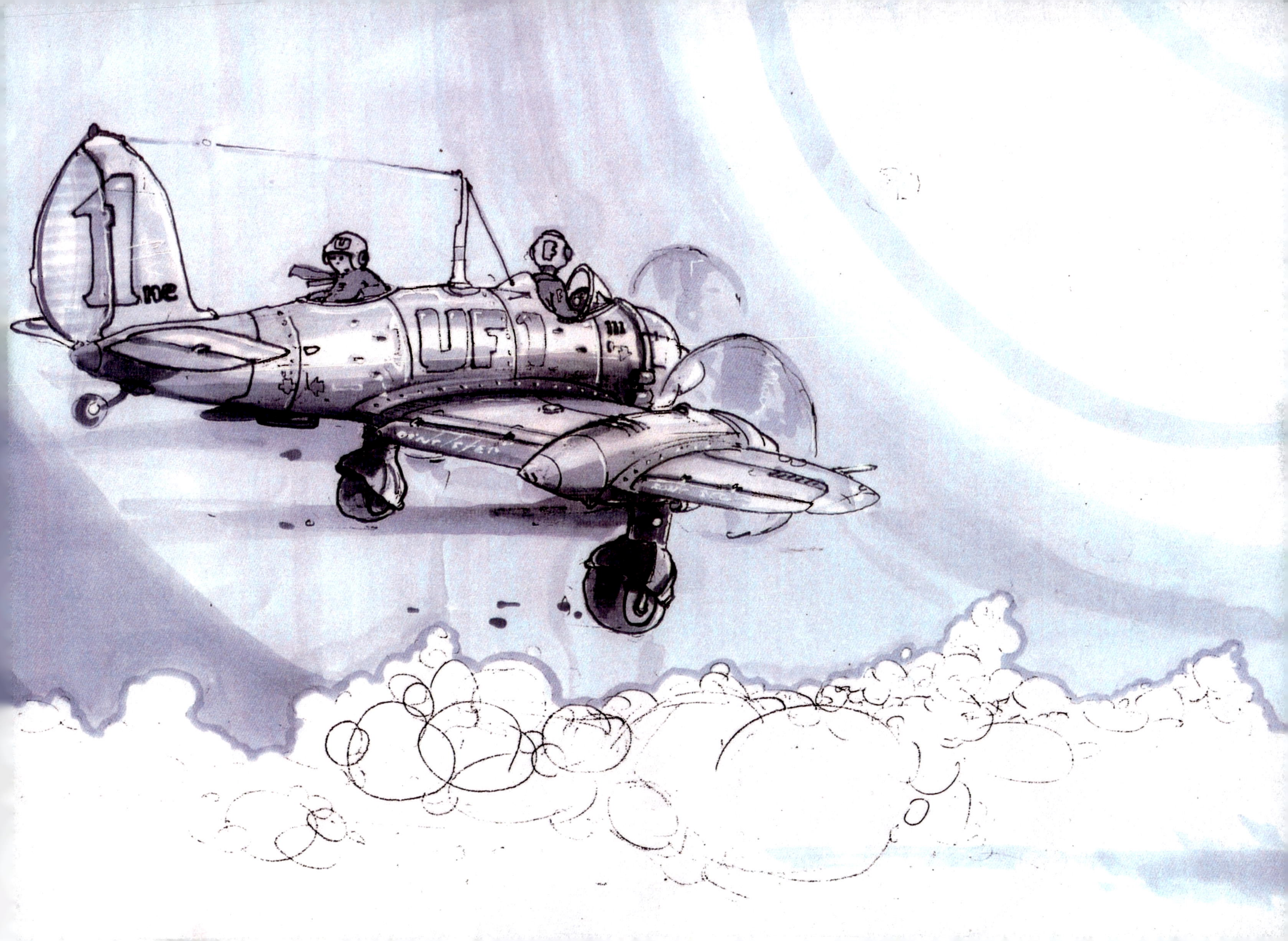
UF1

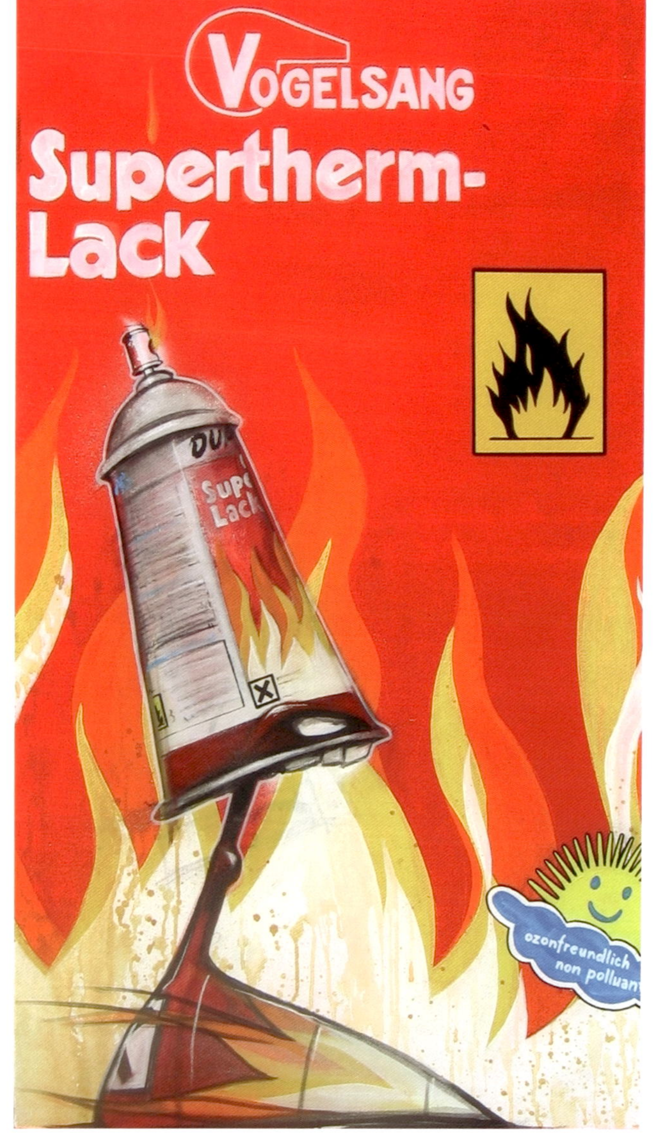
DUPLI-COLO
VOGELSANG
Supertherm-
Lack
ozonfreundlich
non polluant

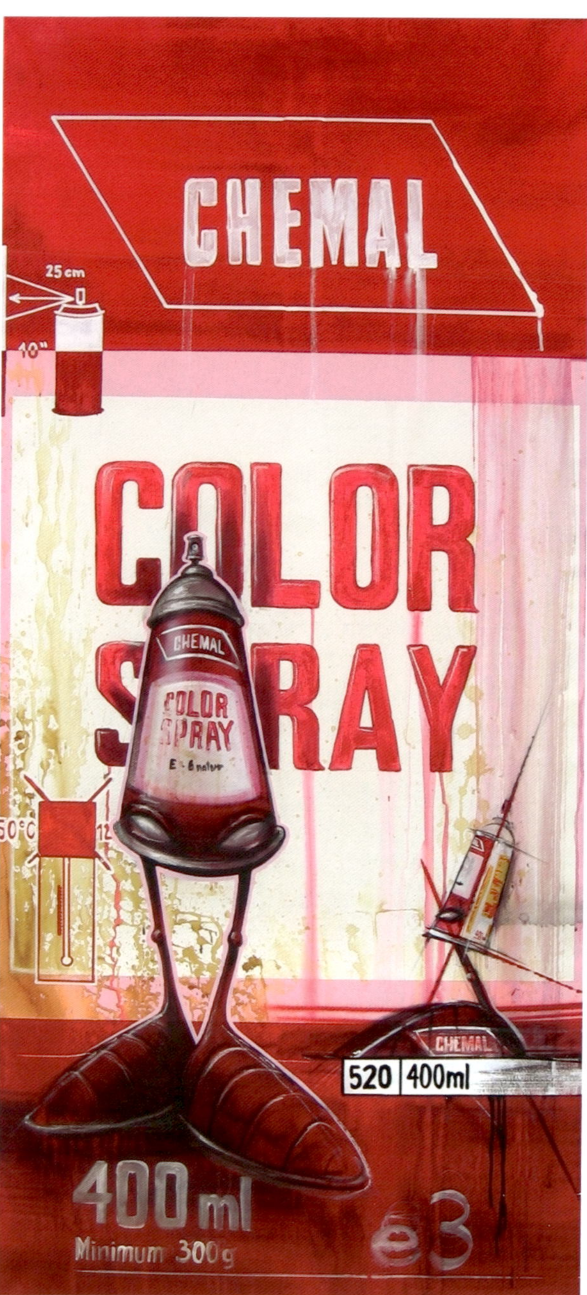
CHEMAL
25 cm
COLOR
SPRAY
CHEMAL
520 400ml
400ml
Minimum 300g

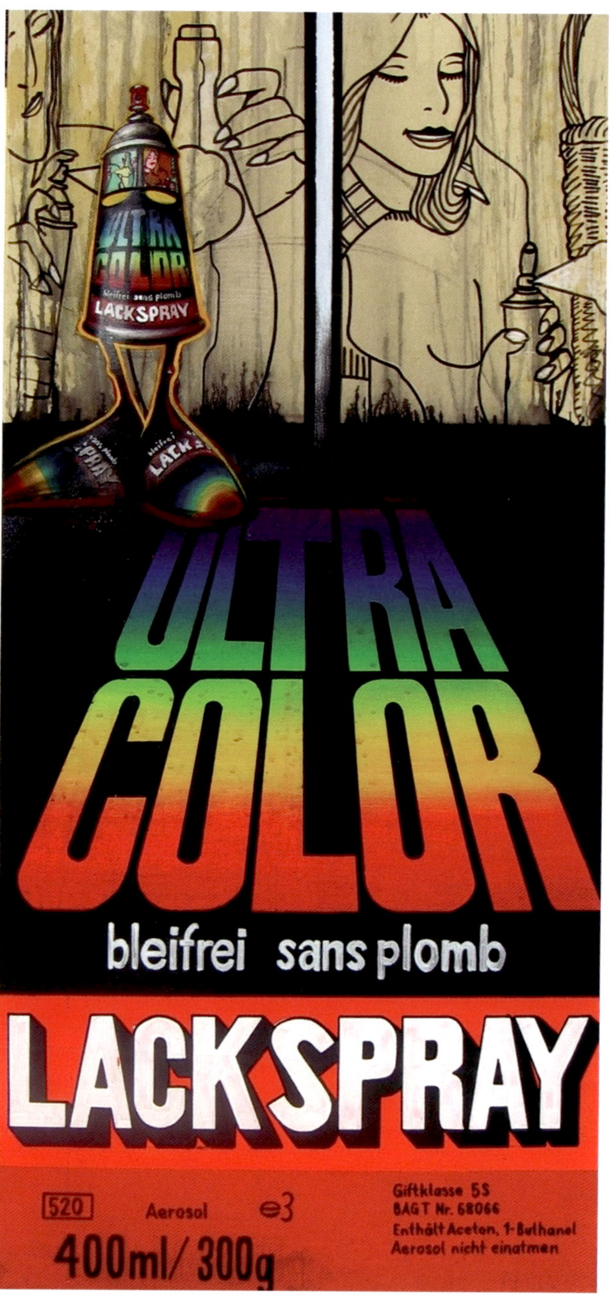
ULTRA
COLOR
bleifrei sans plomb
LACKSPRAY
520
Aerosol
Giftklasse 5S
BAGT Nr. 68066
Enthält Aceton, 1-Buthanol
Aerosol nicht einatmen
400ml/ 300g

DE Meiner Meinung nach treffen die klassischen Definitionen von Illustration und Kunst nach wie vor zu. Das heißt aber nicht, dass man die Illustration nicht auch in künstlerischen Arbeiten einsetzen kann – Illustration ist ein Stilmittel. Die Trennung von Illustration und Kunst geht weniger auf die Kunstschaffenden selbst zurück, sondern vielmehr auf die Gesellschaft, die schlussendlich immer der Kunde ist. In vielen, die heute als Künstler gelten, wurde früher mehr der Dienstleister gesehen. Als Illustrator ist man bei Auftragsarbeiten gezwungen, sich mit Themen zu beschäftigen, mit denen man sich normalerweise nicht auseinandersetzten würde. Das erweitert unfreiwillig den eigenen Horizont und bereichert somit auch die eigenen Arbeiten. Kunst entsteht aus der eigenen Intention heraus, die sich erstmals in der Kindheit als Realitätsflucht in Phantasiewelten äußert. Ich muss zeichnen und malen, so oder so – ob mich jemand dafür bezahlt oder nicht. Wenn das der Fall ist, lasse ich mir den Titel „Illustrator“ gern bezahlen. Ich zitiere Alexander von Humboldt: „Ich wurde von tausenden Schweinen getrieben das zu tun.“

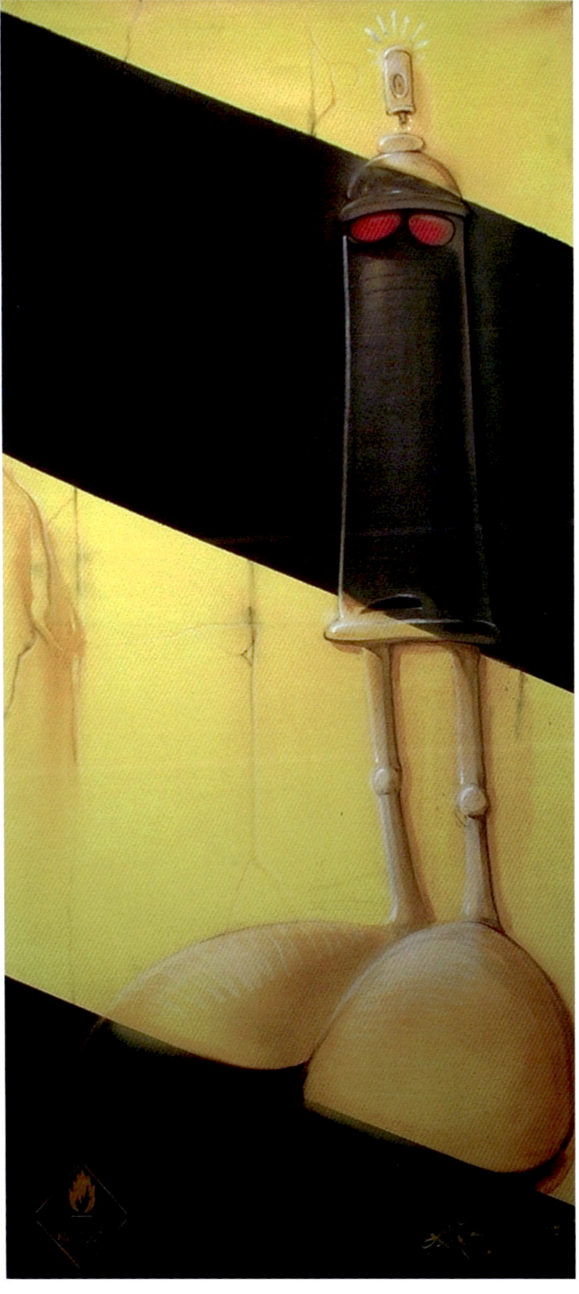

INTRODUCTION: untitled
LEFT PAGE:
LEFT: dupli
MIDDLE: chemal
RIGHT: ultra color
RIGHT PAGE:
LEFT: kontro
RIGHT: camouflage can

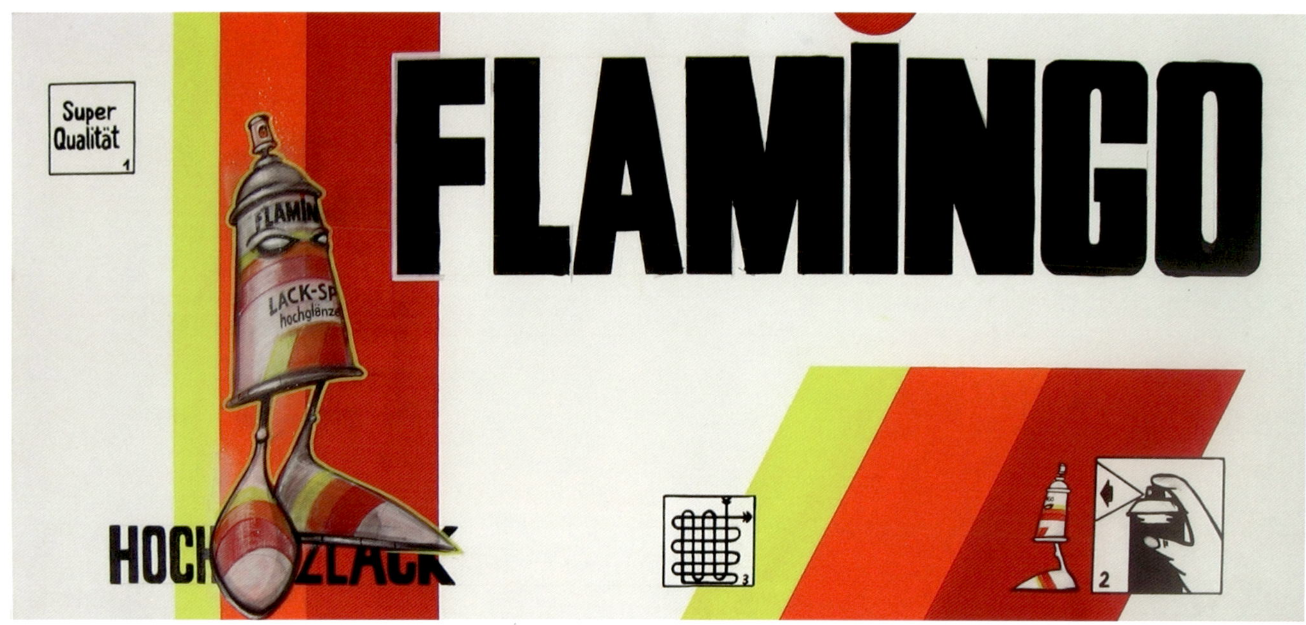

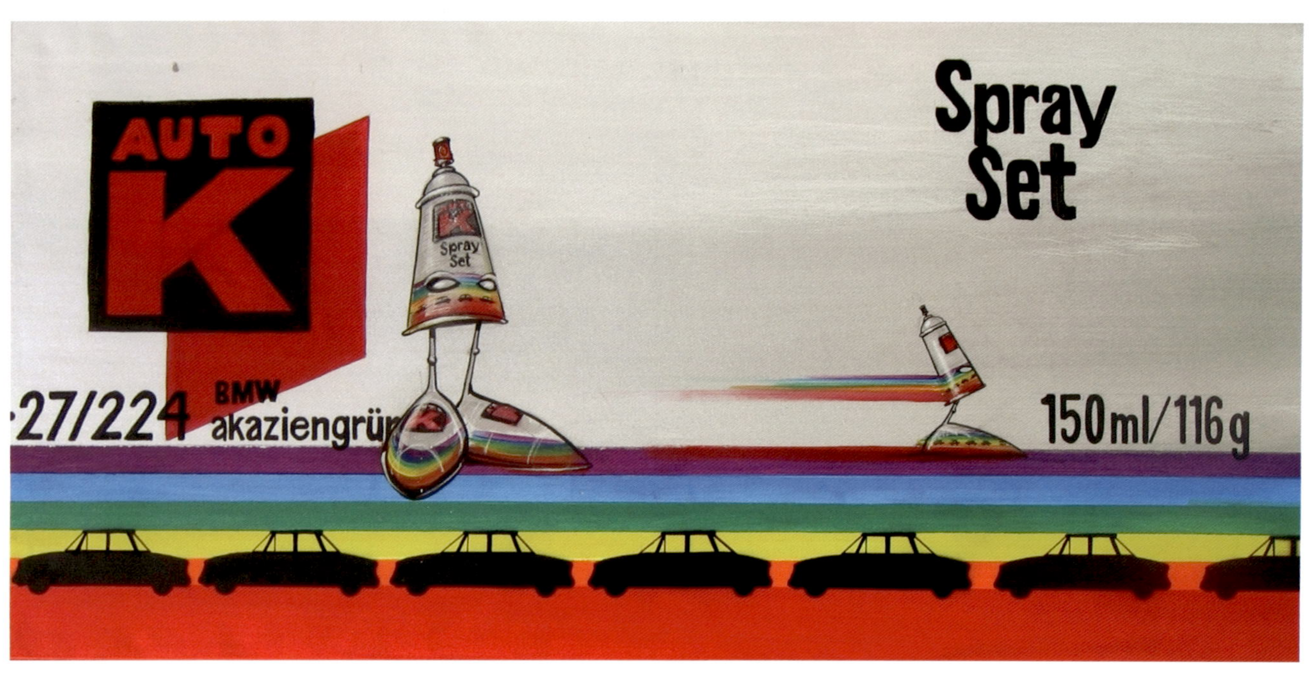

LEFT PAGE:
ABOVE: flamingo
BELOW: auto-k
RIGHT PAGE:
LEFT: throw-up can
MIDDLE: ralley can
RIGHT: red dutch can
NEXT PAGES:
LEFT PAGE:
LEFT: dutch banana can
MIDDLE: fluffy can
RIGHT: joker can
RIGHT PAGE:
LEFT: japanese can
MIDDLE: batcan
RIGHT: swedish can

EN In my opinion, the classical definition of illustration and art is still valid. But that doesn't mean that illustration cannot be used in artistic works – illustration is a stylistic device. The separation of illustration and art was not established by artists themselves but rather by society, which is always the ultimate client. Many who are considered artists today were seen as service providers during their creative careers. As an illustrator you are forced to deal with topics that you would not have chosen to deal with yourself. This inevitably expands your own horizon, and therefore also enriches your works. Art begins with your own intentions which first manifest themselves in childhood as an escape from reality into an imaginary world. I need to sketch and paint, regardless if someone pays me or not. If that is the case, I am willing to be paid as an "illustrator." I quote Alexander von Humboldt: "I was forced by thousands of pigs to do this."

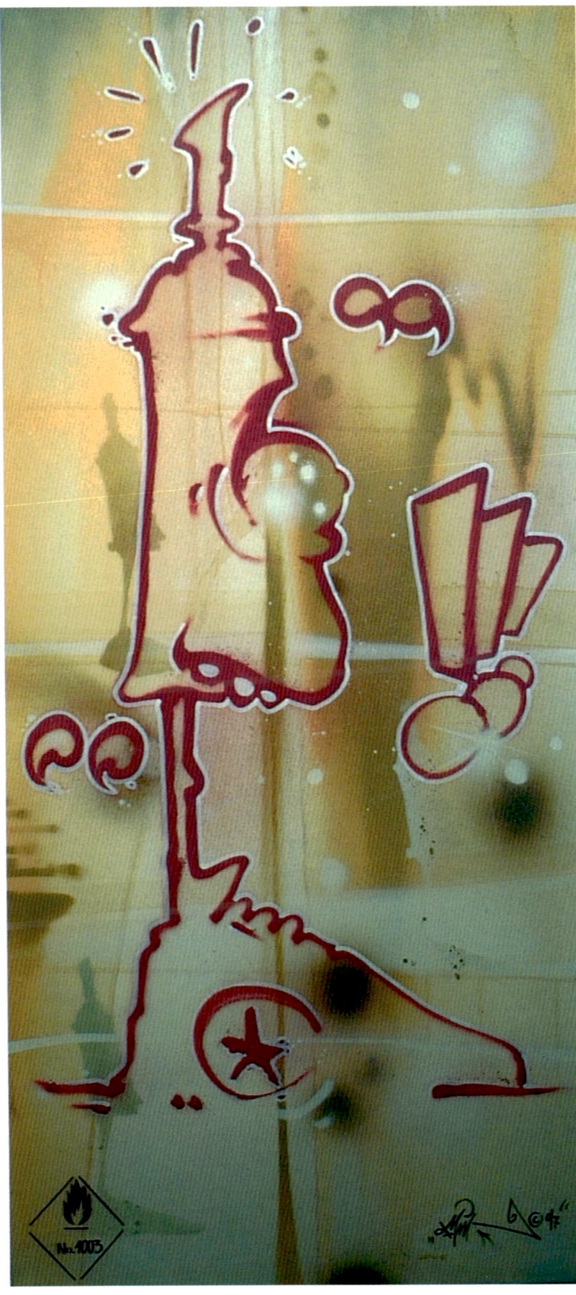

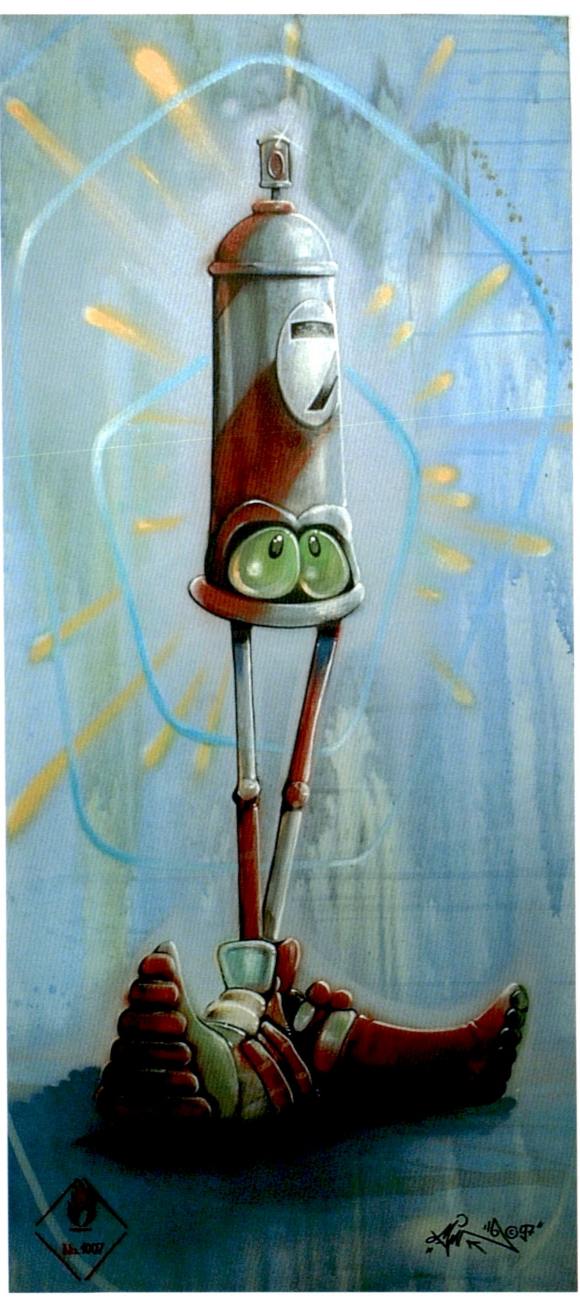

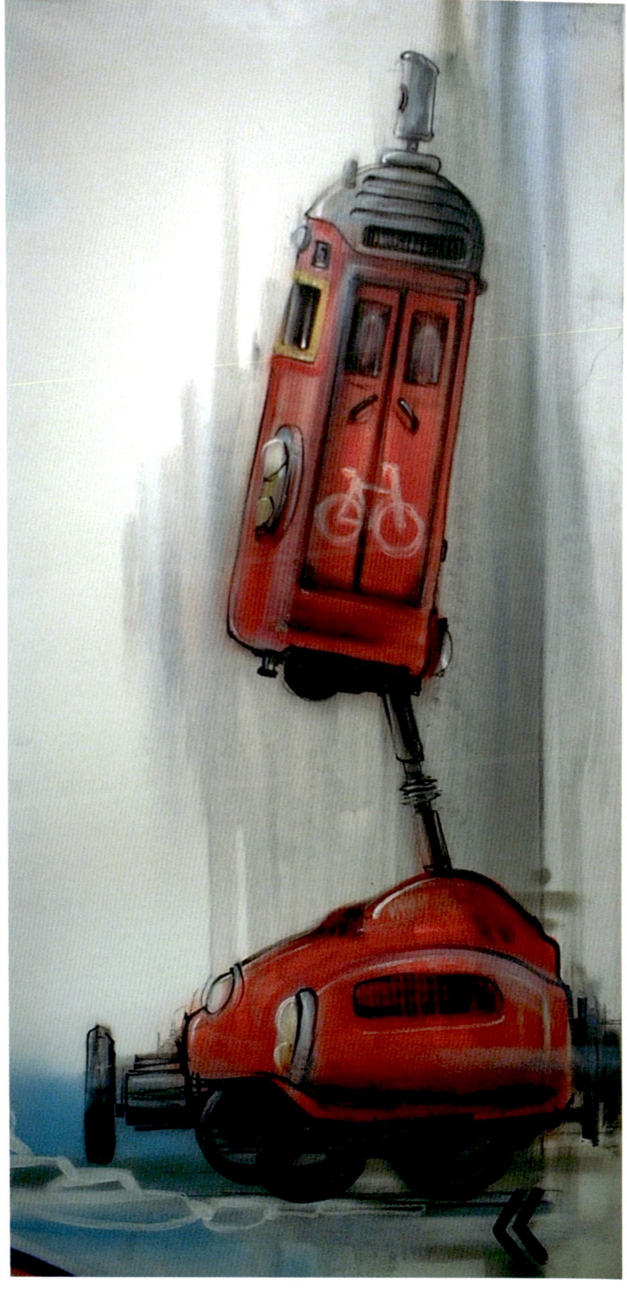

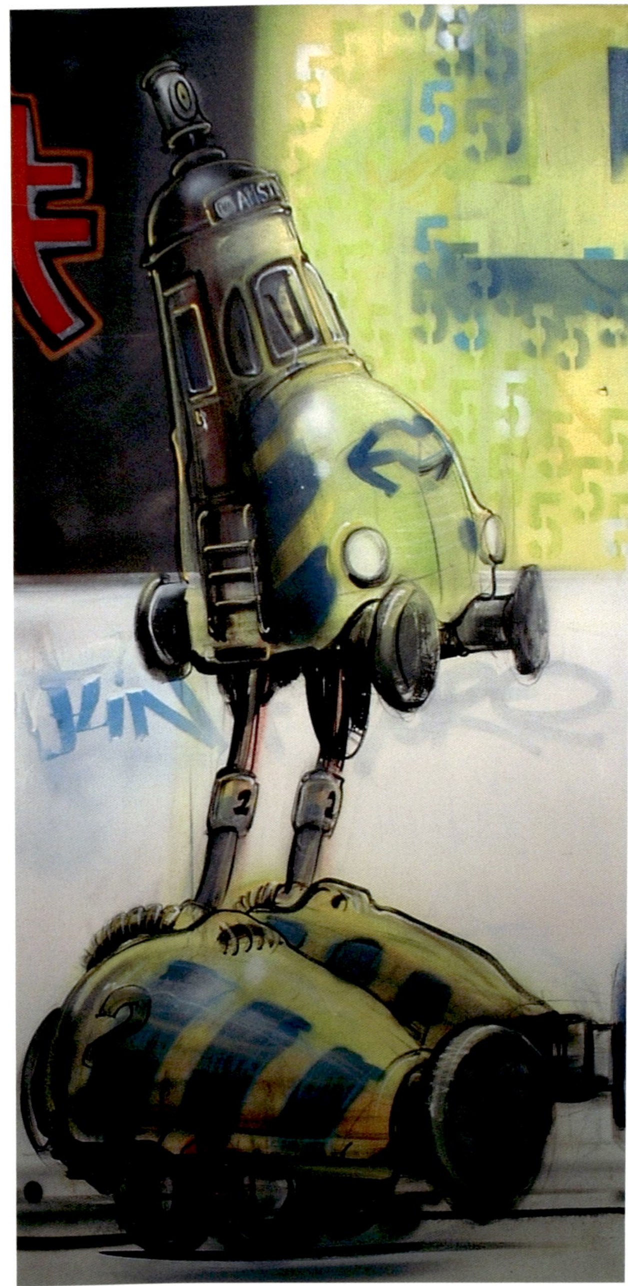

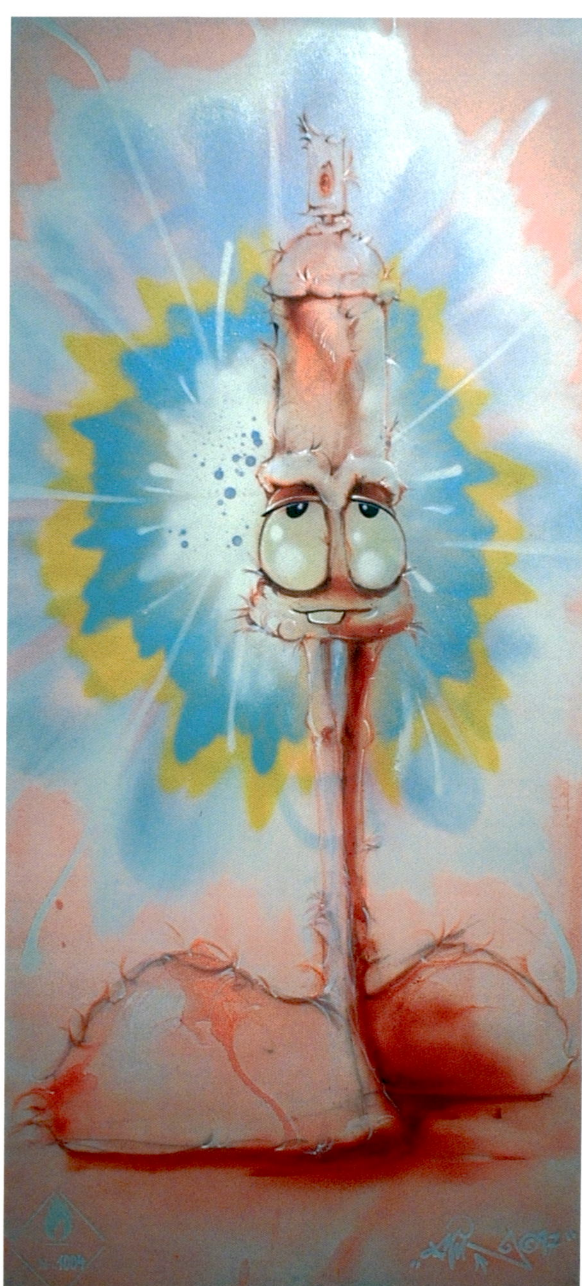

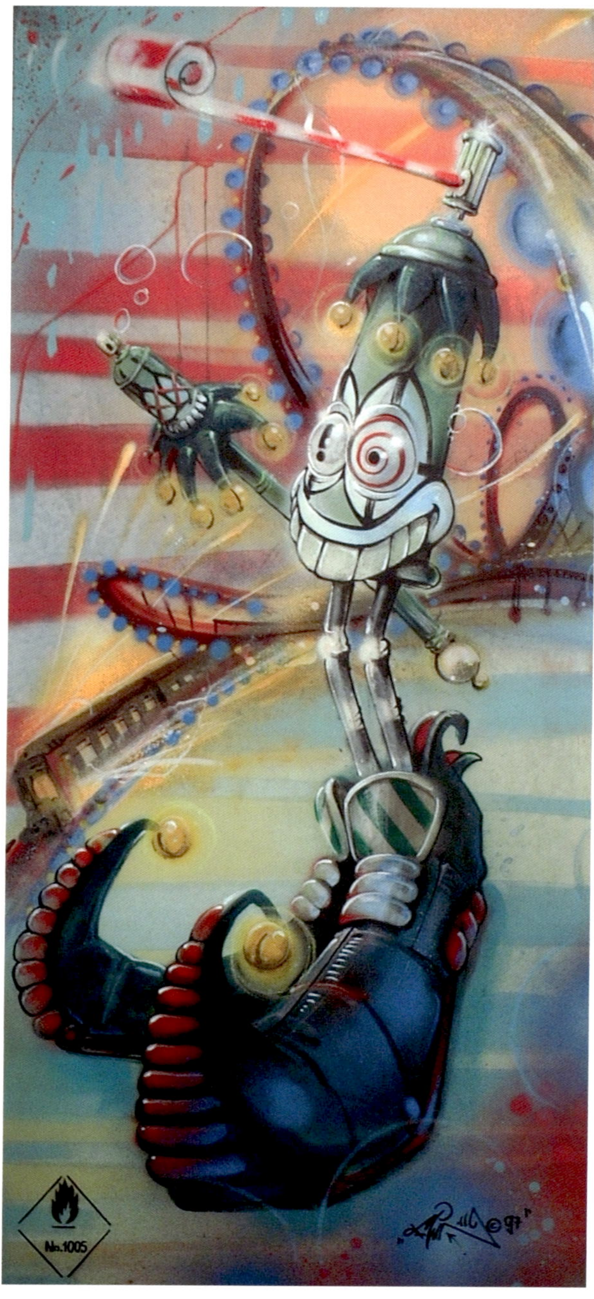
No.1005

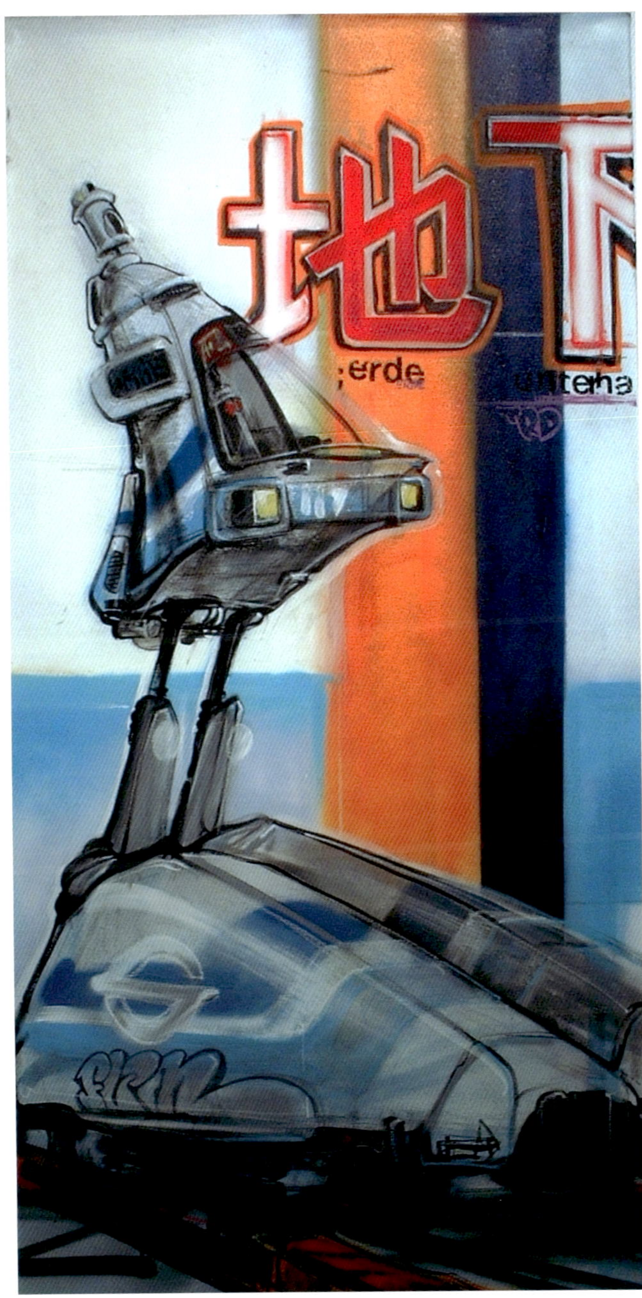
地
;erde

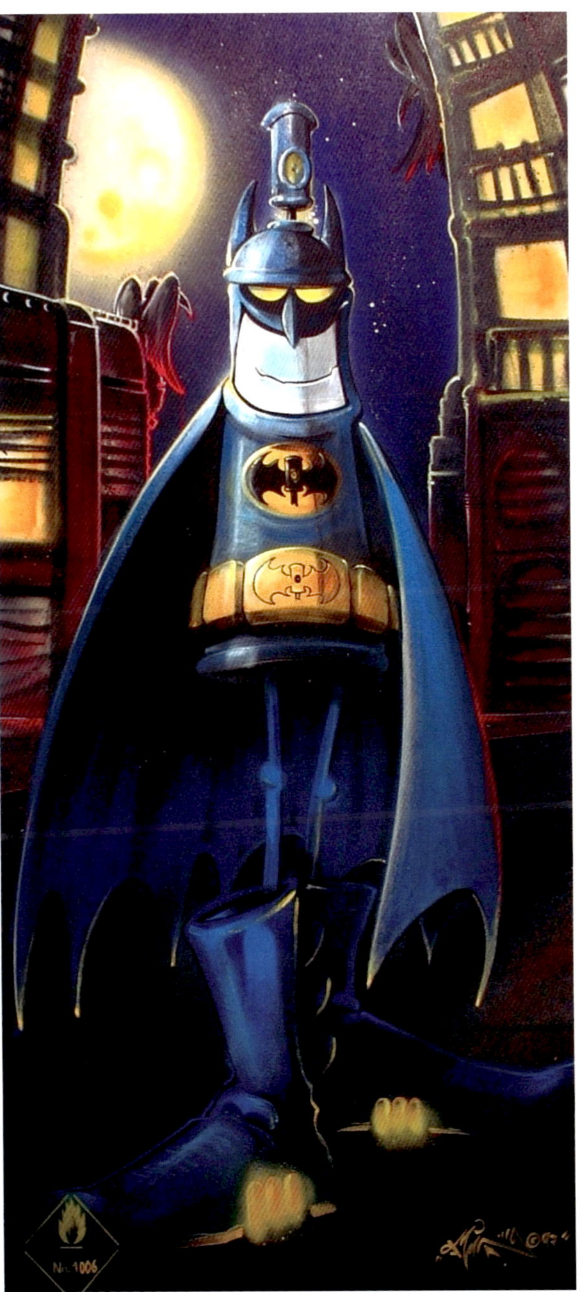

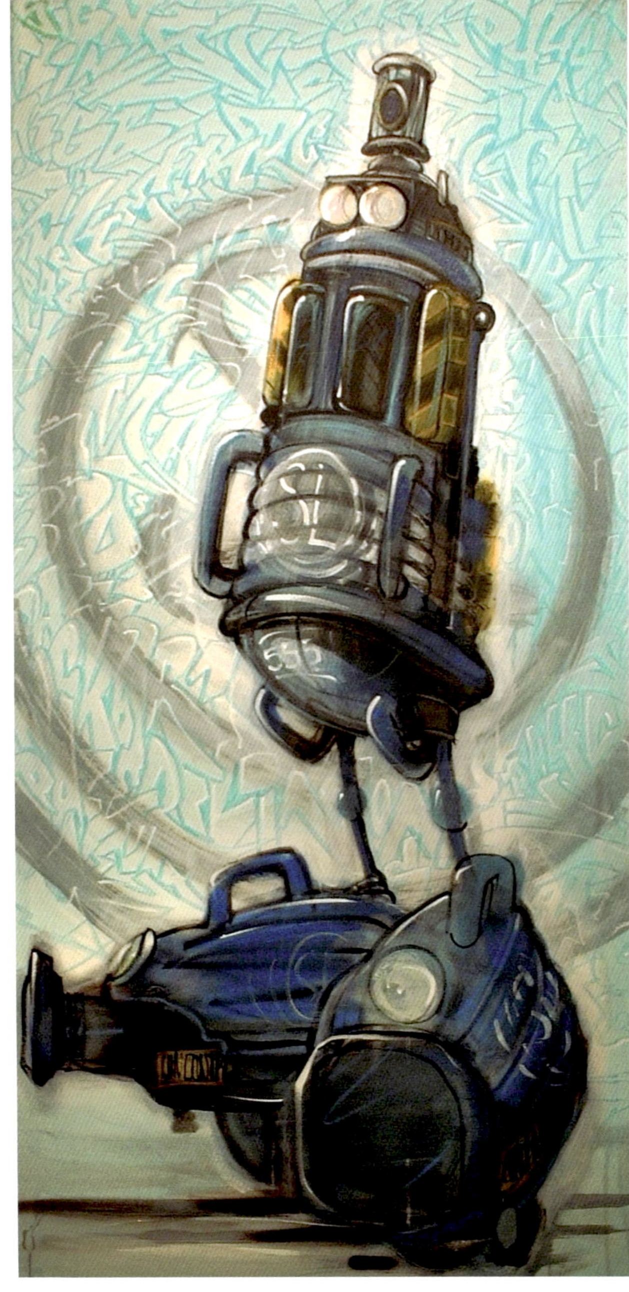

»JEFF FÄRBER

NATIONALITY:	UNITED STATES
LOCATION:	BROOKLYN | NY
PUBLICATIONS:	CASTLEMAGAZINE.DE
REFERENCES:	AMERICAN SCHOOL BOARD JOURNAL | THE AVE BALTIMORE MAGAZINE | CHICAGO SUNTIMES DELAWARE TODAY | ETC. MAGAZINE | HIDDEN AGENDA PRESS | THE INDYPENDENT | JIVE RECORDS KNIGHT RIDDER | MULTICULTURAL FORUM THE PROGRESSIVE | PULSE! MAGAZINE | SPECTRUM STEVE JACKSON GAMES | WIND-UP RECORDS WORKFORCE MAGAZINE | 8 EYE PRESS
EXHIBITIONS:	SHOWS IN SAN FRANCISCO – SAN JOSE | CA SEATTLE | ITALY | KINSEY INSTITUTE DIRTY SHOW (DETROIT) DOZENS IN BROOKLYN AND MANHATTAN AND ON MY MOM'S REFRIGERATOR
REPRESENTIVES:	LANGLEY CREATIVE WWW.LANGLEYCREATIVE.COM
CONTACT:	WWW.JEFFFAERBER.COM
TECHNIQUE:	MIXED MEDIA PAINTING AND DRAWING
BORN:	1974

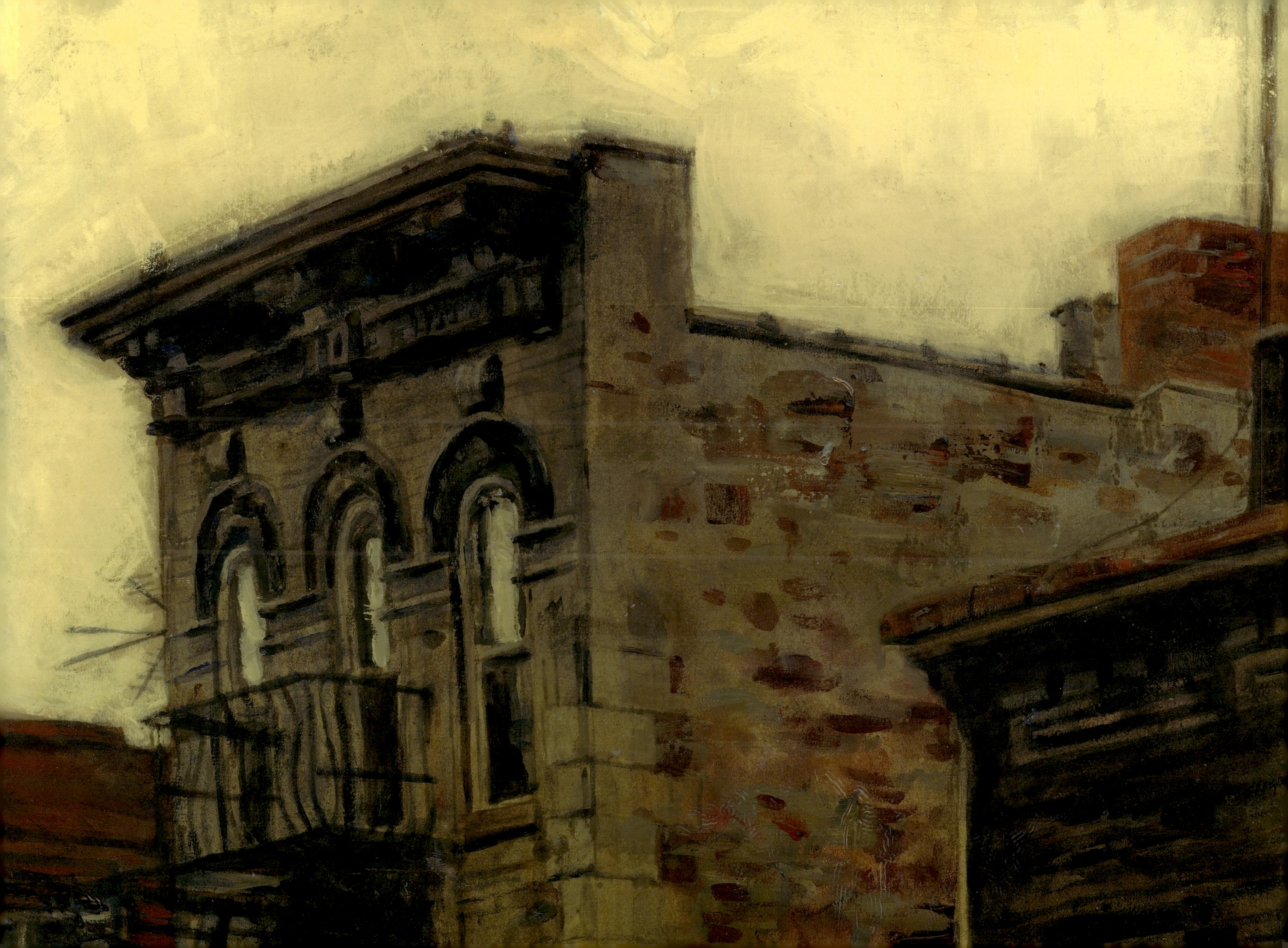

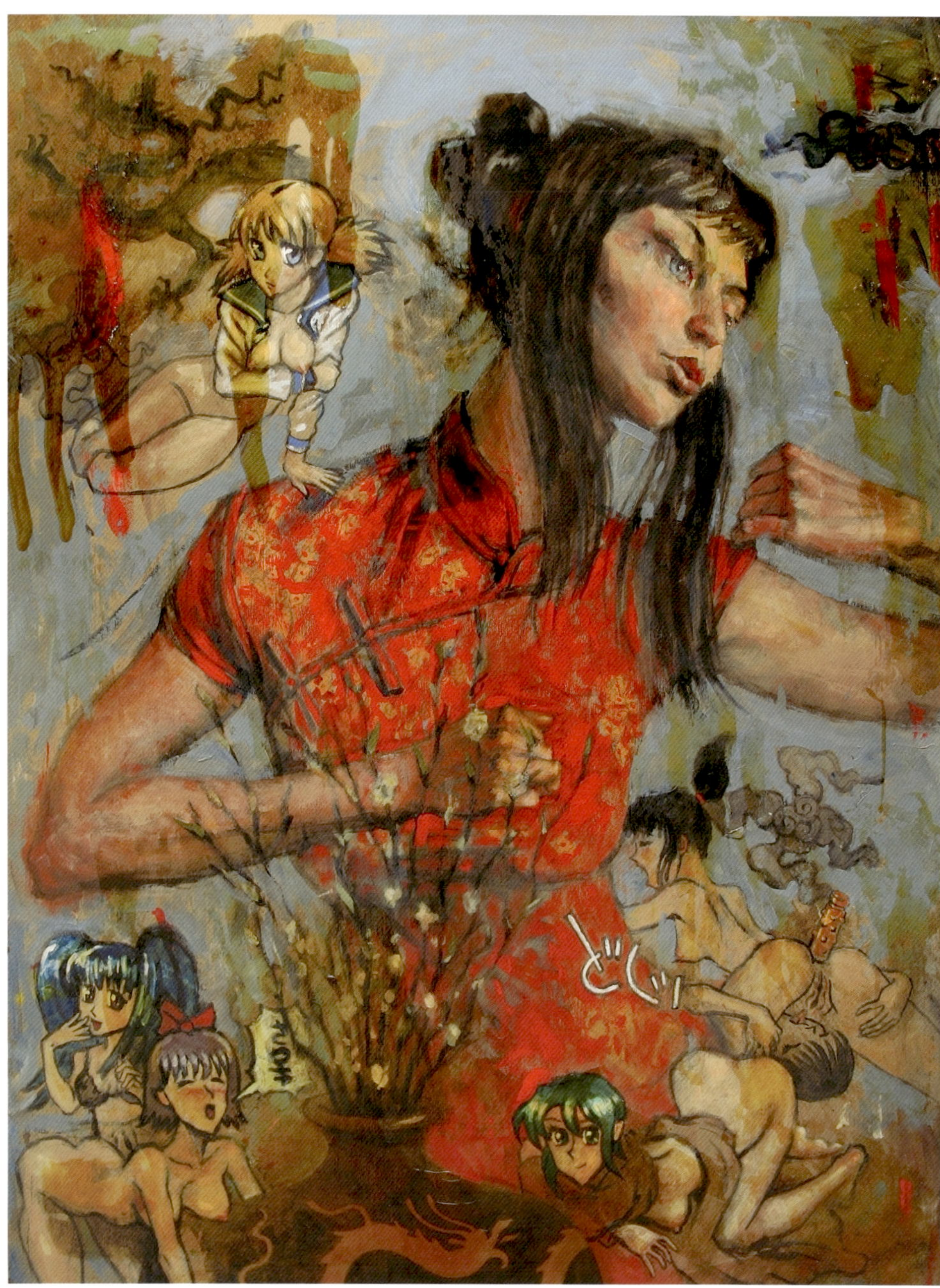

DE Ich glaube, die Grenze zwischen Kunst und Illustration ist nicht eindeutig auszumachen, sie ist fließend. Ich würde zwar eine Unterscheidung zwischen den beiden Begriffen nicht gänzlich von der Hand weisen, aber eigentlich interessiert sie mich nicht. Ich mag den Umstand, dass manche Künstler (und ich falle hoffentlich in diese Kategorie) schwer einzuordnen sind. Es macht Spaß, die Leute zum Denken anzuregen. Leider kann zwischen den Vertretern beider Welten eine feindselige Haltung bestehen (an meiner Kunstakademie begegneten sich diese zwei Lager mit Verachtung). Das ist schade und letztlich nicht sehr hilfreich. Wurden sie als Kind nicht genügend geliebt? Litten sie unter Vitaminmangel? Bin ich Künstler oder Illustrator? Ich bin beides, wenngleich ich, wie gesagt, nicht allzu viel darüber nachdenke. Ich sehe mich als Künstler, der zufällig einen Teil seiner Zeit Auftragsarbeiten erledigt. Illustratoren müssen Kompromisse eingehen oder mit Einschränkungen arbeiten, aber ich persönlich liebe diese Herausforderung. Viele „Künstler“ werden letzten Endes von einem Kunden, der zufällig Galerist oder Mäzen ist, auf einen bestimmten Stil festgenagelt, während sie über Illustratoren die Nase rümpfen. Wir alle suchen nach diesem Gleichgewicht zwischen persönlichem Ausdruck und wie wir damit einen Platz in der Welt finden. Und dabei muss man oft Kompromisse eingehen. Klinge ich, als würde ich mich rechtfertigen? Ich nehme mal lieber meine Vitamintabletten.

INTRODUCTION: williamsburg
LEFT PAGE: koneko
RIGHT PAGE:
LEFT: eli
MIDDLE: kermit
RIGHT: sarah-starwars

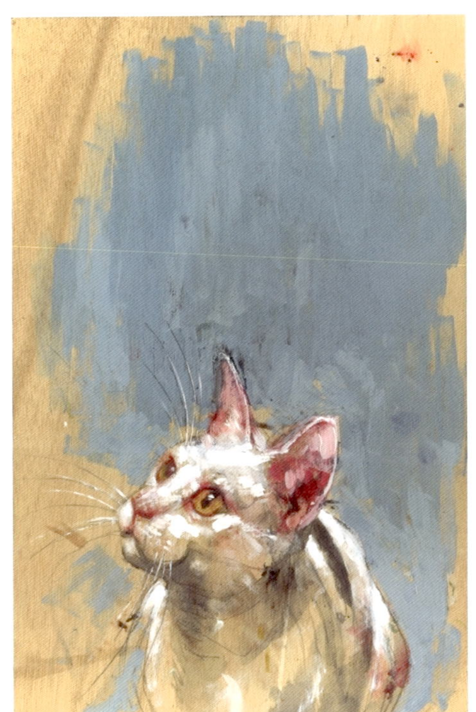

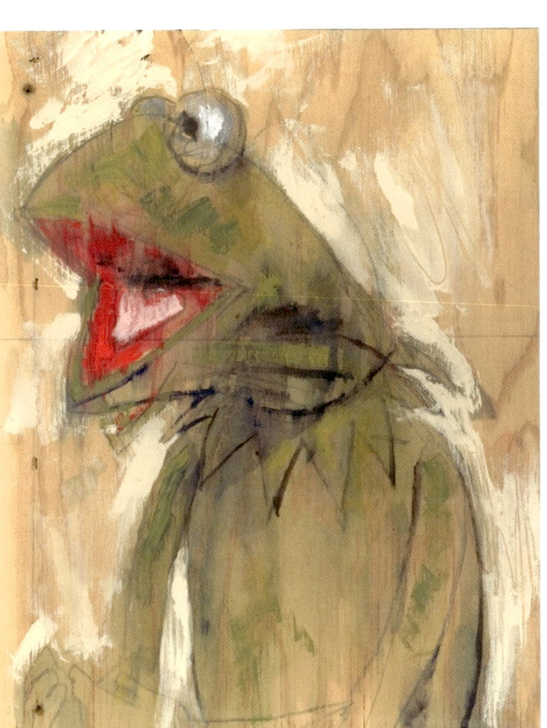

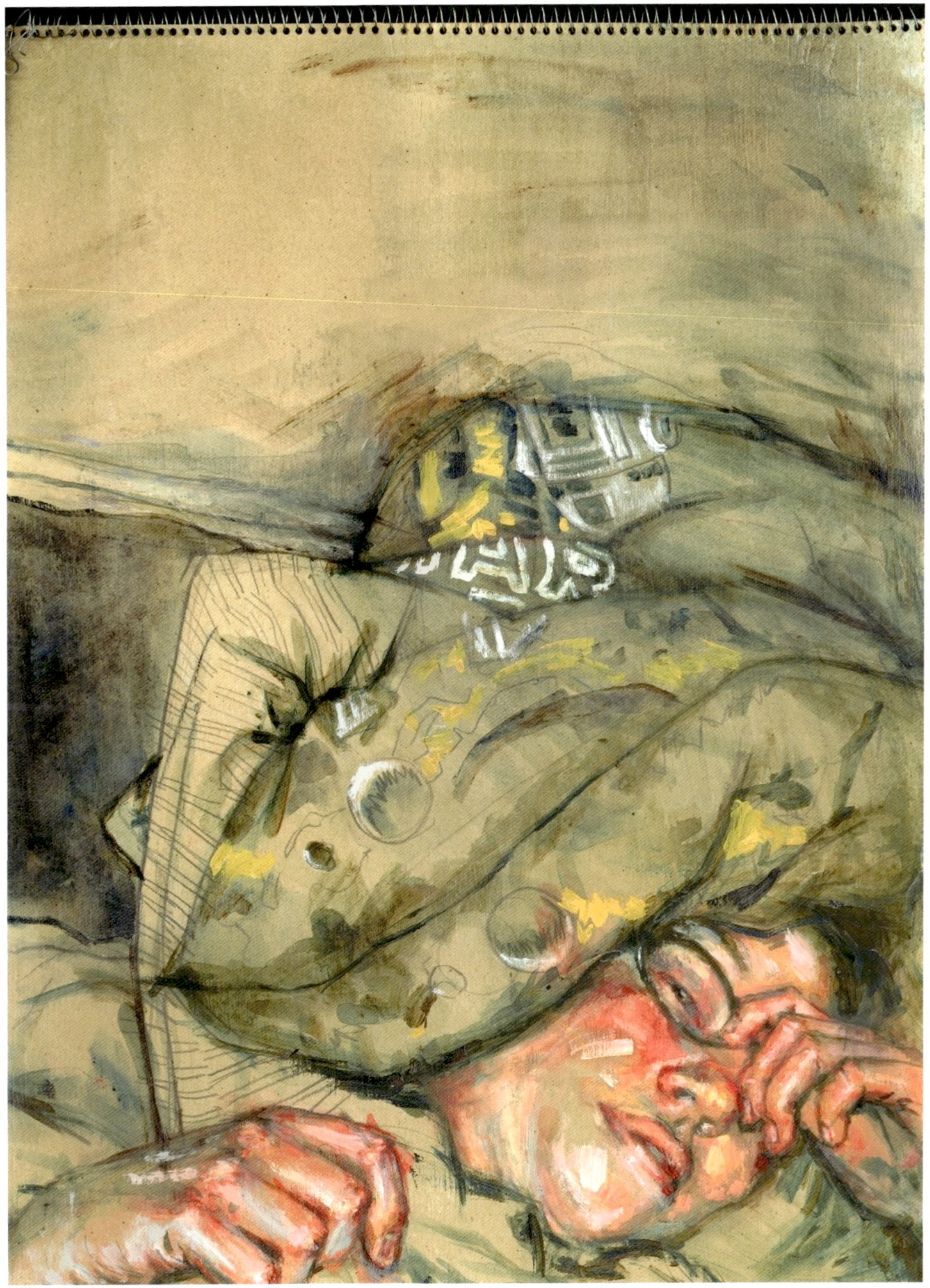

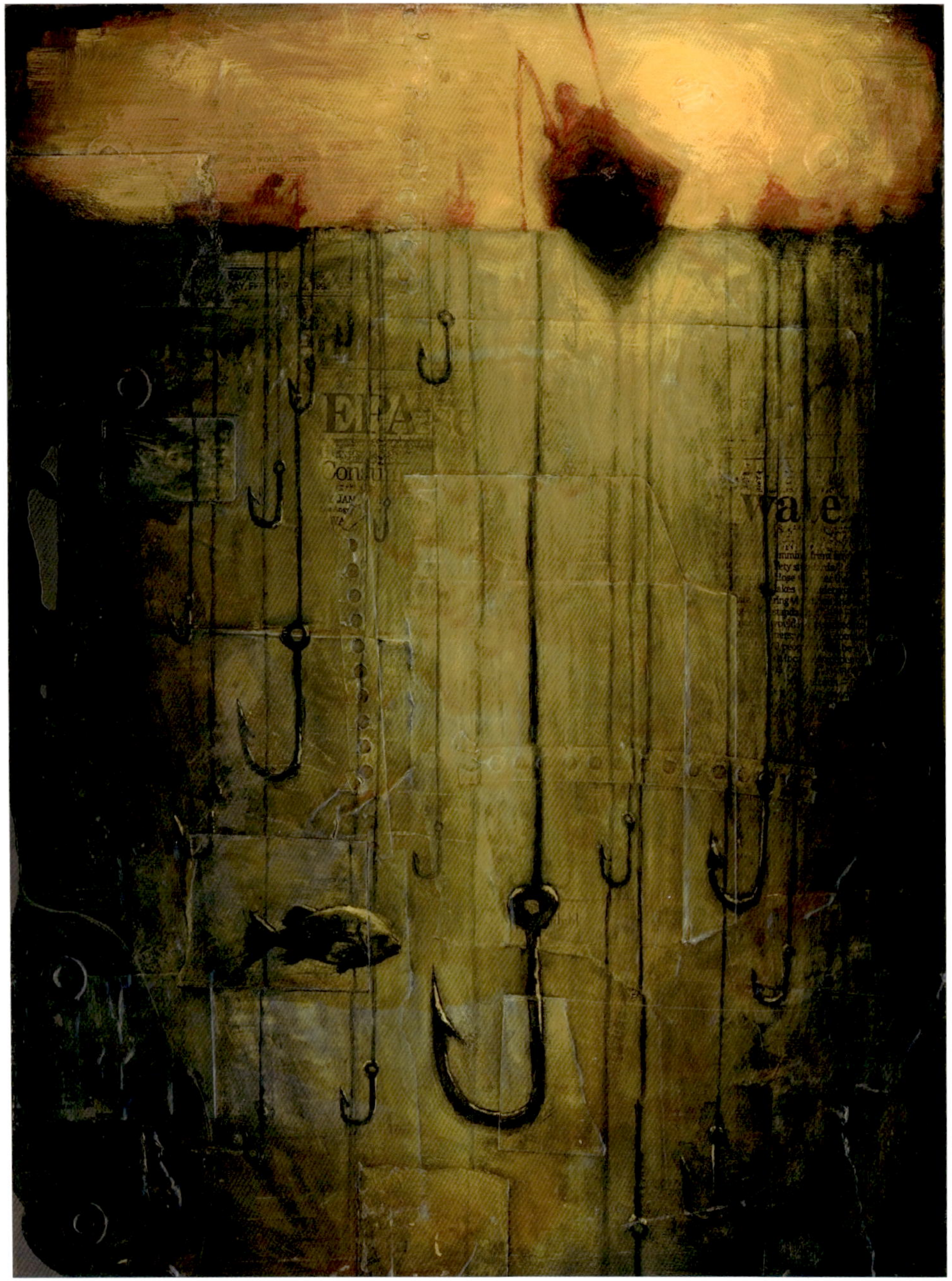

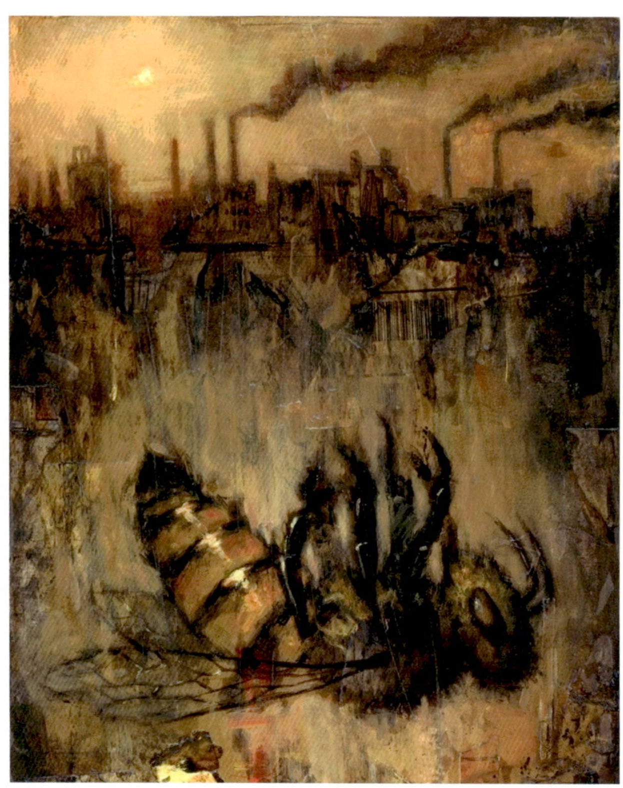

LEFT PAGE:
LEFT: otherfish
RIGHT: bee
RIGHT PAGE:
LEFT: 2conner
RIGHT: death of ajb

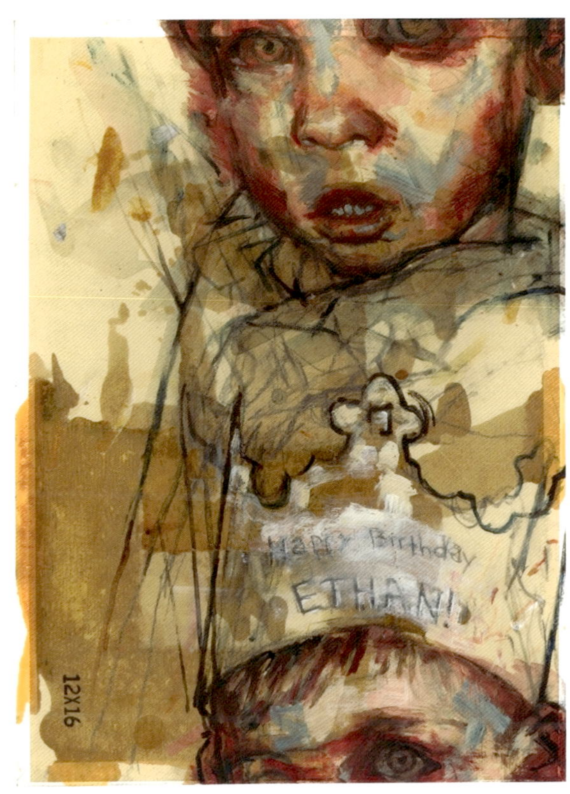
Birthday
ETHAN!

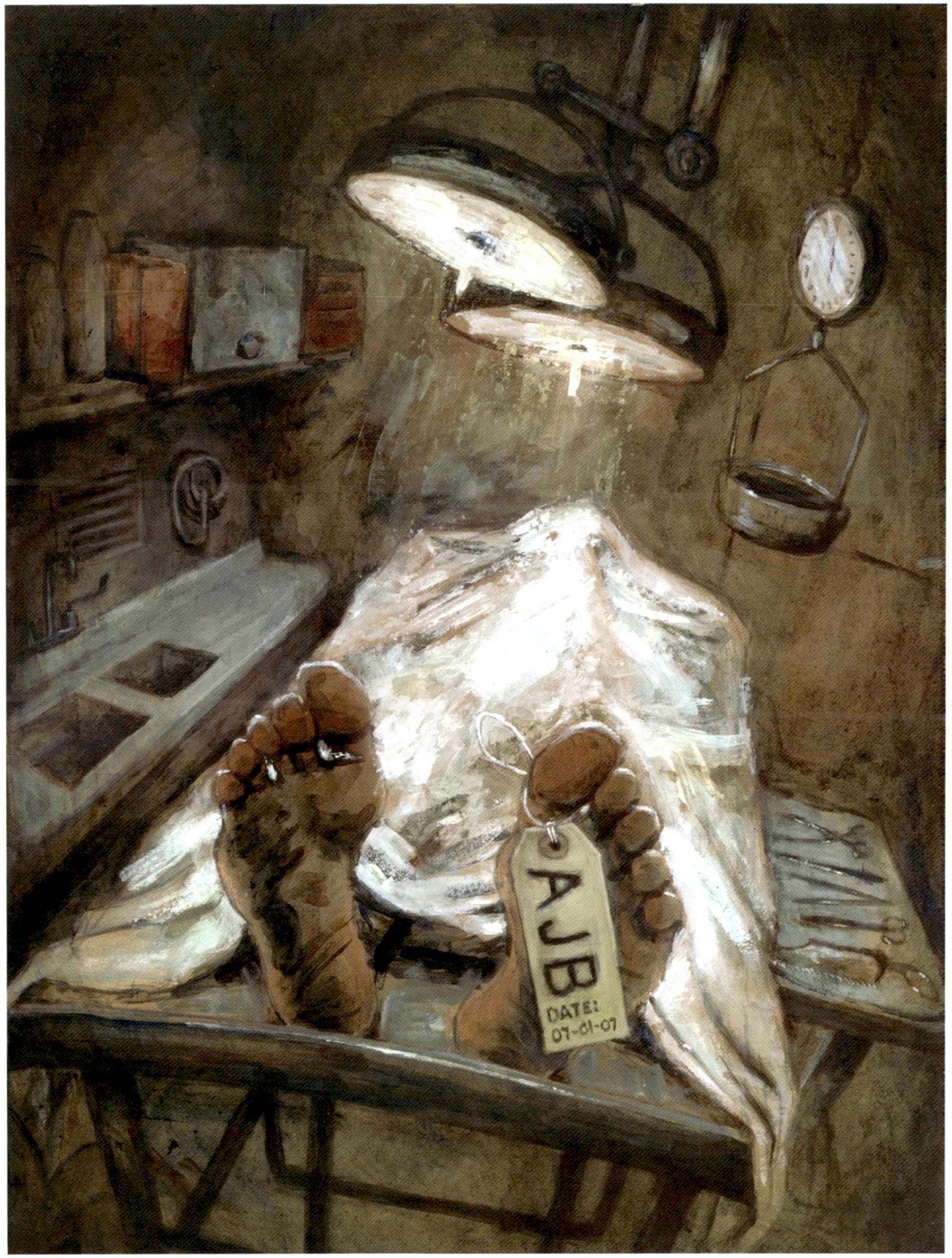

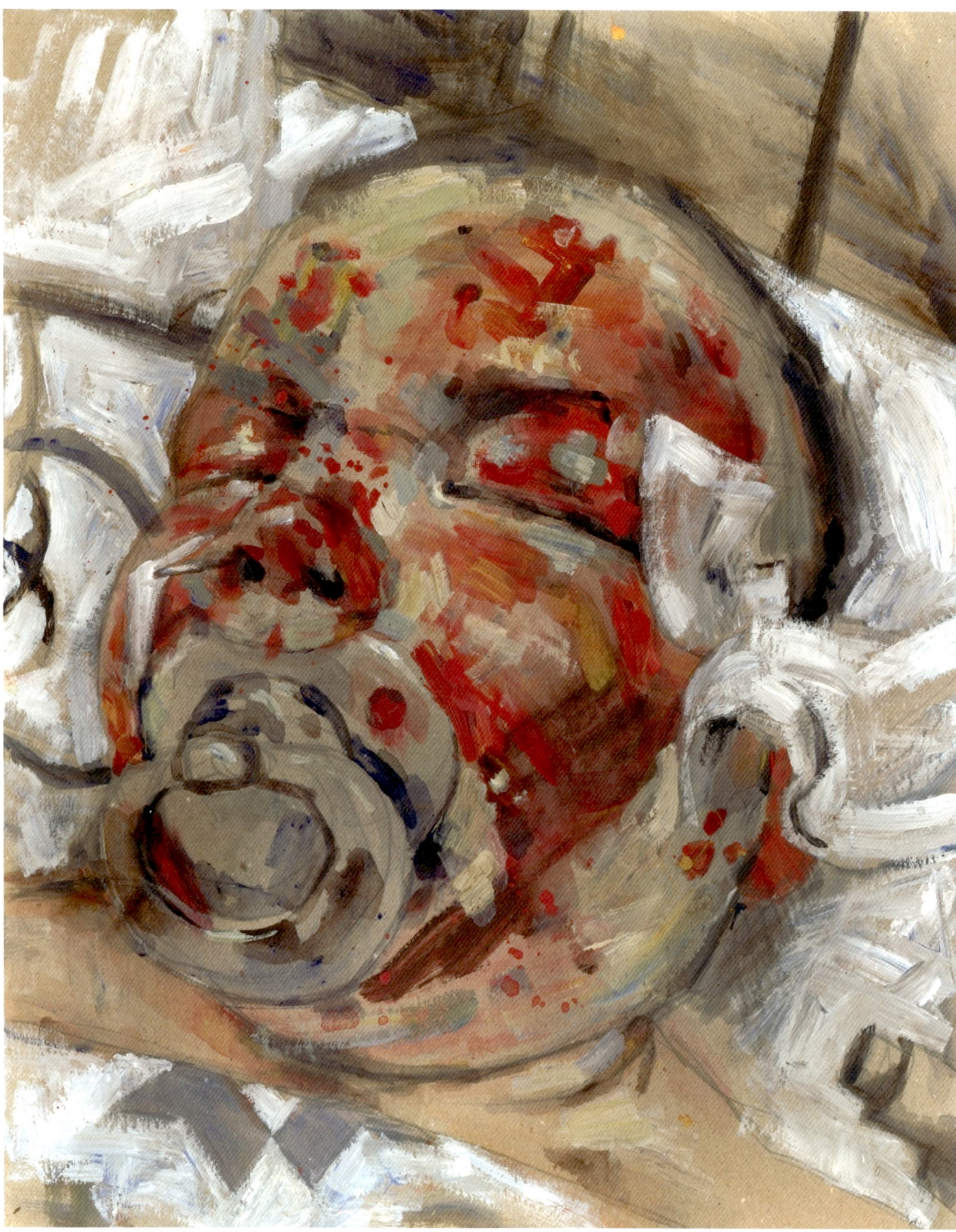

EN I think the line between "art" and "illustration" is very vague with lots free flow between the two sides. While I wouldn't dismiss the difference between the terms completely, I am not really very concerned with it. I like the fact that some artists (and I hope I fit into this category) are hard to classify. It's fun to make people think. Unfortunately, there can be an adversarial stance between people in these two worlds (at my art school, these two camps viewed each other with disdain). This is unfortunate and ultimately not very helpful. Maybe their moms didn't love them enough as children. Or do they suffer from a vitamin deficiency? Am I artist or illustrator? I am both, although, again, I do not spend too much time worrying about it. I think of myself as an artist who happens to do work for clients some of the time. Illustrators do have to compromise or work with constraints, but I personally love that challenge. Ultimately, many "fine artists" end up being just as boxed into a particular style by a client that happens to be a gallery owner or a patron while thumbing their noses at illustrators. We are all trying to find that balance between personal expression and how that fits into the larger world. And it often involves compromise. Do I sound defensive? I'll go take my vitamins.

LEFT PAGE: wounded
RIGHT PAGE: sarah (no mouth)

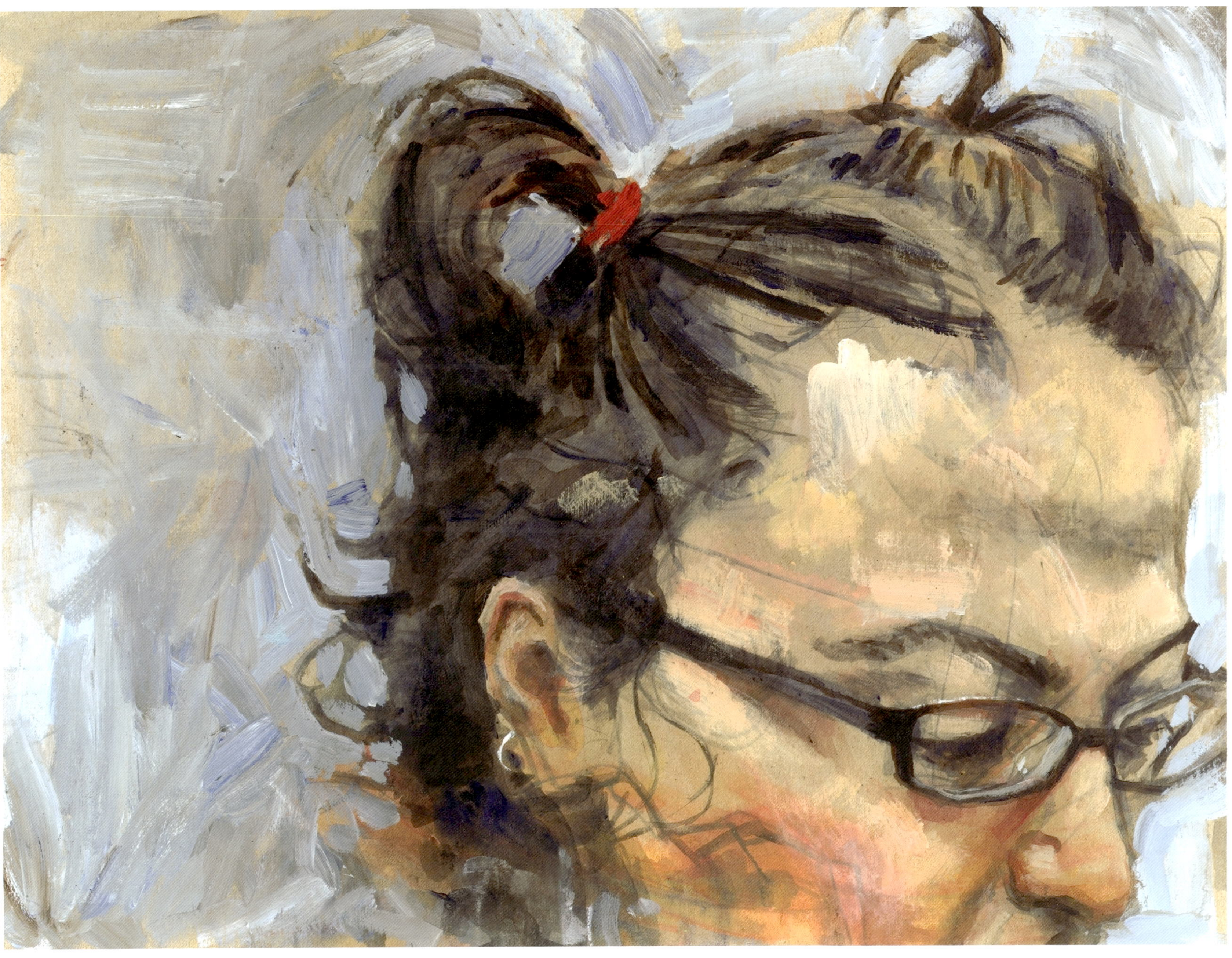

»STARJUMP [ALEXANDER ZÖBISCH]

NATIONALITY:	GERMAN
LOCATION:	AMSTERDAM
PUBLICATIONS:	CASTLEMAGAZINE | JITTER MAGAZIN
REFERENCES:	ANIMATION STUDIOS & ADVERTISING AGENCIES
EXHIBITIONS:	VELVET DA VINCI GALLERY – SAN FRANCISCO CA ART-LOUNGE – VOLKSGARTEN – MUNICH GALERIE AM GRABEN – AUGSBURG WATCH OUT FOR THE THIRD RAIL – MUNICH GÖRRES10 – MUNICH
CONTACT:	ALEX.ZOEBISCH@GMX.DE WWW.STARJUMPENTERTAINMENT.BLOGSPOT.COM
TECHNIQUE:	PENCIL | INK | OIL | ACRYL | WATERCOLOR | PEN TABLET SPRAYCAN & ANYTHING THAT SCRATCHES OR / AND LEAVES MARKS ...
BORN:	1975

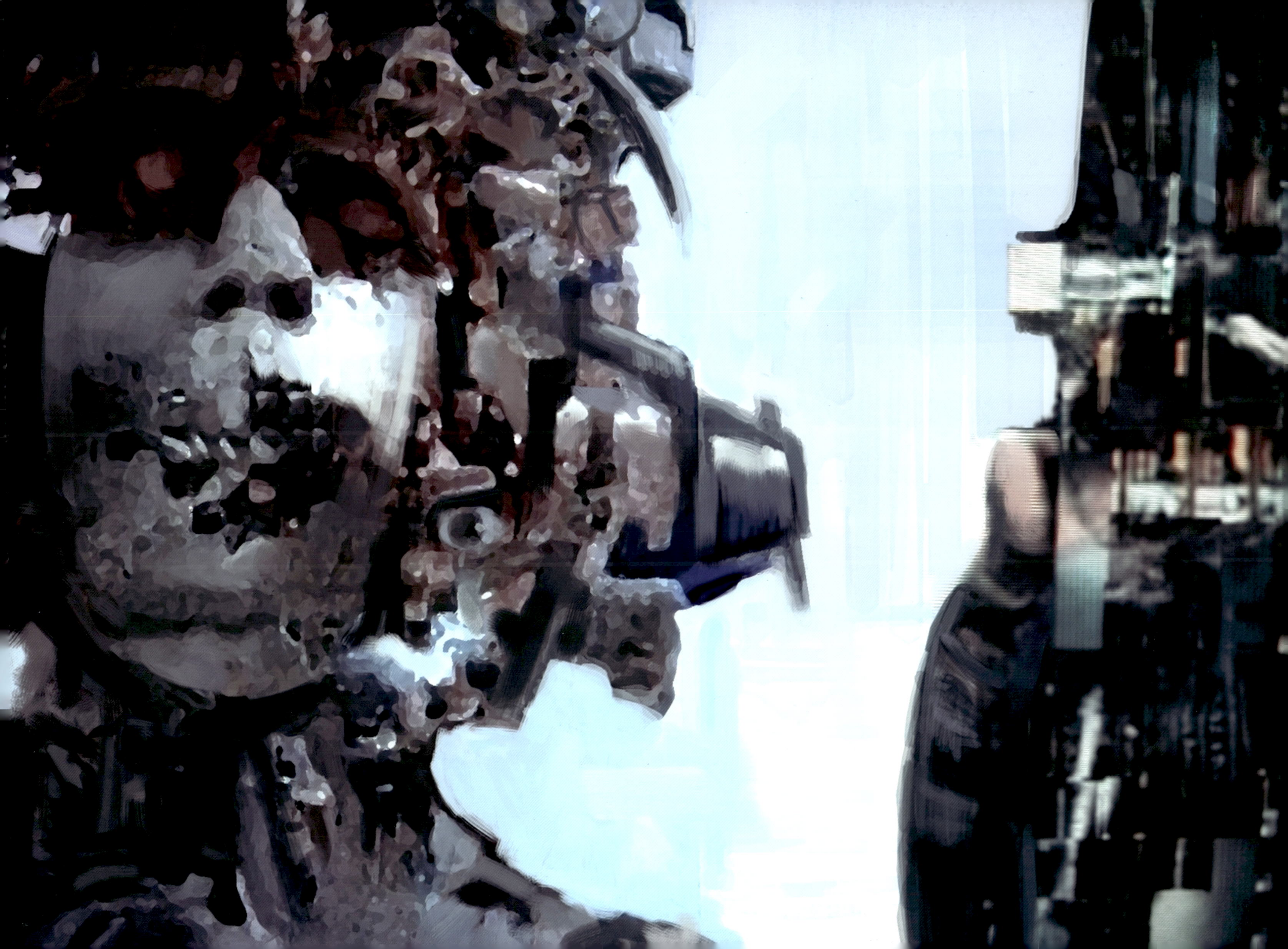

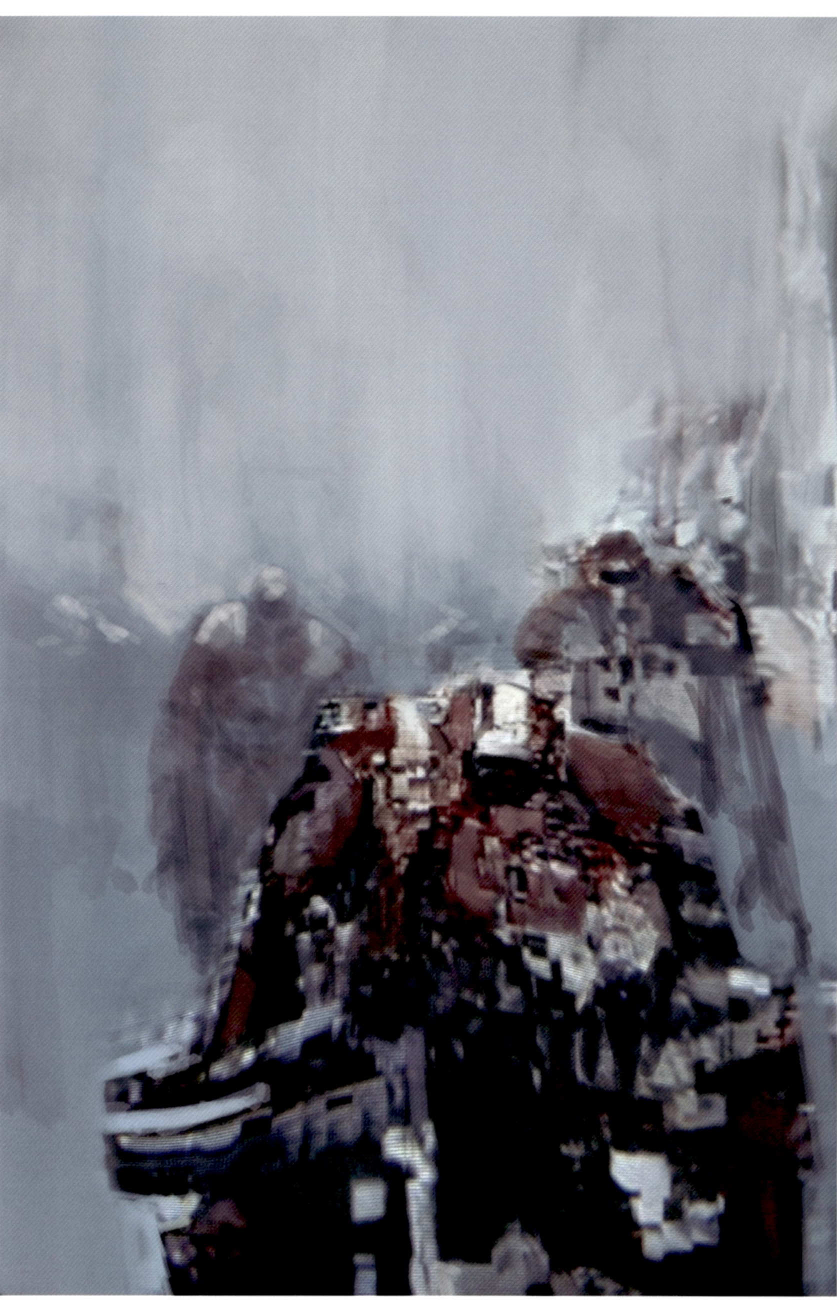

DE Die Definitionen von Illustration und Kunst sind meiner Meinung nach nicht nur aufgrund ihres Auftraggebers zu unterscheiden. Würden wir die Illustration auf kommerzielle Auftragsarbeit reduzieren, müsste man beispielsweise auch alte Kirchenmalereien mit einbeziehen, die heute aber offensichtlich für Kunst gehalten werden. Für mich besteht kein Unterschied, da heutzutage jeder nach etwas „Ausgefallenem", „Ungewöhnlichem" sucht. Deshalb werden selbst illegale „Kunstwerke" wie zum Beispiel Streetart im städtischen Umfeld genutzt, um als nächstes für irgendeine Marke oder Ähnliches zu werben. Ich selbst verstehe mich weder als Illustrator noch als Künstler. Vielleicht ist es einfach diese Sache, mit der ich in der Kindheit begonnen habe. Oder jemand schenkte mir das Talent, im Meer der Träume und anderer Dimensionen zu fischen, wie andere Kreative auch. Verdammt, hätten wir alle einen „vernünftigen" Job erlernt, könnten wir hier die Unterhaltung beenden. Für mich und viele andere ist es jedoch zu spät. Deshalb denke ich, dass wir alle niemals aufhören sollten und unermüdlich unsere Kunst, Illustration oder welchen Namen auch immer man dem geben möchte, fortsetzen. Für mich ist es mein Leben. „Licht sickert durch die Fenster meines Universums."

INTRODUCTION: i love my bombsto
LEFT PAGE: fog
RIGHT PAGE: guards

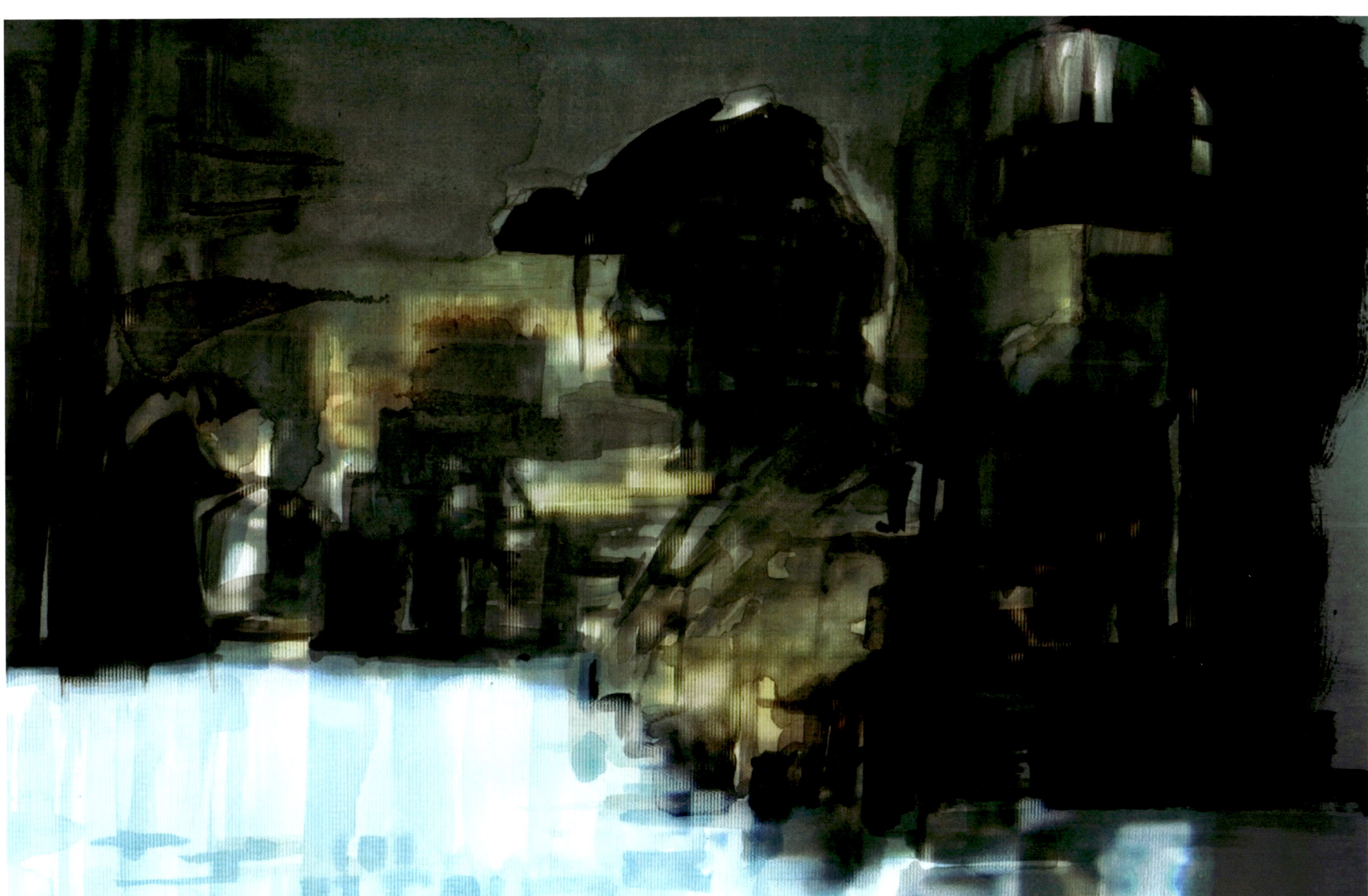

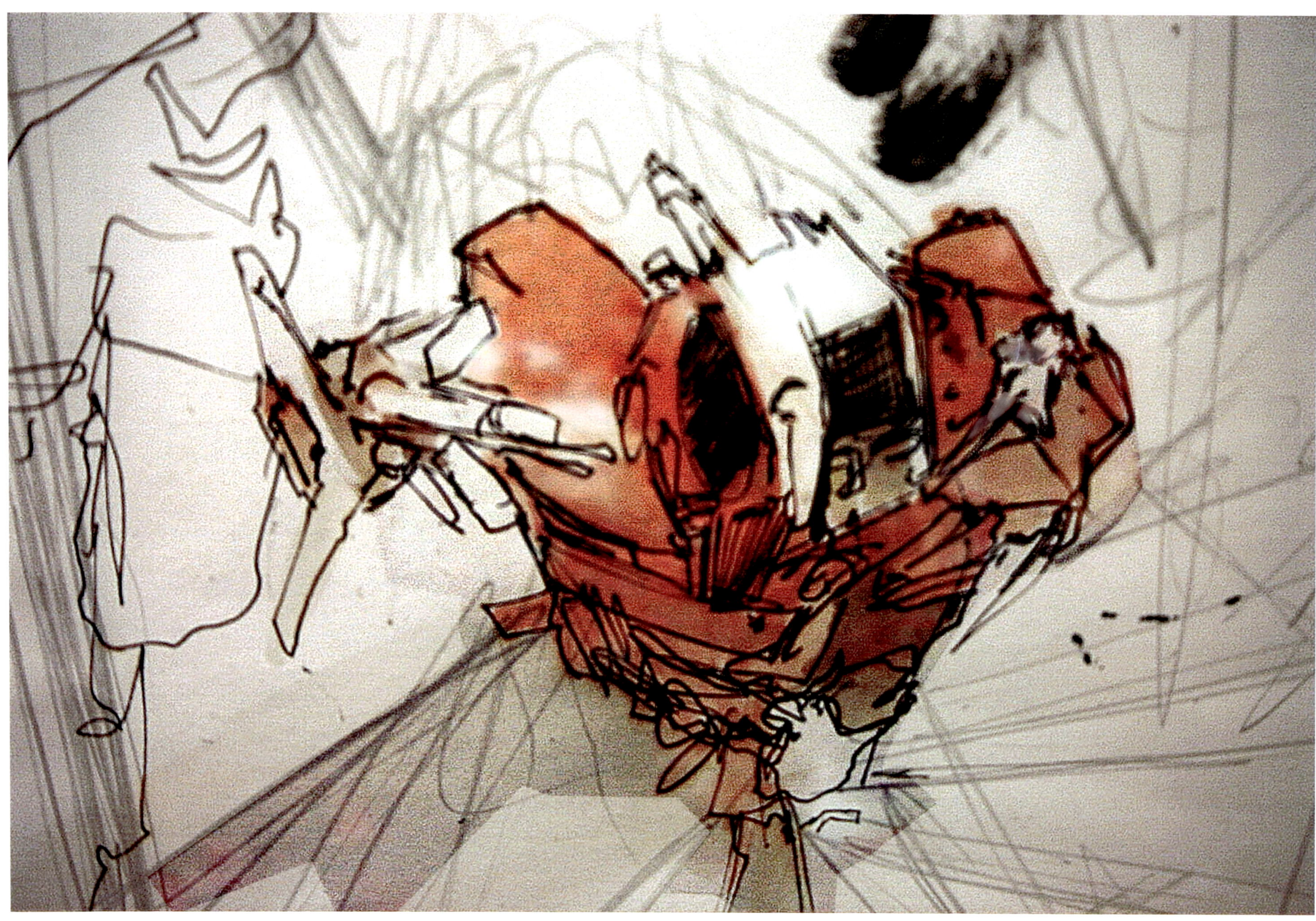

LEFT PAGE: botlabove
RIGHT PAGE:
LEFT: pilots
RIGHT: eyefull

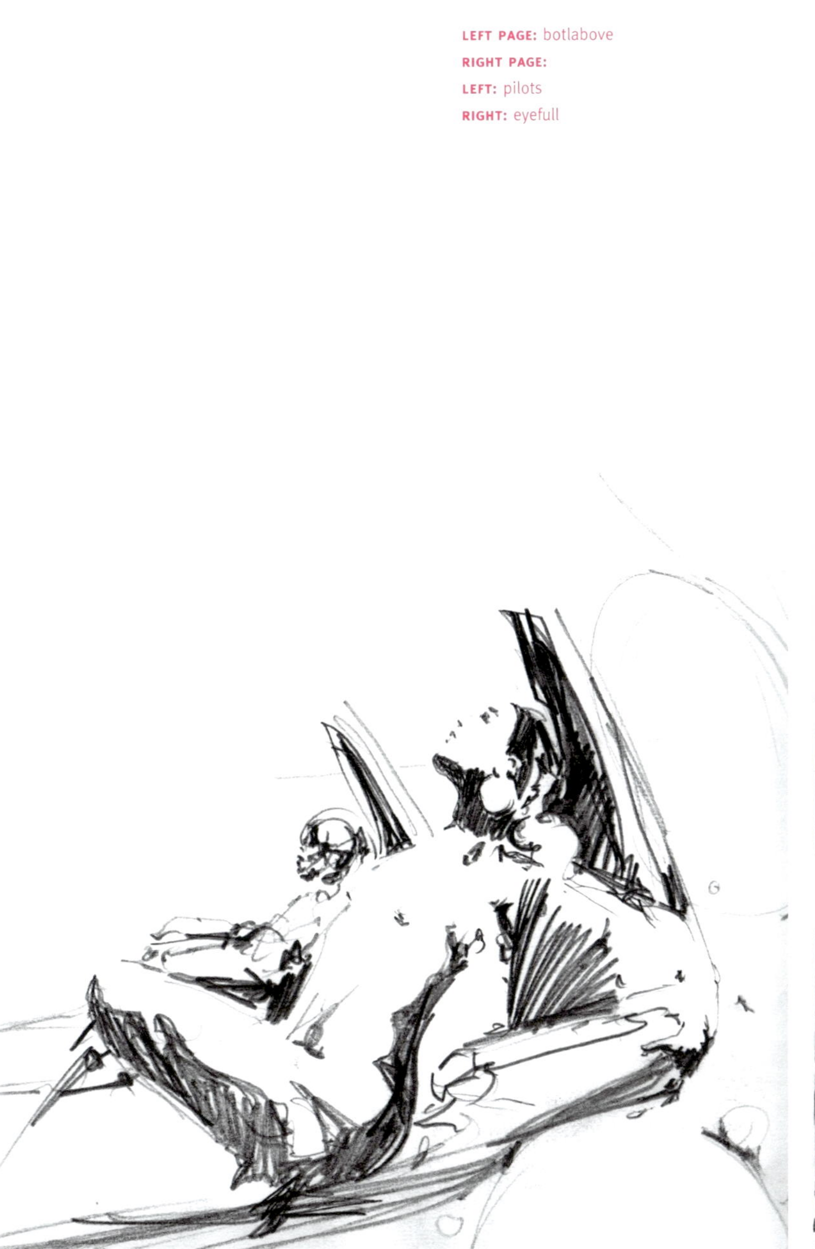

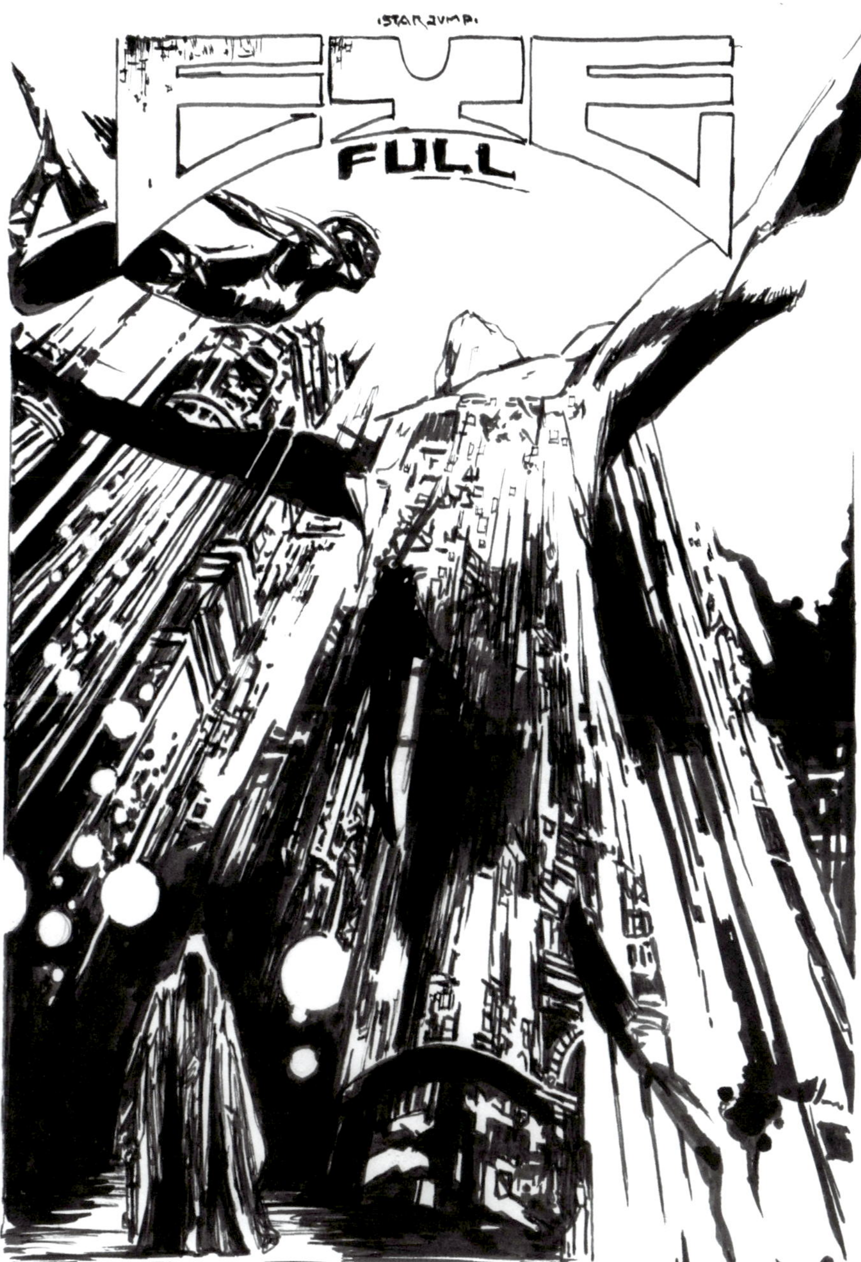

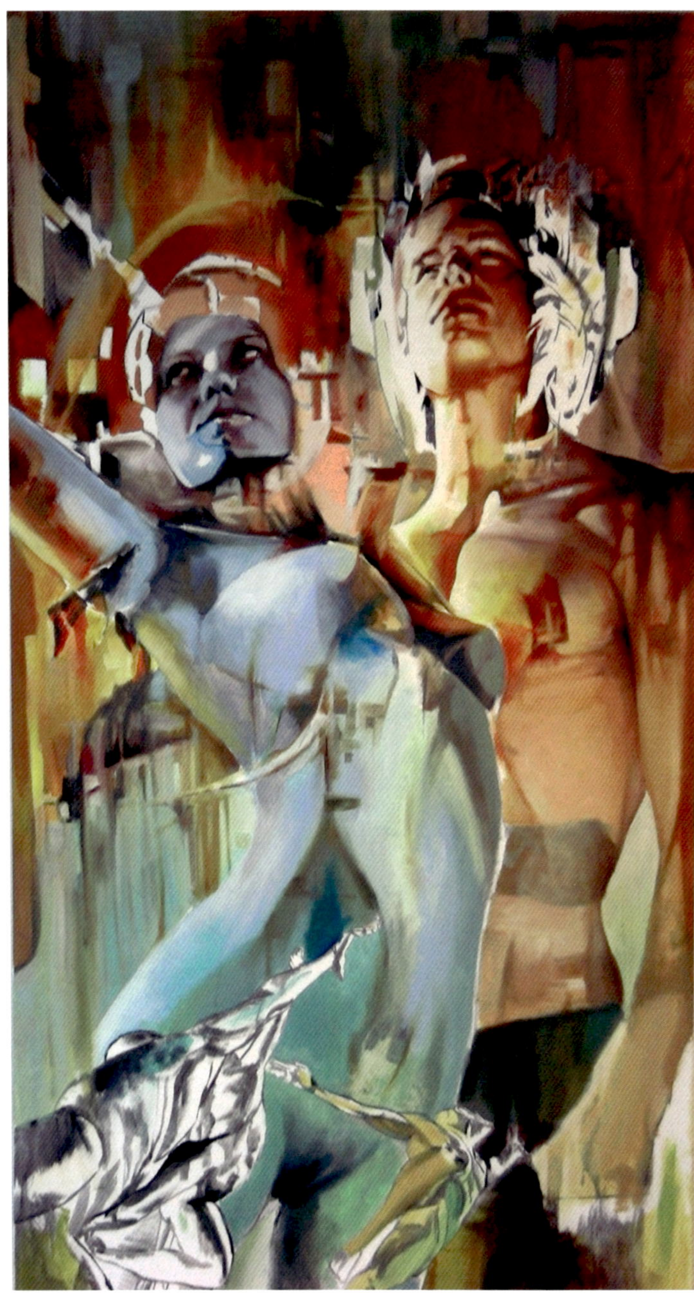

EN In my opinion the definitions of illustration and art are contingent not only on questions of patronage. If we wanted to reduce illustration to commercial works, most paintings in churches, for example, would have to be seen as commissioned illustrations as well, but they are obviously considered as art today. For me there's no difference, because nowadays everyone is after something "special," something "unusual." So even illegal "artworks," such as street art in the urban environment, in the next step, are used to promote some brand. I see myself neither as an illustrator nor as an artist. Maybe it's just the thing I started with in my childhood. Or someone gave me the talent to fish in the sea of dreams and other dimensions, like all other creatives. Damned, if we had learned a "reasonable" job, we could stop talking now. But for me and many others it's "too late" and because of that, I think we should never stop but continue tirelessly doing our arts, illustrations or whatever you want to call it. For me it's my life. "Light sinks through the windows of my universe."

LEFT PAGE: cpt
RIGHT PAGE: mine

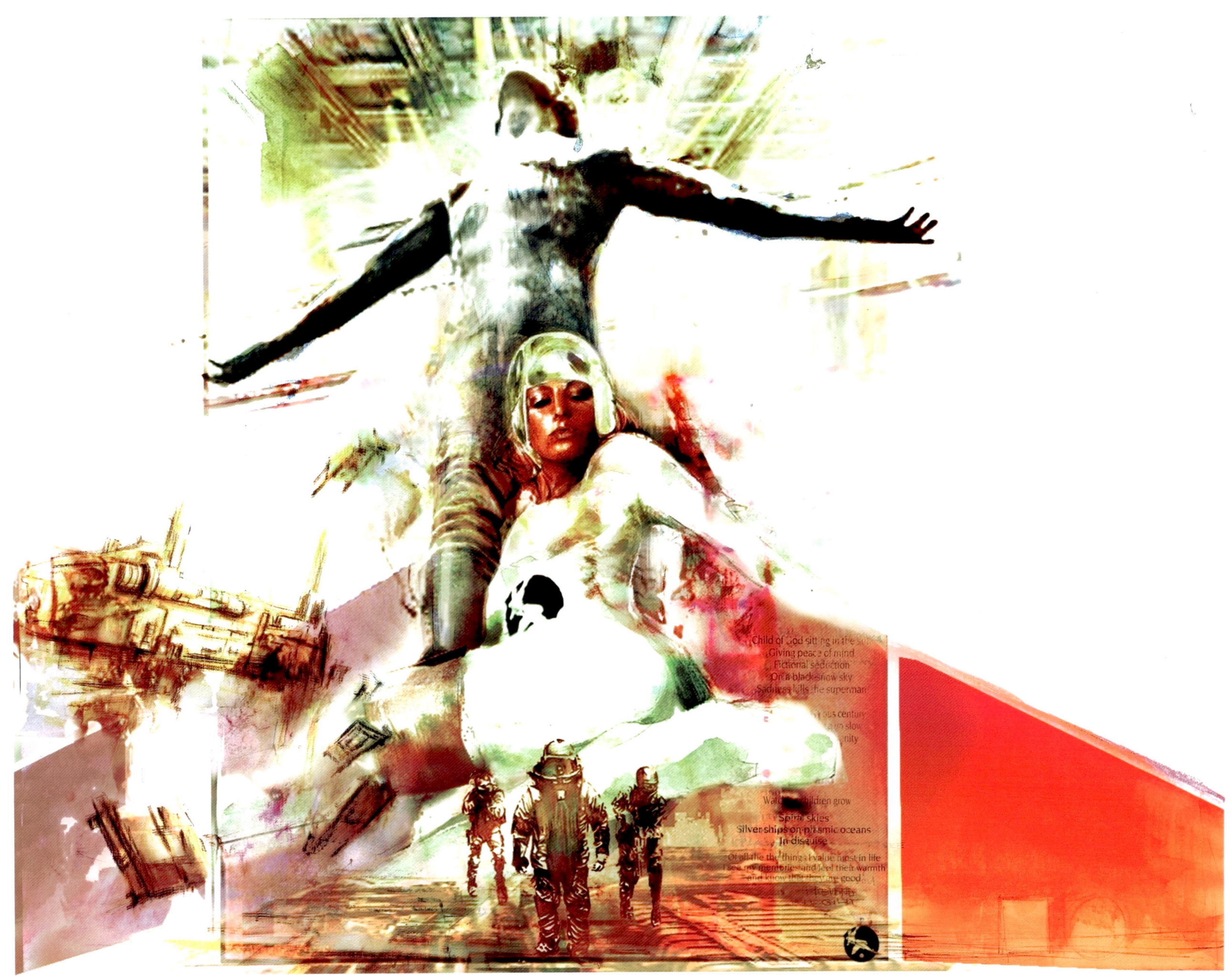
Giving peace of mind
Fictional seduction
Spiral skies
Silver ships on plasmic oceans
In disguise

ECB [HENDRIK BEIKIRCH]

NATIONALITY:	GERMAN
LOCATION:	KOBLENZ
PUBLICATIONS:	STRAIGHT LINES | PUBLIKAT VERLAG
REFERENCES:	DIVERSE
EXHIBITIONS:	NATIONAL AND INTERNATIONAL
REPRESENTIVES:	DIVERSE
CONTACT:	WWW.ECBWORK.DE ECB@ECBWORK.DE
TECHNIQUE:	EXACT
BORN:	1974

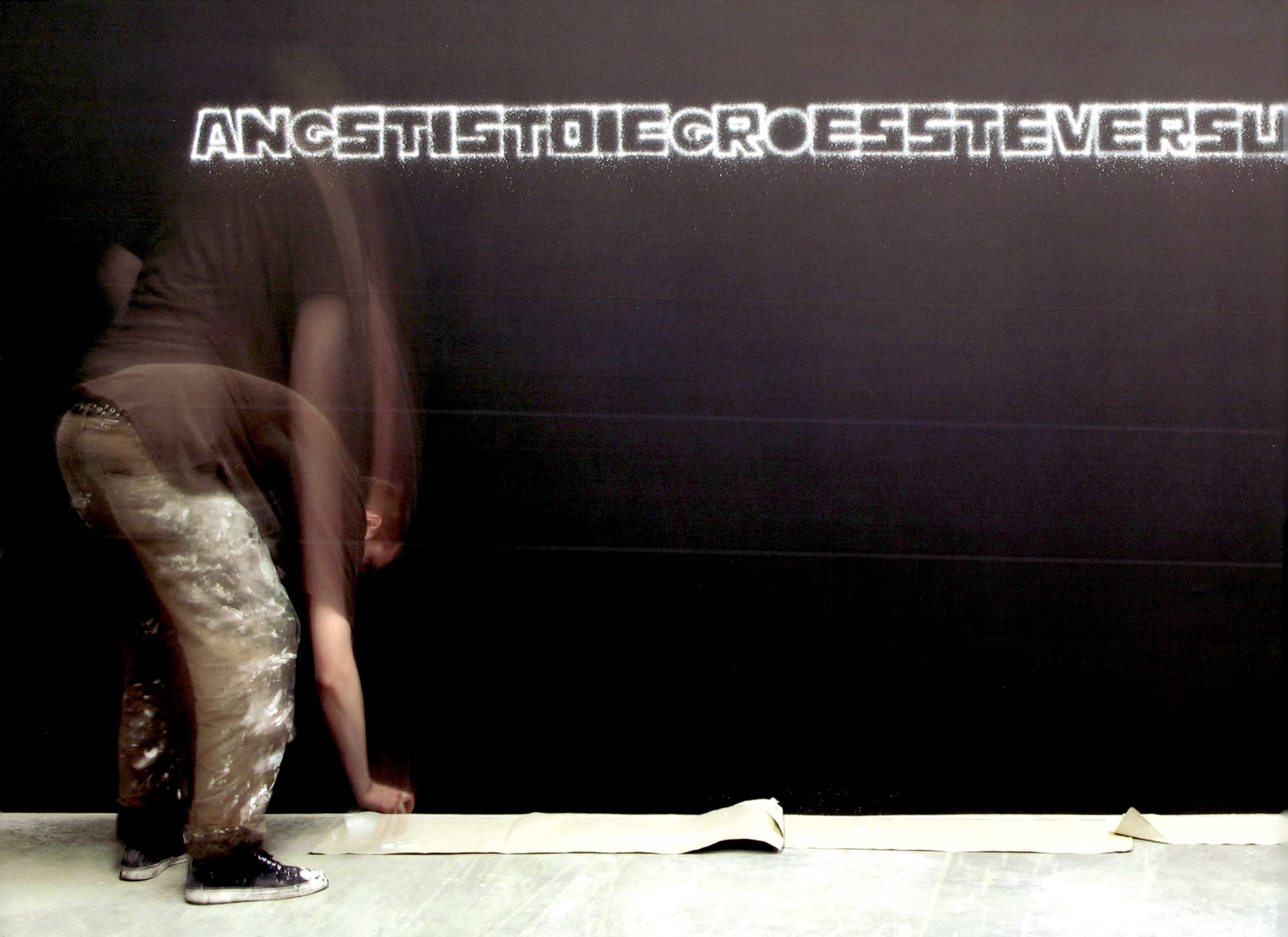
ANGSTISTDIEGROESSTEVERSU

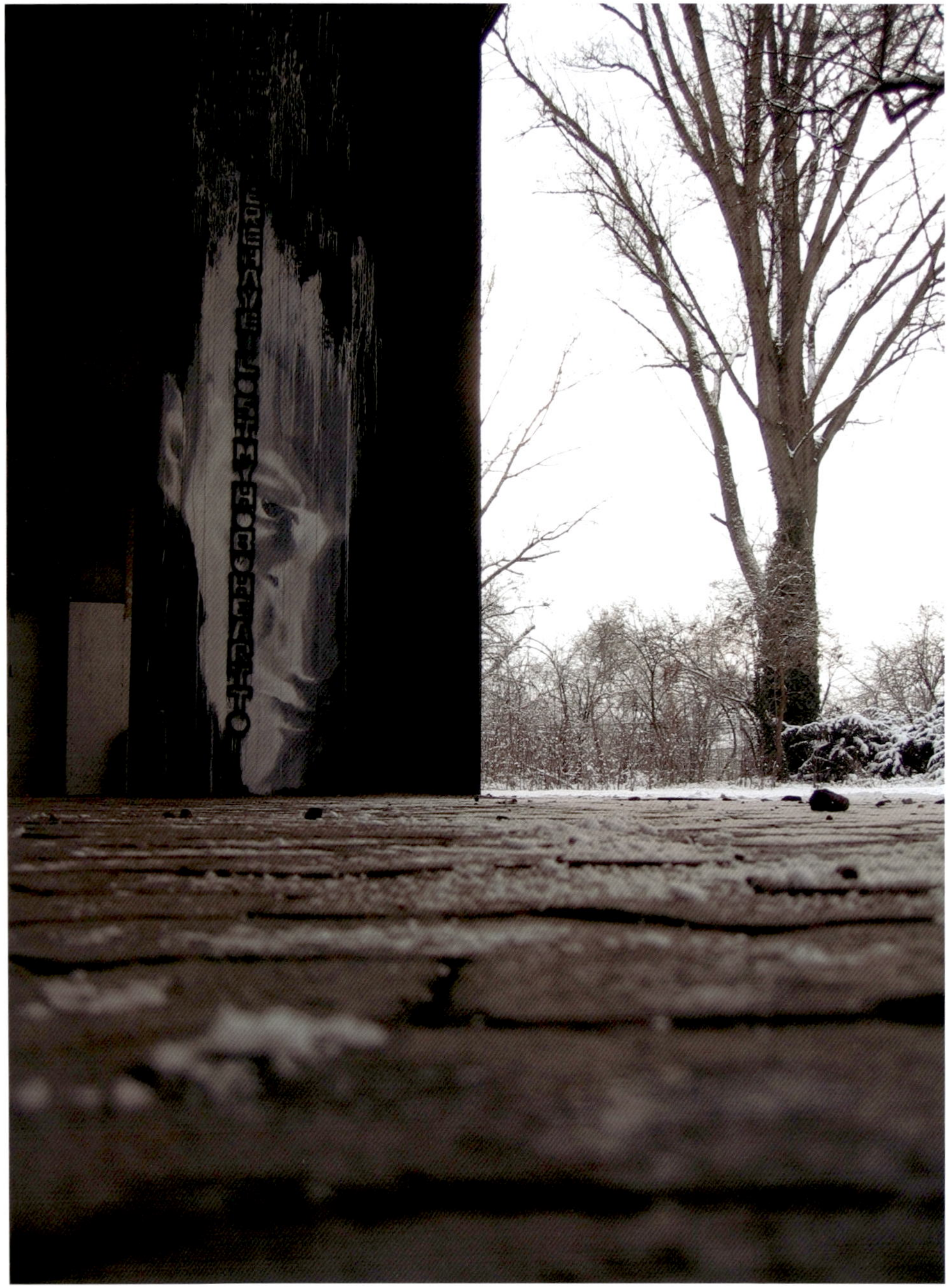

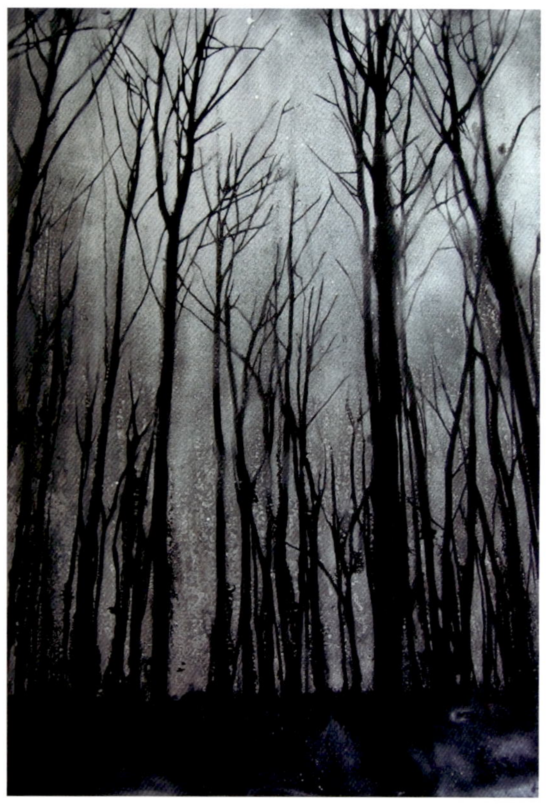

INTRODUCTION: ecb at work
LEFT PAGE:
LEFT: tell me where
RIGHT: riss eines zweifels
RIGHT PAGE:
LEFT: wehmütig
RIGHT: müdenherzens

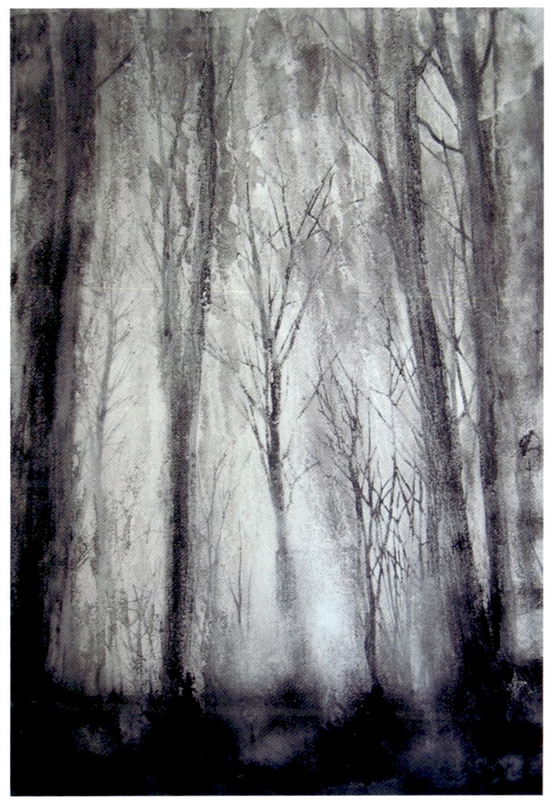

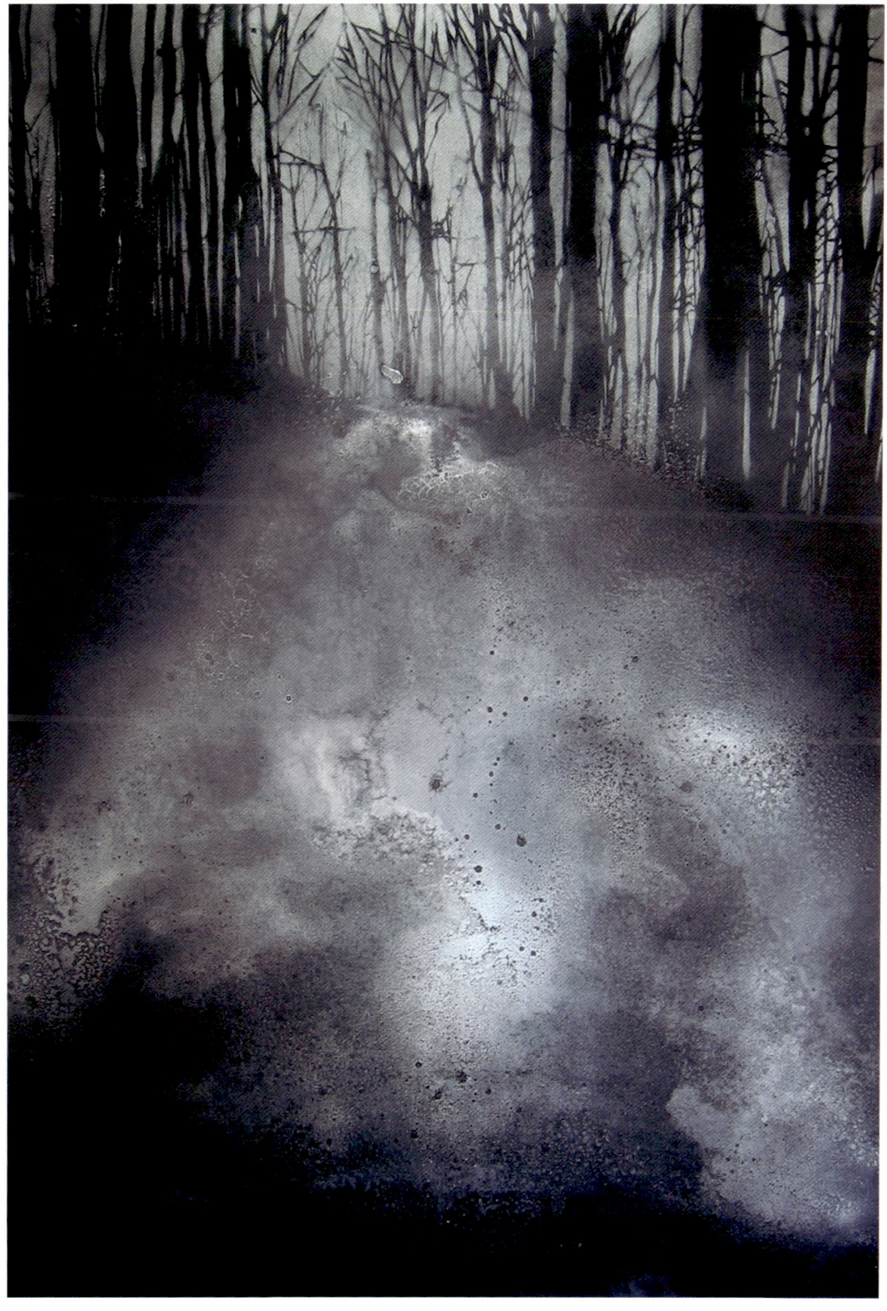

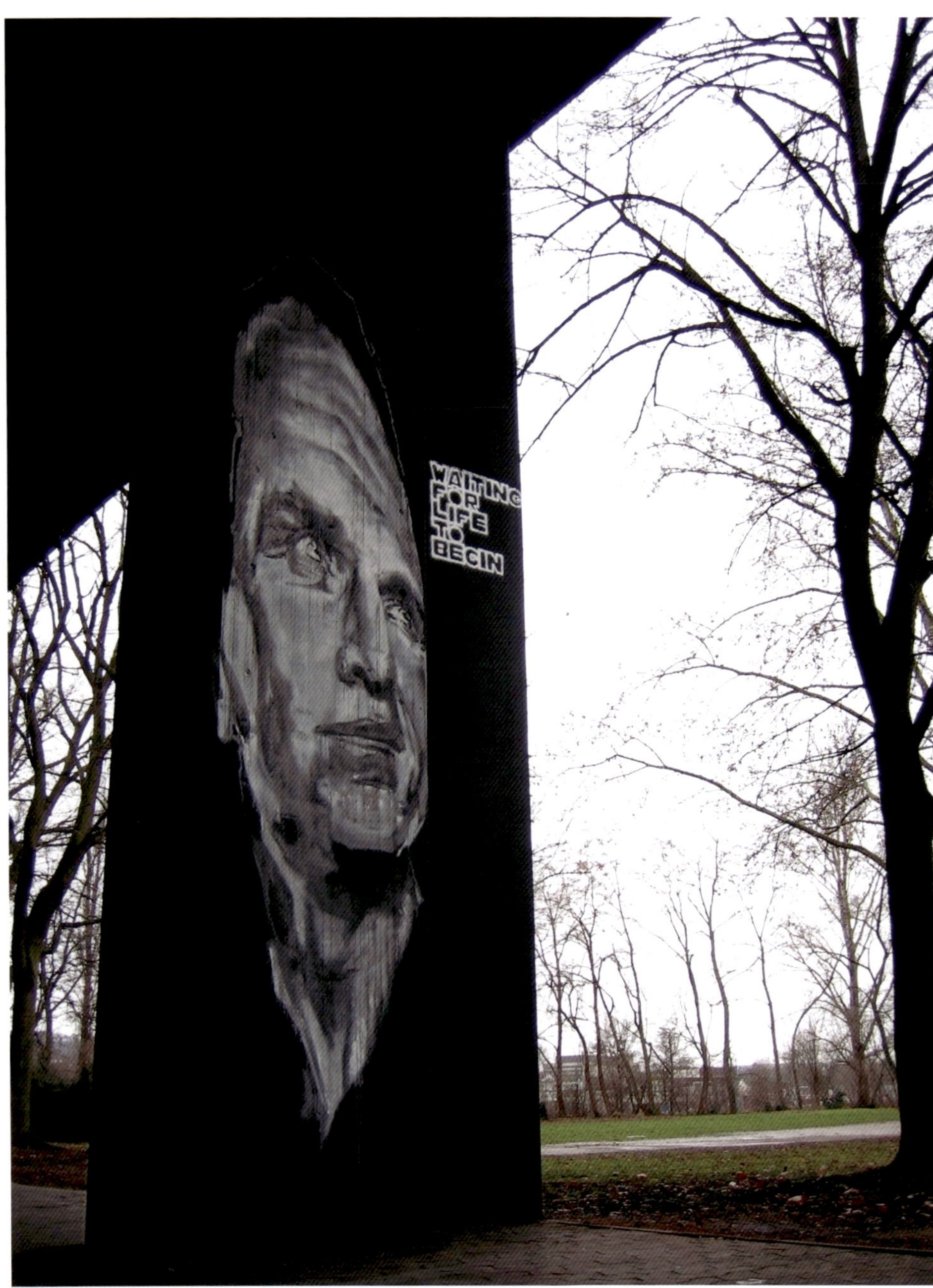

LEFT PAGE: waitingfor
RIGHT PAGE:
LEFT: nothingmore 01
RIGHT: nothingmore 02

DE Sehe ich den Illustrator, Künstler oder beide in mir? Auch meiner Arbeit liegt das Veranschaulichen und Verständlichmachen eines Sachverhalts zugrunde. Die in meinen Bildern enthaltenen Typographien sind der Versuch zu präzisieren. Sie sind eine Synthese aus Word und Bild, um neue, treffendere Bilderwelten zu öffnen. Insofern ergänzen sich auch hier Text und Bild. Letztlich bedeutet mir der Schaffensprozess mehr als das Ergebnis. Die Bilder sind dabei nur Nebenprodukte – Ergebnisse, Beweise für etwas anderes: Dafür, wo ich war und wohin ich gegangen bin. Gesichter, die etwas ausdrücken ... Bilder, die eine Geschichte erzählen. Das ist es, wonach ich suche. Ständig.

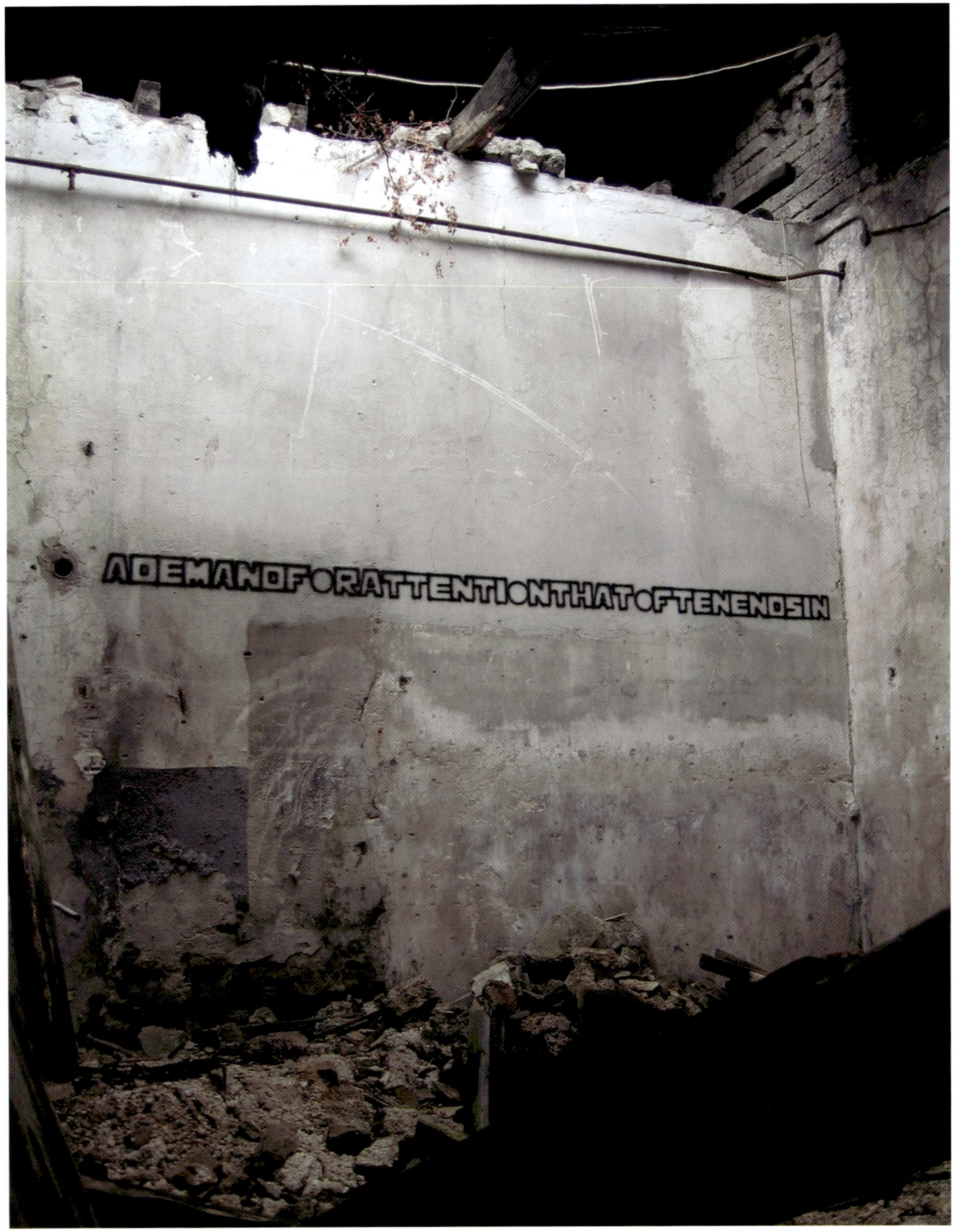
ADEMANDFORATTENTIONTHATOFTENENDSIN

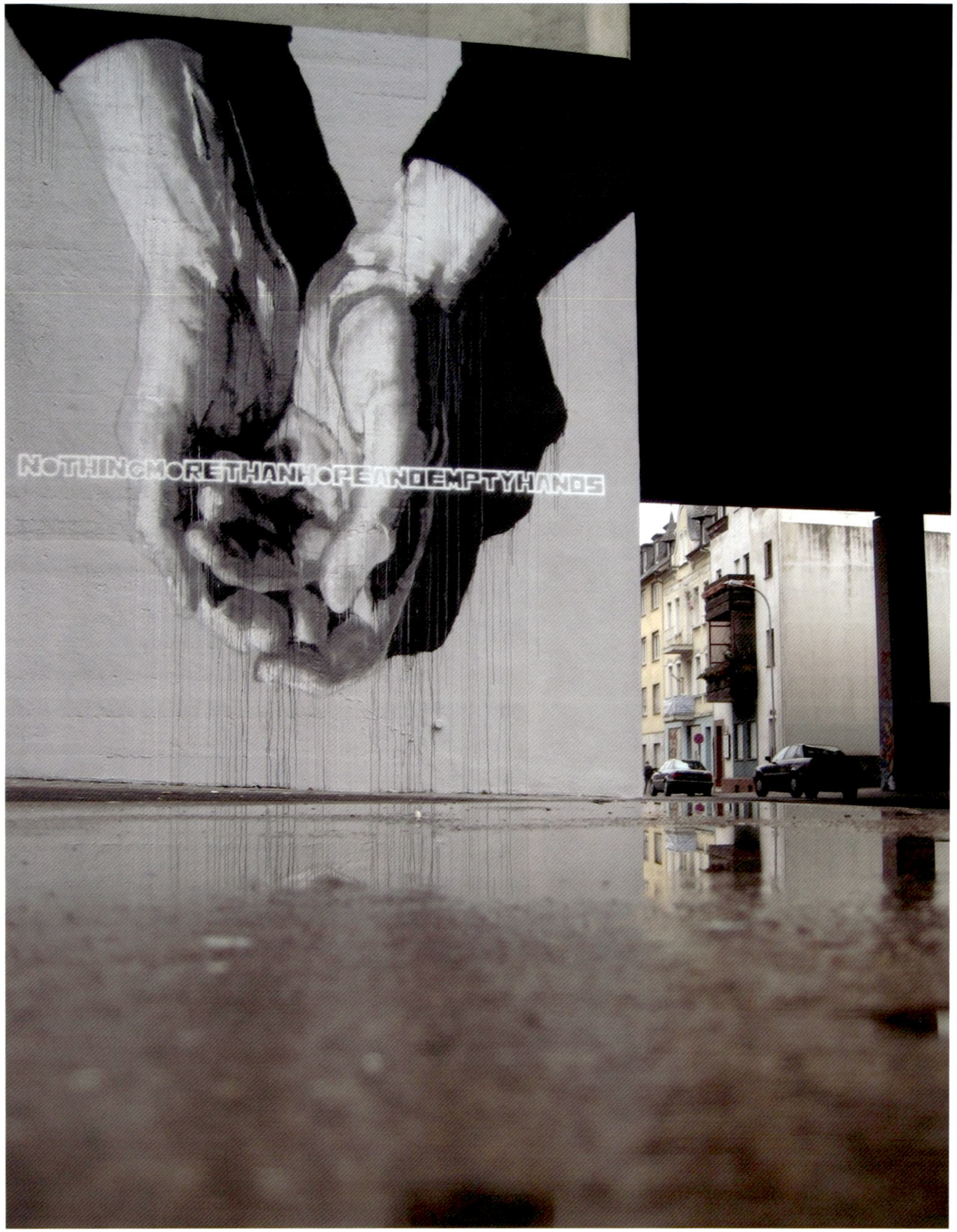
NOTHINGMORETHANHOPEANDEMPTYHANDS

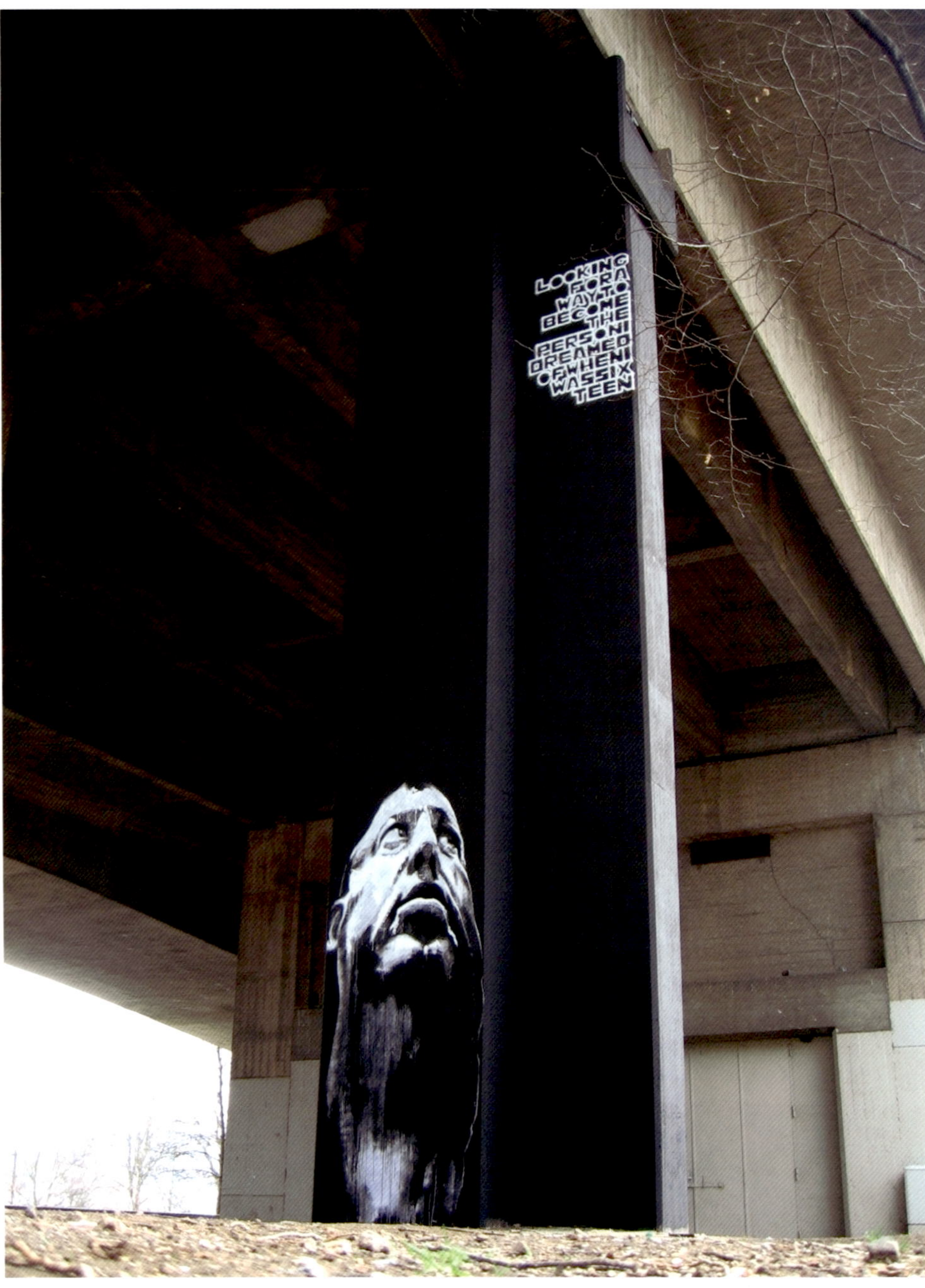

EN Do I see myself as an illustrator, artist, or both? My work is based on illustrating and explaining a subject. The typographies, embedded in my works, are an attempt at precision, a synthesis of image and word in order to achieve new and more accurate worlds of images. Text and image complement each other. In the end, the process of creation matters more to me than the result. My paintings are only by-products of this process – results and evidence of something else: of where I was, and where I was going. Faces expressing something ... Images which tell a story: This is what I am looking for. Always.

LEFT PAGE: looking for
RIGHT PAGE:
LEFT: erstickendes schweigen
RIGHT: all around

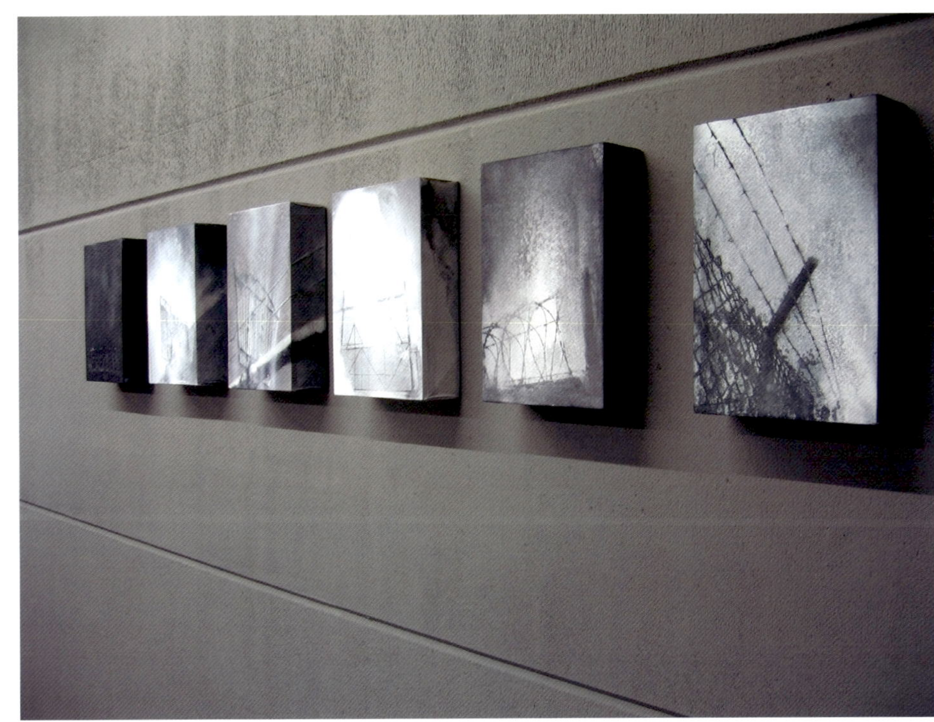

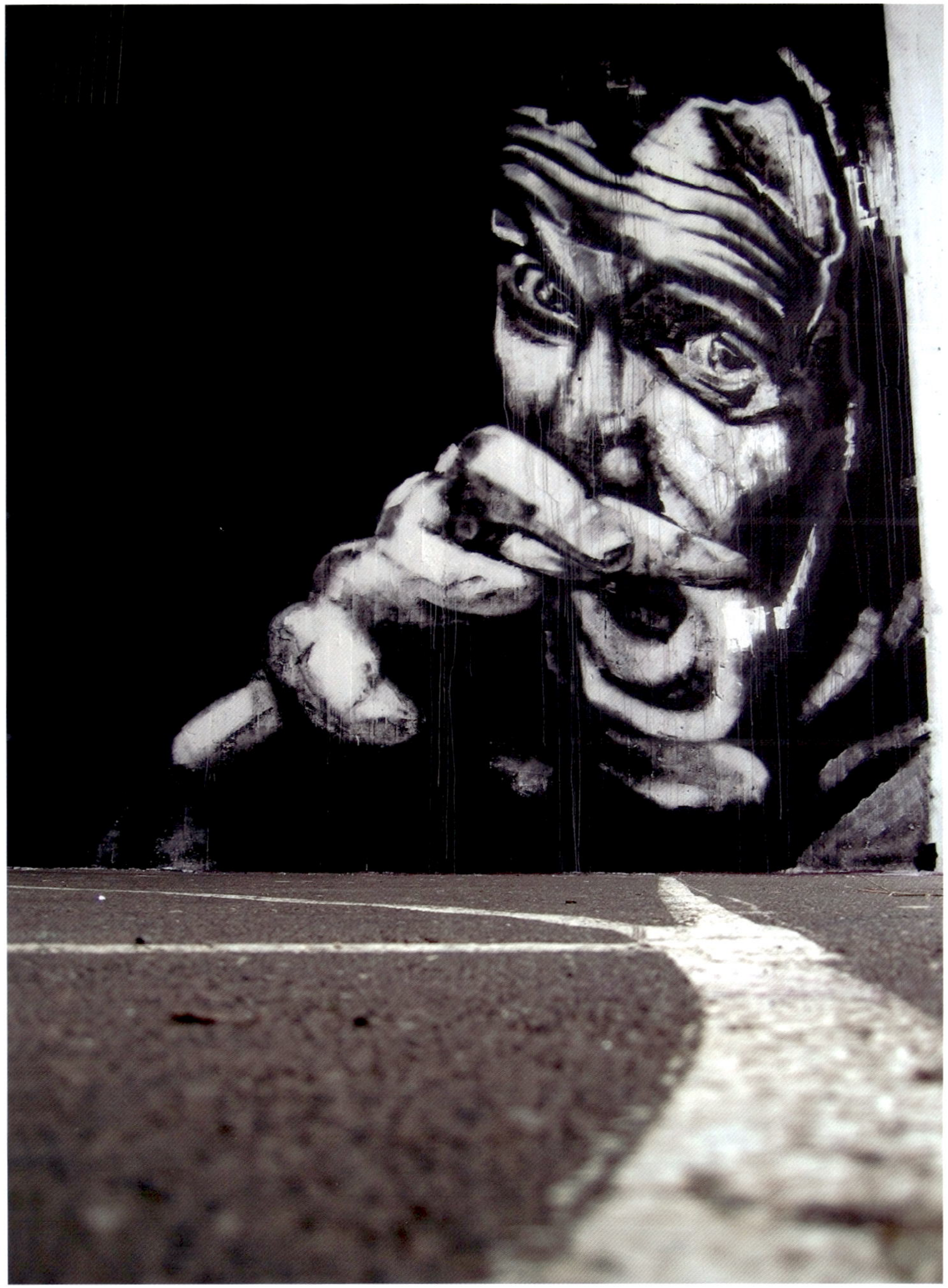

»TOMER HANUKA

NATIONALITY:	ISRAELI
LOCATION:	NEW YORK CITY
PUBLICATIONS:	BIPOLAR (COMICS) | THE PLACEBO MAN (COMICS) MEATHAUS (COMICS)
REFERENCES:	TIME MAGAZINE | THE NEW YORKER | SPIN THE NEW YORK TIMES | ROLLING STONE | MTV SAATCHI & SAATCHI | BBDO | NIKE | GQ | MAXIM WARNER BROS | DC COMICS | MEN'S HEALTH | BUCK TV SCHOLASTIC | RANDOM HOUSE | PENGUIN | MICROSOFT PLAYBOY | FANTAGRAPHICS | THE PROGRESSIVE MOTHER JONES | ENTERTAINMENT WEEKLY | THE REDCROSS SEVENTEEN | COSMO & ESQUIRE TO NAME A FEW
CONTACT:	WWW.THANUKA.COM
TECHNIQUE:	MIXED MEDIA
BORN:	1974

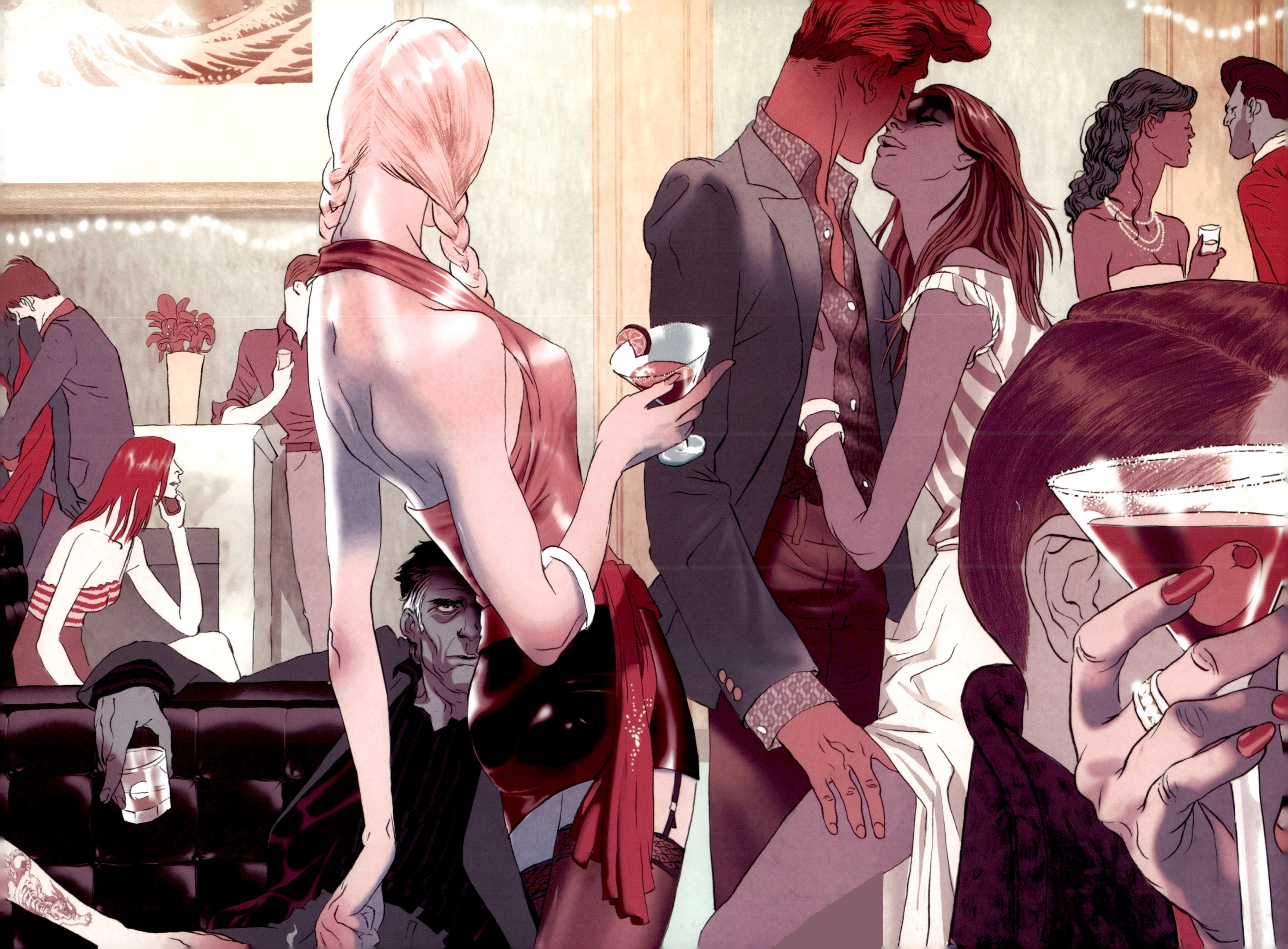

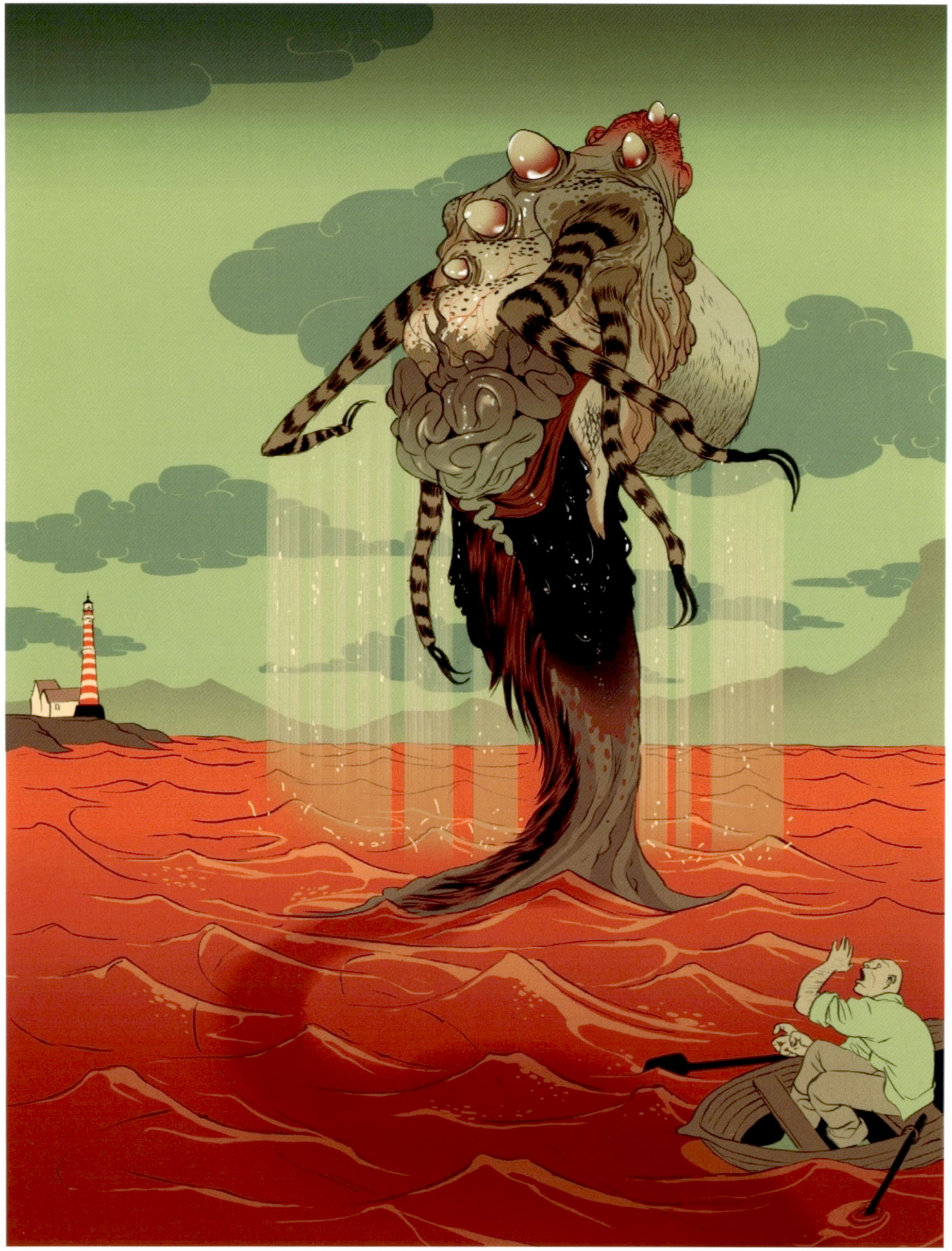

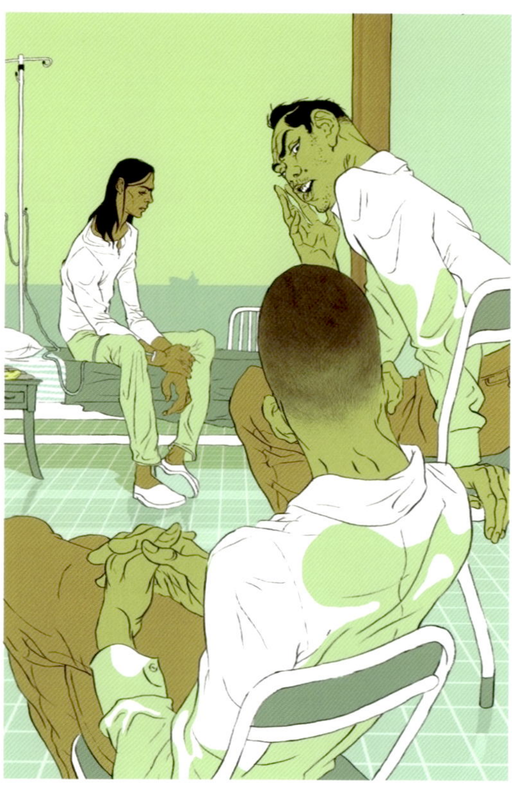

INTRODUCTION:
the possibility of an island
LEFT PAGE:
LEFT: cholera
RIGHT: memory
RIGHT PAGE:
LEFT: safe
RIGHT: life of pi

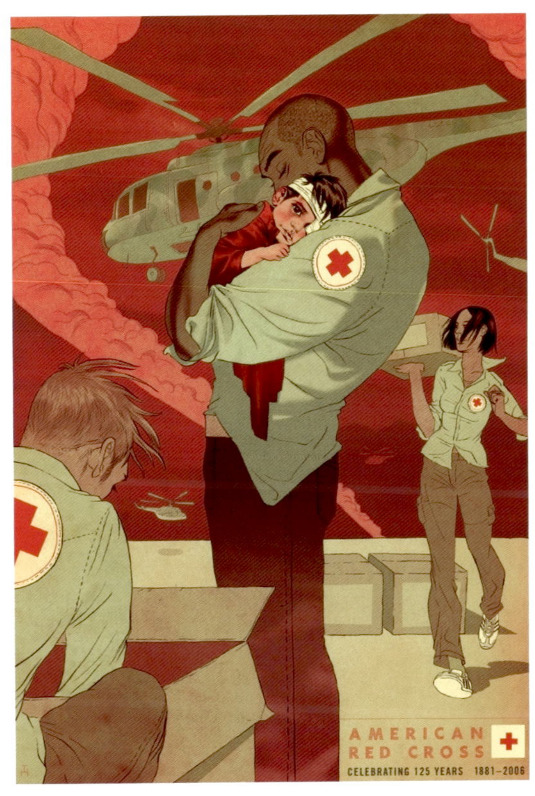
AMERICAN
RED CROSS
CELEBRATING 125 YEARS 1881–2006

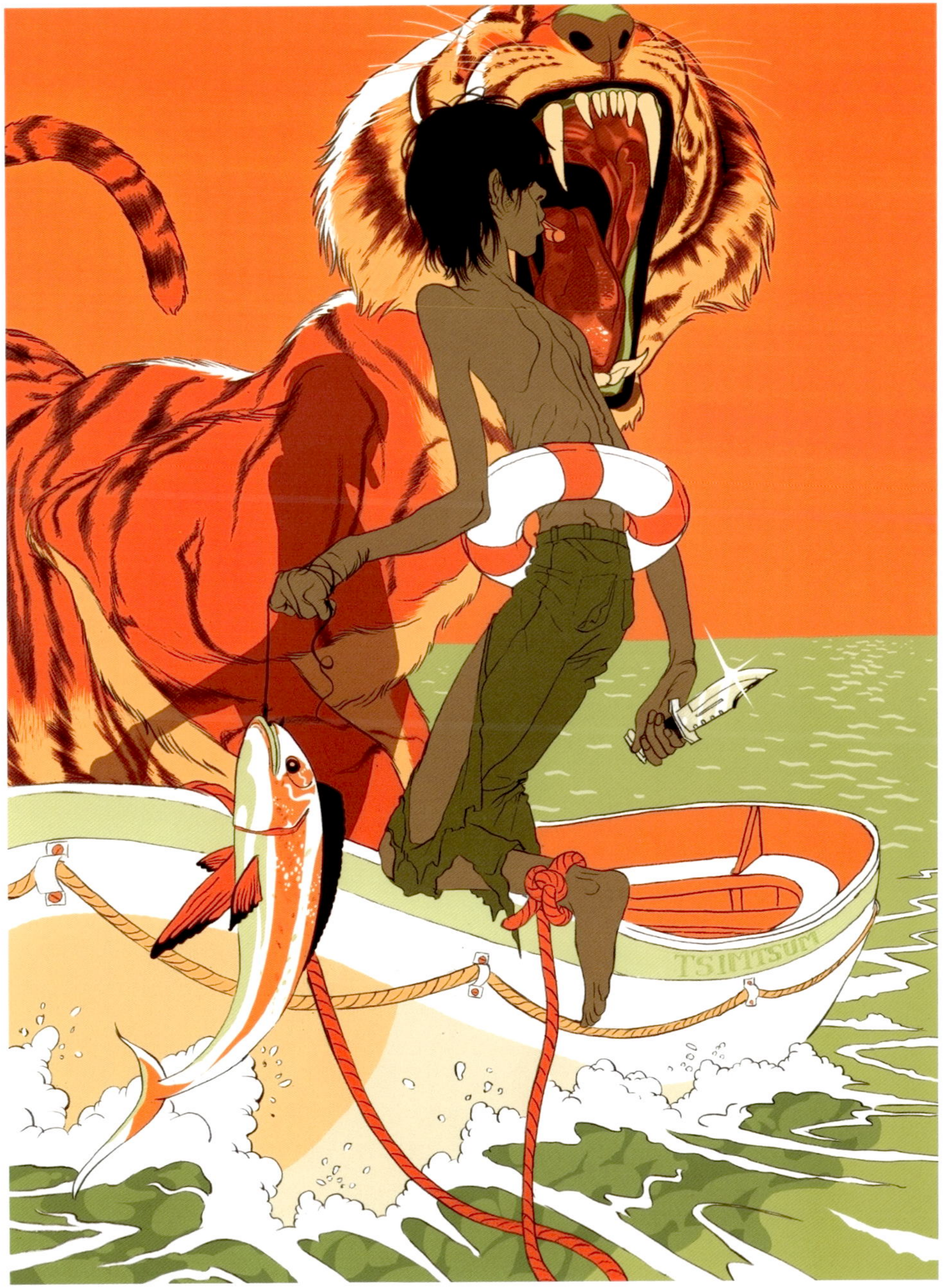

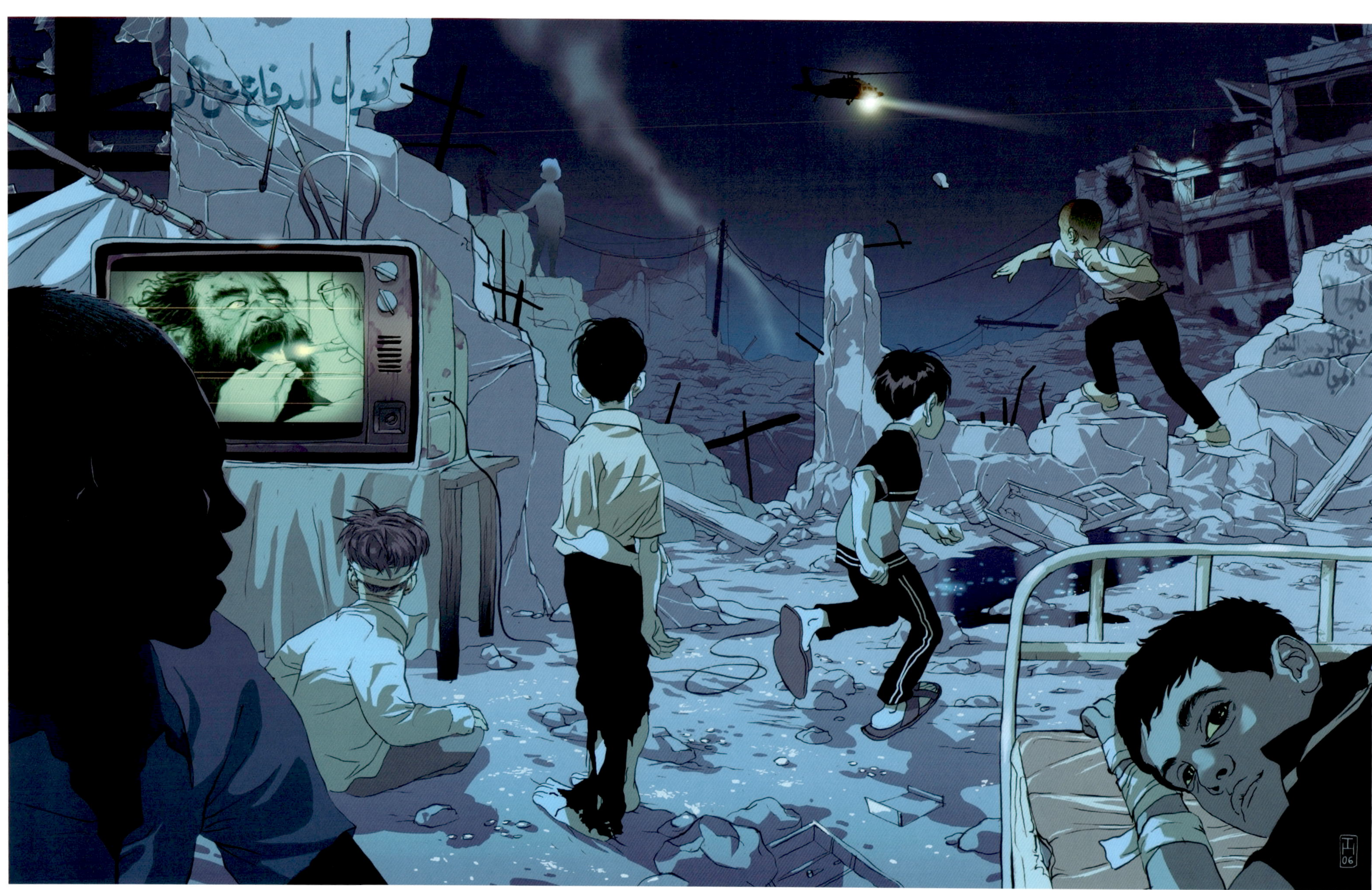

LEFT PAGE: night probe
RIGHT PAGE: the road

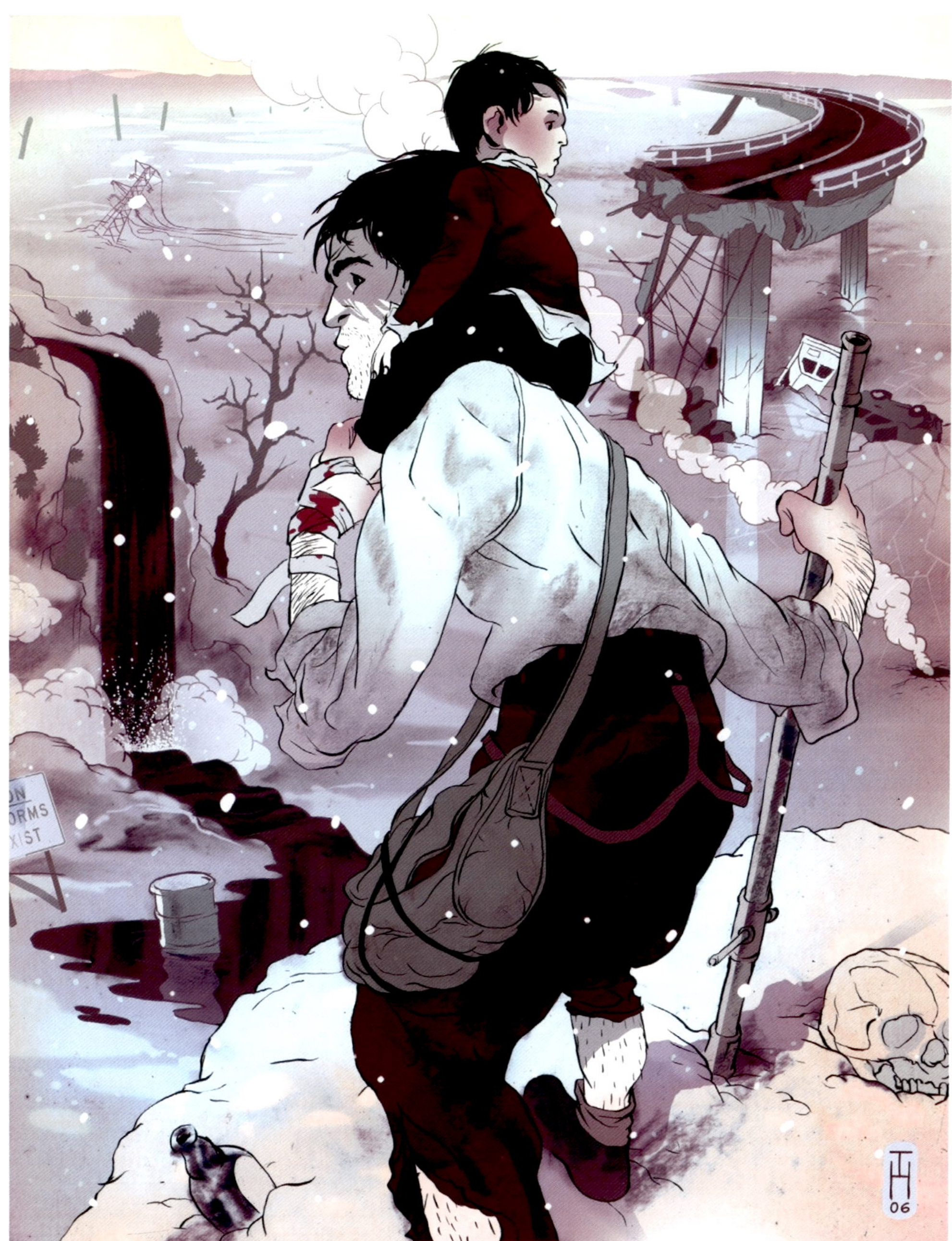

DE Von Zeit zu Zeit sehen wir Dinge, die unser Herz berühren. Das kann eine bestimmte Einstellung in einem Film oder das Logo einer Fast-Food-Kette sein, ein altes Foto von irgendjemanden, an einem beliebigen Ort aufgenommen, das Farbstift-Gekritzel des Neffen, der gerade dabei ist zu entdecken, wie man Kreise zeichnet, oder die Welt, gespleißt durch die Aussicht aus unserem Schlafzimmerfenster. Ich weiß nicht, ob eines dieser Beispiele Kunst ist und ich kann nicht beurteilen, weshalb das von Bedeutung sein könnte.

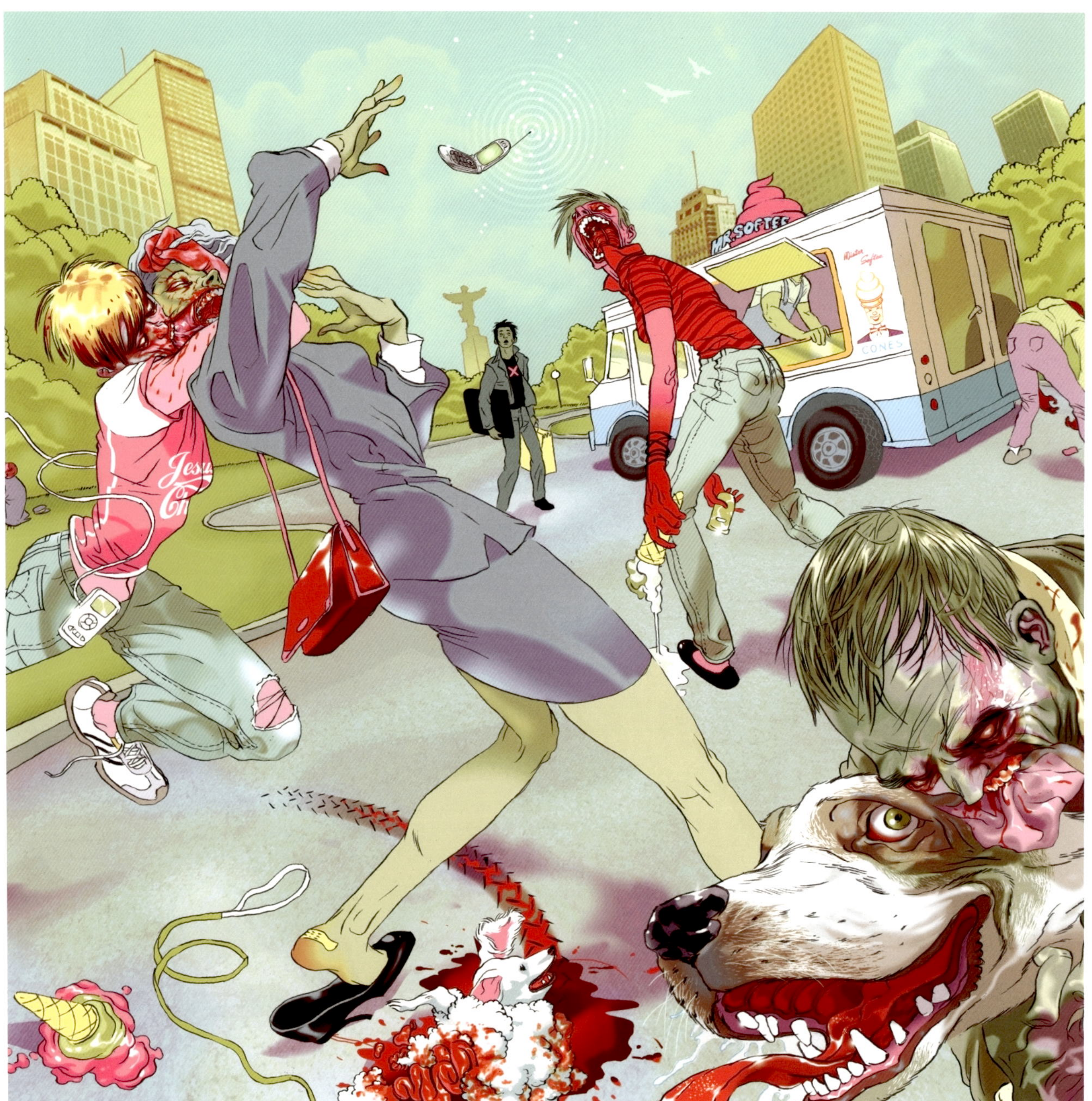

LEFT PAGE: cell
RIGHT PAGE:
LEFT: no fare, no well
RIGHT: food chain

EN Once in a while we see something that breaks our heart. It can be a certain frame in a movie, a fast food character logo, an old photo of someone somewhere, a nephew's crayon doodle on the cusp of discovering circles or the world spliced through our bedroom window. I don't know if any of these examples are art, and I can't see why it should matter.

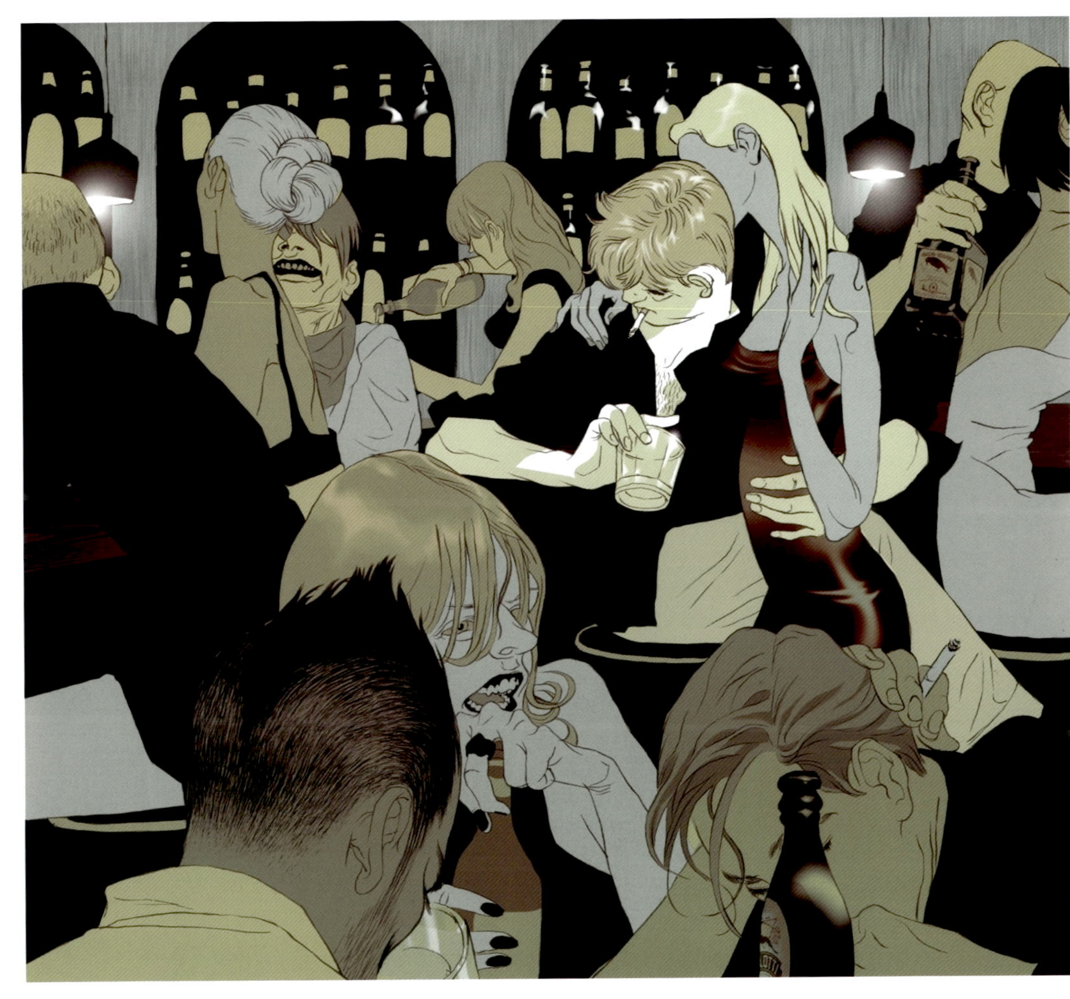

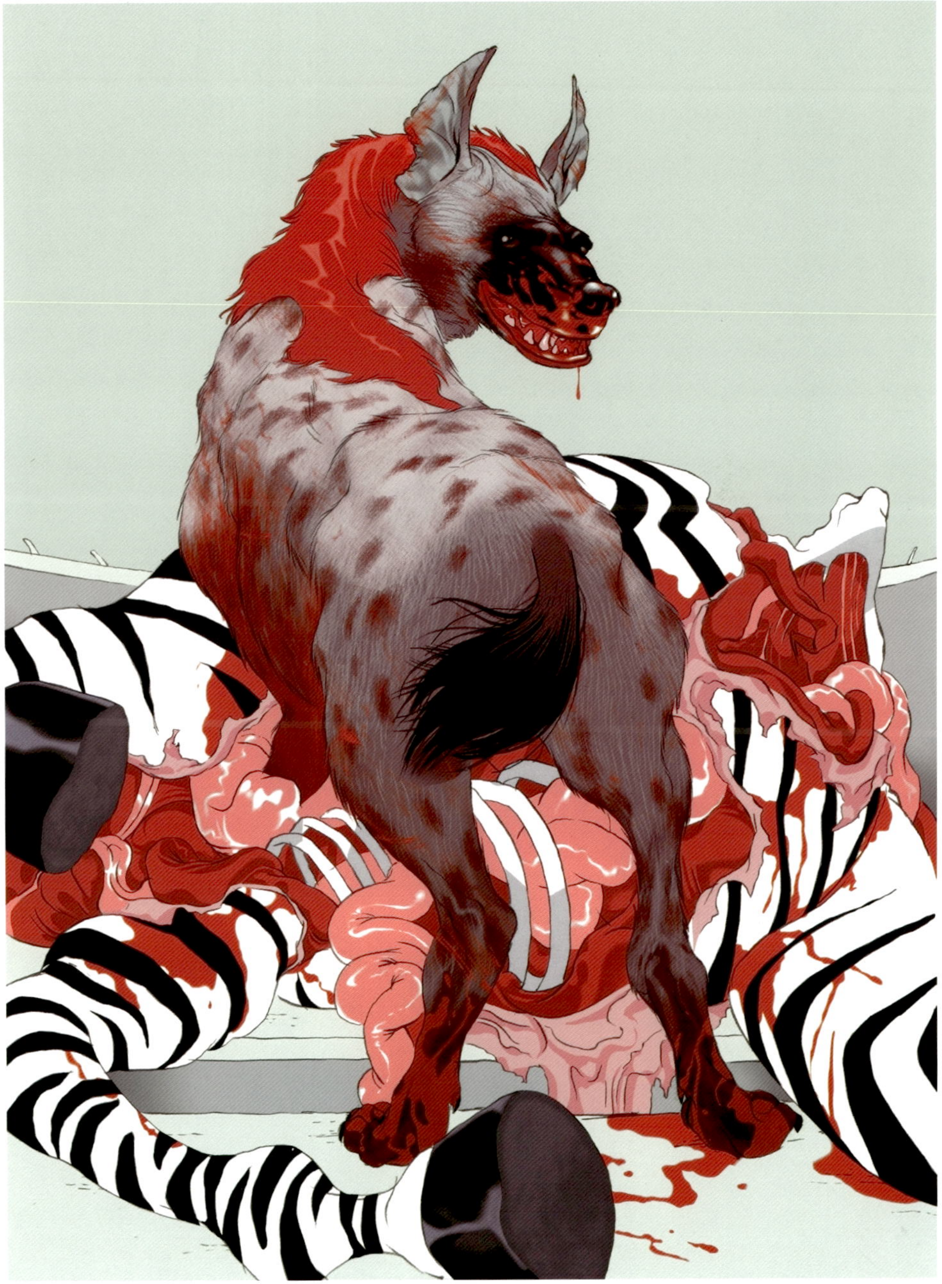

»CLIFFORD URBAN

NATIONALITY:	EUROPEAN
LOCATION:	BRUSSELS
PUBLICATIONS:	DONT KNOW
REFERENCES:	MANY
EXHIBITIONS:	NOT SO MANY
REPRESENTIVES:	NONE
CONTACT:	CLIFFORDURBAN@WEB.DE
TECHNIQUE:	HARD TO SAY
BORN:	MUCH TO EARLY

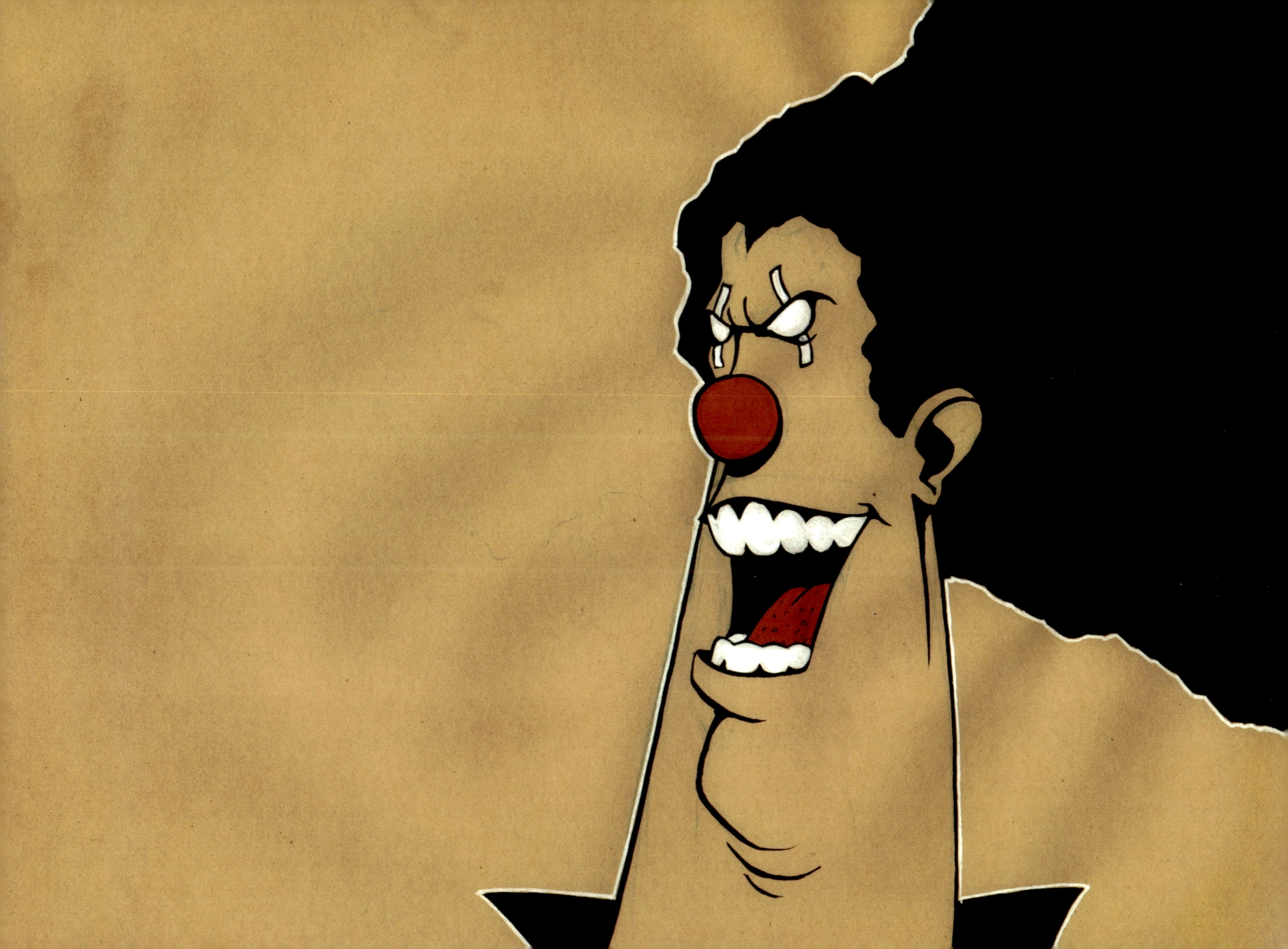

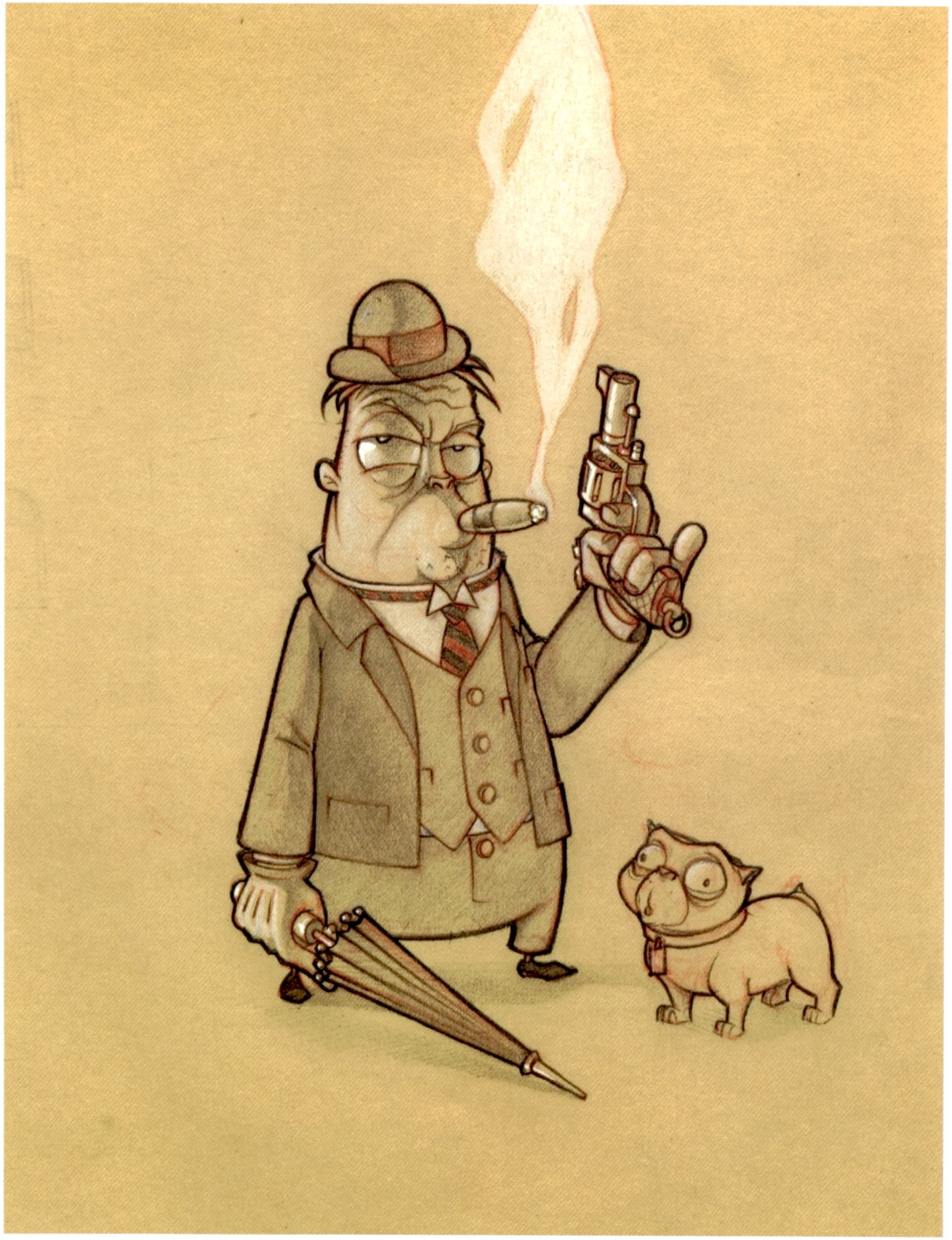

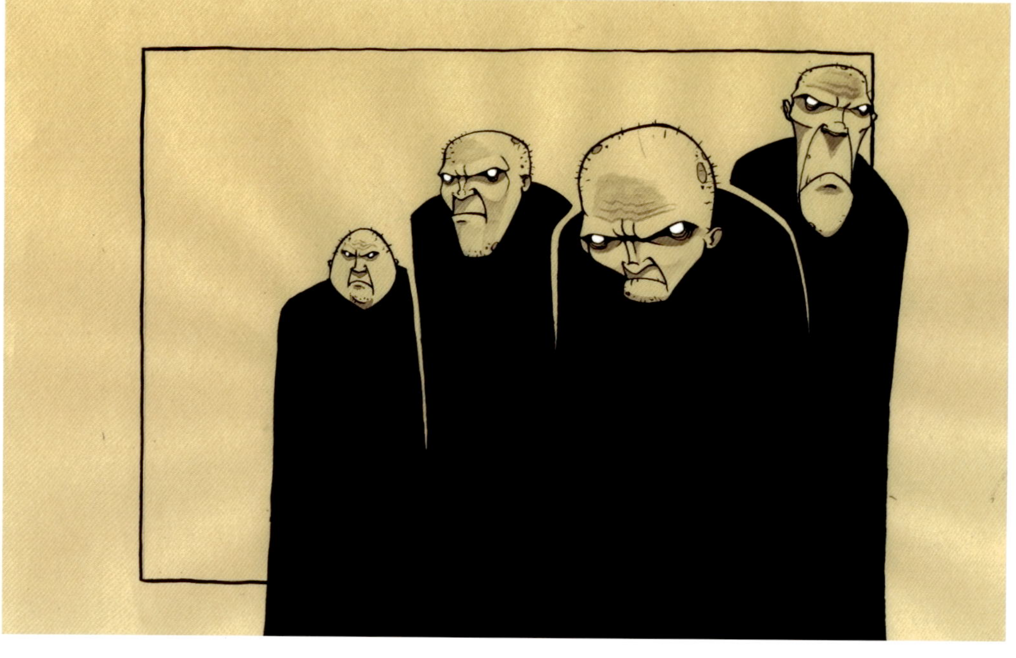

INTRODUCTION: clown 2

LEFT PAGE:

LEFT: character 4

RIGHT: character 2

RIGHT PAGE: clown 1

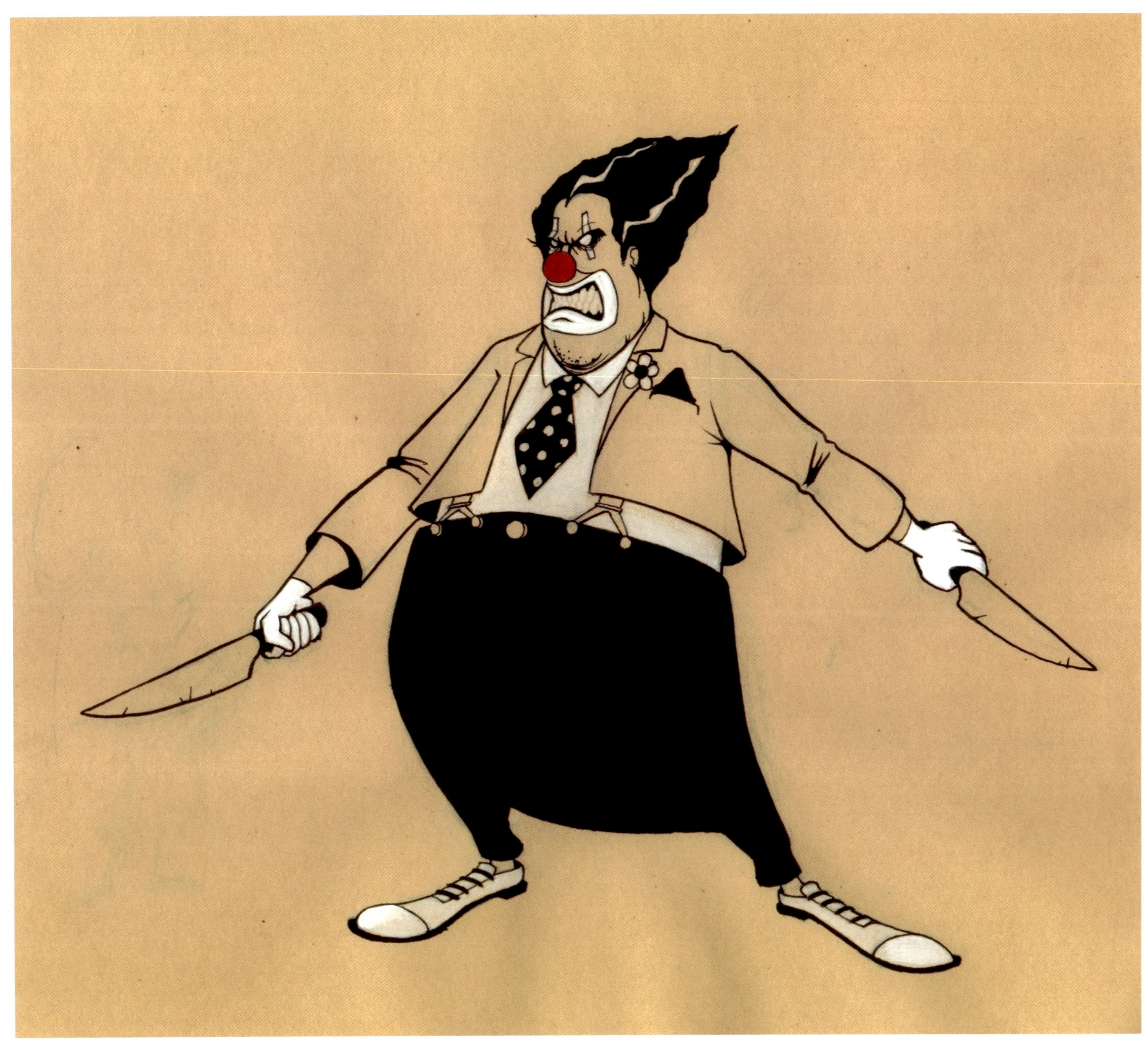

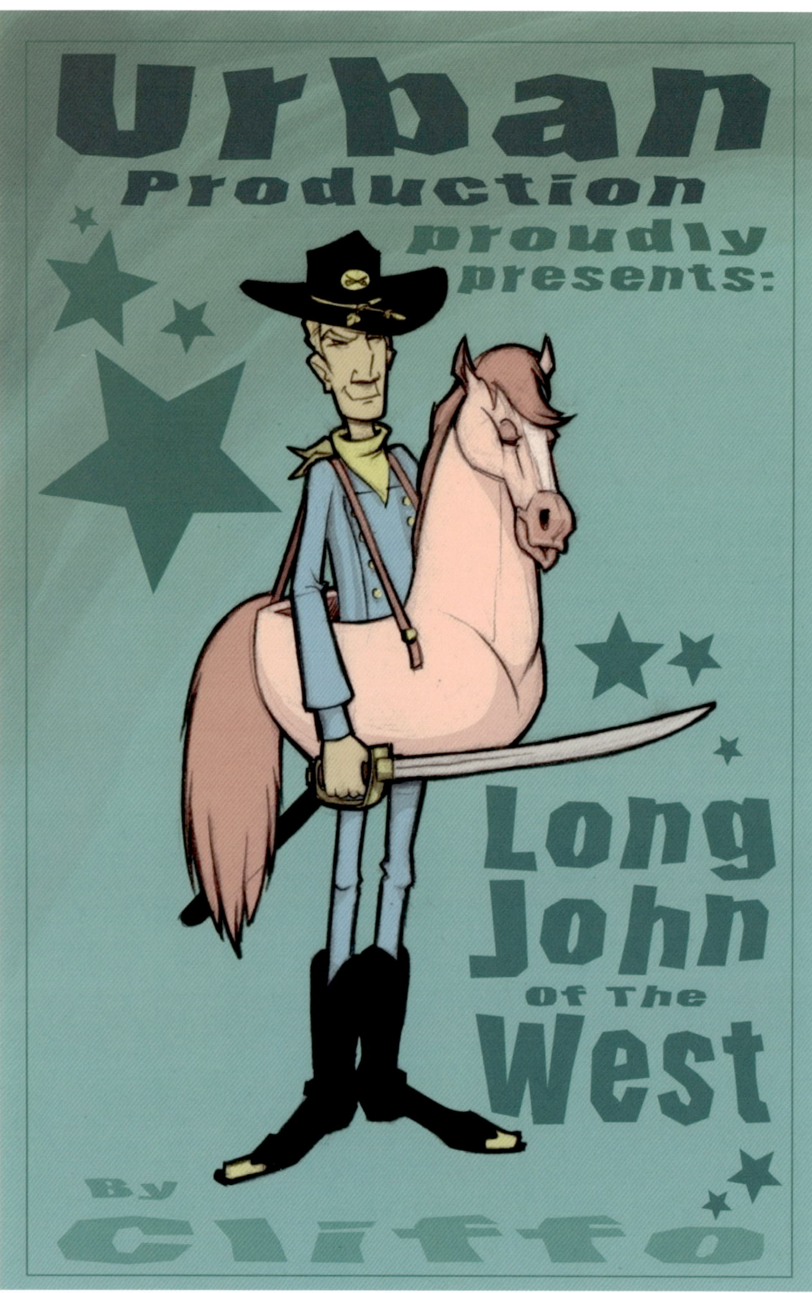

DE Fest steht nach wie vor, dass der Illustrator auftragsbezogen und der Künstler frei arbeitet. Für mich hat sich lediglich die Zahl der zur Auswahl stehenden Medien bezüglich der Umsetzung geändert. Meiner Einschätzung nach spielt die Frage, inwiefern eine Unterscheidung zwischen Illustration und Kunst existent, nötig oder obsolet ist, keine Rolle, da sehr viele Illustrationen durch ihre hochwertige Umsetzung einem „frei" entstandenen Werk kaum oder in nichts nachstehen. Gleichzeitig haben viele Kunstobjekte durch den gewählten Stil einen sehr illustratorischen Charakter, was sie nicht zu Auftragsarbeiten macht. Theoretisch hingegen sagt eine Unterscheidung etwas über den Beweggrund für die Entstehung einer Arbeit aus. Ich persönlich verstehe mich dabei als König oder Hure, und das ändert sich täglich.

LEFT PAGE: cowboy 1
RIGHT PAGE:
LEFT: soldat
TOP RIGHT: cowboy 2
DOWN RIGHT: indianer

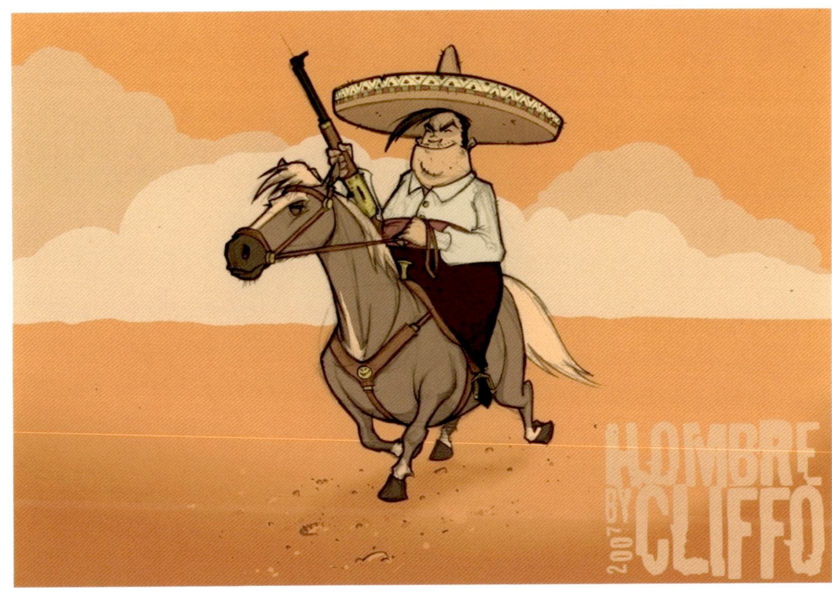

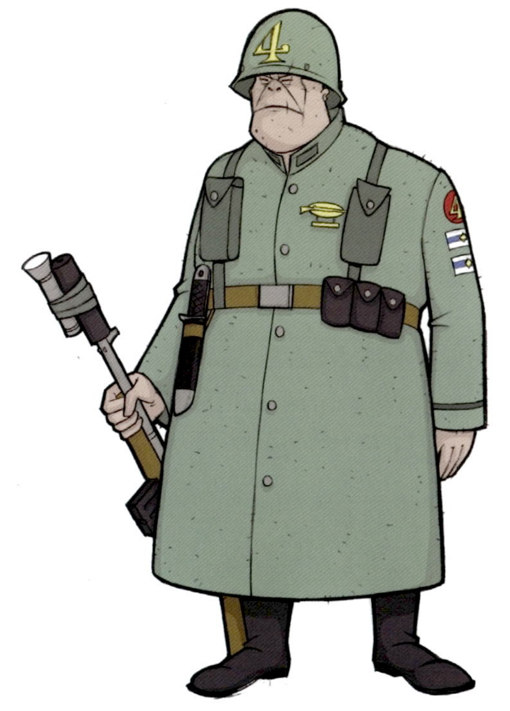

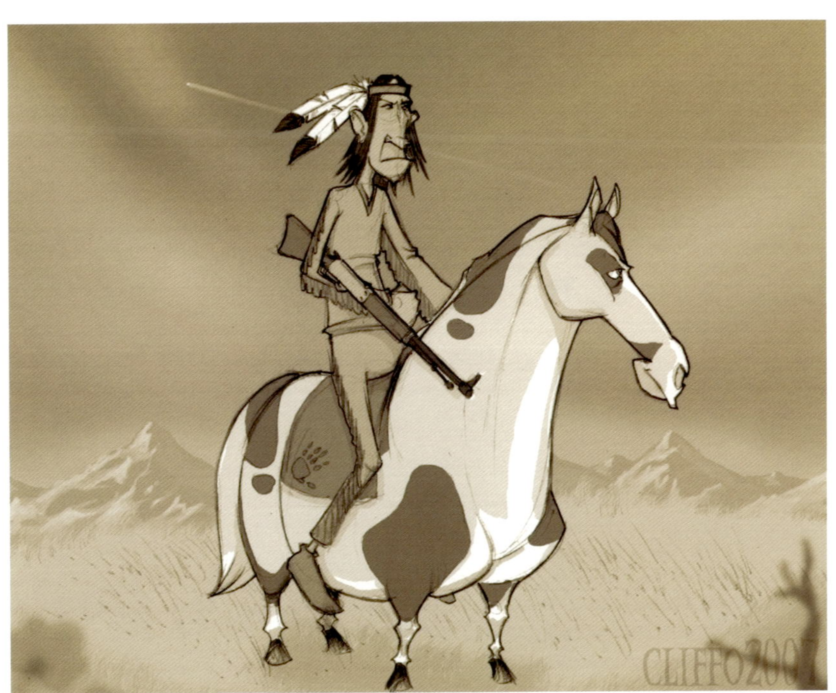

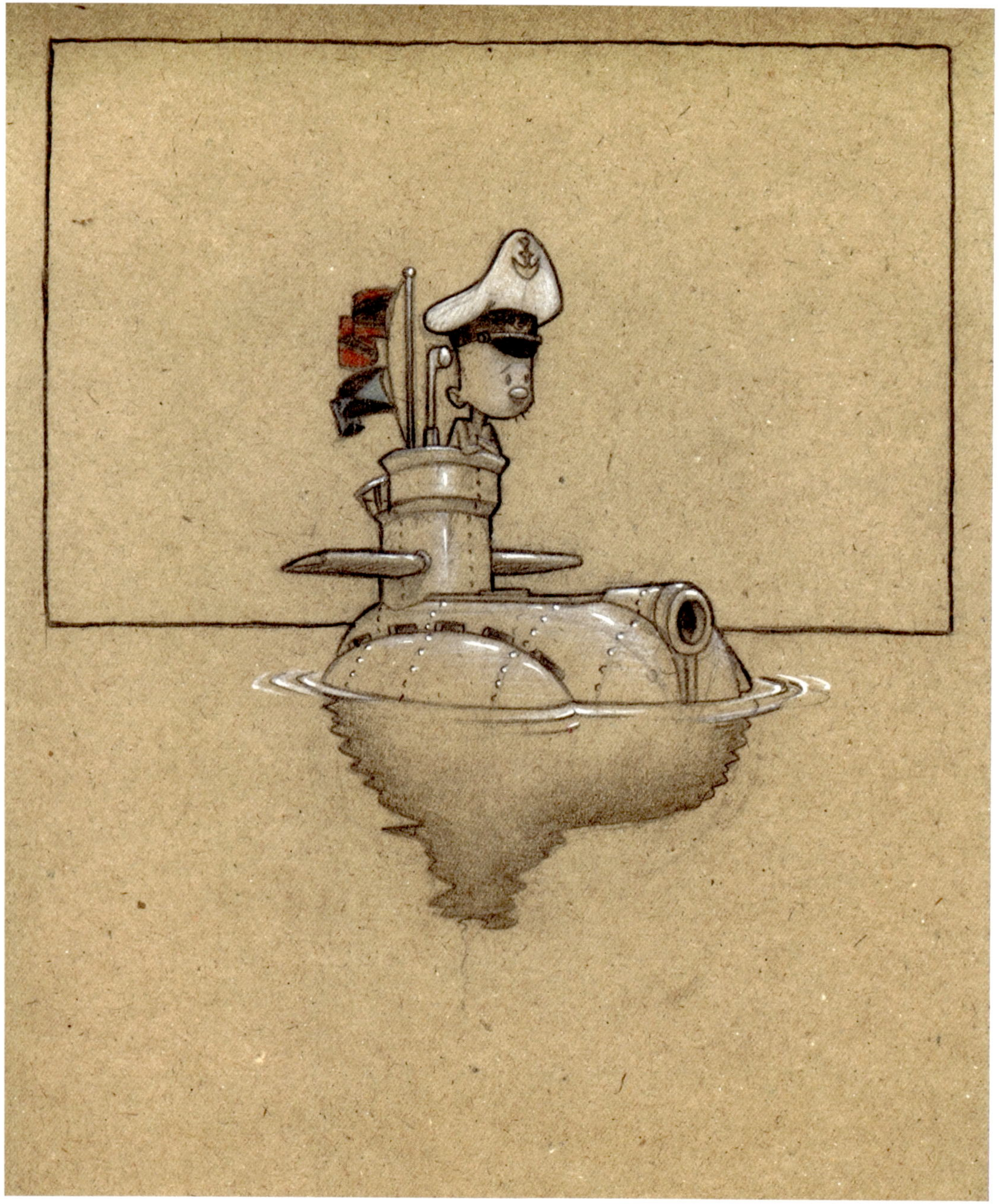

LEFT: matrose
TOP RIGHT: landser
DOWN RIGHT: tank

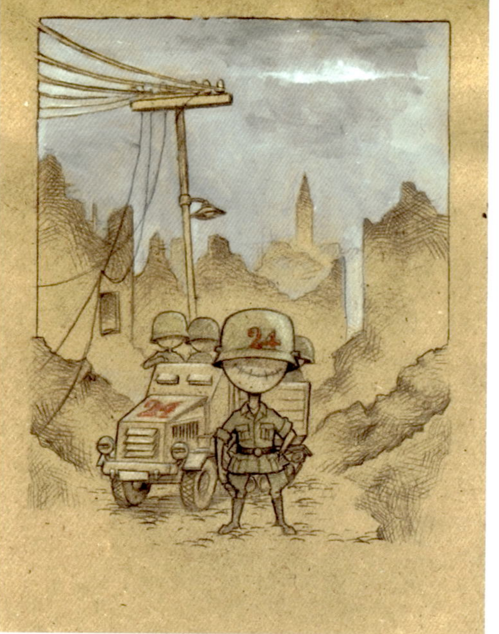

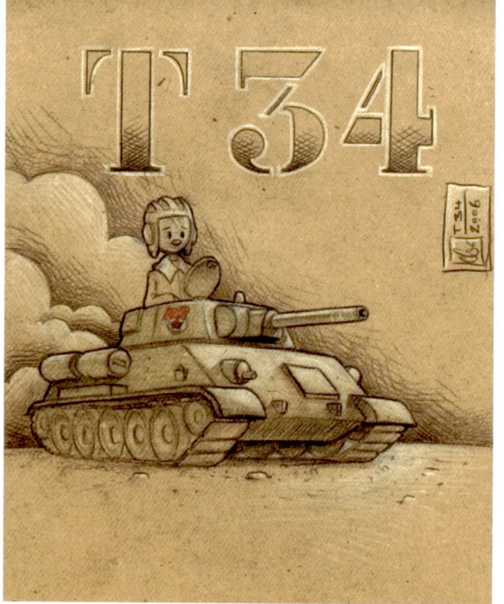

EN It still holds true that the illustrator works on commission and the artist on a free-lanced basis. What has changed is simply the number of media that we can use. In my opinion, the question whether a distinction between illustration and art exists, is necessary or obsolete, is not that relevant as many illustrations, due to the high quality of their execution, are in no way worse than independently produced works. On the other hand, many art objects do display a very illustrative character because of their style, which doesn't mean that they are commissioned works. In theory the distinction is based on the reason for the work's creation. I see myself as a king or a whore – different every day.

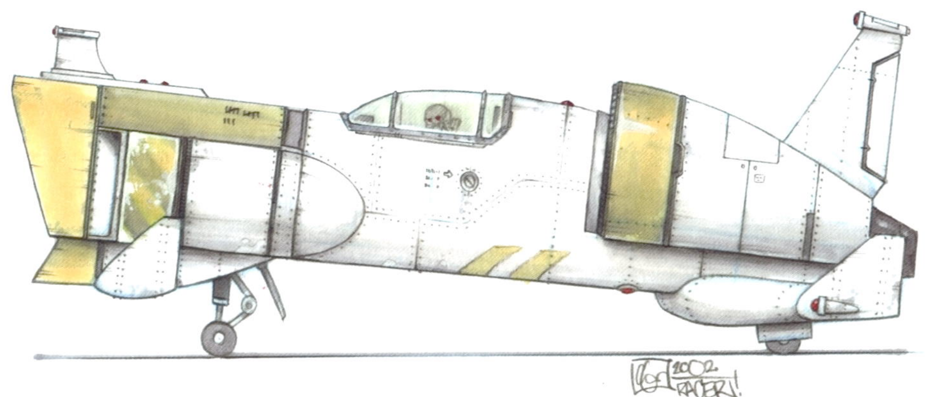

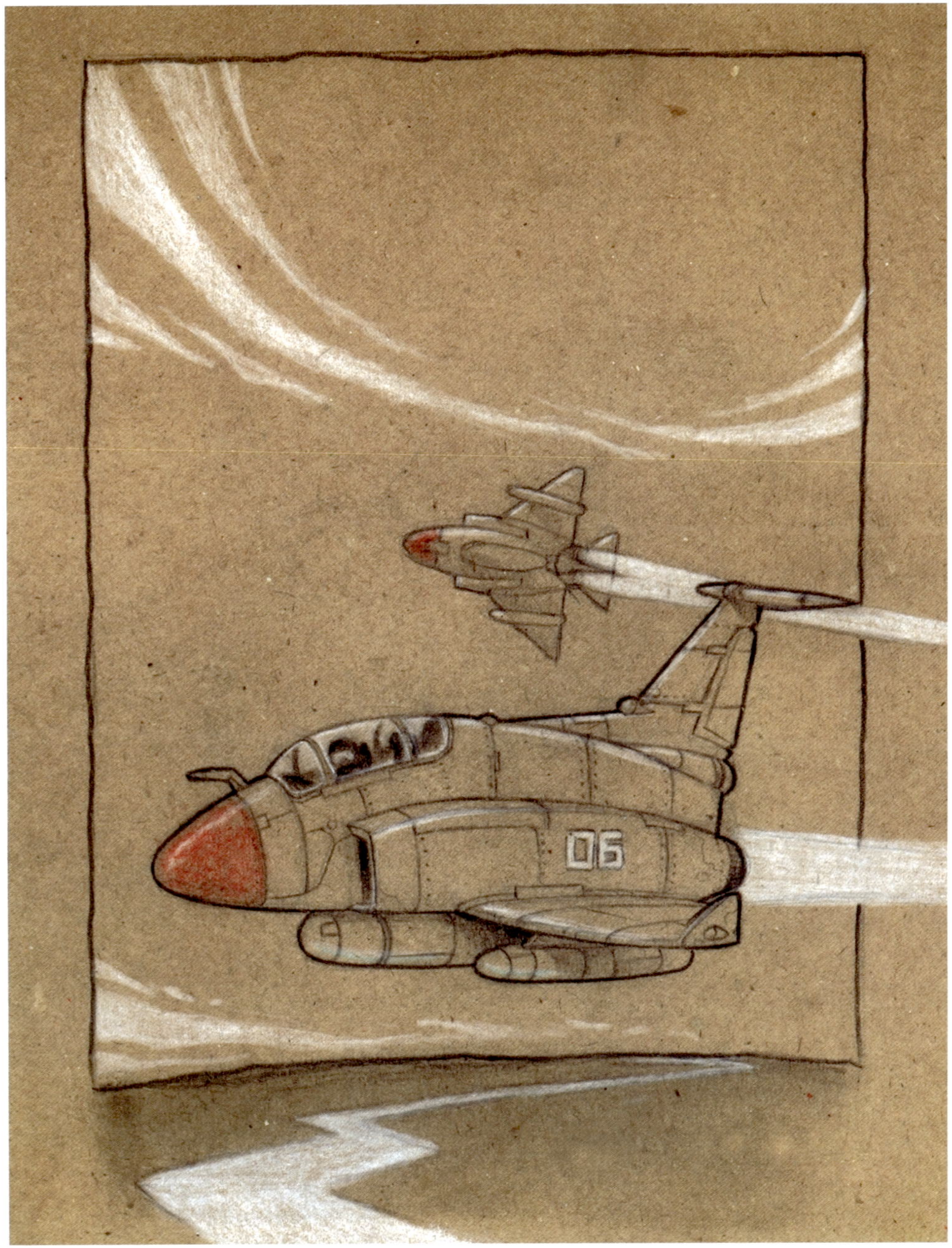

» JOSHUA HAGLER

NATIONALITY:	UNITED STATES
LOCATION:	SAN FRANCISCO | CA
PUBLICATIONS:	COMICS WORKED ON: THE BOY WHO MADE SILENCE | MY INNER BIMBO THE ESCAPIST | THE MISSIONARY (SPEAKEASY) "THE QUIET ENEMY" FIRST APPEARING IN KITCHEN SINK MAGAZINE ART APPEARED IN: THE GUARDIAN (UK) | AUSTRALIAN ART MARKET REPORT FOURTEEN HILLS LIT MAG | RAISEUP VOL. 2 | SPECTRUM AMERICAN ILLUSTRATION | CASTLEMAGAZINE.DE
REFERENCES:	DC COMICS | UPPER DECK | WIZARDS OF THE COAST HASBRO | DARK HORSE COMICS | ONI PRESS | IMAGE COMICS SPEAKEASY | LEVI STRAUSS | IRONPORT SYSTEMS ETC.
EXHIBITIONS:	WORD OF MOUTH – RHYS GALLERY – BOSTON ARTSFEST | NOMINATED FOR EMERGING ARTIST OF 2005 AWARD CENTER FOR DESIGN GALLERIA – SAN FRANCISCO CONTEMPORARY PERSPECTIVES – JURIED SHOW AT THE MUSEUM OF CONTEMPORARY ART – SANTA ROSA | CA
CONTACT:	5MINEDFIELDS@GMAIL.COM WWW.5MINEDFIELDS.COM
TECHNIQUE:	NOT SPECIFIED
BORN:	1979

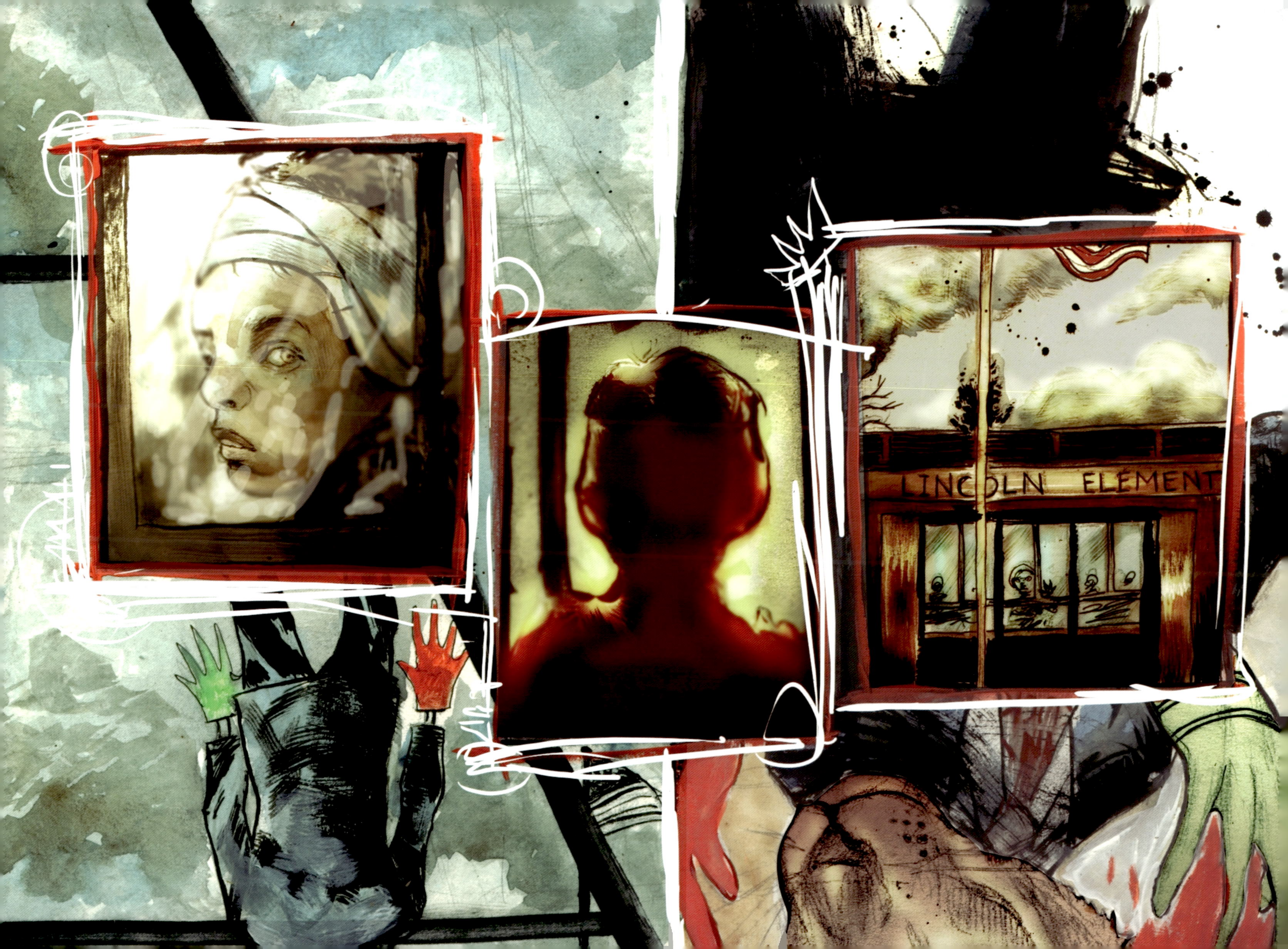
LINCOLN ELEMENT

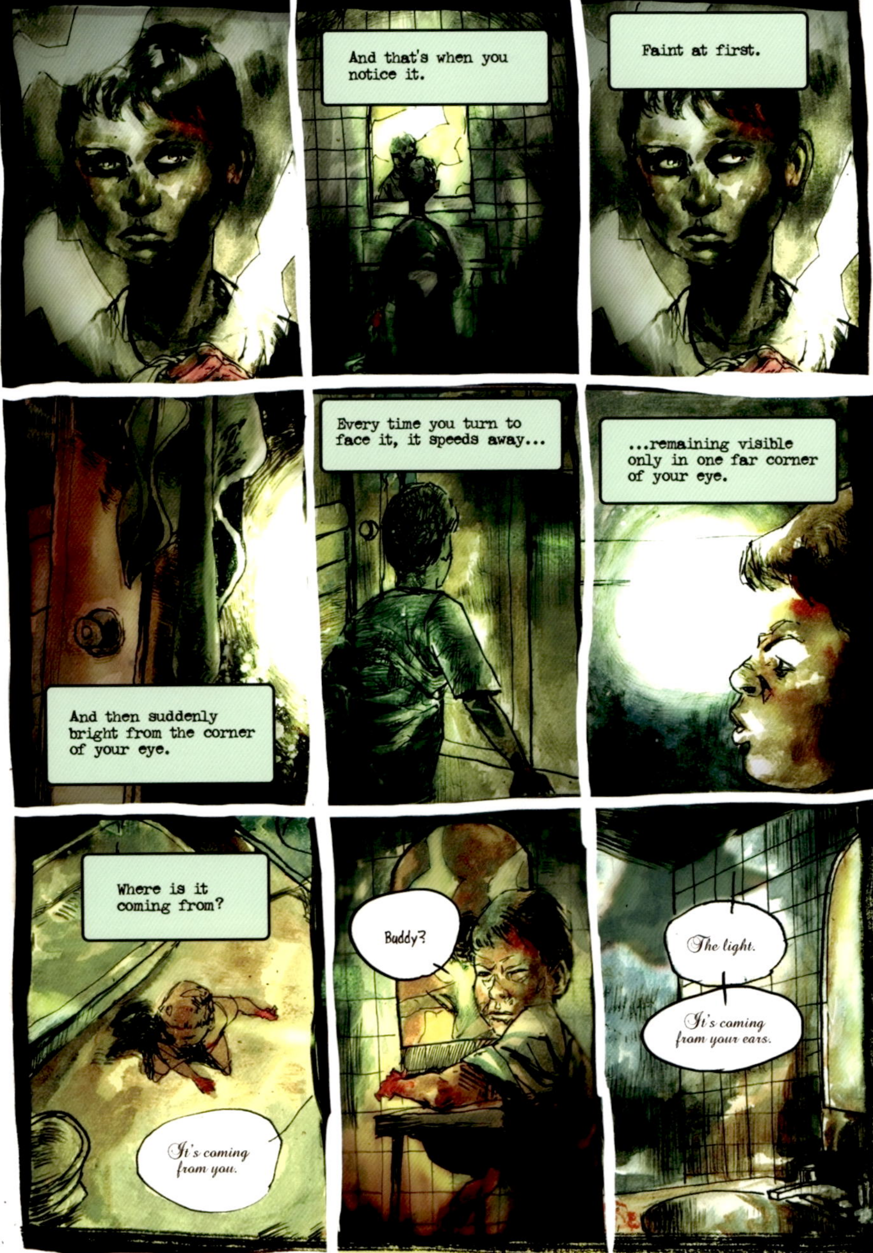

DE Ich habe an der University of Arizona in Tucson Illustration studiert und war damals überzeugt, dass ich mir genau damit meinen Lebensunterhalt verdienen möchte. Ich blickte auf zu Illustratoren wie Ralph Steadman, Marshall Arisman, Barron Storey und Dave McKean, die großen Einfluss auf die Illustration hatten. Ich glaubte naiverweise, dass wenn man nur überzeugend genug auftritt, könnte man im kommerziellen Kunstbetrieb arbeiten und das tun, was einem wichtig ist, und gleichzeitig mit der Unterstützung einer großen Zielgruppe rechnen, die die Arbeit als Illustrator automatisch mit sich bringt. Vielleicht war ich nicht überzeugend genug und habe deshalb diese Freiheit im Bereich Illustration nie entwickeln können. Selbst wenn ich heute als Illustrator arbeite, finde ich selten Erfüllung in den Aufträgen. Stil scheint bei der Arbeit, mit der man mich betraut, mehr zu zählen als Substanz. In den letzten Jahren habe ich auf ästhetische und konzeptionelle Art und Weise rebelliert gegen die Erwartungen, denen man im Bereich Illustration zwangsläufig begegnet. Bei meiner Comicbuchreihe *The Boy Who Made Silence* setze ich ein, was ich als Illustrator wie auch als Künstler gelernt habe, um meine Geschichte zu erzählen. In gewisser Weise ist es immer noch Illustration, da ich eine Geschichte illustriere, aber es ist eine selbst bestimmte, komplexe, von einer Idee angetriebene Arbeit und damit genau das, was mich an der bildenden Kunst anzieht. Ich denke, eine Abgrenzung zwischen Illustration und Kunst existiert und ist notwendig. Da diese Grenze häufig verwischt wird, mag sie hinfällig erscheinen, aber ich glaube, Arbeiten aus dieser „Grauzone“ sind weitgehend in der Minderheit im Vergleich zu den eindeutig der Kunst oder der Illustration zuzuordnenden Arbeiten. In der heutigen globalen Konsumgesellschaft ist die Unterscheidung zwischen einer vom Künstler bestimmten und einer

INTRODUCTION: from *the boy who made silence*
LEFT PAGE: from *the boy who made silence*
RIGHT PAGE:
LEFT: from *the boy who made silence*
RIGHT: from *the boy who made silence*

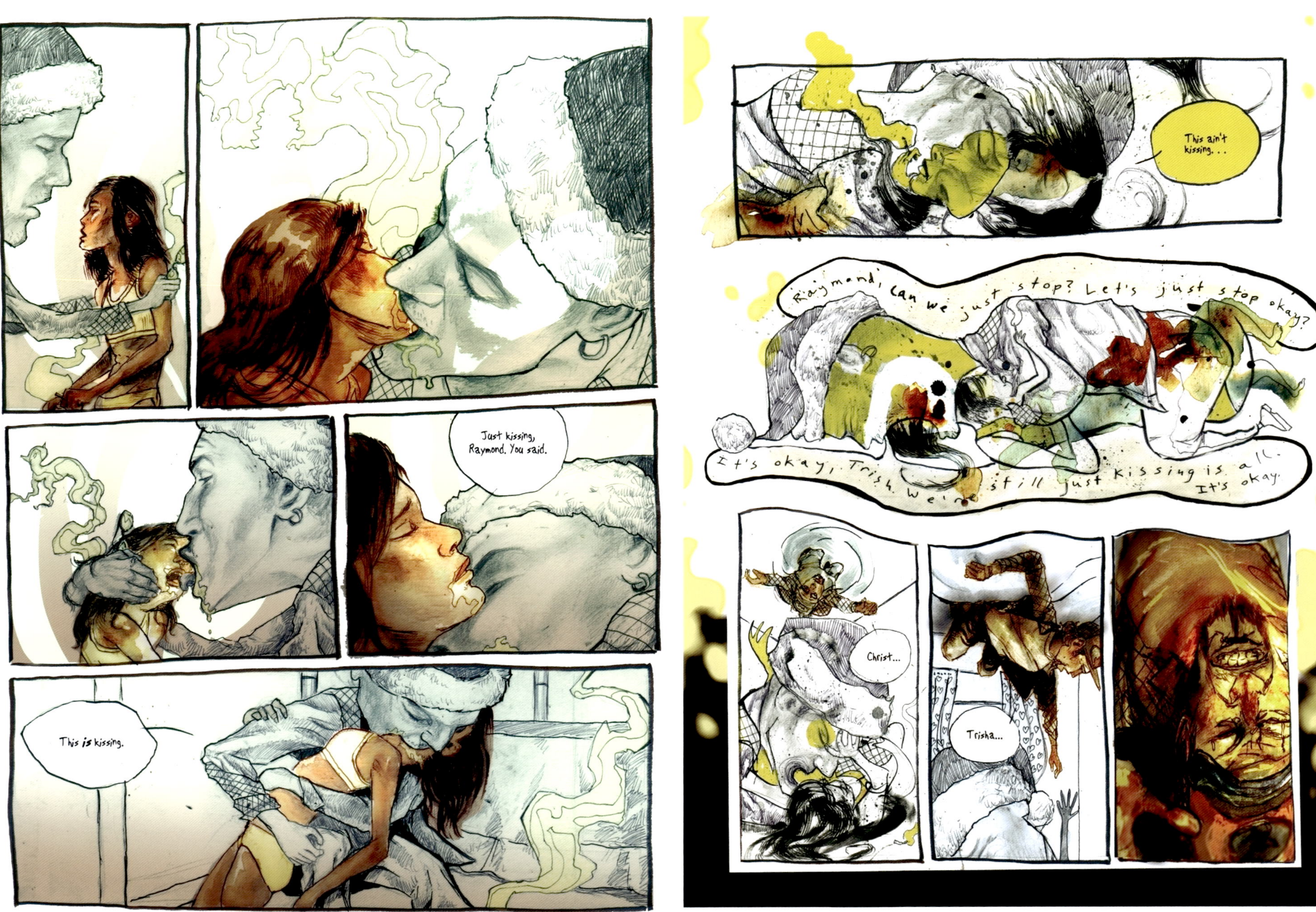
Just kissing, Raymond. You said.
This **is** kissing.
This ain't kissing. . .
Raymond, can we just stop? Let's just stop okay?
It's okay, Trish. We're still just kissing is all. It's okay.
Christ...
Trisha...

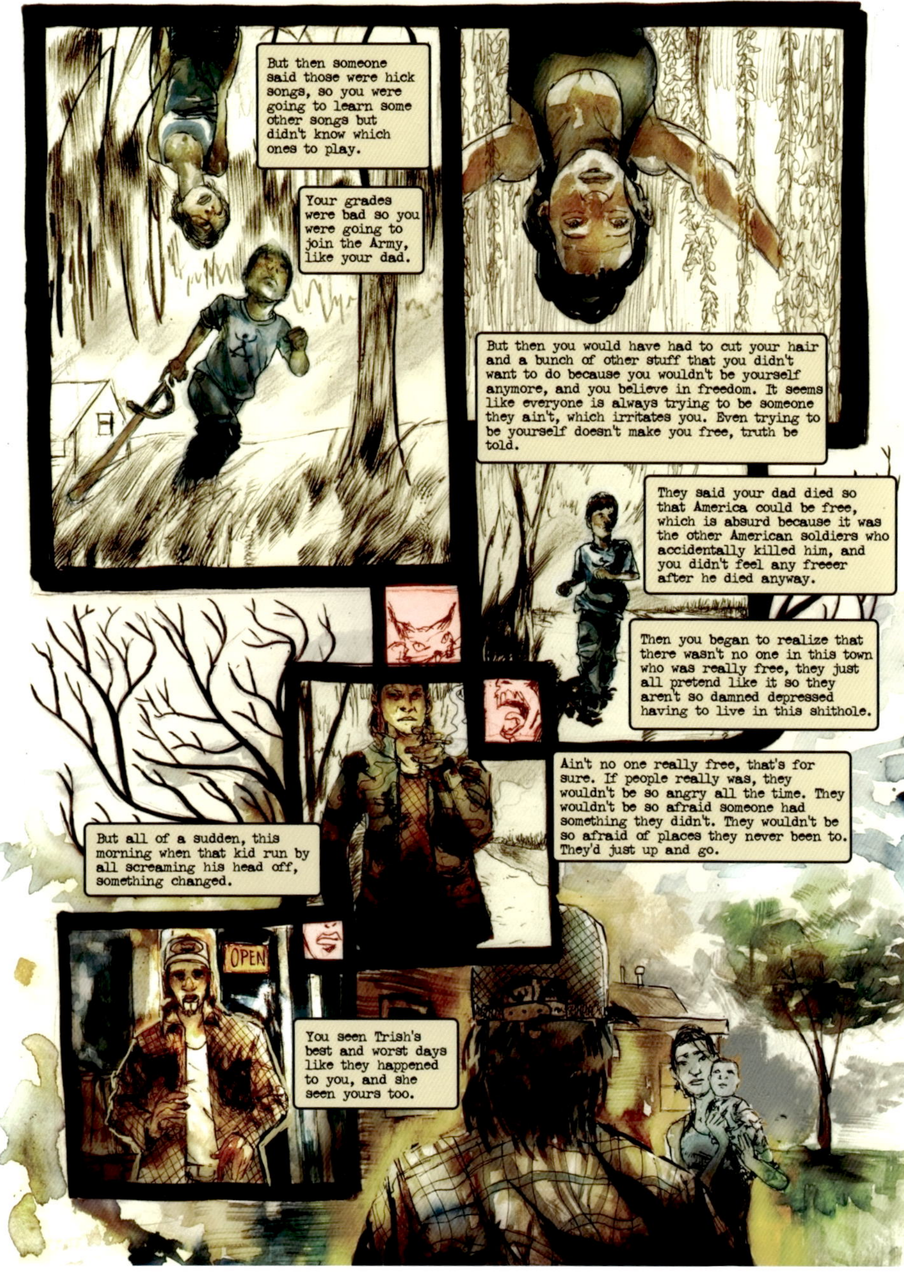

zweckbestimmten Bildsprache zur Steigerung von Unternehmensprofiten, nicht hinfällig, sondern relevanter denn je. Ich glaube, die Sache wird klarer, wenn wir den weiten Begriff „Kunst" im konkreteren Zusammenhang von „zeitgenössischer Kunst" betrachten. Diese existiert notwendigerweise an der Schnittstelle des gesellschaftlichen Dialogs und bestimmt häufig dessen Richtung, sie erforscht neues ästhetisches und konzeptionelles Terrain. Tut sie es nicht, ist sie keine zeitgenössische Kunst. Der Nebeneffekt eines Werks, das seine Aufgabe als zeitgenössische Kunst zufriedenstellend erfüllt, ist, dass es für das breite Publikum weniger zugänglich ist, da es mehr die intellektuelle und kulturelle Elite anspricht und die breite Masse hinter sich lässt. Zeitgenössische Kunst kommt nicht auf demokratischem Weg zustande. Illustration ist dagegen weitaus demokratischer als zeitgenössische Kunst. Sie verfehlt ihr Ziel etwas zu verbildlichen, wenn sie so komplex ist, dass sie sich dem Betrachter nicht schnell erschließt. Sie verlangt vorbehaltlos die uneingeschränkte Zustimmung des Publikums, um fortbestehen zu können. Und sie formt nicht den öffentlichen Geschmack, sie folgt ihm. Kein Artdirector wird die Dienste eines Illustrators in Anspruch nehmen, der nicht bereit ist ein Bild zu gestalten, das man binnen fünf Sekunden versteht. Illustration ist für ein breites Publikum zugänglich, aber sie ist normalerweise nicht in der Lage, das Bewusstsein eines Betrachters zu erweitern, da die im Bild enthaltene Idee sowohl durch die Erwartungen des nach Profit strebenden Kunden als auch durch die allgemeinen Erwartungen des Markts vorgefiltert wurden. Letzten Endes verstehe ich mich gleichermaßen als Künstler und als Illustrator.

LEFT PAGE: from *the boy who made silence*
RIGHT PAGE:
LEFT: from *the boy who made silence*
RIGHT: from *the boy who made silence*

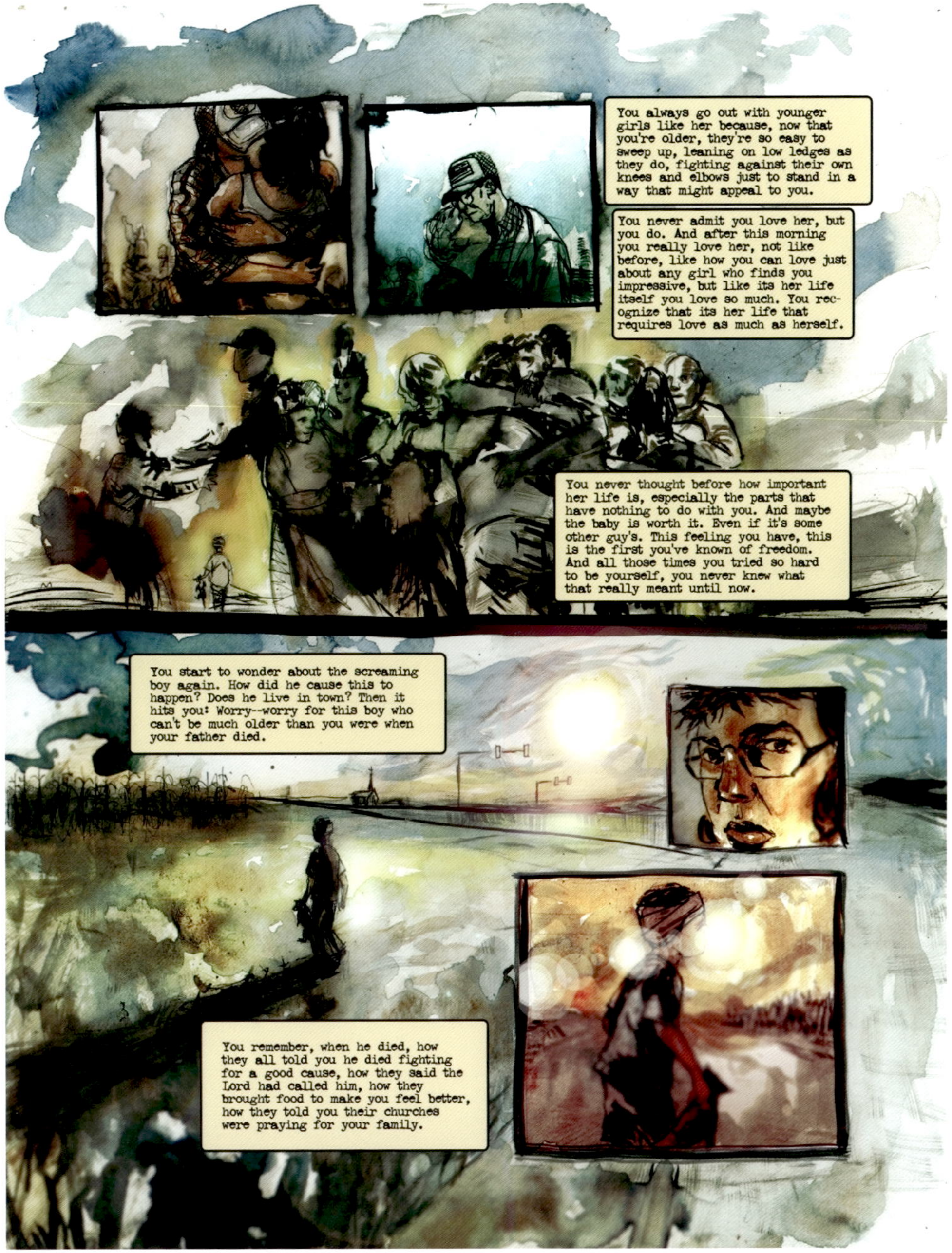

You always go out with younger girls like her because, now that you're older, they're so easy to sweep up, leaning on low ledges as they do, fighting against their own knees and elbows just to stand in a way that might appeal to you.

You never admit you love her, but you do. And after this morning you really love her, not like before, like how you can love just about any girl who finds you impressive, but like its her life itself you love so much. You recognize that its her life that requires love as much as herself.

You never thought before how important her life is, especially the parts that have nothing to do with you. And maybe the baby is worth it. Even if it's some other guy's. This feeling you have, this is the first you've known of freedom. And all those times you tried so hard to be yourself, you never knew what that really meant until now.

You start to wonder about the screaming boy again. How did he cause this to happen? Does he live in town? Then it hits you: Worry--worry for this boy who can't be much older than you were when your father died.

You remember, when he died, how they all told you he died fighting for a good cause, how they said the Lord had called him, how they brought food to make you feel better, how they told you their churches were praying for your family.

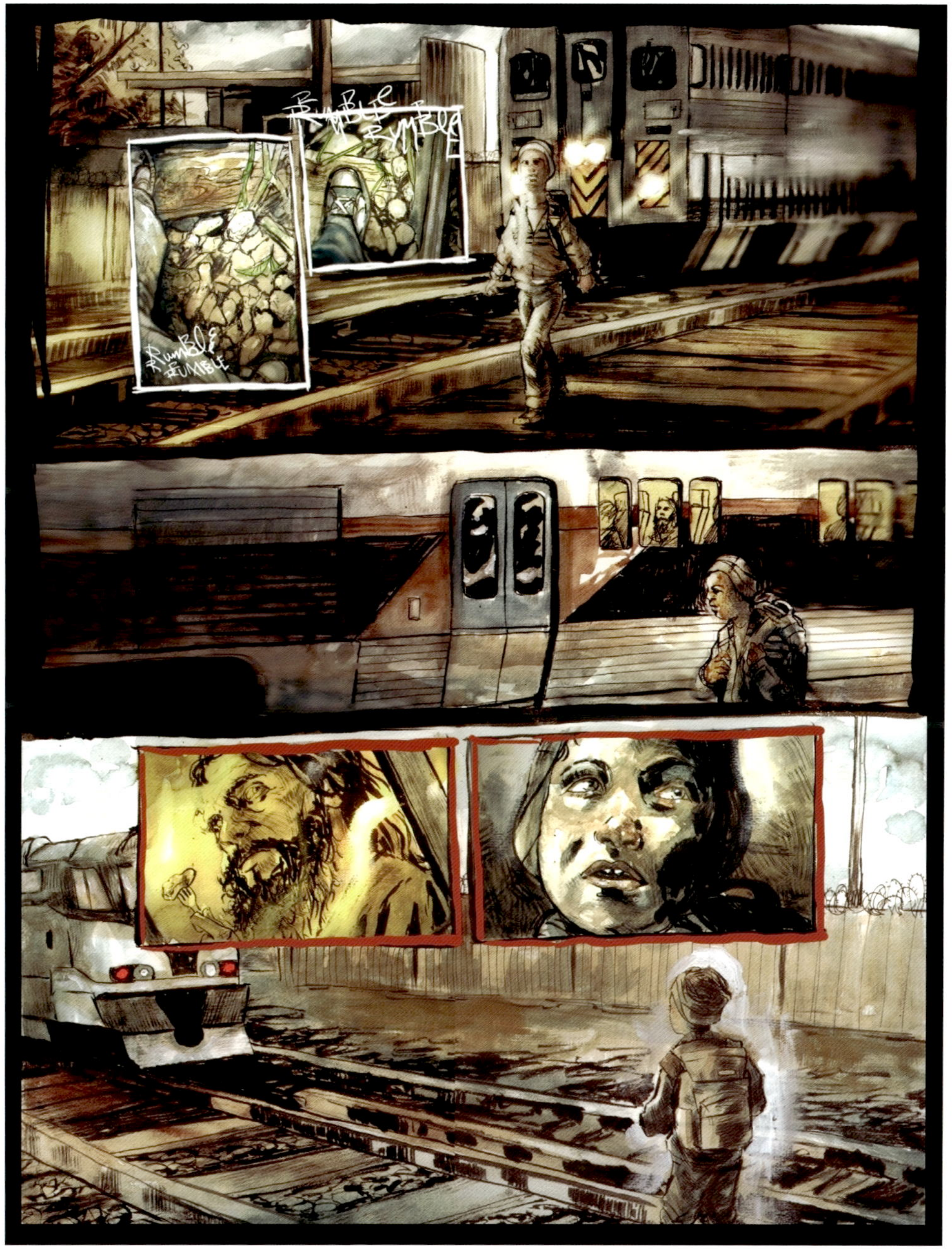

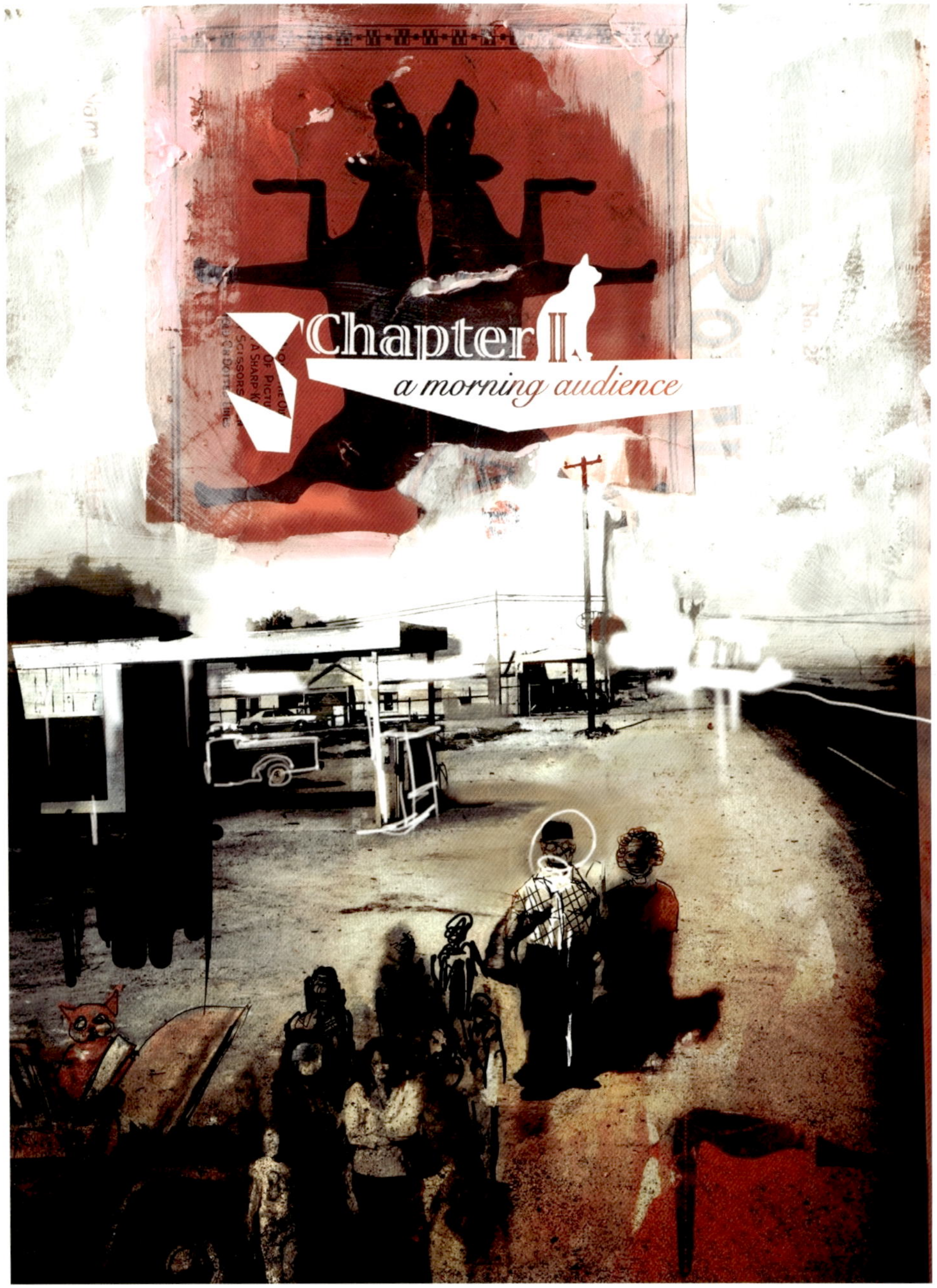

Chapter II
a morning audience

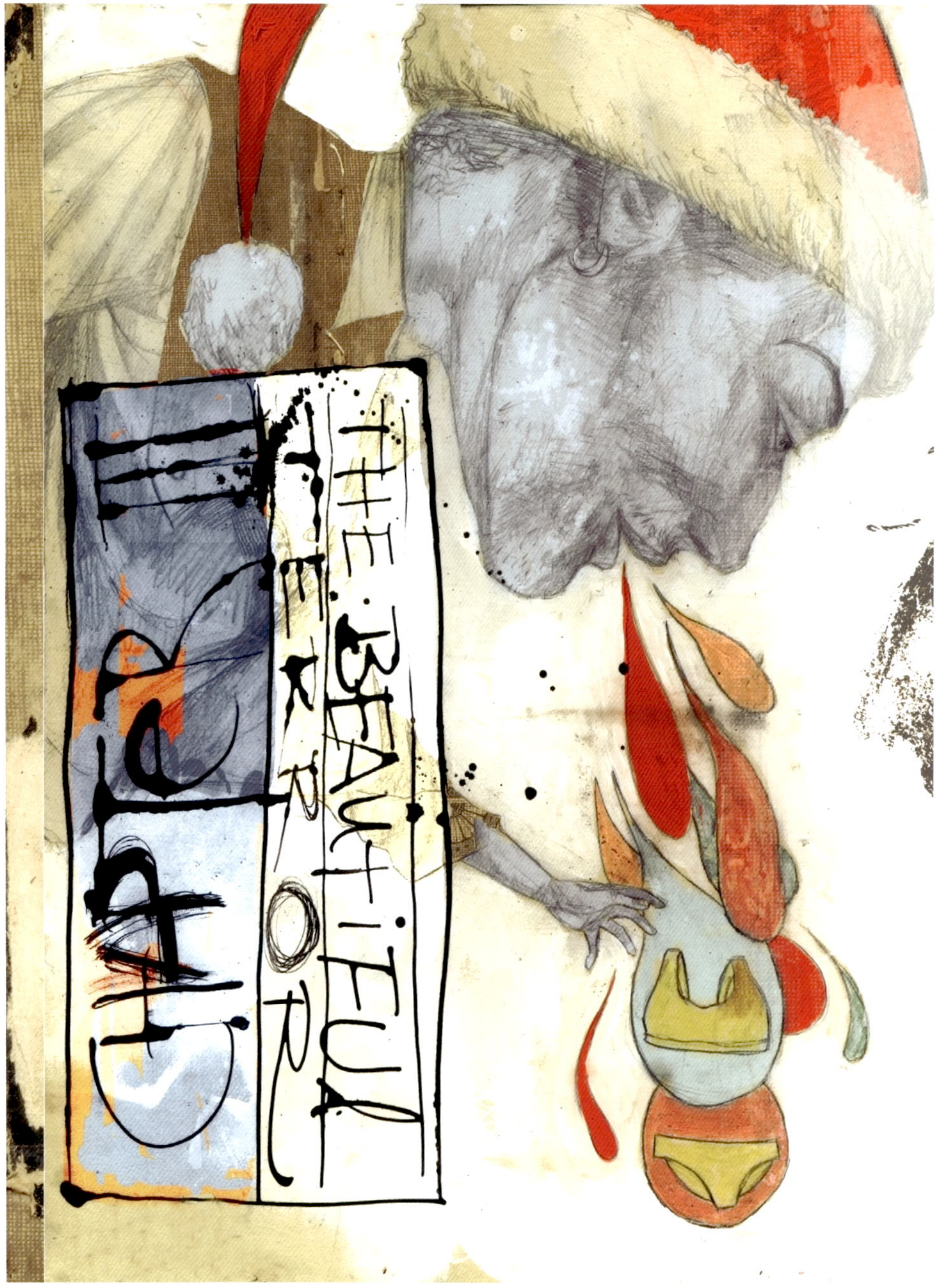

EN I got my degree in illustration at the University of Arizona in Tucson and had, at the time, believed, that this is what I wanted to do for living. I looked up to illustrators such as Ralph Steadman, Marshall Arisman, Barron Storey, and Dave McKean who have strong voices within the field of illustration. I had naively believed that if your voice is strong enough, you could work within the commercial art world being able to do the kind of work that's important to you and have the benefit of the large audience that illustration has built into it. Perhaps my voice was not strong enough and this is why I could never find that freedom within illustration. Even when I do illustration work now, I rarely find fulfillment in the assignments. Style seems to be of higher value than substance with the work that I get assigned to do. Over the past couple of years, I've had a sort of aesthetic and conceptual rebellion against the expectations that are built into the illustration world. With my comic book series "The Boy Who Made Silence," I'm using what I've learned as both an illustrator and a fine artist and applying that to the story that I want to tell. In a sense, it's still illustration, because I'm illustrating a story, but it is self-initiated, complex, concept-driven work, which is what attracts me to the fine art world. I think a differentiation between illustration and fine art is present and necessary. Because the differentiation is often blurred, it might seem to be obsolete, but I think work being created in the "blurry zone" is in the vast minority compared to the work being created in the hard and fast "illustration" or "fine art" zones. In the global consumer economy, the difference between artist-determined imagery and committee-determined imagery used to increase corporate profit, the differentiation between fine art and illustration is not obsolete, but, on the contrary, more relevant than ever. I think the case is made more obvious when we discuss the broad term "fine art" within the more specific context of "contemporary art." Contemporary art necessarily exists on the cutting edge of and often defines the direction of social dialogue and explores new aesthetic and conceptual territory. To fail at this is to fail at making contemporary art. The side effect of creating work that functions well as contemporary art is that it's less accessible to the general public because it appeals more to the intellectual and cultural elite, leaving the general public behind. It does not come into existence through democratic channels. Illustration, on the other hand, is far more democratic than contemporary art. It fails at being illustration if it is too complex to digest quickly. It implicitly asks for majority permission of the audience to perpetuate. It does not form public taste, it follows it. No art director is going to call on the service of an illustrator who is not willing to make an image that is seen and understood within five seconds. It is palatable to a larger audience, but is usually unable to compel the viewer toward a broader consciousness because the ideas contained in the image have been filtered both by the expectations of the profit-seeking client and the general expectations of the marketplace. Finally I see myself as an illustrator as well as an artist.

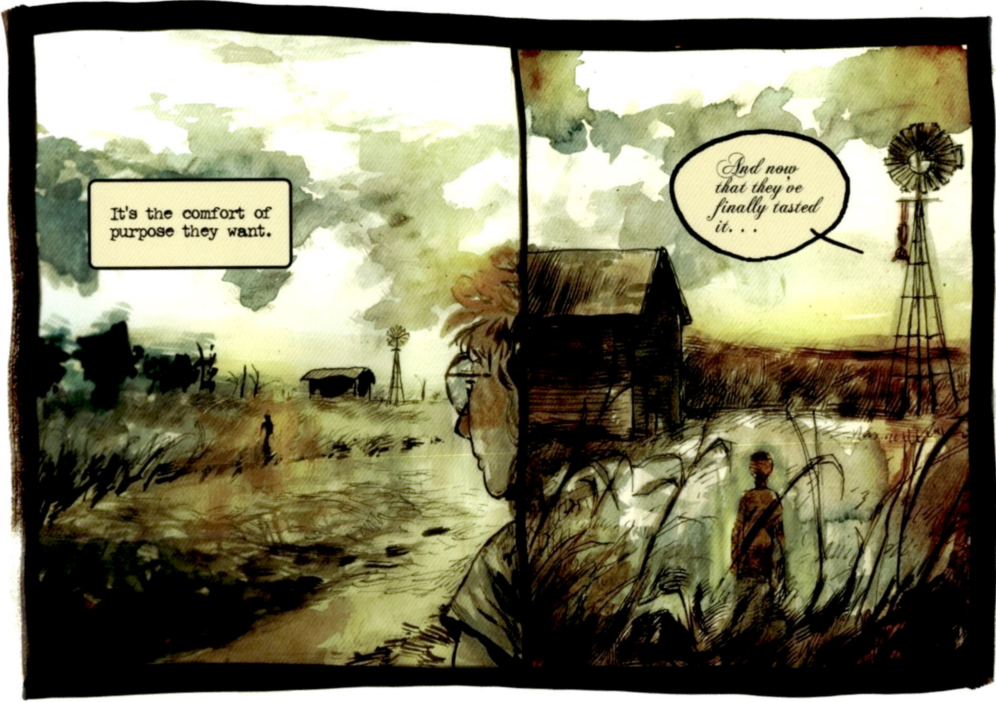

LEFT PAGE / LEFT:
from *the boy who made silence*
LEFT PAGE / RIGHT:
from *the boy who made silence*
RIGHT PAGE:
TOP RIGHT:
from *the boy who made silence*

» CONTENT PROVIDER IMAGE GROUP

NATIONALITY:	NONE (OF REAL INTEREST)
LOCATION:	DIVERSE
REFERENCES:	A NUMBER OF CONTRIBUTIONS TO THE EVER GROWING ART-LOSS-REGISTER
CONTACT:	WWW.CPI-GROUP.BLOGSPOT.COM
TECHNIQUE:	MIXED MEDIA ON VARIOUS SUPPORT
BORN:	IN THE INFAMOUS 20TH CENTURY

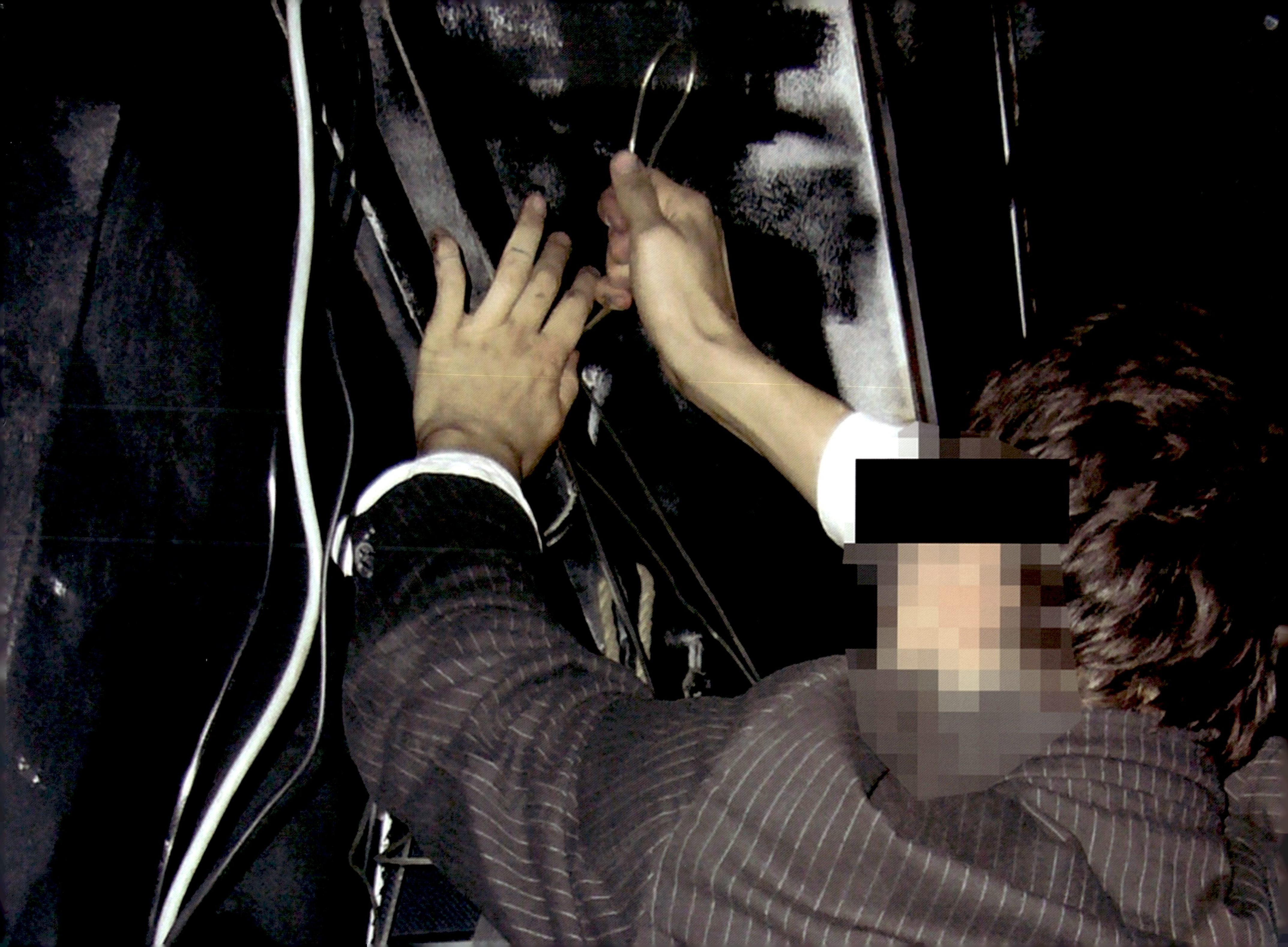

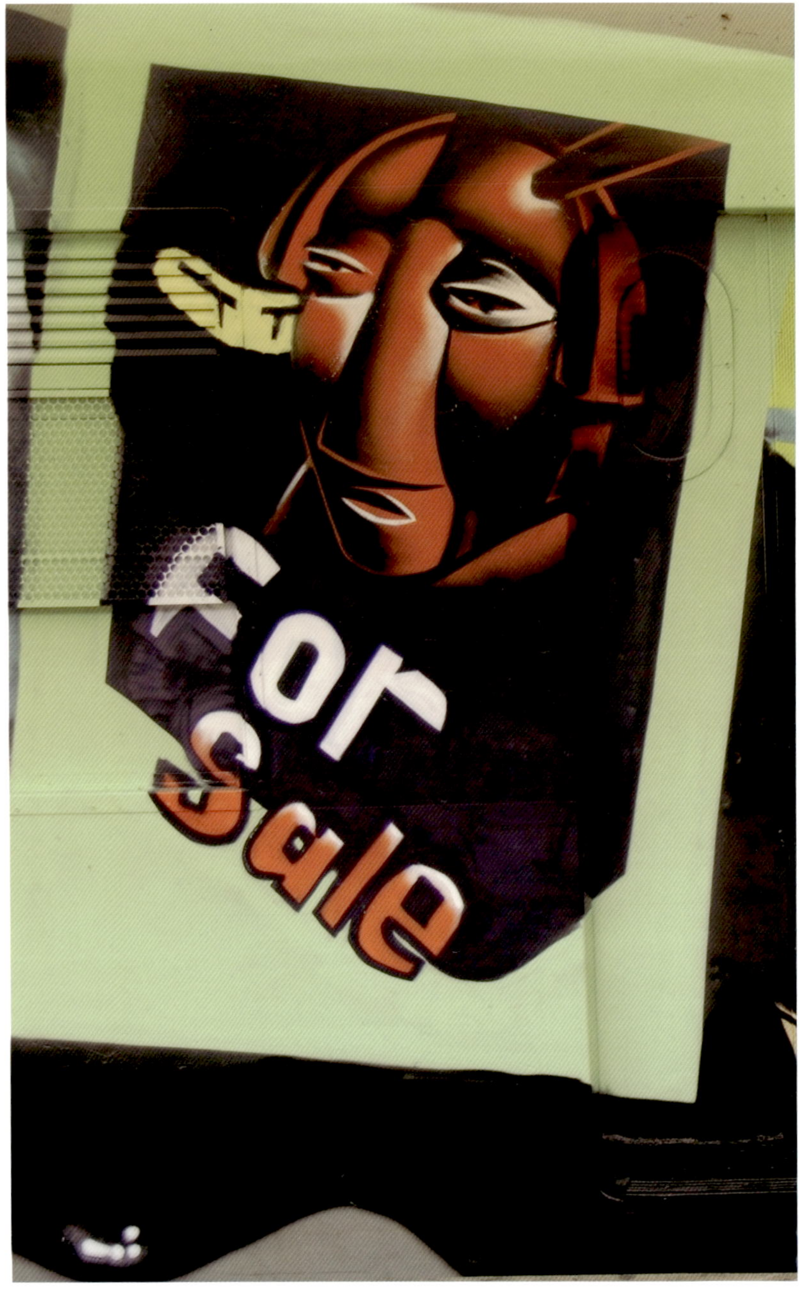
For
Sale

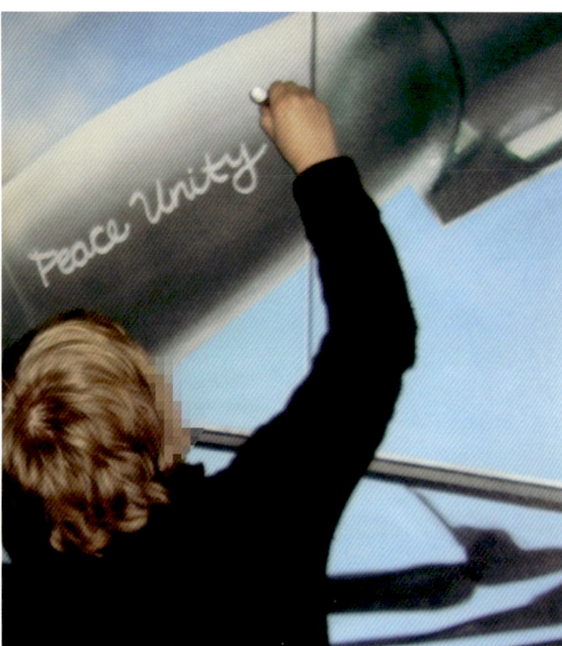
Peace Unity

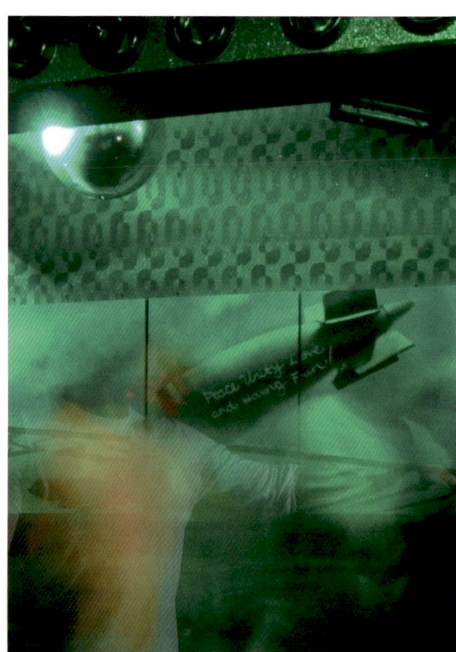

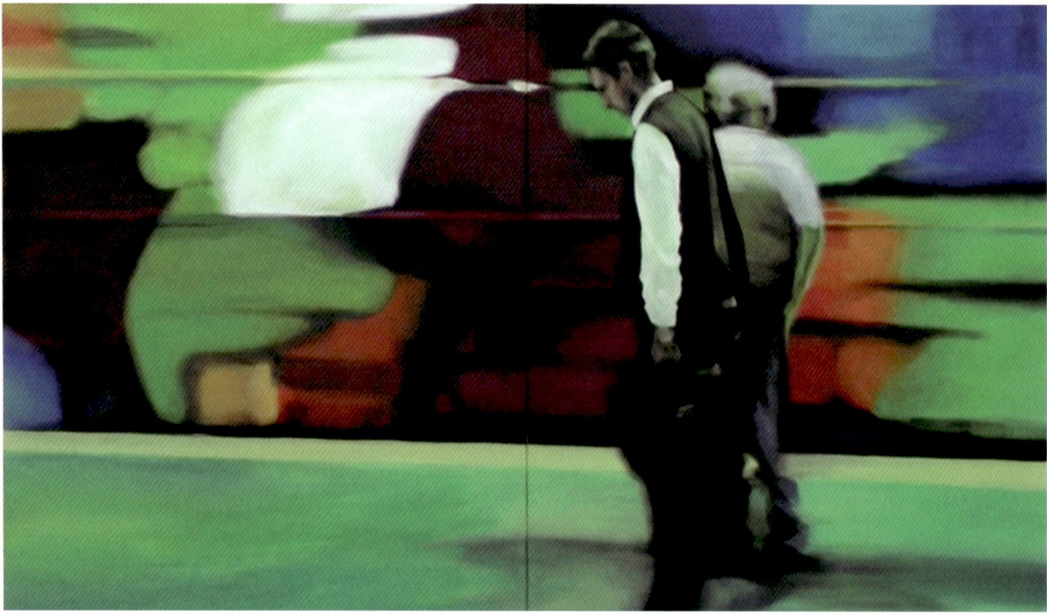

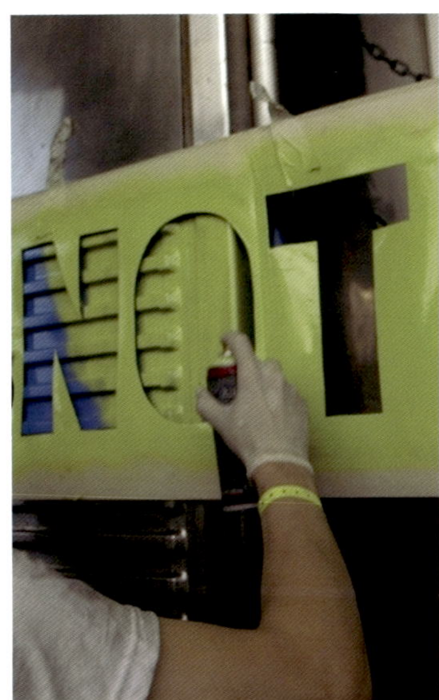

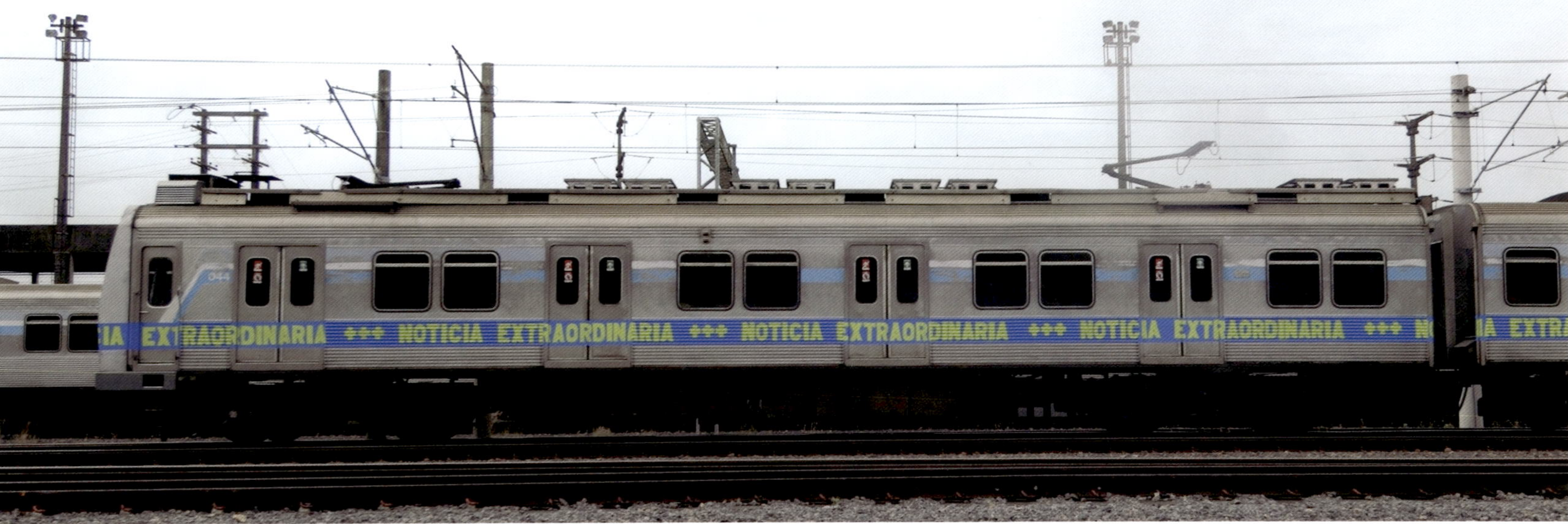

DE Ich muss wohl einer Streife der Londoner Transit Police einen verdächtigen Eindruck gemacht haben. Zwei Beamte durchsuchten mich und meine Tasche, deren Inhalt ihren Eindruck offensichtlich noch verstärkte, und befragten mich, wobei sie die Daten und Angaben in einen tragbaren Minicomputer eintippten. „Name? Adresse? Ausweisnummer?", damit konnte ich dienen. „Self defined ethnicity?" – meinen Sie Rasse? Diese Frage stellt die Polizei in Deutschland seit einiger Zeit eher selten. Ich nutzte die Gelegenheit und machte darüber einen Scherz, der Lacherfolg war mäßig. Sie zeigten mir die verschiedenen Möglichkeiten, die der kleine Computer bereithält: „Caucasian", „asian", „african" und viele mehr. Die weiteren Assoziationen, die sich beim historisch interessierten Deutschen einstellen können, waren zu meiner Enttäuschung nicht darunter. Bald erteilten mir die Polizisten mit einem gönnerhaften Spruch à la „Wir wissen, was Sie hier vorhatten und könnten Sie jetzt verhaften, aber wir wollen mal nicht so sein", einen Platzverweis. Zur Bestätigung meiner Durchsuchung bekam ich eine Art Kassenzettel ausgedruckt: „Damage caused: none" hatten sie sich darauf selbst bestätigt und während meiner Bemerkungen zur Weltgeschichte bei der Kategorie „self defined ethnicity" eigenmächtig „W9: Any other white" ausgewählt. Ihr Computer hatte für alles eine Lösung und ohne ihn hätten sie ihre Arbeit wohl unmöglich machen können. Diese kleine Episode kommt mir in den Sinn, wenn ich mich bei einer Fragestellung wie der hier zugrunde liegenden festlegen muss. Es mag anderen nicht so gehen – bei mir provoziert der Wunsch nach Reinheitsgeboten und Zugehörigkeitsdefinitionen immer eine Trotzreaktion, obwohl vorauszusehen ist, dass die pflichtbewussten Beamtenseelen die Definition dann eben selbst vornehmen.

INTRODUCTION: in action
LEFT PAGE:
LEFT: for sale (with nunca, spraypaint on commuter train)
TOP LEFT:
peace, unity, action
TOP RIGHT:
peace, unity, love, and having fun (spraypaint and marker on canvas, handwriting by k.u.s.s.)
DOWN RIGHT:
circumvesuviana (acrylic on canvas)
RIGHT PAGE:
extraordinaria metro (spraypaint on metro train)

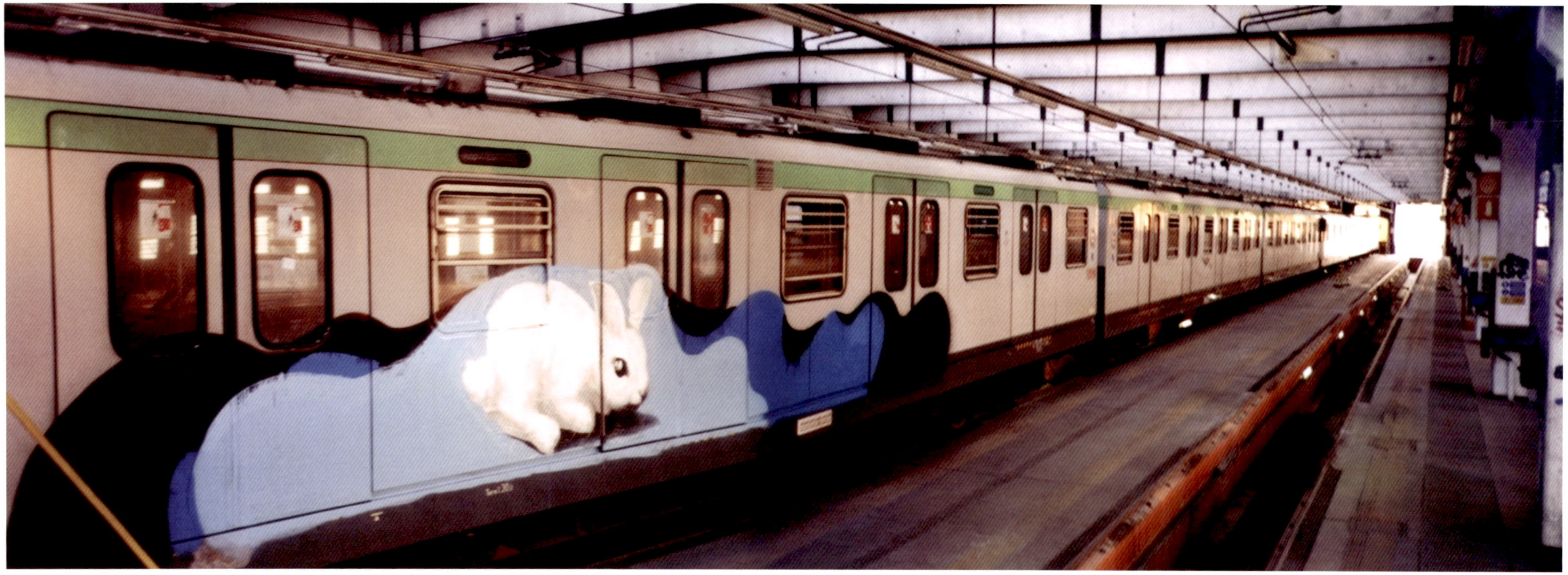

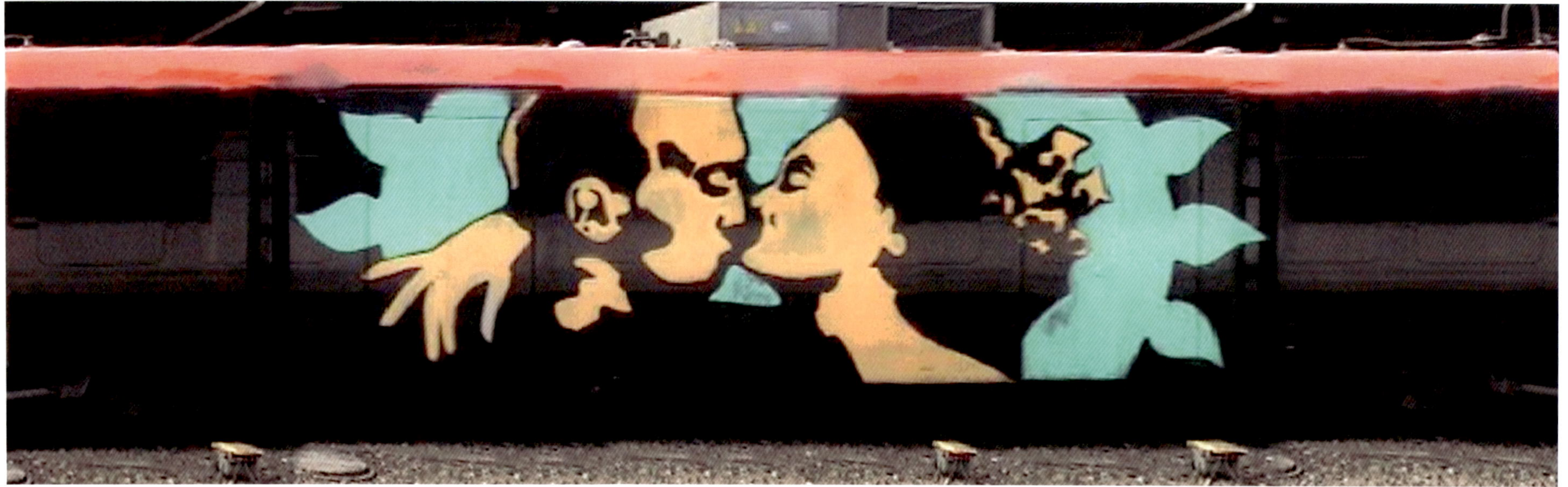

I must have looked suspicious to a London Transit Police patrol. Two officers searched my bag and body, and what they found obviously confirmed this impression. They questioned me, while feeding a portable mini-computer with my data and answers. "Name? Address? Passport number?" I could deliver. "Self defined ethnicity?" – You mean race? A question German police would hardly ever ask you. I answered with a little joke about that very fact, but my audience was not amused. They showed me the various options available on their little computer: "Caucasian," "Asian," "African," and many more. Various other options that a German person with an interest in history may have come up with were, to my disappointment, not on the menu. Shortly thereafter the officers officially let me go with some patronizing remark, like: "We know what you were up to and we could easily arrest you for that, but we'll let you go." They simply printed a little receipt documenting their search. They awarded themselves a "Damage caused: none," and during my remarks on German history they had arbitrarily selected: "W9: Any other white." Their computer obviously had a solution for anything, and without it they probably wouldn't have been able to do their work at all. This little episode comes to my mind every time I have to face a question like the one we try to answer here. Others might be able to cope easily with it, but for me the ever-present calls for purity and affiliation makes me defiant, even though it's perfectly clear that the conscientious bureaucrat will find a proper definition by themselves in those cases.

LEFT PAGE:
TOP:
follow me
(spraypaint, paper, enamel
on subway train)
BOTTOM:
kiss me, kiss me
(photoshop collage
of digital video stills)
RIGHT PAGE:
vietato venezia
(acrylic on canvas)

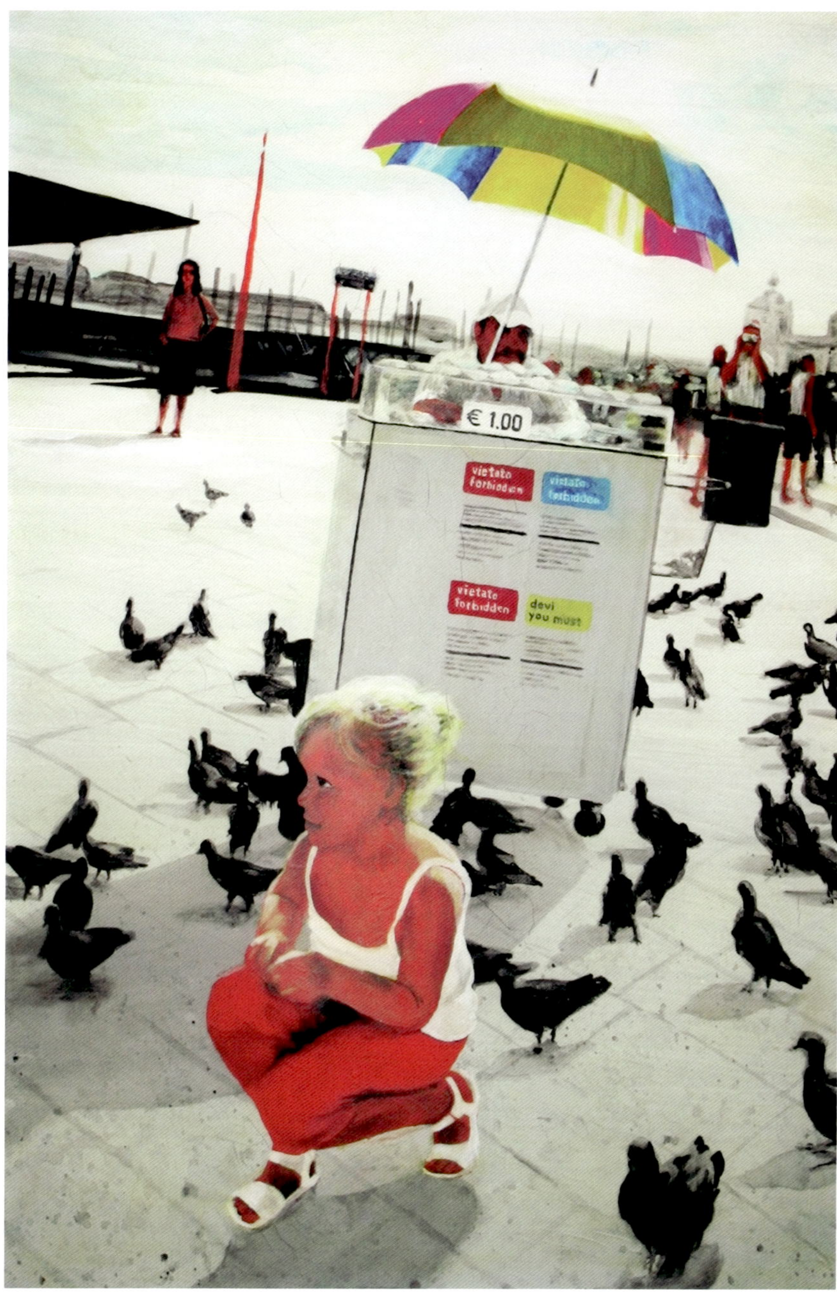

»VANDATA [MICHAEL MATTHIAS]

NATIONALITY: GERMAN

LOCATION: HAMBURG

PUBLICATIONS: NOVUM | PAGE | MAX | BOLERO

REFERENCES: RED BULL | PREMIERE | SÜDDEUTSCHE ZEITUNG

EXHIBITIONS: BLACK ON WHITE – MUNICH
VANDATA WALLPAINTING – MUNICH UNDERGROUND

CONTACT: PHONE +49 (0) 176 450 32 907
MICKEY@VANDATA.DE

TECHNIQUE: DIGITAL | SCRATCHY | PENCIL
STRUCTURES | FOUND STUFF

BORN: 1979

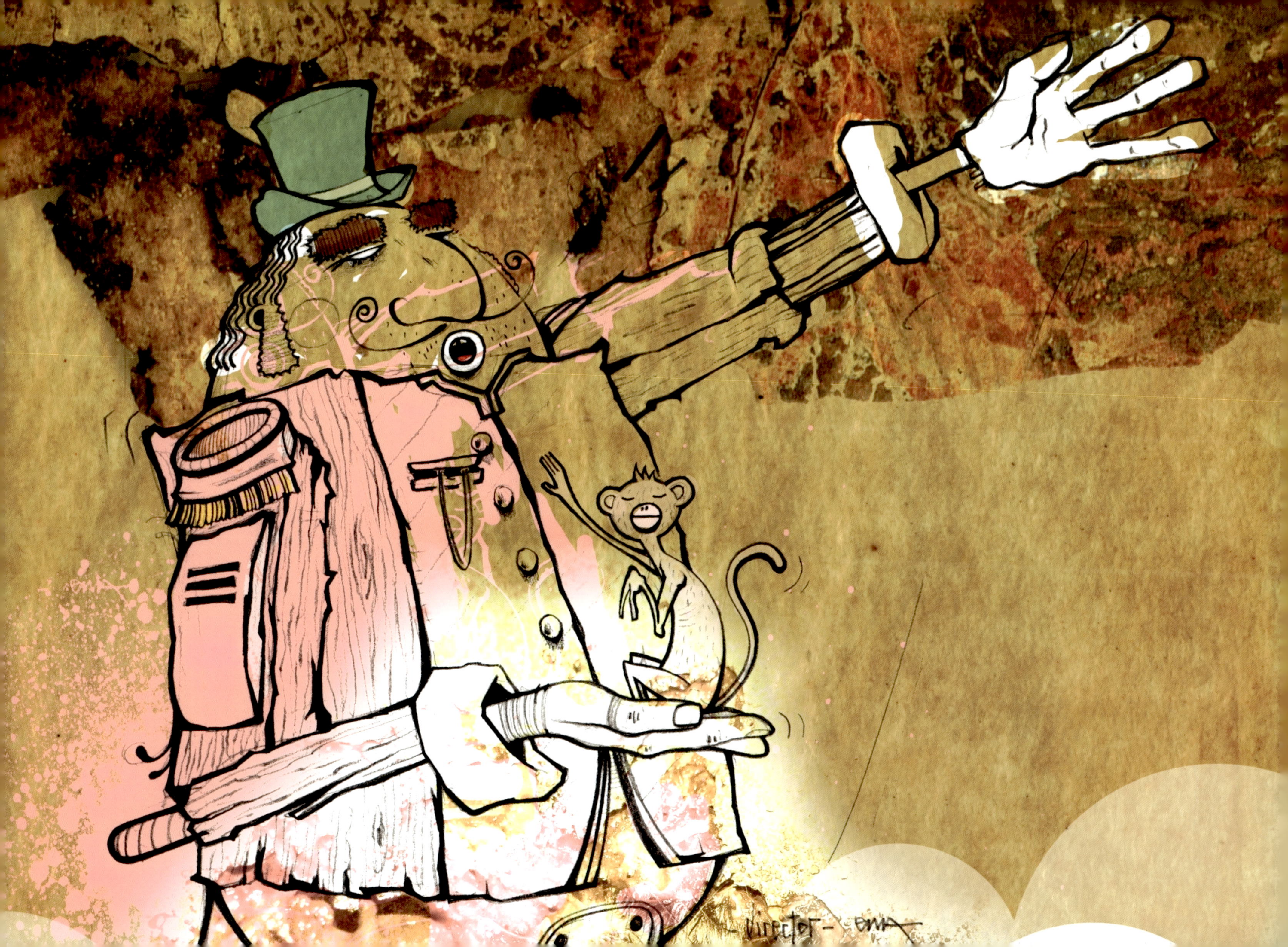
Director-

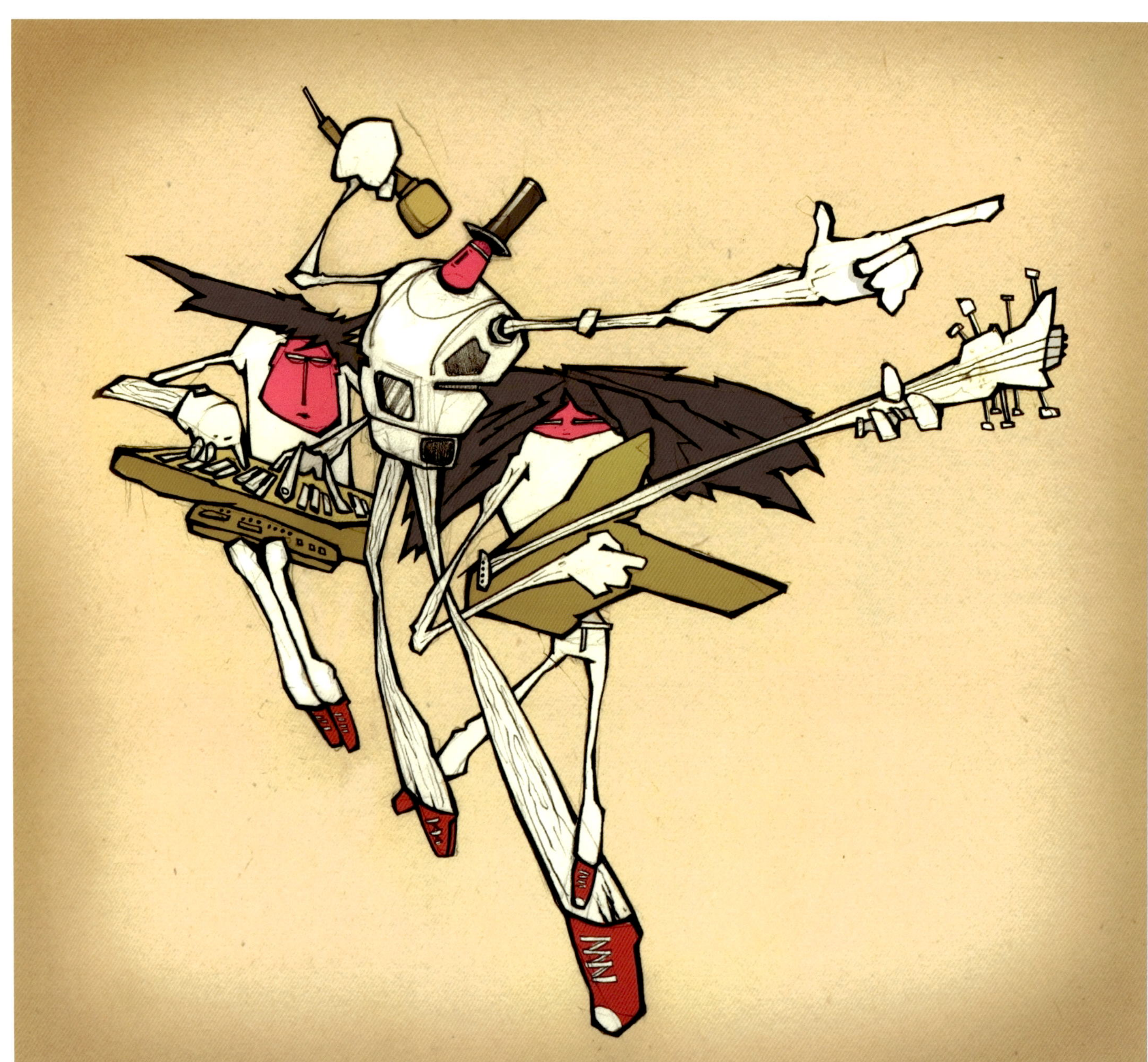

INTRODUCTION: director
LEFT PAGE: the unforgotten
RIGHT PAGE: blockwurst

DE Kunst behauptet oft das Gegenteil zu sein und doch betreiben viele selbst ernannte Künstler ein noch viel subtileres Spiel der allgemeinen Anpassung, als ihnen vielleicht selbst bewusst ist. Ich denke, dass kein Mensch vom Urteil anderer unabhängig ist, sofern er kein Autist ist. Deshalb produziert ein Künstler, genauso wie ein Illustrator, nichts frei von Gedanken an spätere Betrachter. Wenn man sich einzig und allein mit sich selbst und der Kunst austauschen müsste, als führe man eine Beziehung zu einer Frau ohne einen weiteren anderen Menschen auf der Welt – oh Gott, wie langweilig das wäre. Folglich gehe ich davon aus, dass beide Gruppen – Illustratoren sowie Künstler –, jede auf ihre Art, mehr oder weniger für eine Zielgruppe arbeitet. Früher fanden Künstler am Hof des Königs ihre Zielgruppe und ihre Auftraggeber – heute sind Marken und die Werbung die Geldgeber der Illustratoren und Mäzene und reiche Säcke die der Künstler. Dabei haben sich Letztere in den vergangenen Jahren immer mehr vermischt. Ich denke, dass die Unterscheidung zwischen diesen beiden Bereichen vor allem für Kunstsammler und Investoren wichtig ist, denn sie wollen ja mit der massenweise vervielfältigten Schnelllebigkeit der Illustration nichts zu tun haben, weil sonst das Elitäre und somit das Rare, also Teure, schwer Erreichbare fehlt. Die Künstler selbst stehen der Illustration vielleicht gar nicht so feindlich gegenüber – werden aber durch diesen Zugzwang in eine konfrontative Rolle gepresst. Das Wort „art" ist mit so viel Schund behaftet. Also bin ich wohl eher Illustrator – diese Schublade ist noch ein wenig unverbrauchter.

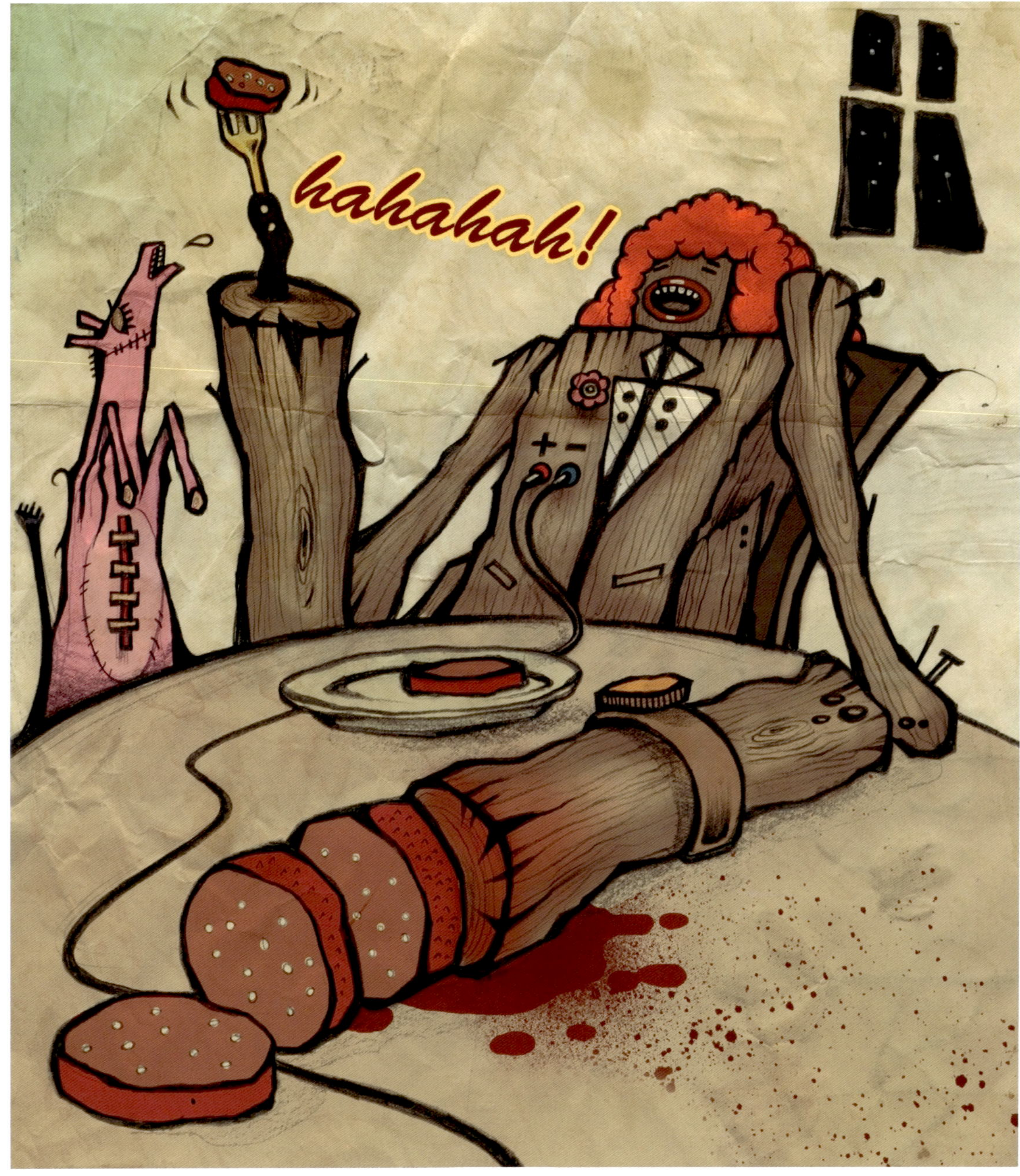

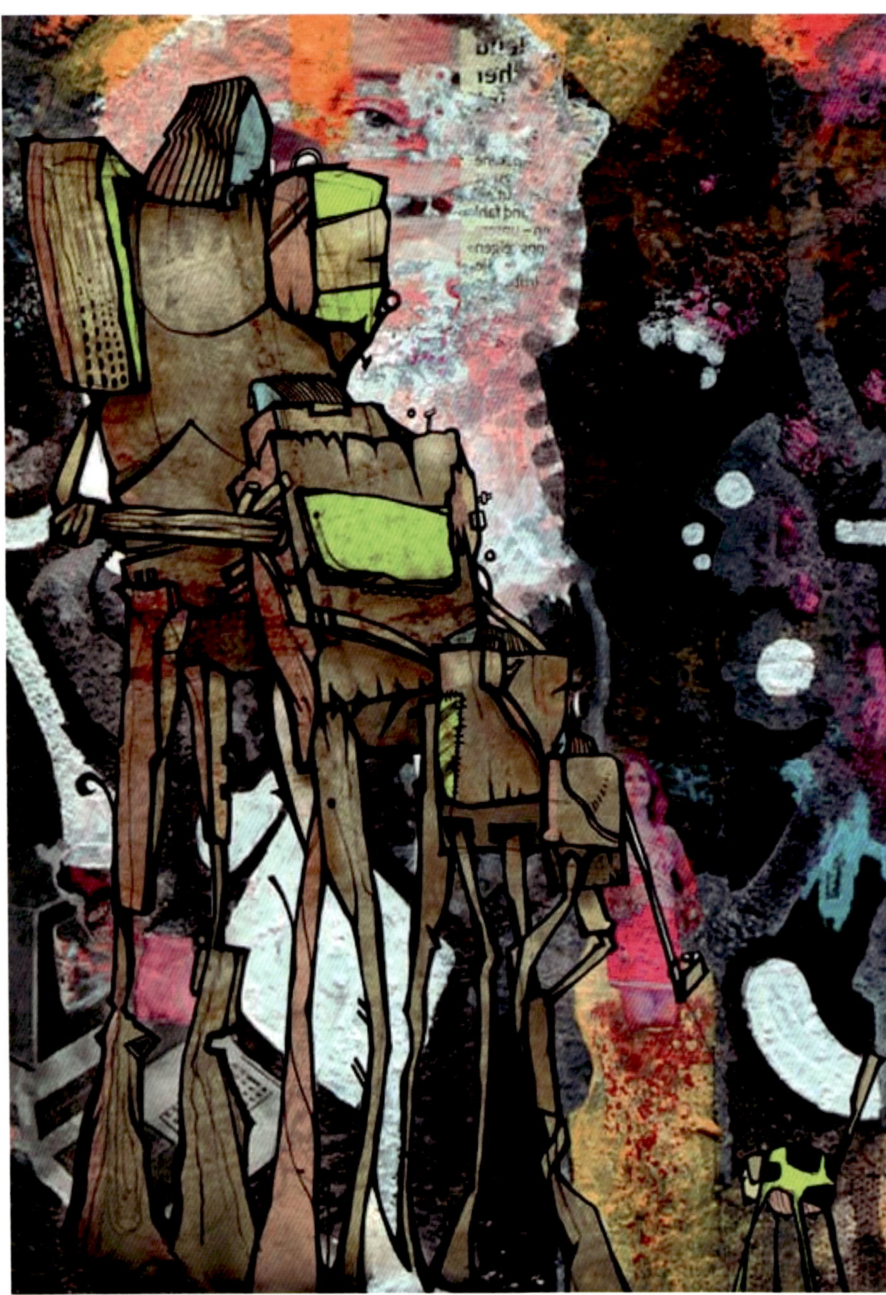

EN Illustration is often associated with commerce and suitability for the masses. Art often claims to be the opposite and yet a lot of self-appointed artists play an even more subtle game of adaptation than they might be aware of. I don't think that anybody totally disregards the opinions of other people, not unless that person is autistic. For this reason artists and illustrators alike don't produce anything without considering those who will later view their work. Oh God, how boring that would be – like a relationship with a woman and no-one else in the world. So, I think that both groups – illustrators and artists – each in their own way, more or less work for a target group. In former times artists found their target group and their clients in the royal courts – today the financiers for illustrations are brands and advertising and for artists they're the patrons and wealthy people. However, this aspect has blended more and more over the last years. I think that a differentiation between these two spheres is especially important for art collectors and investors. These people don't want to have anything to do with the mass copied transience of illustrations because the aspect of being elite, hence rare, costly and hard to get is missing. Artists themselves might not even be so hostile towards illustrators but are being pressed into a role of confrontation by these norms. The word "art" is associated with so much trash. So maybe I prefer illustrator – that pigeonhole hasn't been used as much.

LEFT PAGE: family
RIGHT PAGE:
LEFT: bloeckler23
RIGHT: contorsion

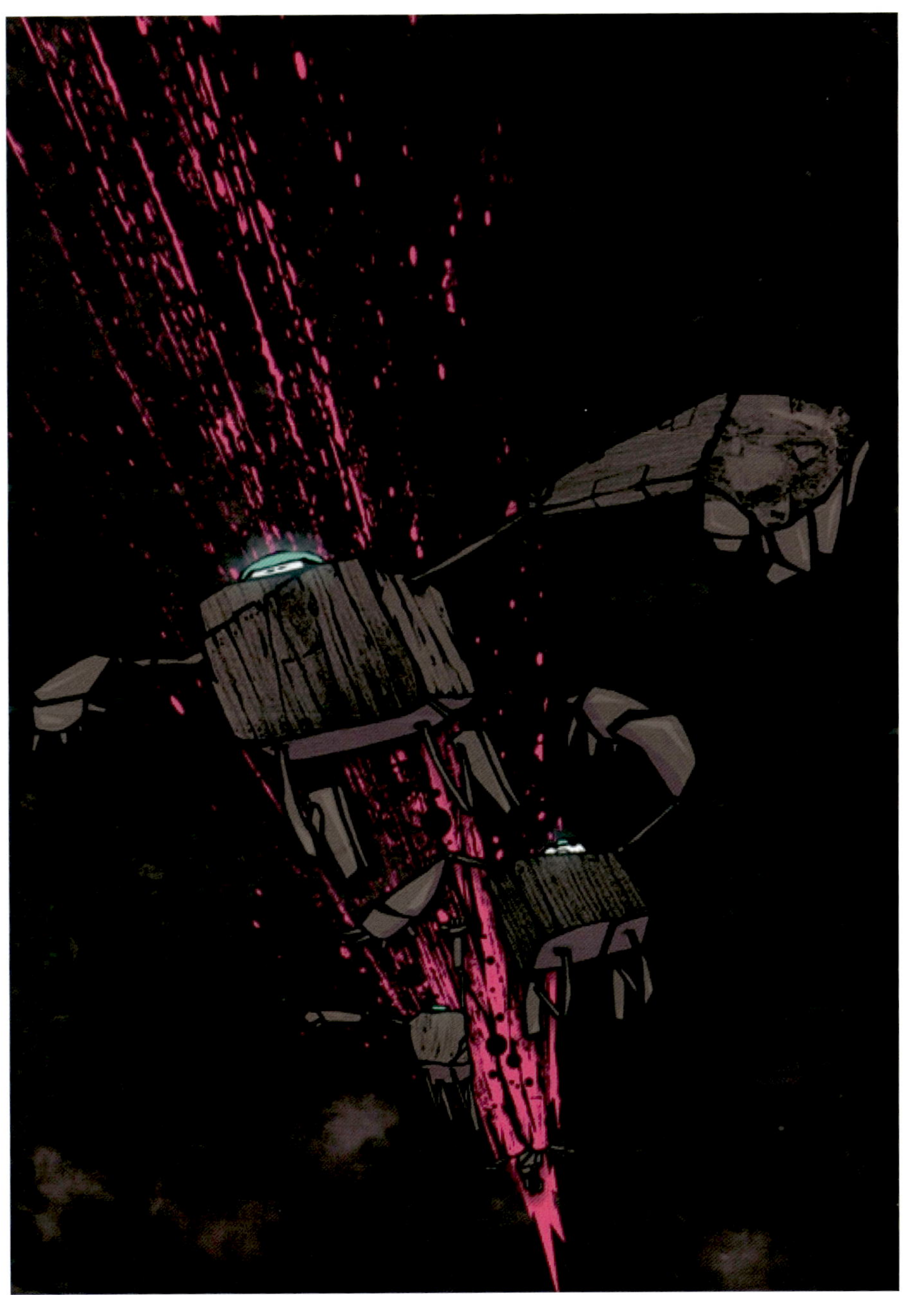

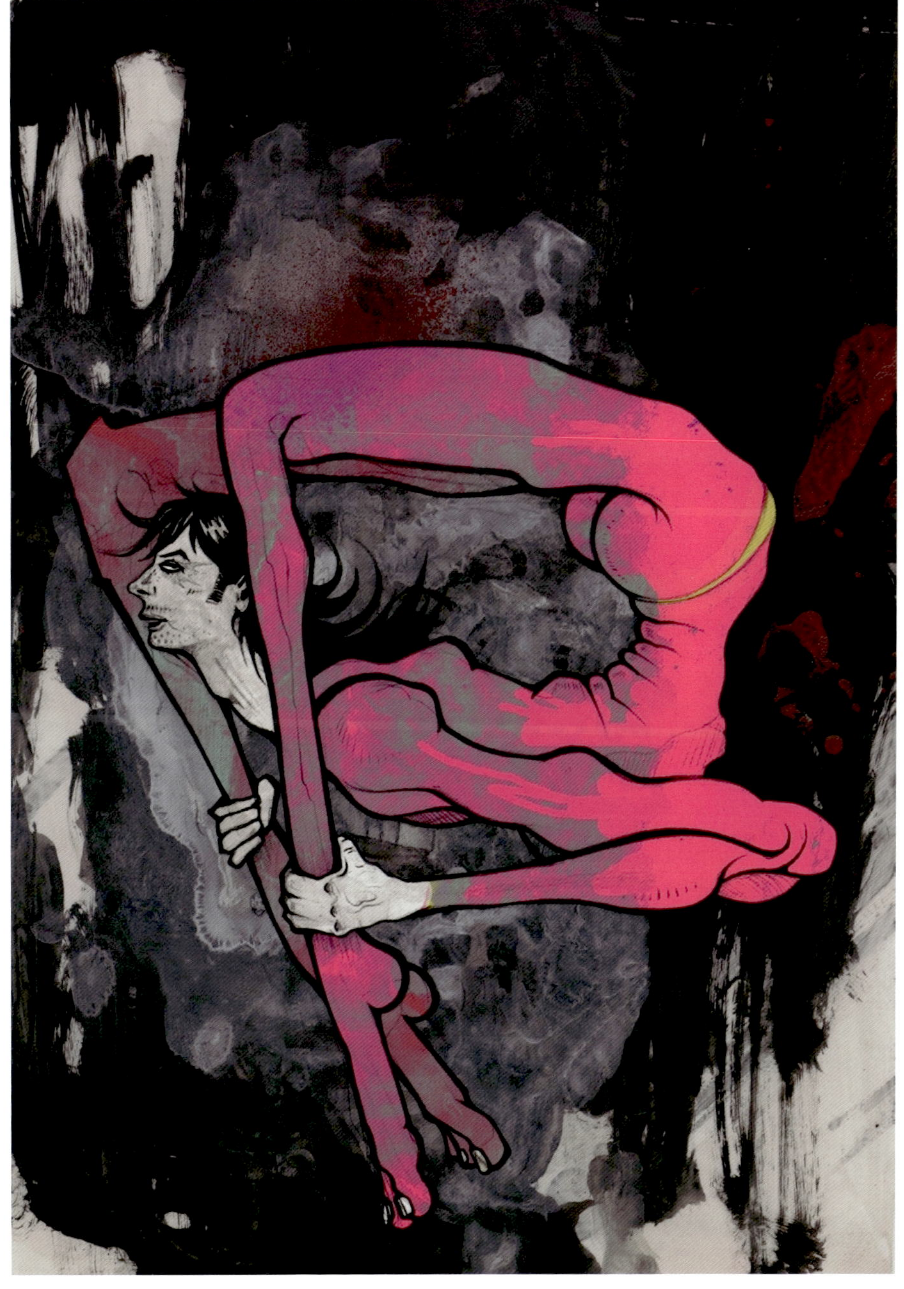

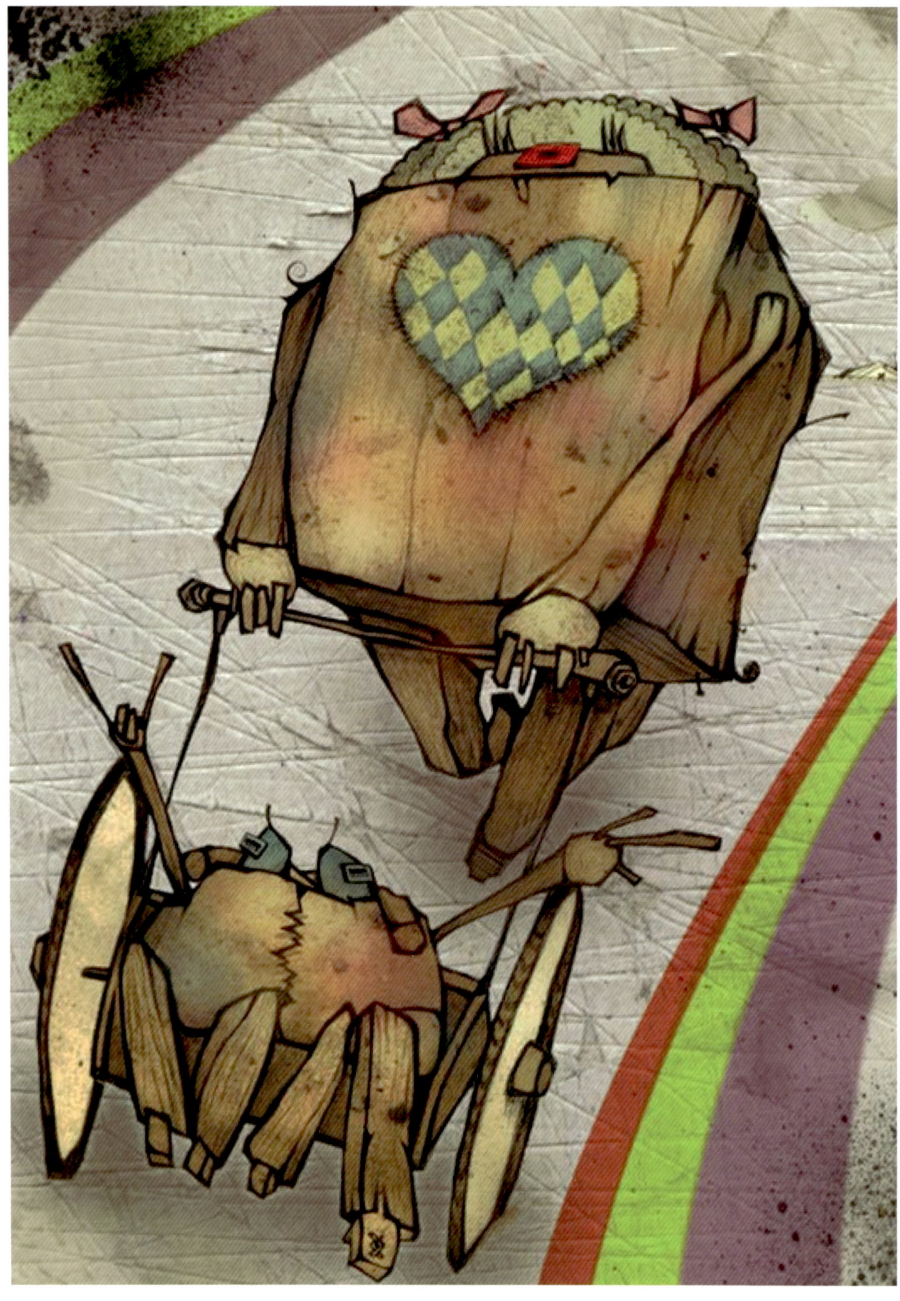

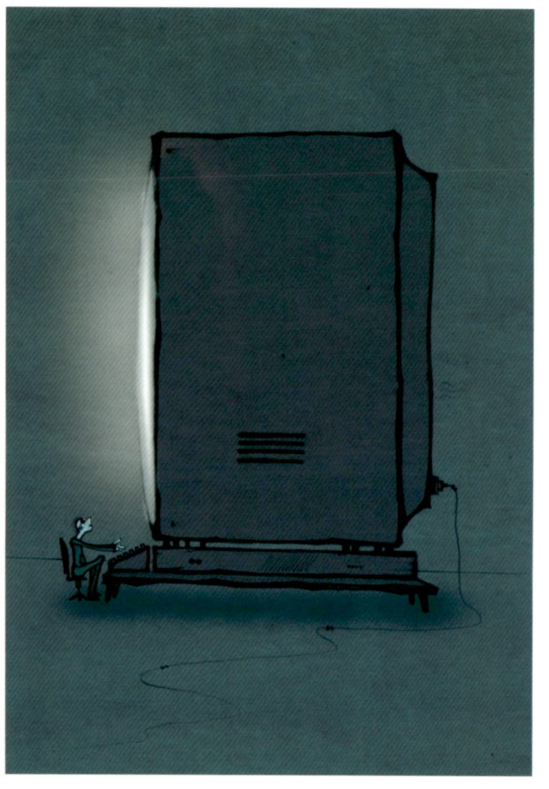

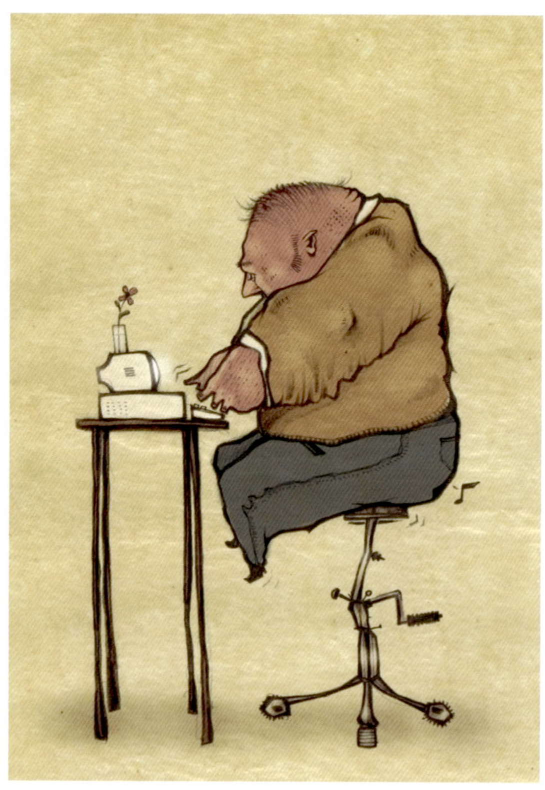

LEFT PAGE:
LEFT: blockmama
MIDDLE: user smaller
RIGHT: user bigger
RIGHT PAGE:
professional insurance agent

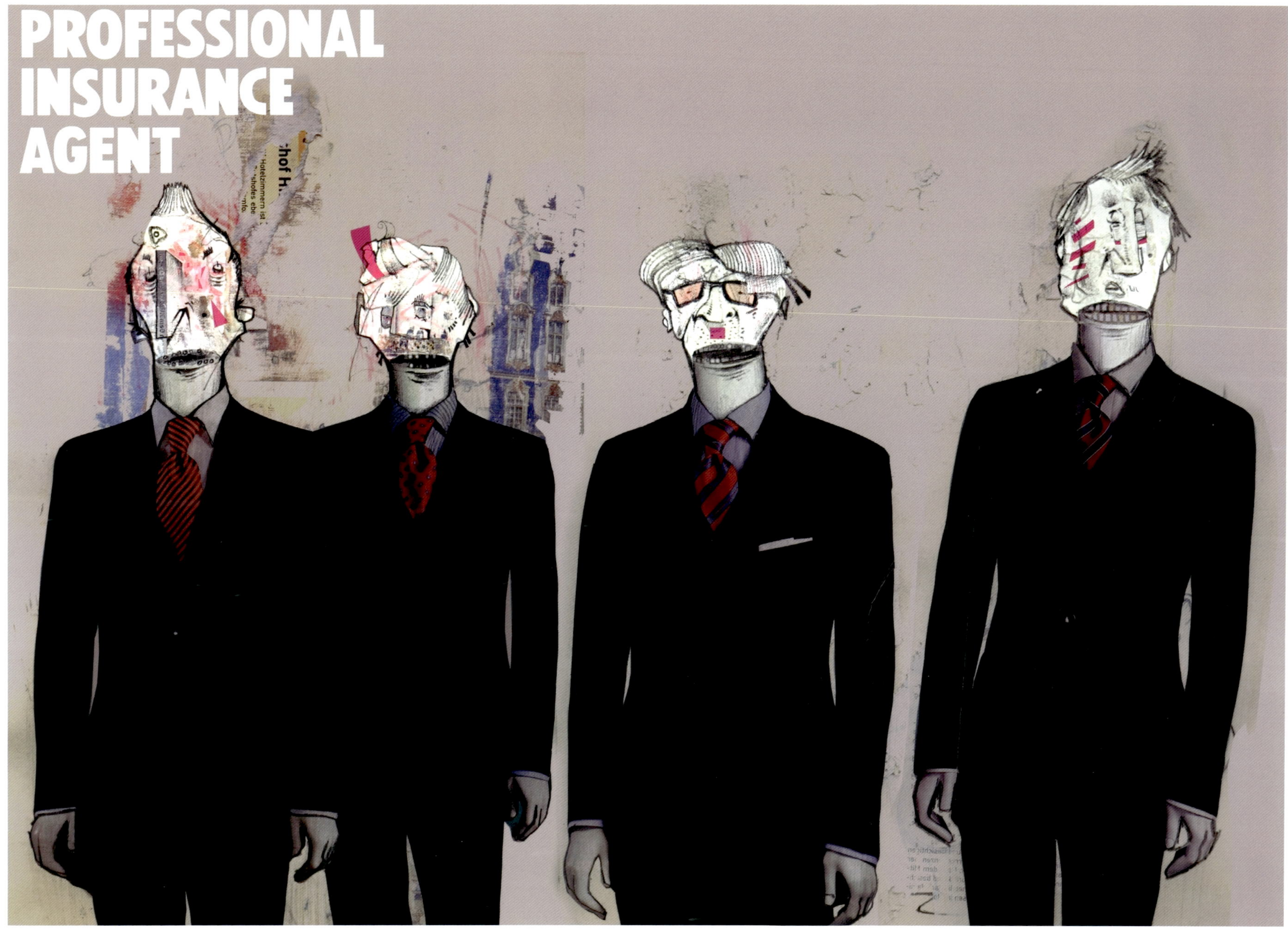
PROFESSIONAL
INSURANCE
AGENT

LUCAS AGUIRRE

NATIONALITY:	ARGENTINIAN
LOCATION:	CORDOBA
PUBLICATIONS:	BALLISTIC PUBLISHING (AUSTRALIA) | FRONTZINE (BELGIUM) DEFISH (BELGIUM) | DELIROPOLIS (SPAIN) ECLECTICZINE (AUSTRALIA) | THEFORGOTTEN (AUSTRALIA)
REFERENCES:	ERASERHEADPRESS BOOKS (USA) | AFTERBIRTH BOOKS (USA) RENAISSANCE HOUSE (USA/MEXICO) | LLANTO DE MUDO (ARG) THE LOOP (ARG) | DOLORES (ARG) | FORGOTTEN BMX (AUSTRALIA) GRAFICA LATINA (ARG) | CREATING DUCKS (ARG)
EXHIBITIONS:	VARIOUS SOLO AND GROUPAL EXHIBITIONS IN ARGENTINA
CONTACT:	LUCASAGUIRRE@GMAIL.COM
TECHNIQUE:	DIGITAL AND TRADITIONAL MEDIA
BORN:	1979

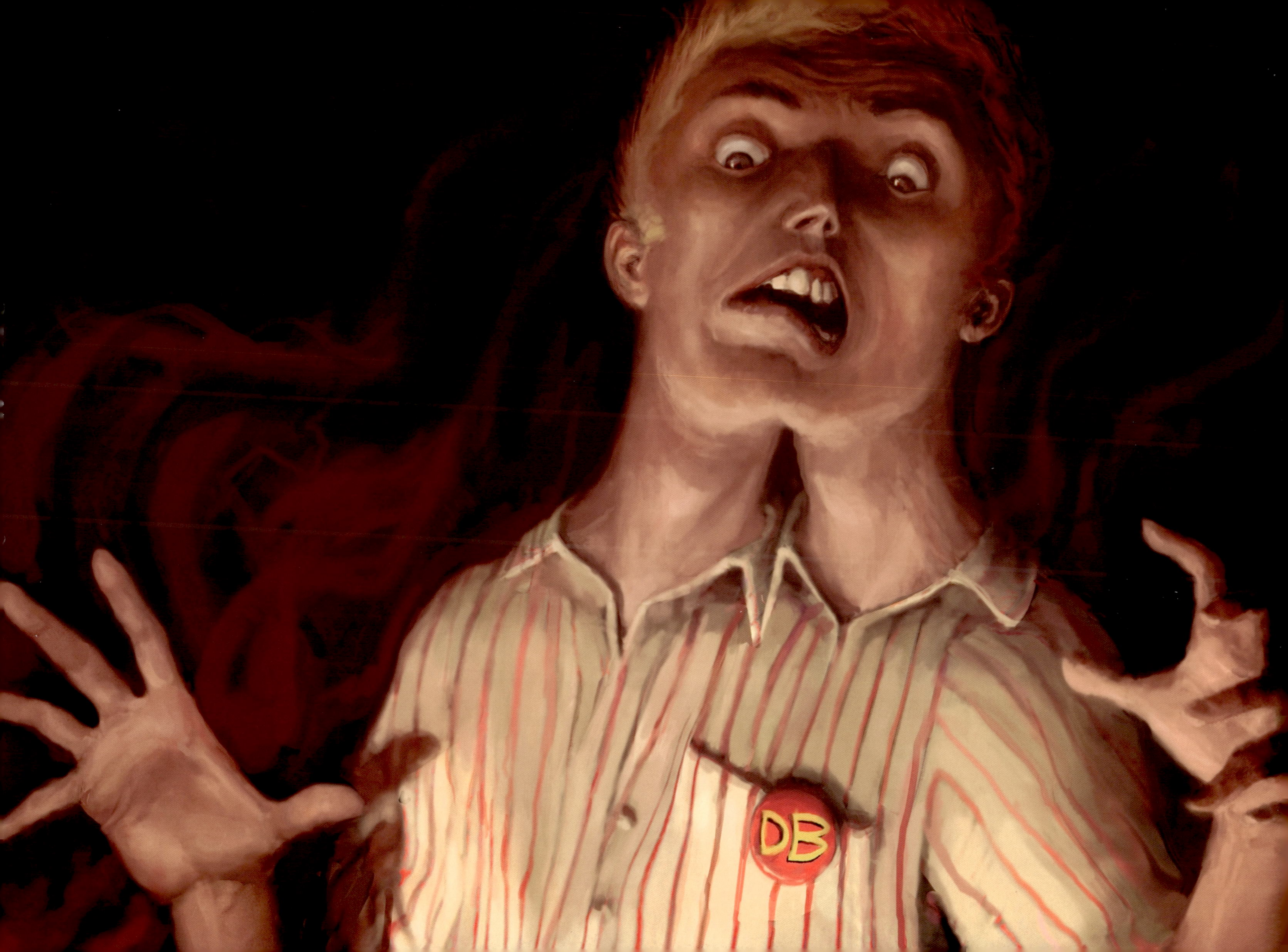
DB

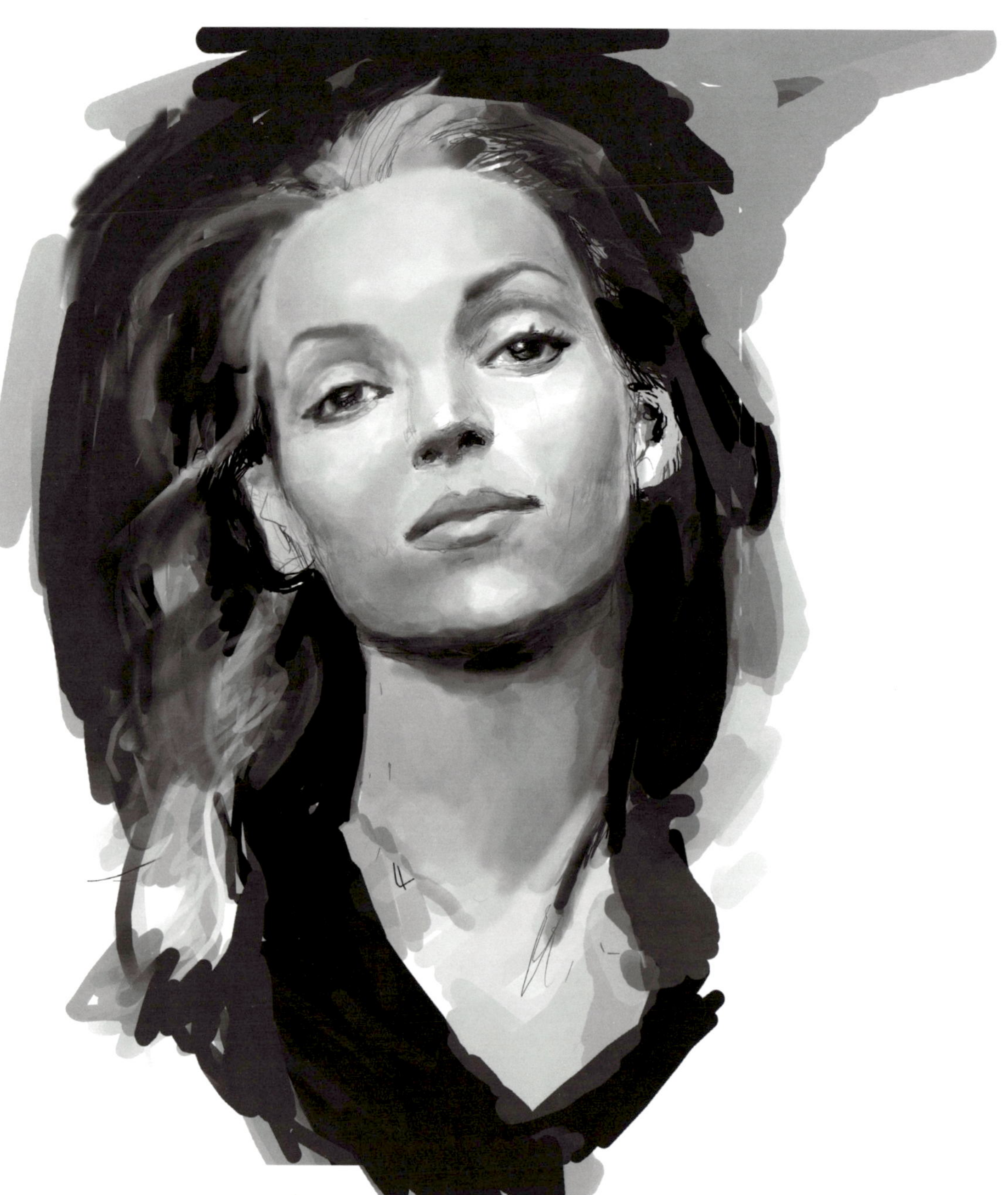

DE Ich denke, Kunst entspringt der Persönlichkeit des jeweiligen Künstlers, und wenn sie aufrichtig ist, ist sie eine einzigartige Sache. Illustration kann dem sehr ähnlich sein, wenn der Künstler etwas für sich macht, sie kann aber auch etwas völlig anderes sein. Ich glaube, dass in vielen Fällen die Bedürfnisse des Kunden das Endergebnis beeinflussen, insbesondere wenn etwas zweckbestimmt ist und ihm eine Richtung vorgegeben wird. Die eigene Kunst ist meist frei von diesen Fesseln, wenn auch nicht immer, so entsteht sie doch aus den Tiefen unseres Wesens. Für mich ist sie eine geheimnisvollere Art zu arbeiten, meine persönliche Angelegenheit, aber manchmal bin ich schon bei Auftragsarbeiten auf Dinge gestoßen, die ich nicht entdeckt hätte, wenn ich nur mein eigenes Zeug gemacht hätte. Ich betrachte mich als Künstler, der illustrieren kann, aber hauptsächlich geht es mir um meine persönliche Arbeit. Sie ist der Bereich, in dem ich mich vor allem mitteilen und der Welt das Beste geben möchte, was ich zu bieten habe.

INTRODUCTION:
it came from below the belt
LEFT PAGE: uma mia
RIGHT PAGE:
LEFT: skaltrio
RIGHT: la idea

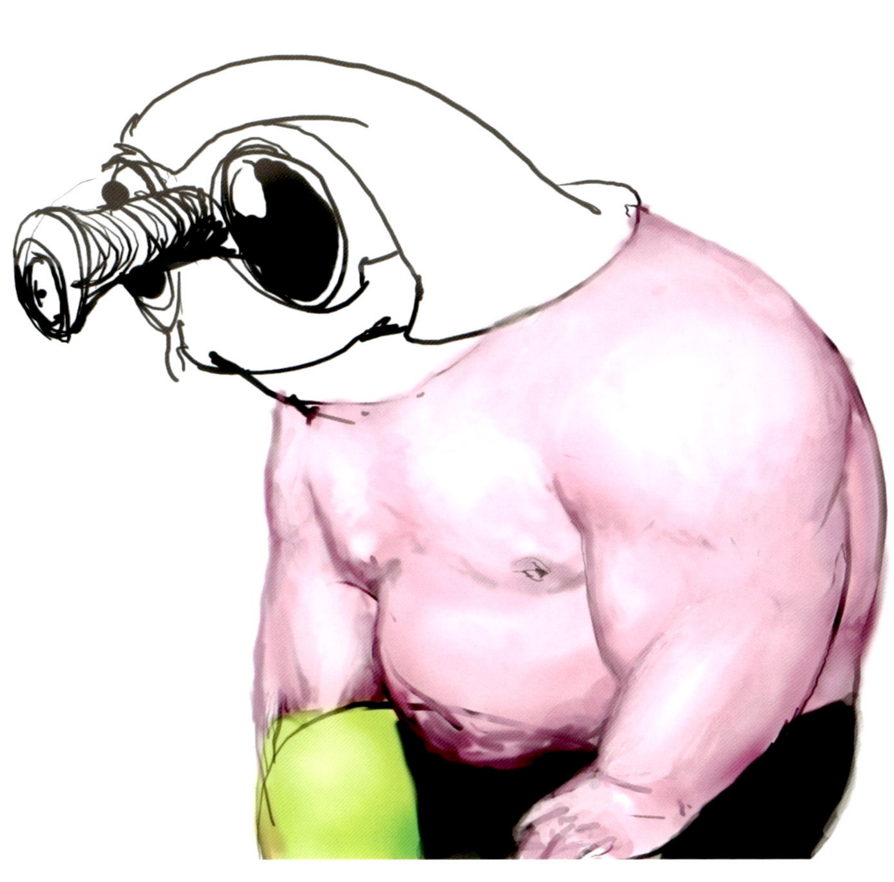

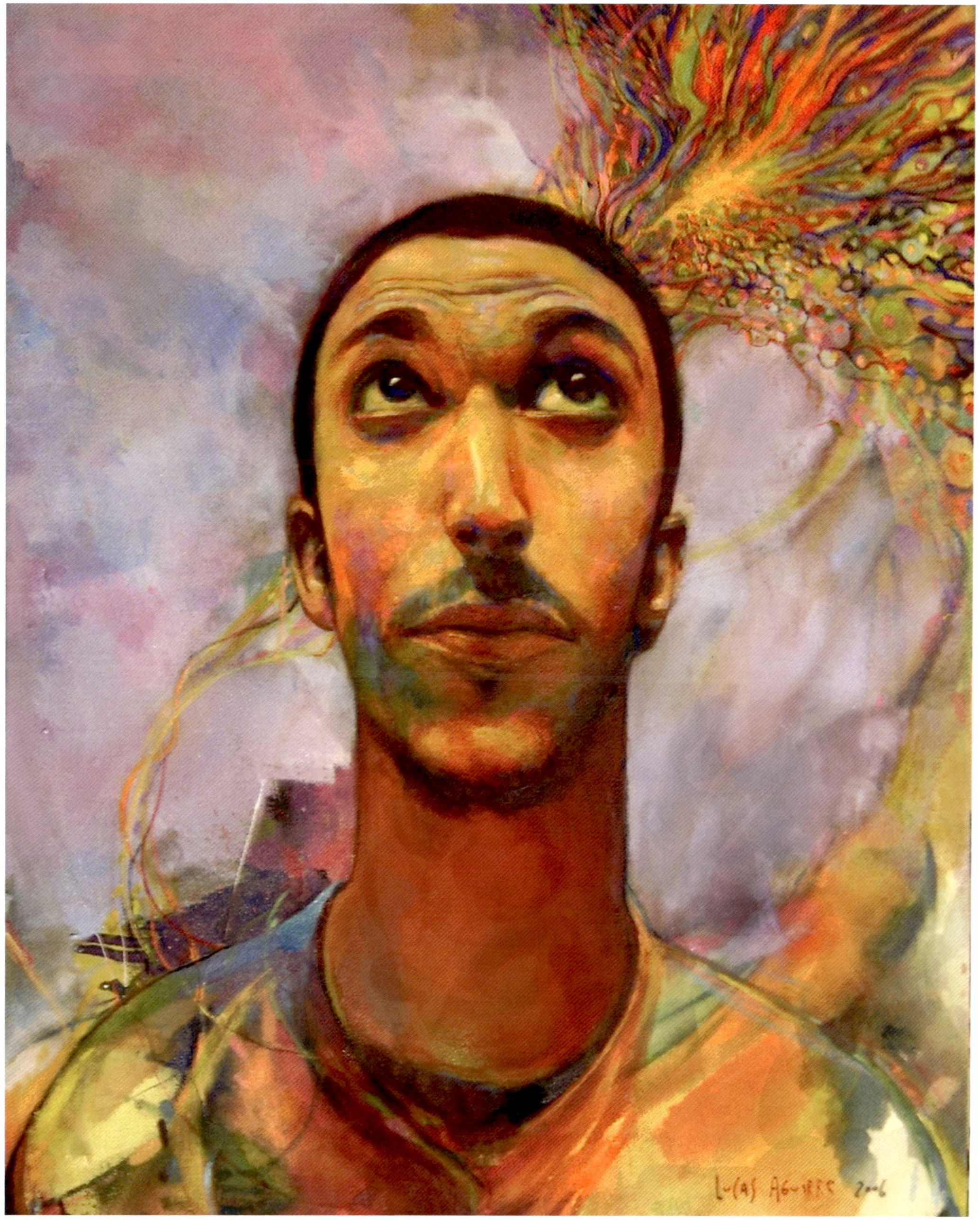

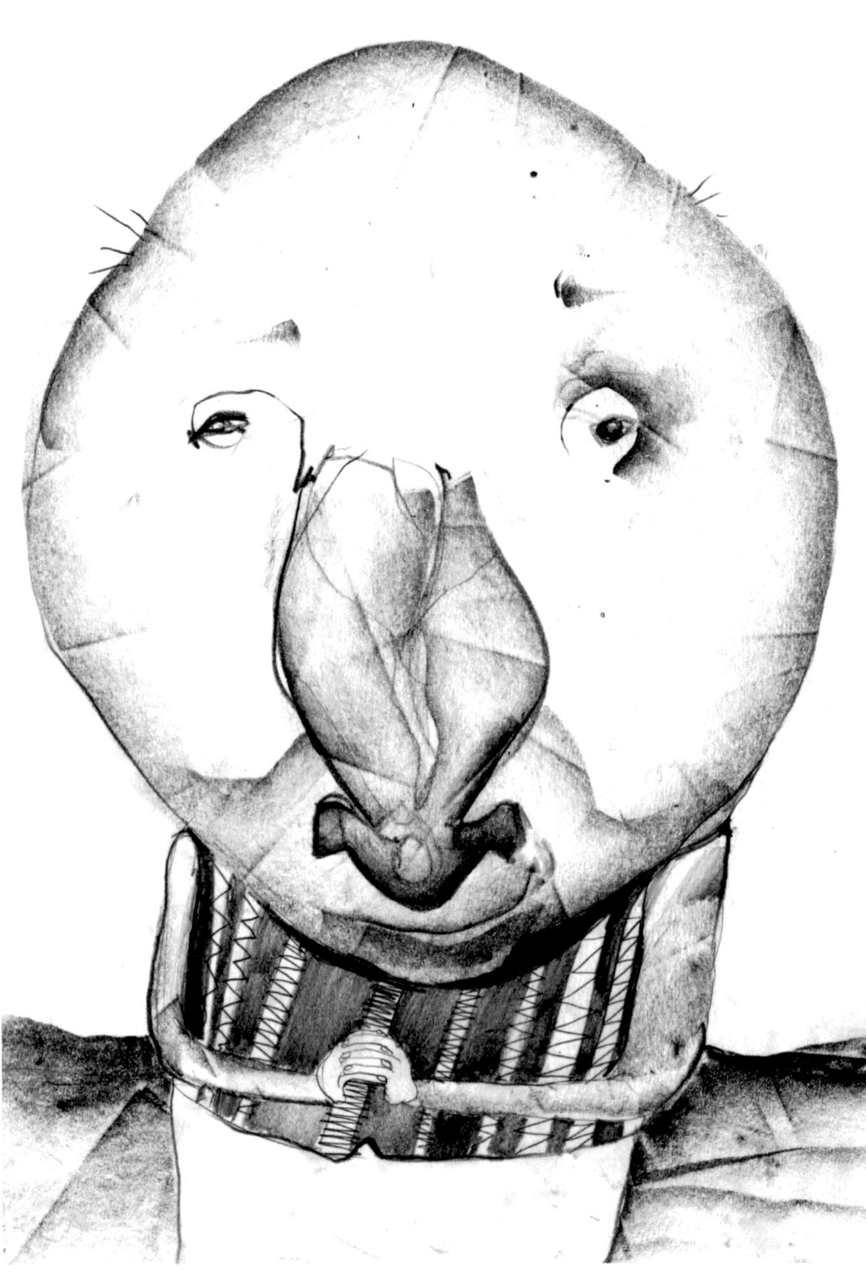

EN I think art comes from the personality of each artist, and if it's done honestly, it's a very unique thing. Illustration can be very similar to what the artist personally does for himself, but it can also be something quite different. I think in most cases the client's needs change the final result, in fact doing something for a specific purpose or destination modifies the subject most of the time. Personal art is more often free from these restrictions, not always, but it is created more from the depth of everyone's nature. For me it is a more mysterious way of work, it is my personal affair, but sometimes I found things while working on commissioned illustrations that I wouldn't have discovered by just doing my own stuff. I consider myself as an artist who is able to do illustrations, but my main topic is my personal work; it is the field where I primarily want to communicate, where I want to give my best to the world.

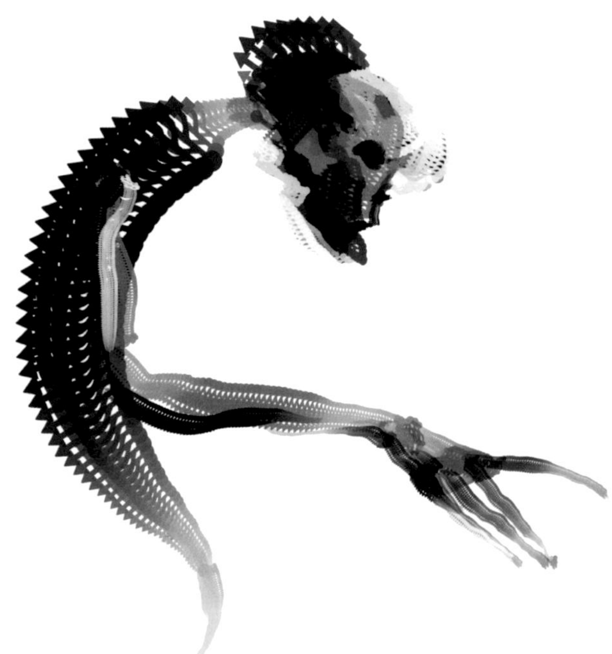

LEFT: cabezon1
RIGHT: esqueleto usb

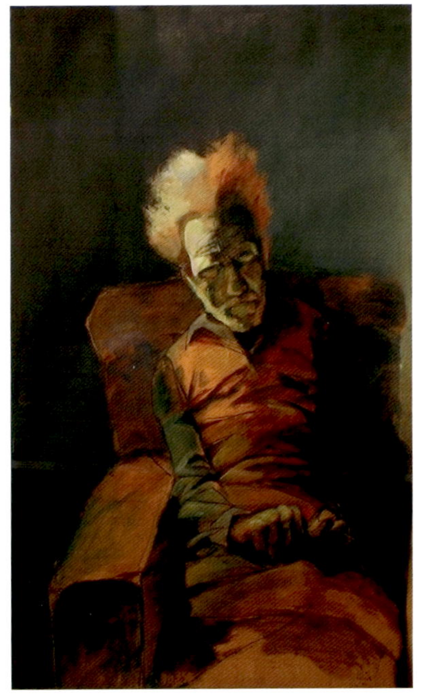

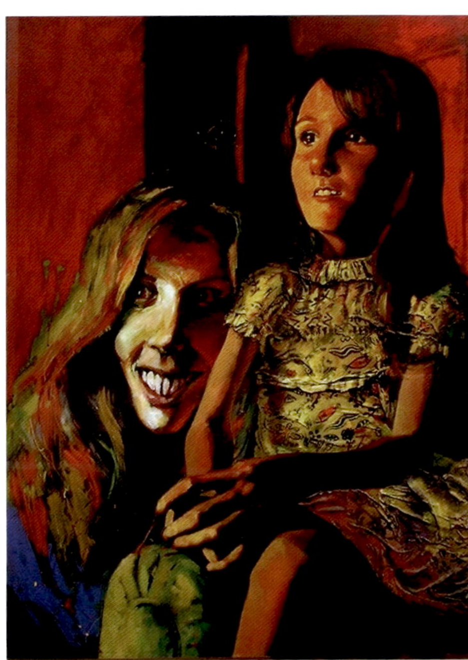

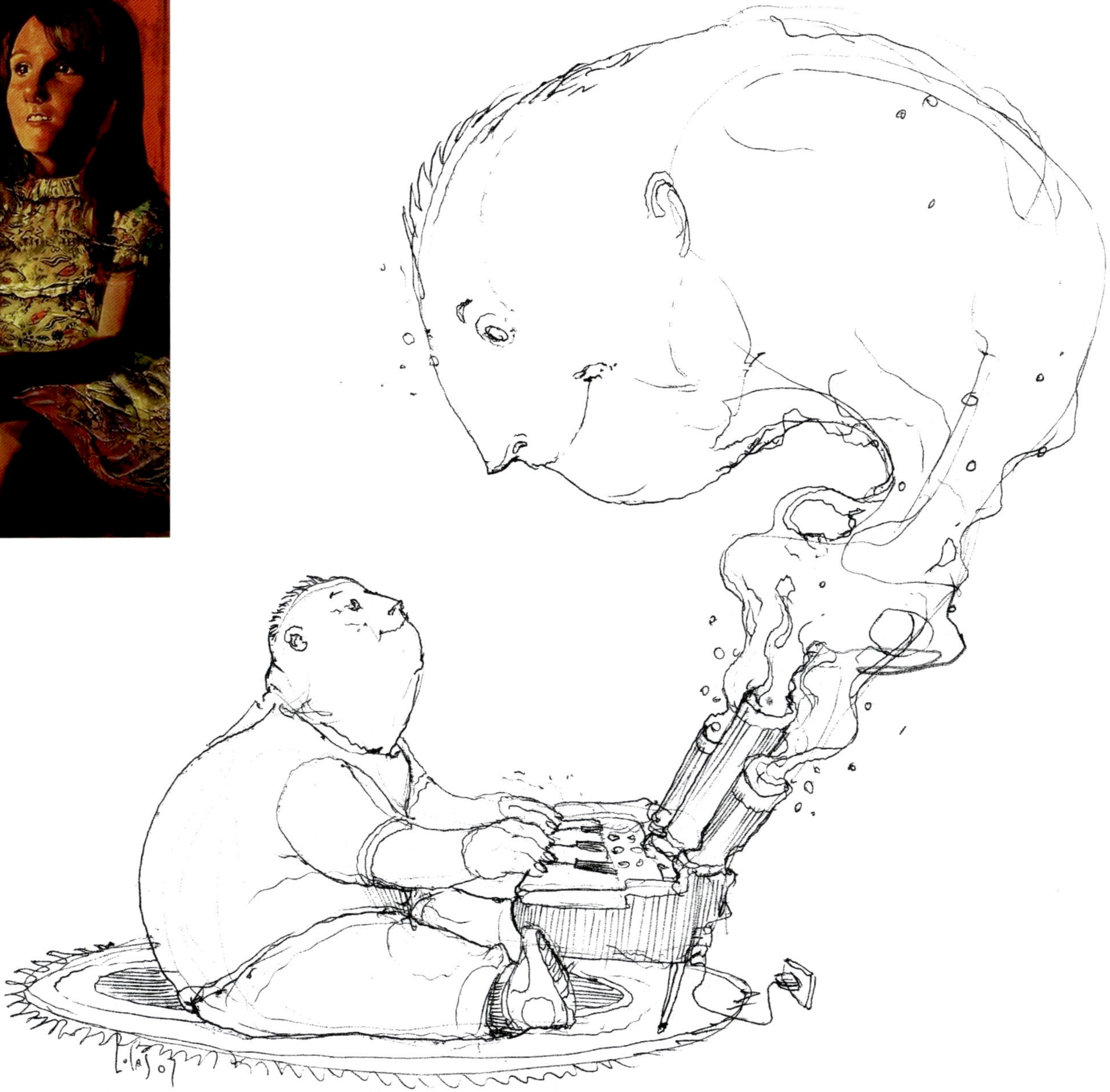

LEFT: ezra
MIDDLE: susana sell
her daughters soul to satan
RIGHT: musica

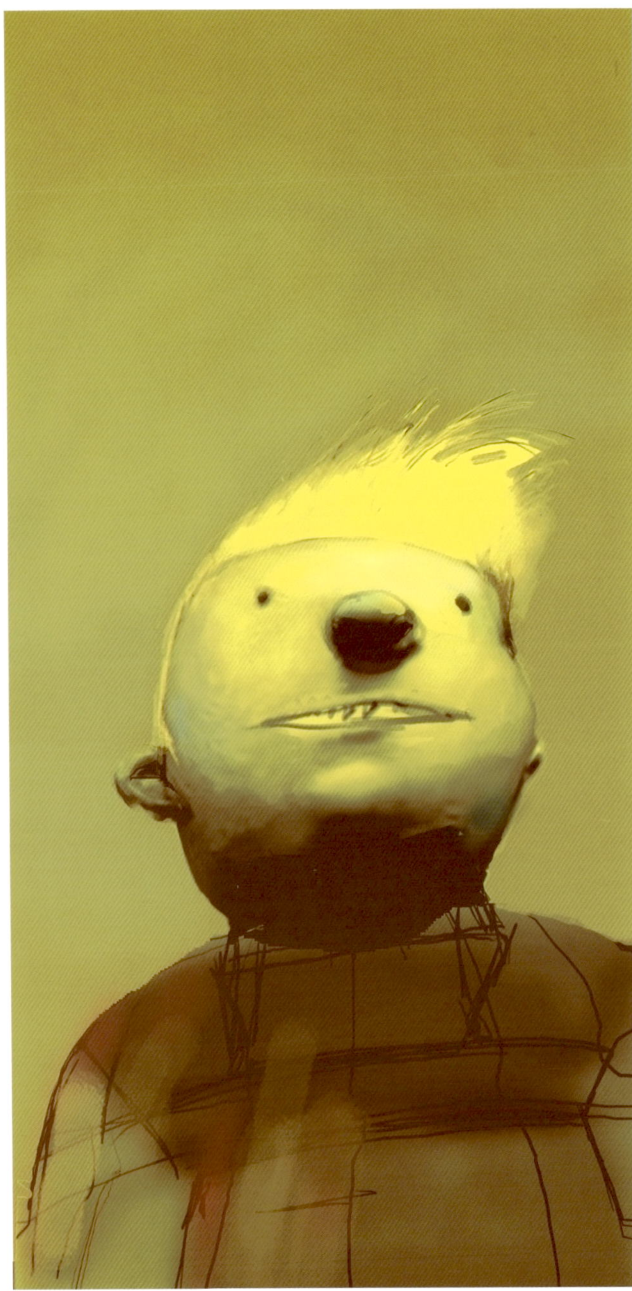

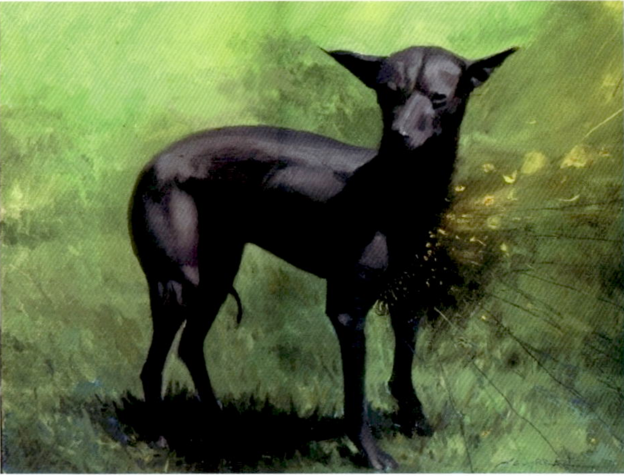

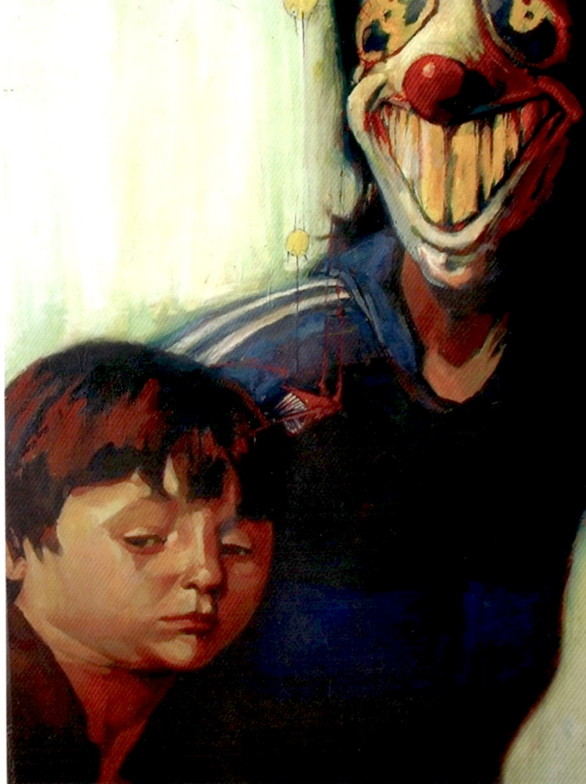

LEFT PAGE:
LEFT: cabeza
TOP RIGHT:
mexican hairless dog chapulin win the first prize
DOWN RIGHT: careta
RIGHT PAGE: ludo is friend of rocks

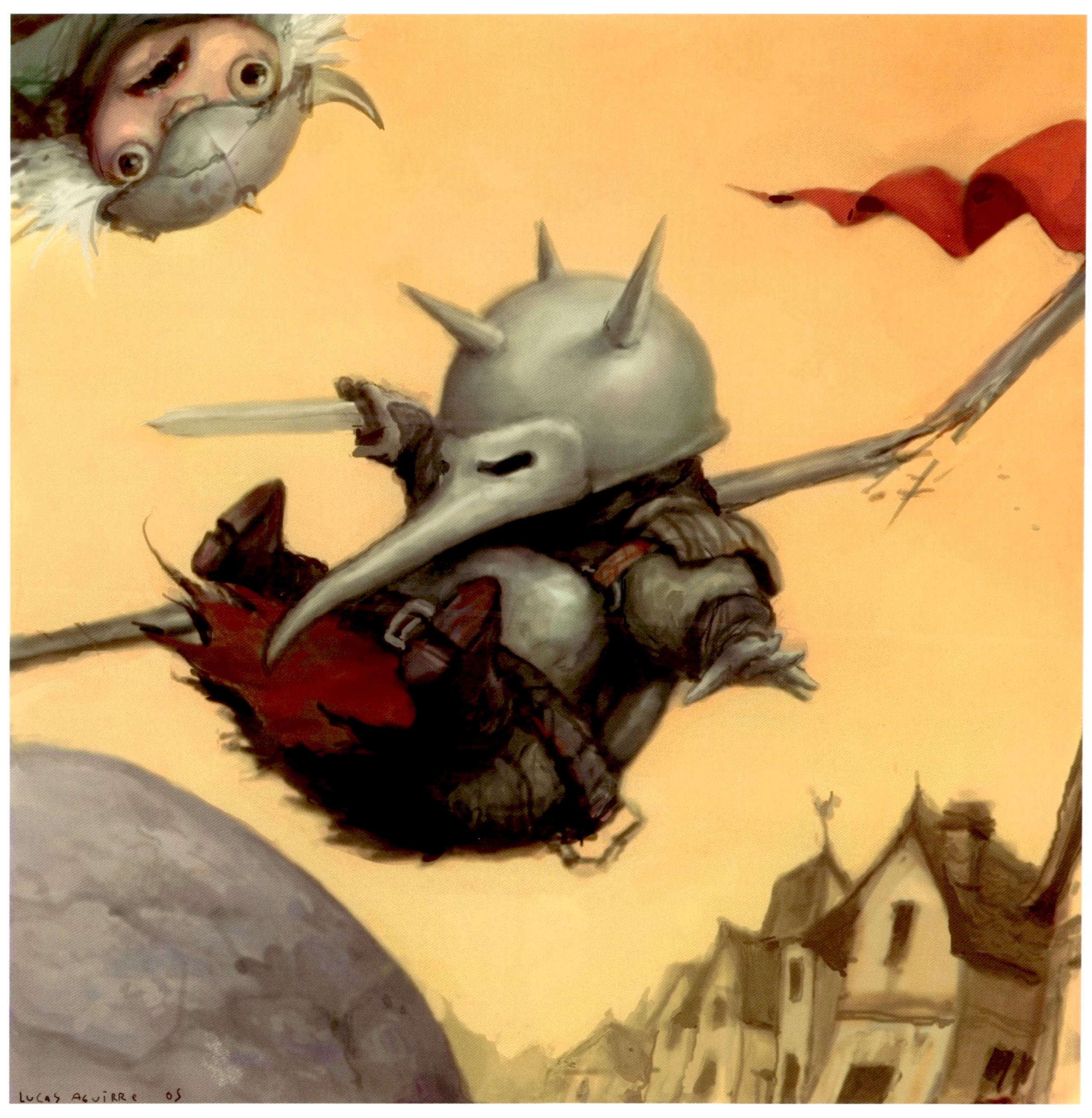
LUCAS AGUIRRE 05

»FONS SCHIEDON

Nationality:	DUTCH
Location:	AMSTERDAM
Publications:	PICTOPLASMA ENCYCLOPEDIA | HIDDEN TRACK ILLUSIVE 1 AND 2 | FREISTIL 2 | 3X3 MAGAZINE
References:	MTV ASIA | SUBMARINECHANNEL | PARK AVENUE VOLKSKRANT MAGAZINE
Exhibitions:	MU – EINDHOVEN | WIMP – LONDON AND HONG KONG EXTRAFEIN – BERLIN
Contact:	PHONE +31 6 41555017 OFFICE@FONZTV.NL WWW.FONZTV.NL
Technique:	DIGITAL | ANIMATION
Born:	1980

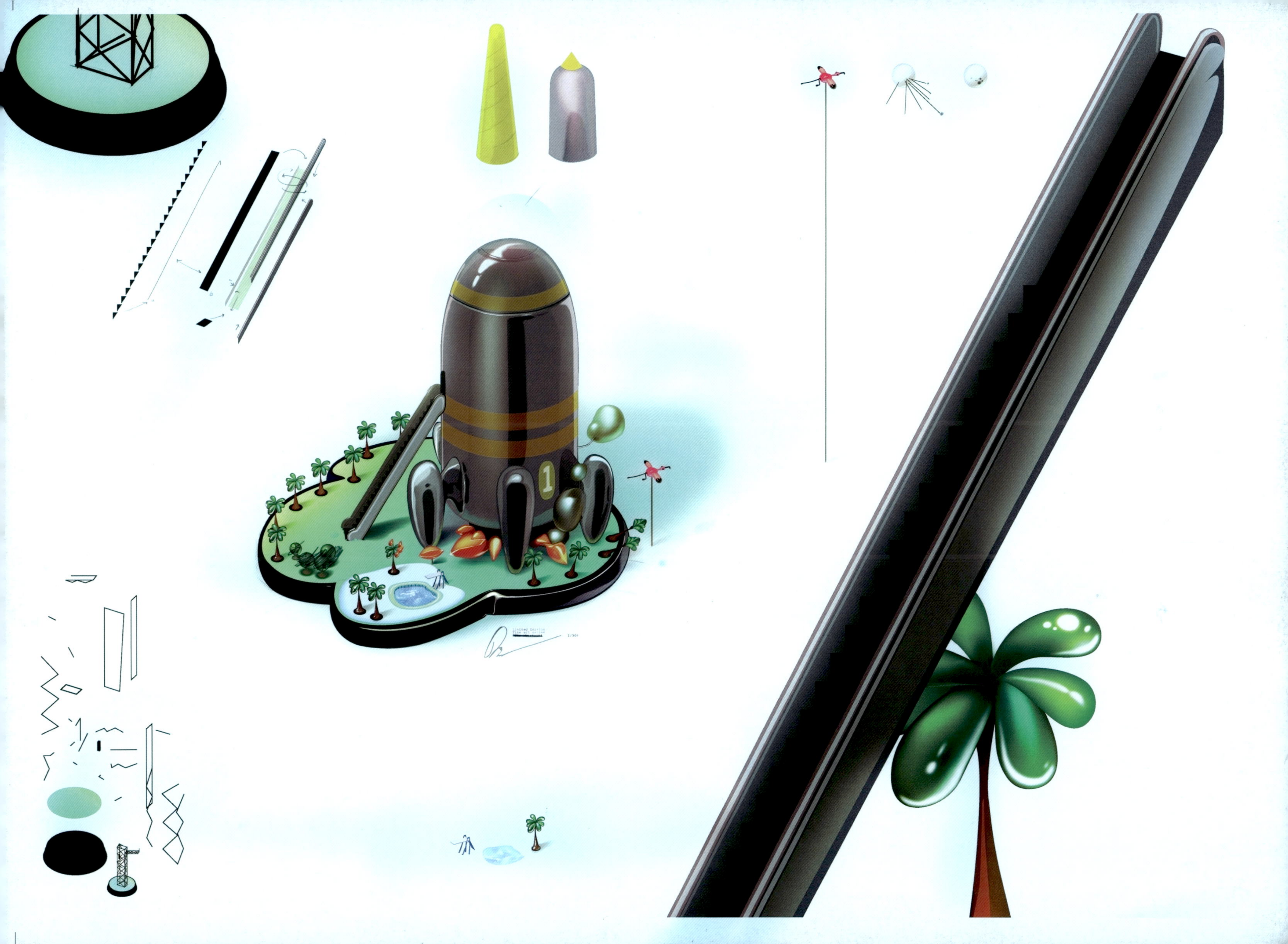

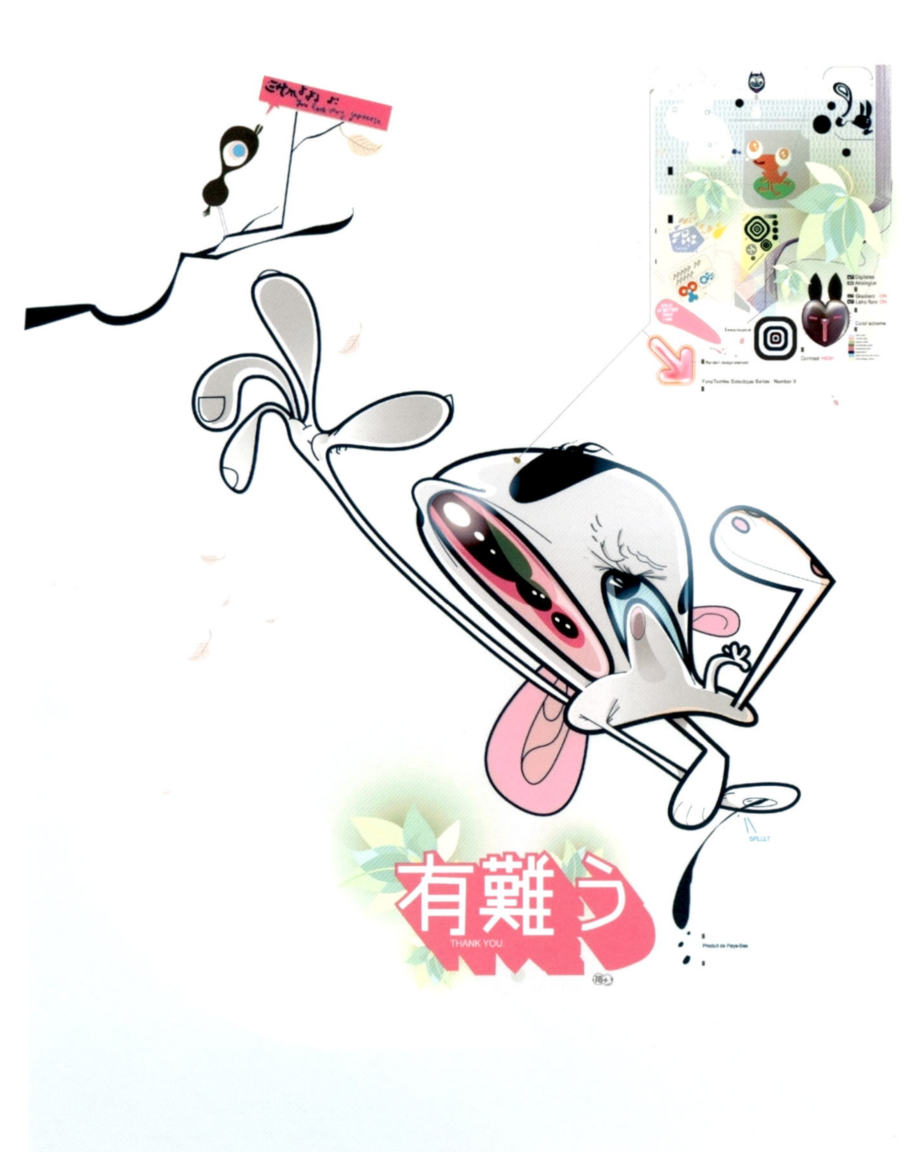
有難う
THANK YOU.

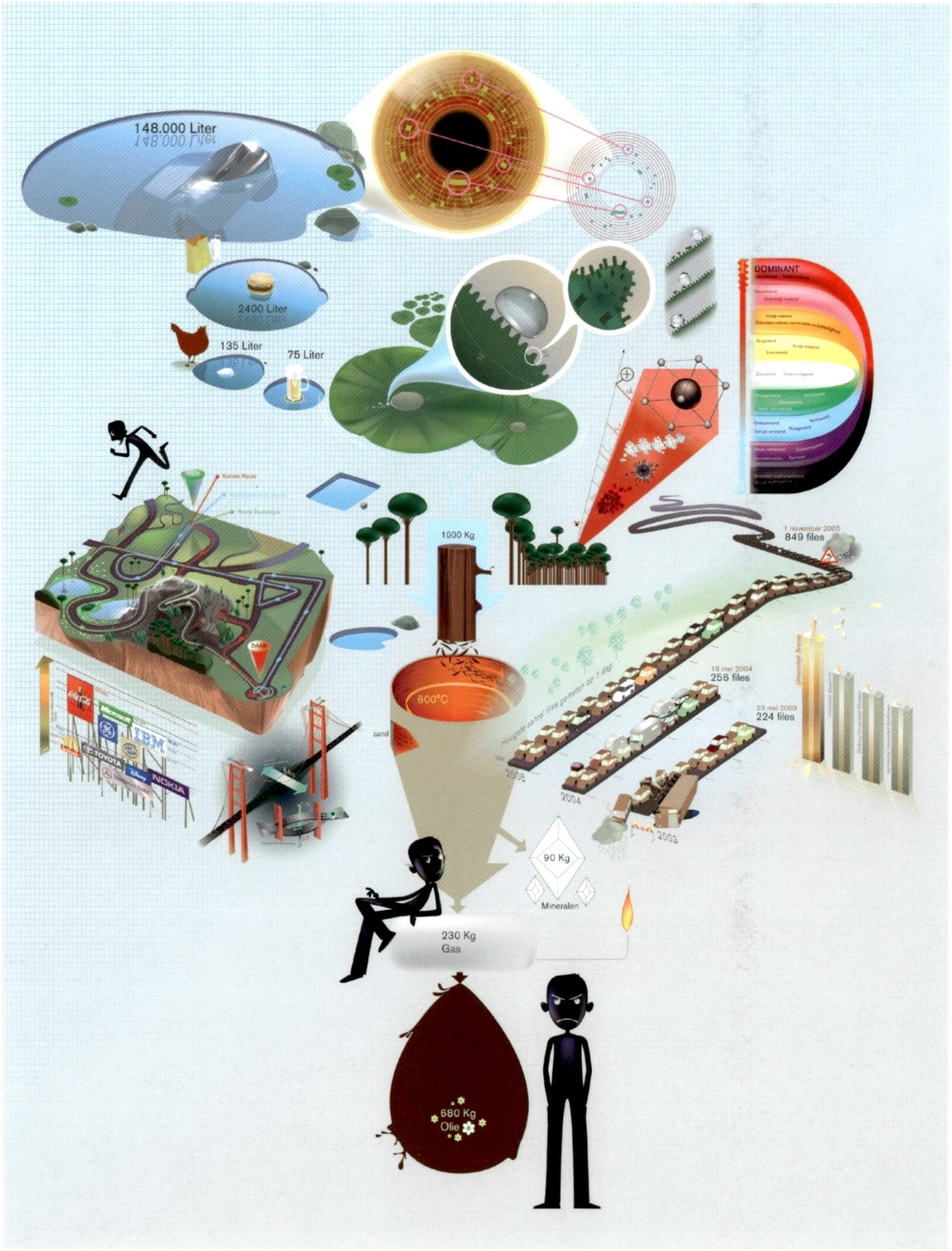

148.000 Liter
2400 Liter
135 Liter
75 Liter
DOMINANT
1000 Kg
1 november 2005
849 files
19 mei 2004
256 files
23 mei 2003
224 files
600°C
90 Kg
Mineralen
230 Kg
Gas
680 Kg
Olie

INTRODUCTION: rocket
LEFT PAGE:
LEFT: arigato
RIGHT:
bachelor campaign-compilation
RIGHT PAGE:
LEFT: submarinechannel-squirrel
RIGHT: monkey

DE Kunst und Illustration können von derselben Person geschaffen werden, und das ist so ziemlich das Einzige, was sie gemeinsam haben. Illustration ist viel einfacher und unkomplizierter zu definieren als Kunst, denn der Unterschied liegt ganz allein in der Motivation. Kunst kann persönlich motiviert oder auch in Auftrag gegeben sein. Kunst kann vieles sein. Aber Illustration ist nichts weiter als Illustration. Der Dienstleistungsaspekt ist natürlich immer da und er ist es, der Illustration erst entstehen lässt. Bei jeder Art von angewandter Kunst arbeitet man mit bestimmten Anforderungen und Beschränkungen. Deine Arbeit ist Teil einer größeren Sache und muss hinsichtlich dessen funktionieren. Aber der Umstand, dass es Einschränkungen gibt, bedeutet nicht notwendigerweise, dass kein Raum für persönlichen Ausdruck ist. Bei Buchillustrationen ist es eher üblich, dass der Illustrator eine subjektive, in hohem Maße persönliche Sicht auf das Thema liefert. In anderen Fällen wird eine zu persönliche Herangehensweise möglicherweise schlicht nicht im Interesse der gesamten Kommunikation liegen. Es kommt auch darauf an, in welcher Branche man arbeitet. In der Werbung sind Ideen und künstlerische Gestaltung meist so weit entwickelt, dass sich die Arbeit eines Illustrators oder Fotografen mehr oder weniger auf die Ausführung beschränkt. Die Frage, inwieweit eine Abgrenzung zwischen Kunst und Illustration existiert beziehungsweise notwendig oder hinfällig ist, muss jeder Künstler oder Illustrator für sich entscheiden. Solche Definitionen sind im Tagesgeschäft nicht von Belang, nur bei Interviews wie diesem. Es geht einzig darum, dass deine Arbeit mit dem zu tun hat, woran du glaubst, was du magst oder was du gut kannst. Und du musst dir bei jeder Arbeit – ob Auftragsarbeit oder nicht – überlegen, wie du an sie herangehst und auf welche Befriedigung von Bedürfnissen du überhaupt abzielst. Viele meiner Auftragsarbeiten hätte ich ebenso als persönliches Projekt in Angriff nehmen können, da sie mir Gelegenheit boten, mich auf meine Weise mit einem Thema zu befassen, wobei die Anforderungen des Auftraggebers dennoch erfüllt wurden. Eine Sache an diesen Definitionen verwirrt mich allerdings. Ich halte es für sinnvoll, etwas Illustration zu nennen, wenn es eine ist, aber es befremdet mich, wenn manche Leute ihre eigene Arbeit als Illustration bezeichnen, nur weil sie so aussieht. Eine solche Art von Illustration existiert nicht, das ist Unsinn. Illustration muss in Auftrag gegeben sein, basta.

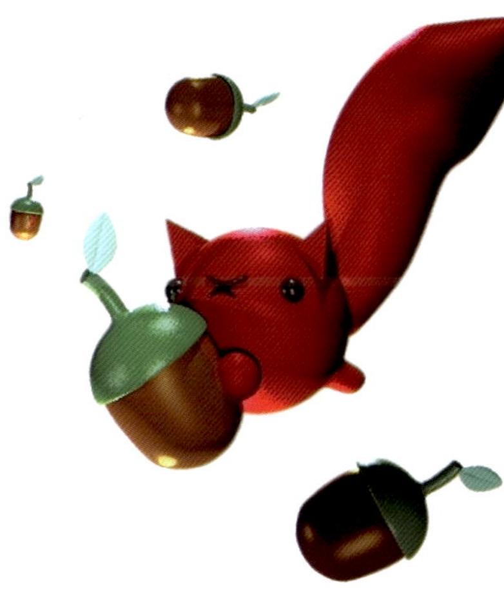

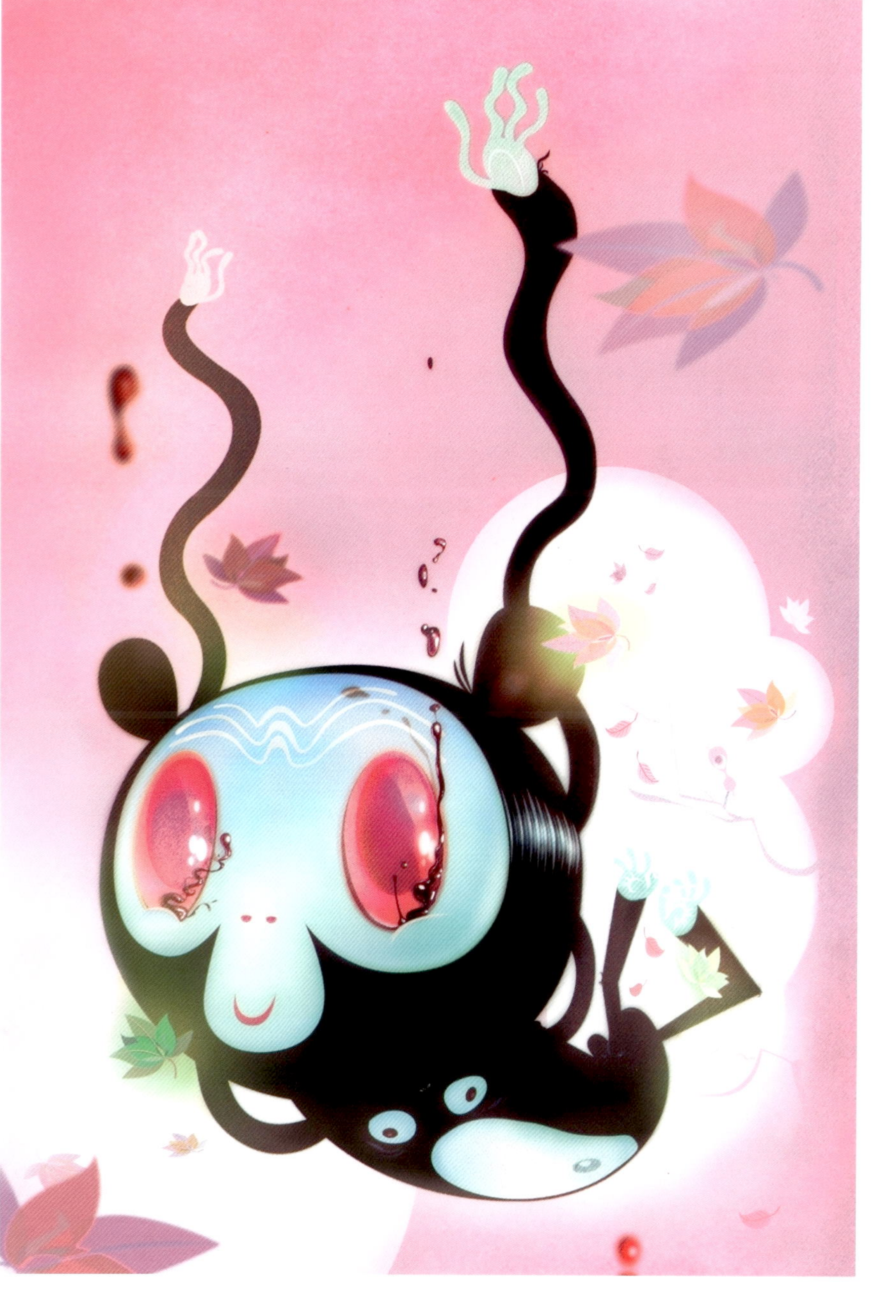

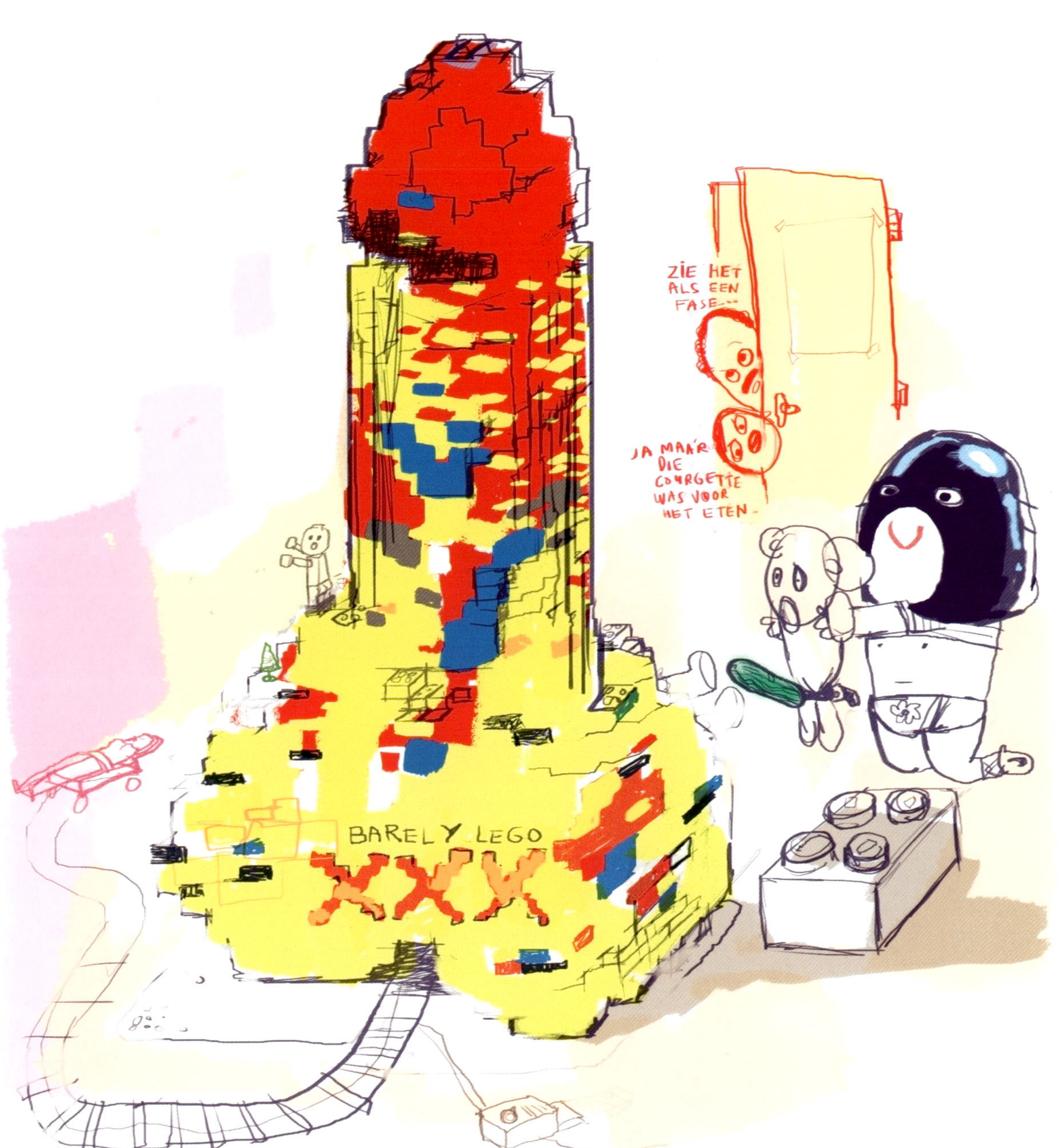

EN Art and illustration can be made by the same people, that's pretty much the only thing they share. Illustration is much easier to define than art, because the difference is all in the motivation. Art can be personal as well as commissioned, art can be a lot of things. But illustration is just illustration. The service aspect is still there of course and is exactly what makes illustration be illustration. In any of the applied arts you're working with certain demands and limitations. Your work is part of something bigger and has to function in that respect. But the fact that there are limitations does not necessarily mean that there's no room for personal expression. In editorial illustration it is more common for illustrators to deliver a subjective, highly personal view on a subject. In other cases, it might simply not be in the best interest of the overall communication to have too much of a personalized approach. It's also a matter of which part of the industry you're working in. In advertising, the concepts and art direction are usually developed to such an extent that the job of an illustrator or photographer is almost only on the level of execution. On the question to what extent a differentiation between art and illustration exists, is necessary or obsolete, I can just say that's merely a personal judgment for the illustrators/artists to make. Definitions are not important for my daily work, only for interviews like this one. It's all about doing work that connects to what you believe in or like or are good at. And every job, whether commissioned or not, requires you to think about your approach and which needs you are aiming to fulfill anyway. I've done plenty of commissioned work that I could have easily made as a personal project, just because it provided me with an opportunity to explore a subject in a personal way, and still fulfill the requirements. There's one thing about those definitions though that I've been puzzled about. To me it makes sense to call something an illustration if it is one, but I am not convinced when some people call their personal work illustration just because it looks like it. Personal illustration or art illustration is non-existent, it's nonsense. Illustration has to be commissioned, period.

LEFT PAGE: sex
RIGHT PAGE: violently happy bugs alltogethernow

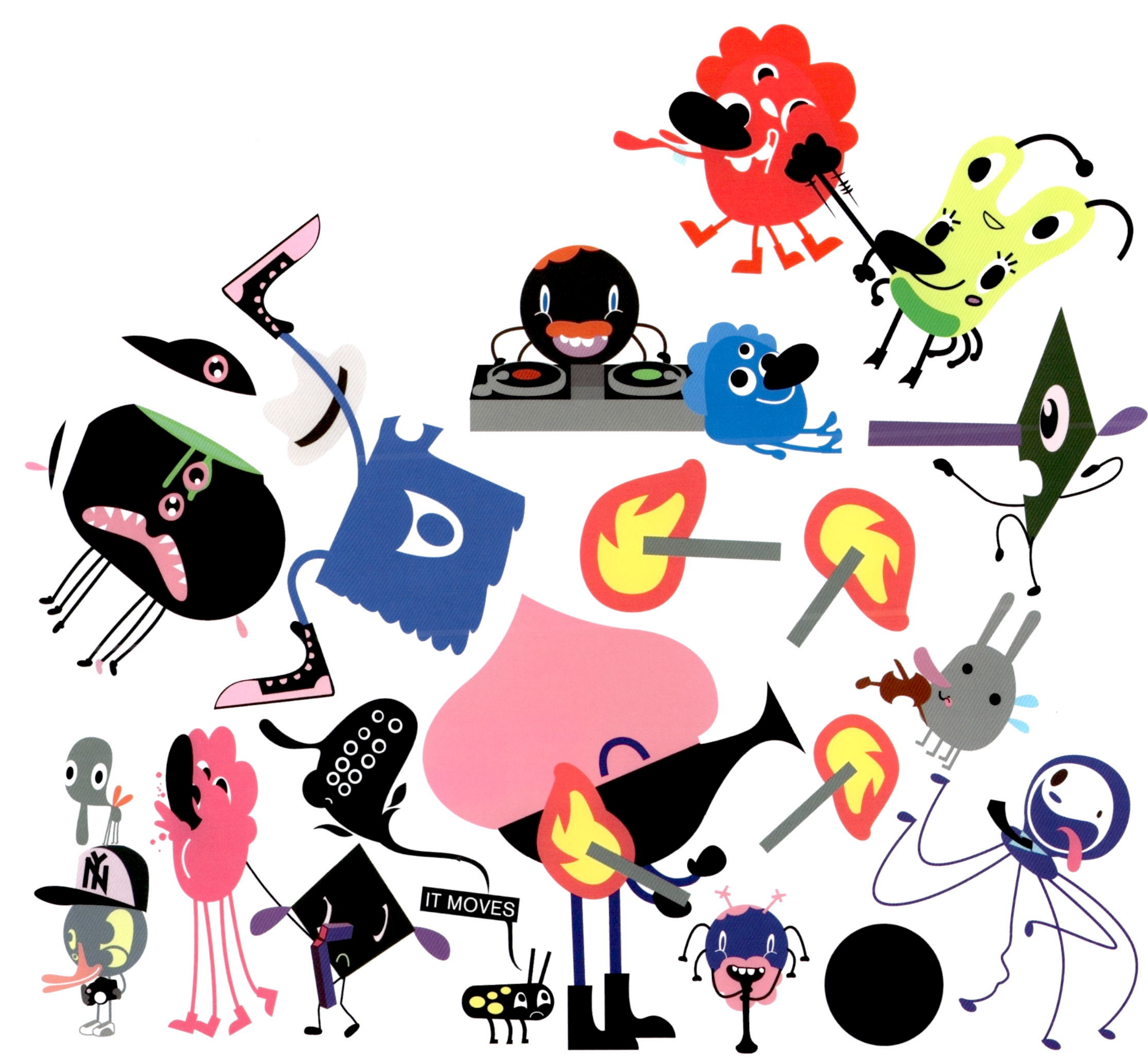
IT MOVES

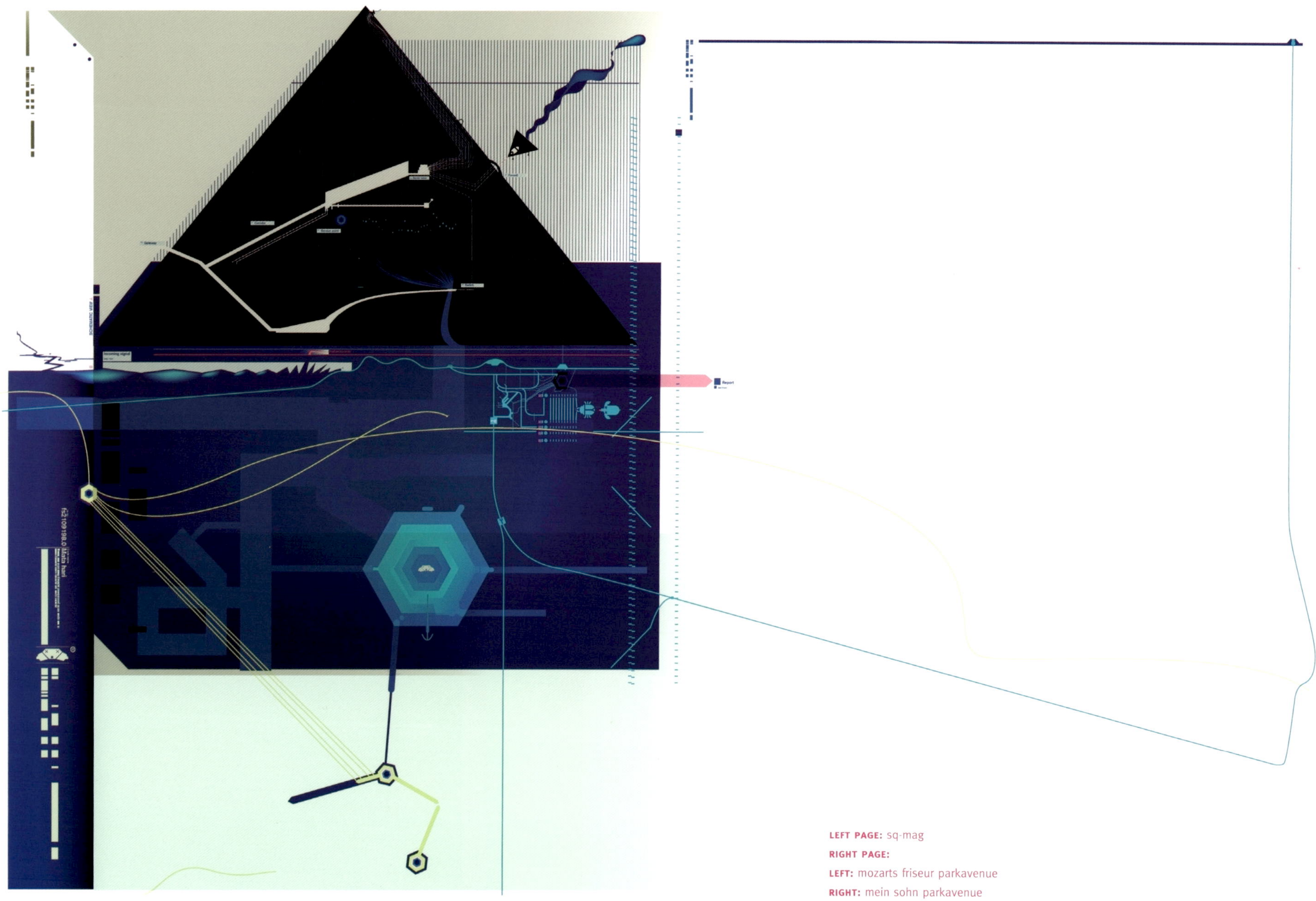

LEFT PAGE: sq-mag
RIGHT PAGE:
LEFT: mozarts friseur parkavenue
RIGHT: mein sohn parkavenue

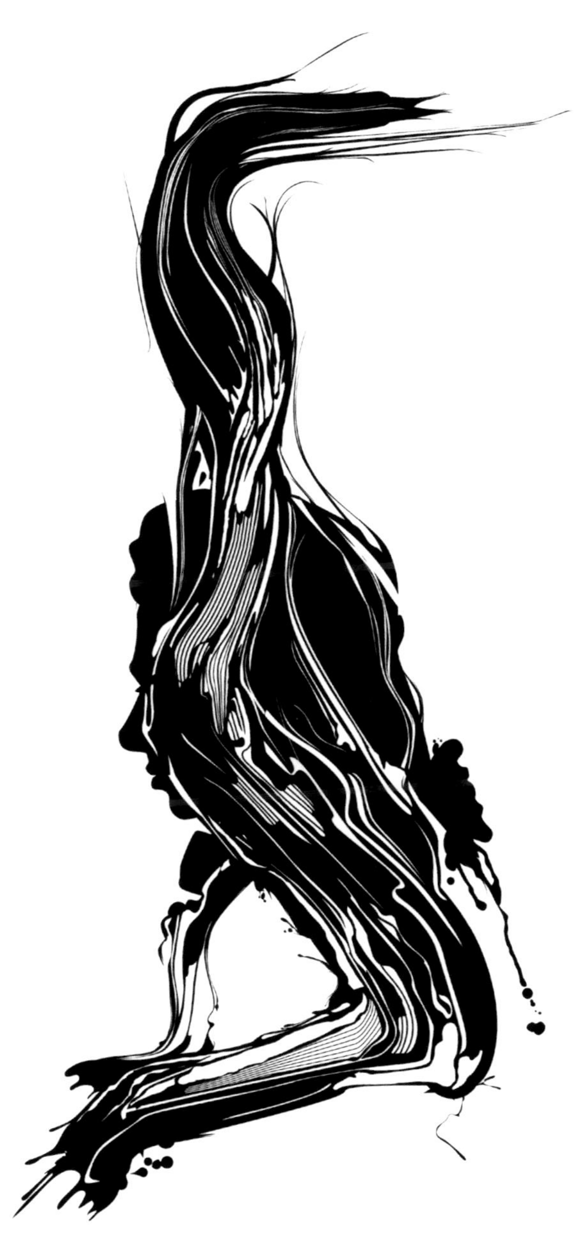

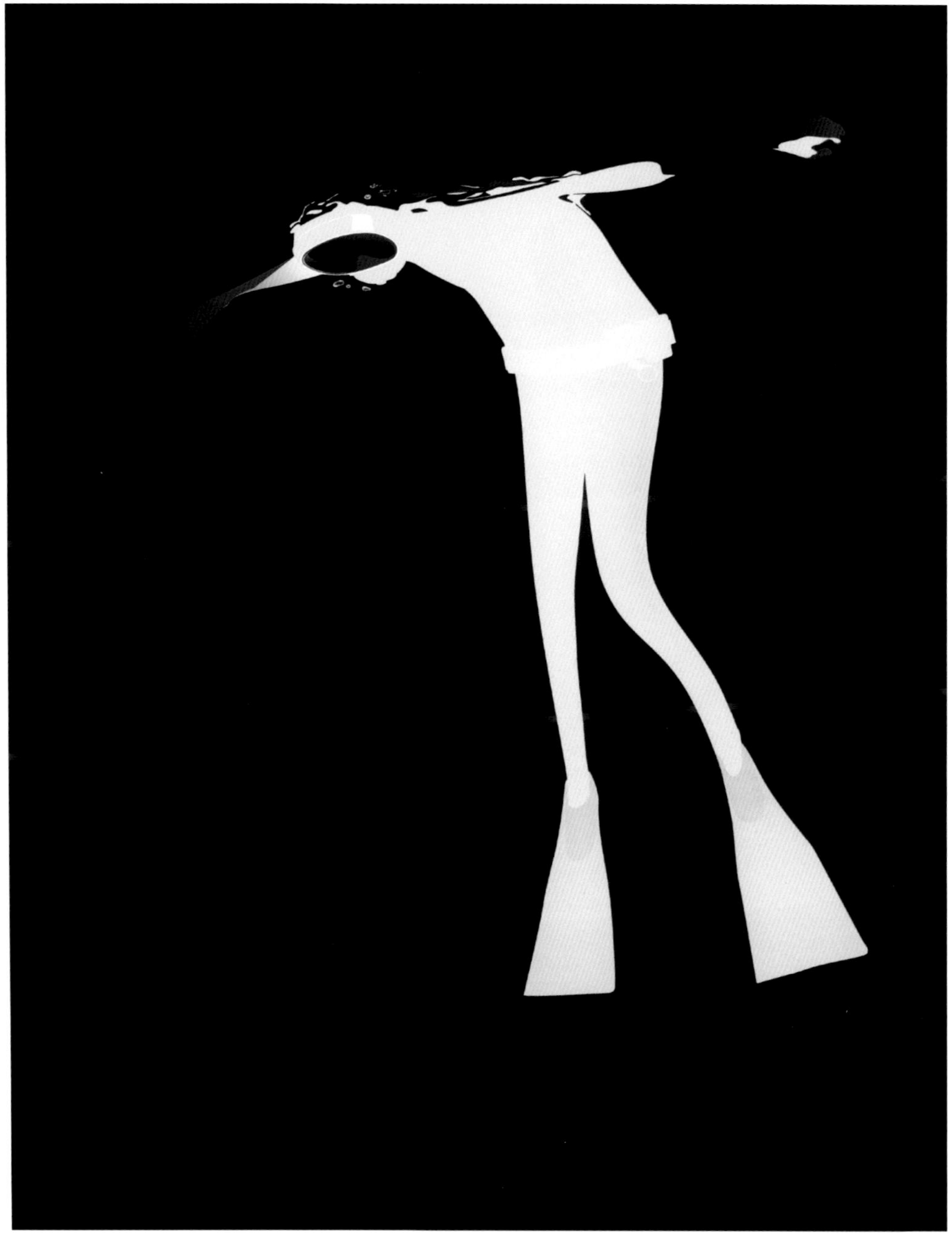

» KONSTANZE SCHÖFFL

NATIONALITY:	GERMAN
LOCATION:	AUGSBURG
PUBLICATIONS:	FREISTIL 3 | CASTLE MAGAZINE
EXHIBITIONS:	GALERIE AM UNTEREN SCHLÖSSCHEN – BOBINGEN KULTURHAUS – SENDEN
CONTACT:	WWW.KONNI-S.DE MAIL@KONNI-S.DE
TECHNIQUE:	DIGITAL COLLAGE | 3-D POP-UP | GLOSSY PRINTS NEON COLOR | STYROPOR | DEPA FIT
BORN:	1980

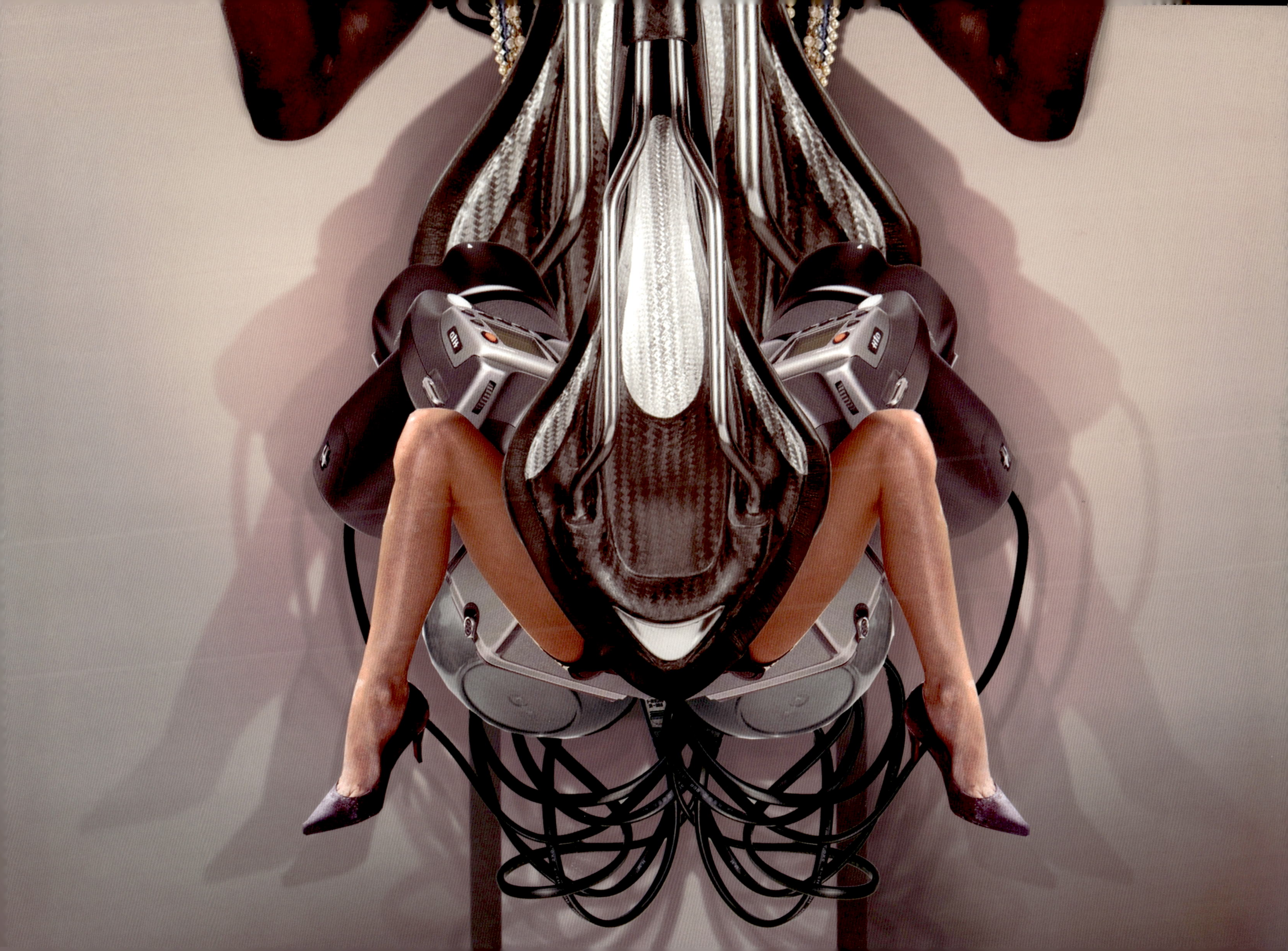

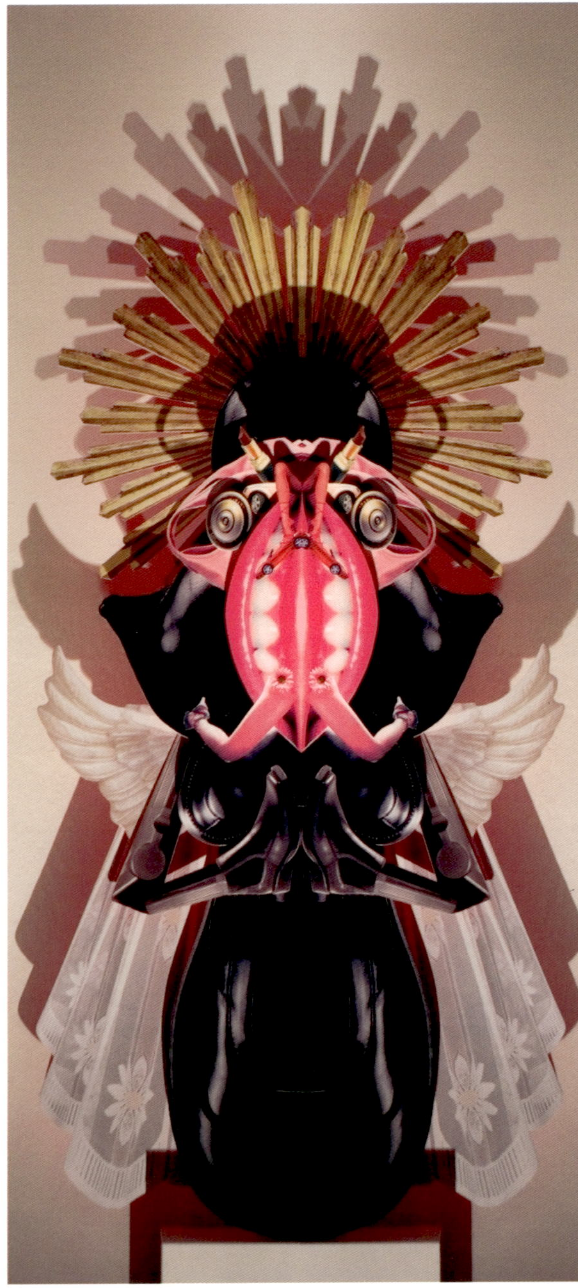

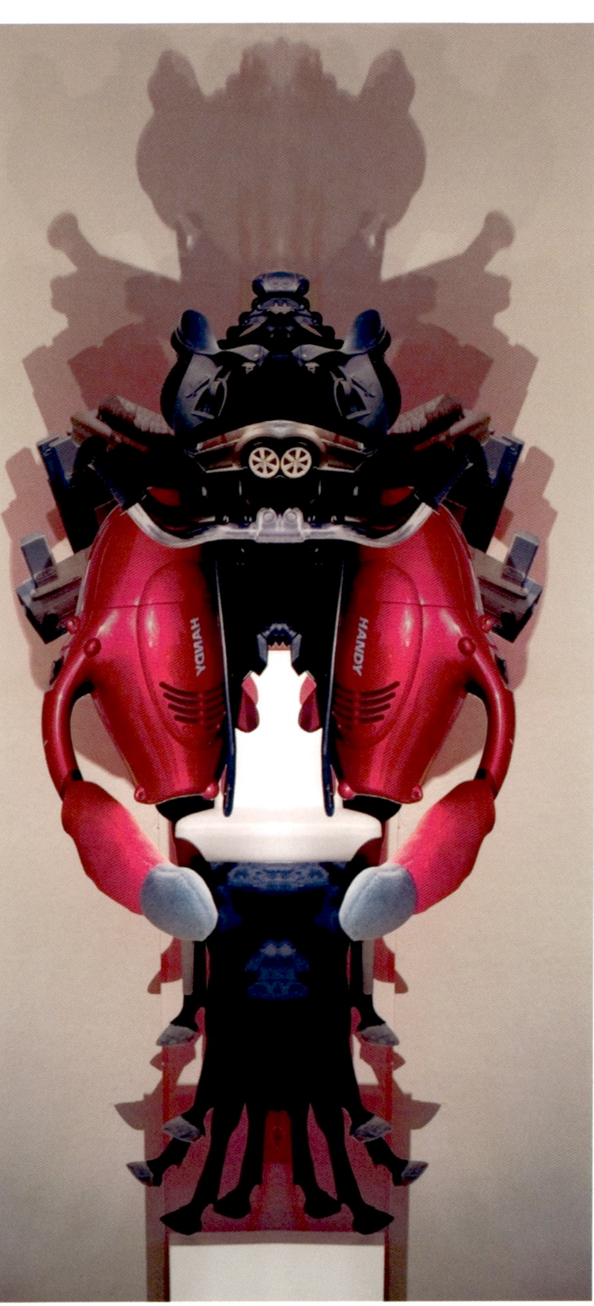

Illustration hat immer eine Funktion, wie zum Beispiel die Veranschaulichung eines Textes, und wendet sich meist an ein breites Publikum. Darum sollten Illustrationen eindeutig zu verstehen sein. Illustration ist also Mittel zum Zweck und wird unter anderem auch daran gemessen, ob sie ihren Zweck erfüllt. Freie Kunst hingegen ist nicht durch eine Funktion festgelegt und frei von jeglicher Zweckbindung. Sie kann ambivalent und verschlüsselt sein und muss nicht den Anspruch haben, verstanden zu werden. Zeitgenössische Kunst kann es sich leisten, auf Breitenwirkung zu verzichten und nur einen kleinen Kreis intellektueller und ästhetisch interessierter Personen anzusprechen. Die Arbeitsvoraussetzungen eines angewandten Künstlers und eines freien Künstlers sind deshalb unterschiedlich. Illustratoren werden in ihrer Arbeit mehr durch äußere Faktoren wie beispielsweise Auftraggeber, Vorgaben und Zielsetzungen bestimmt. Außerdem müssen sie sich immer wieder auf neue Aufgabenstellungen einlassen. Im Gegensatz dazu kann der freie Künstler sein Thema selbst wählen und sich ein ganzes Leben lang nur mit einer Idee auseinandersetzten. Zeitgenössische Kunst ist deshalb freier und persönlicher als Illustration. Unsere Gesellschaft trennt bis heute zwischen dem Berufsbild des Künstlers und dem des Illustrators, obwohl es auch viele Mischformen zwischen beiden Bereichen gibt und auch schon immer gab. Oft werden kreativ schaffende Menschen aufgrund ihres Werdegangs auf eines dieser Berufsbilder reduziert. So ist es etwa für eine Person, die nicht an der Akademie studiert hat, schwer, in der Kunstszene Beachtung zu finden. Allerdings kann man beobachten, dass sich die Grenze zwischen den beiden Bereichen immer mehr auflöst. So waren in den letzten Jahren immer häufiger kommerzielle Arbeiten in Galerien zu sehen – ein Zeichen dafür, dass sich die Kunstszene auch für angewandte Kunst öffnet, ebenso wie Werbeagenturen immer häufiger Interesse an freien Künstlern zeigen.

INTRODUCTION: product-nr.: dkf j06 008
RIGHT: produkt-nr.: dkf j06 004
LEFT: produkt-nr.: dkf j06 001

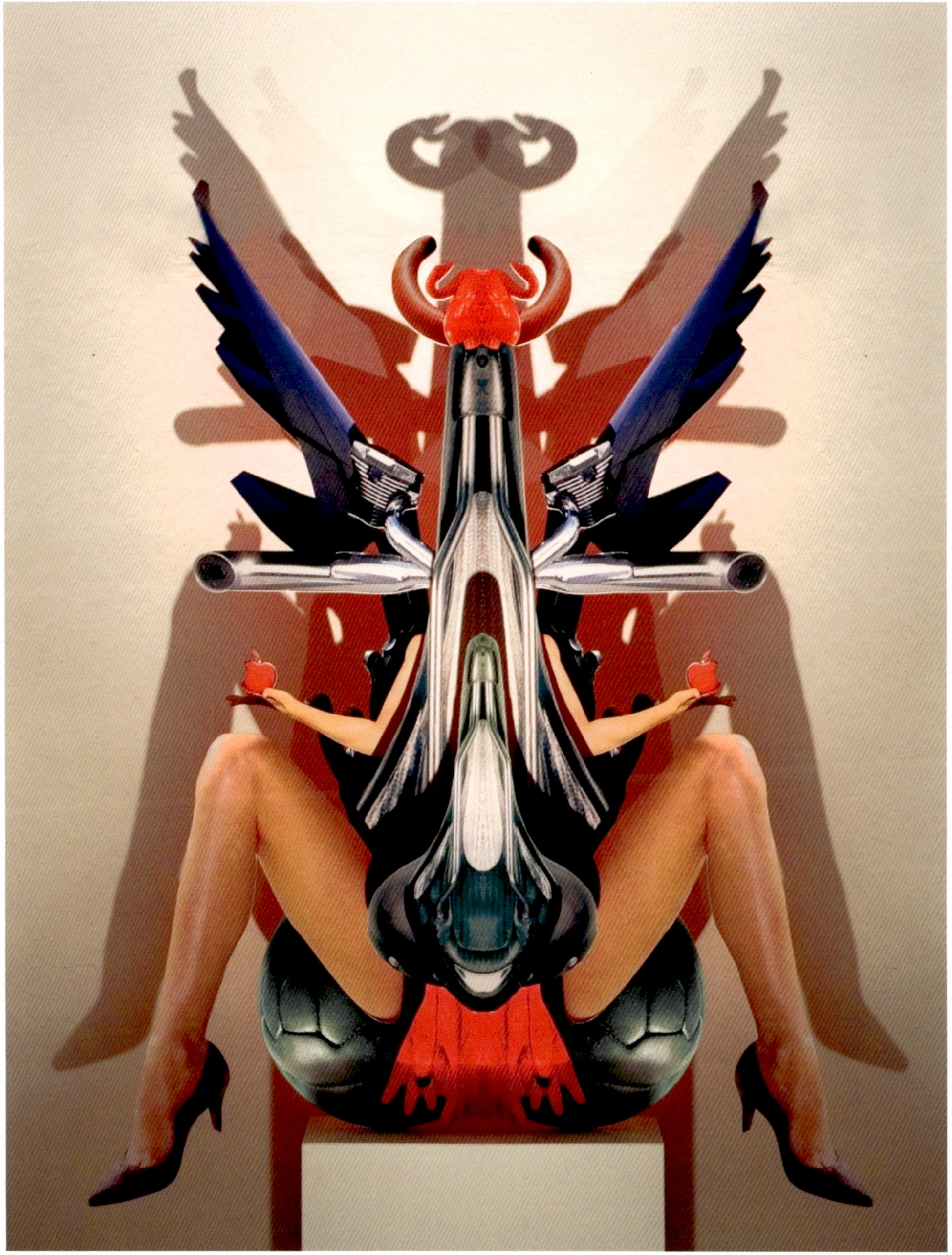

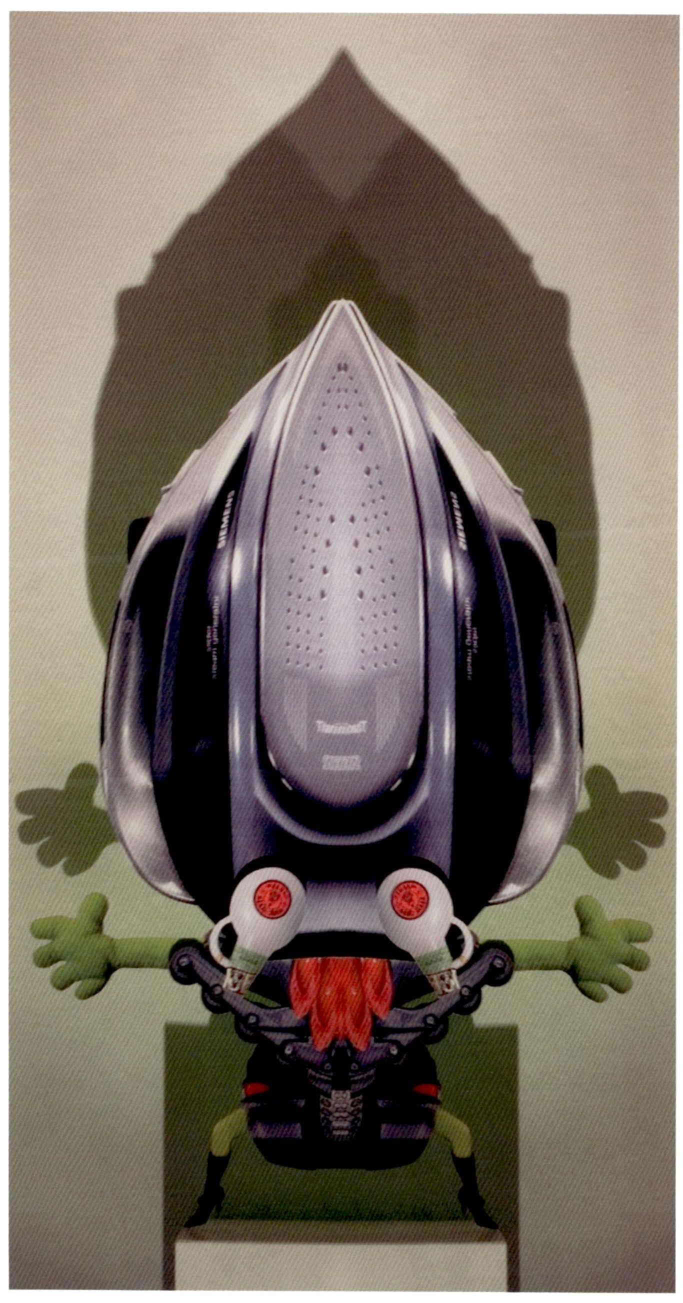

LEFT: produkt-nr.: dkf j06 003
RIGHT: produkt-nr.: dkf j06 002

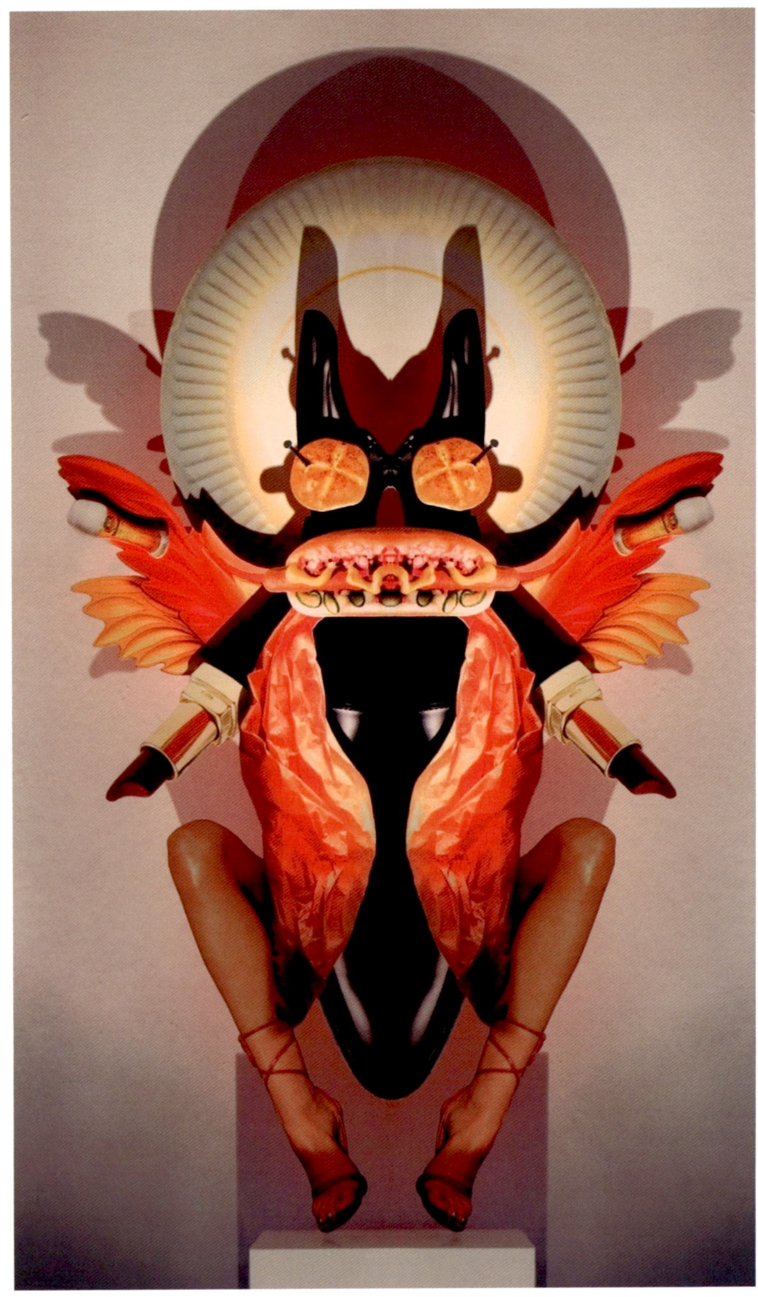

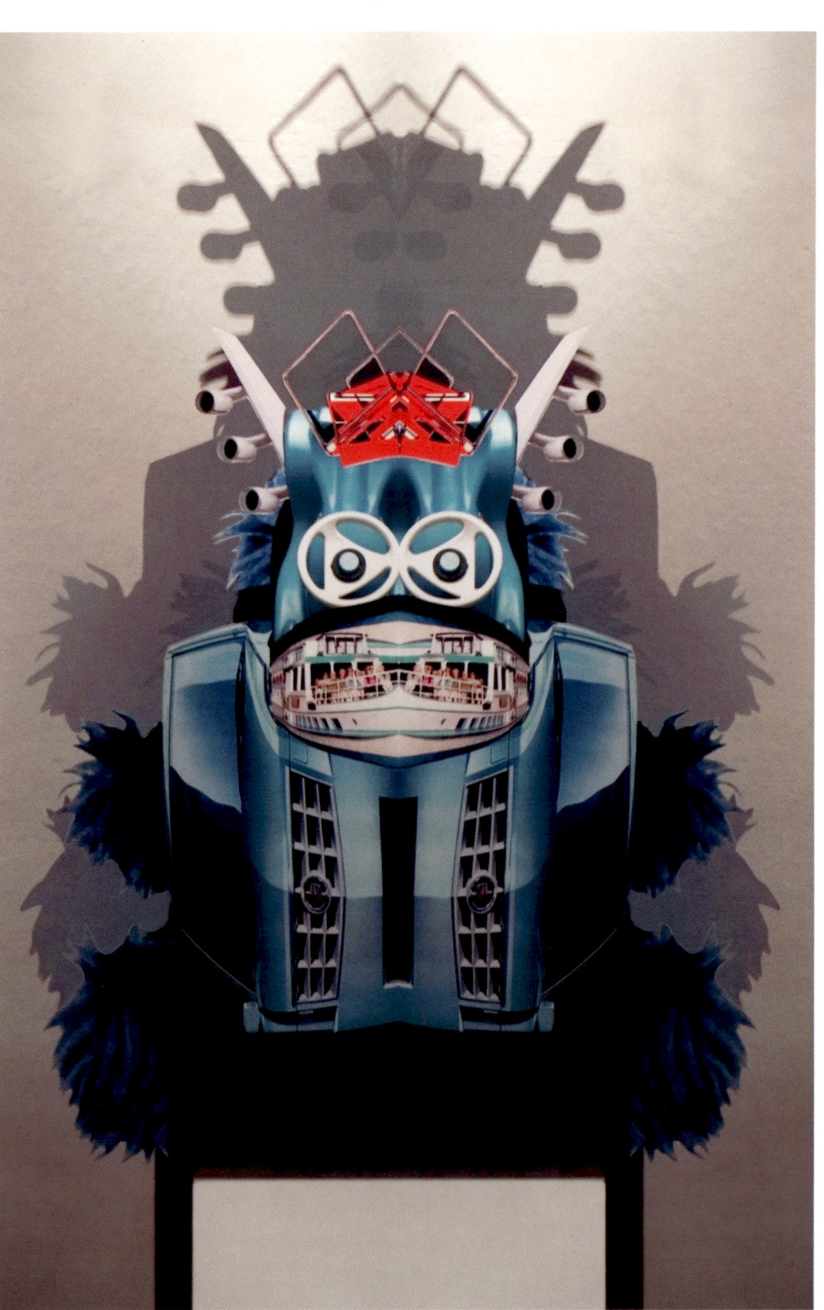

LEFT PAGE:
LEFT: produkt-nr.: dkf j06 006
RIGHT: produkt-nr.: dkf j06 005
RIGHT PAGE: produkt-nr.: dkf j06 007

EN In my opinion illustration is an artistic discipline that could also be called applied arts. An illustrator is therefore also an artist who is facing certain restrictions and works under different conditions. Illustration always follows a function, like the visualization of a text, and attempts to appeal to a large audience. Therefore an illustration should be easy to read. Illustration is a means to an end and is judged mainly by whether or not it serves its purpose. Independent art is not defined by a function, and does not have to fulfill a purpose. Art can be ambivalent and enigmatic and does not need to be easily comprehensible. Contemporary art can afford not to appeal to the masses but rather appeal to a small group of people who are intellectually and aesthetically interested. For that reason the working conditions of an applied artist and an independent artist are different. The work of illustrators is more defined by external factors like the employer, guidelines and objectives. Furthermore, illustrators have to face different objectives each time. The independent artist on the other hand can choose his own subject and dedicated the rest of his life to it. Contemporary art offers more liberty and is much more personal than illustration. Our society differentiates between the job profiles of the artist and the illustrator, even though there are and always have been many things that they have in common. Creative people are often allowed only one of the two labels dependent on their professional background and career. It is for example quite hard for someone who has not studied at an academy of fine arts to gain attention in the art scene. Nevertheless, the fine line between the two is gradually dissolving. In recent years a growing number of commercial works have been on display in galleries which is a sign that the art scene is opening itself up to applied arts, just as design agencies are showing a growing interest in independent artists.

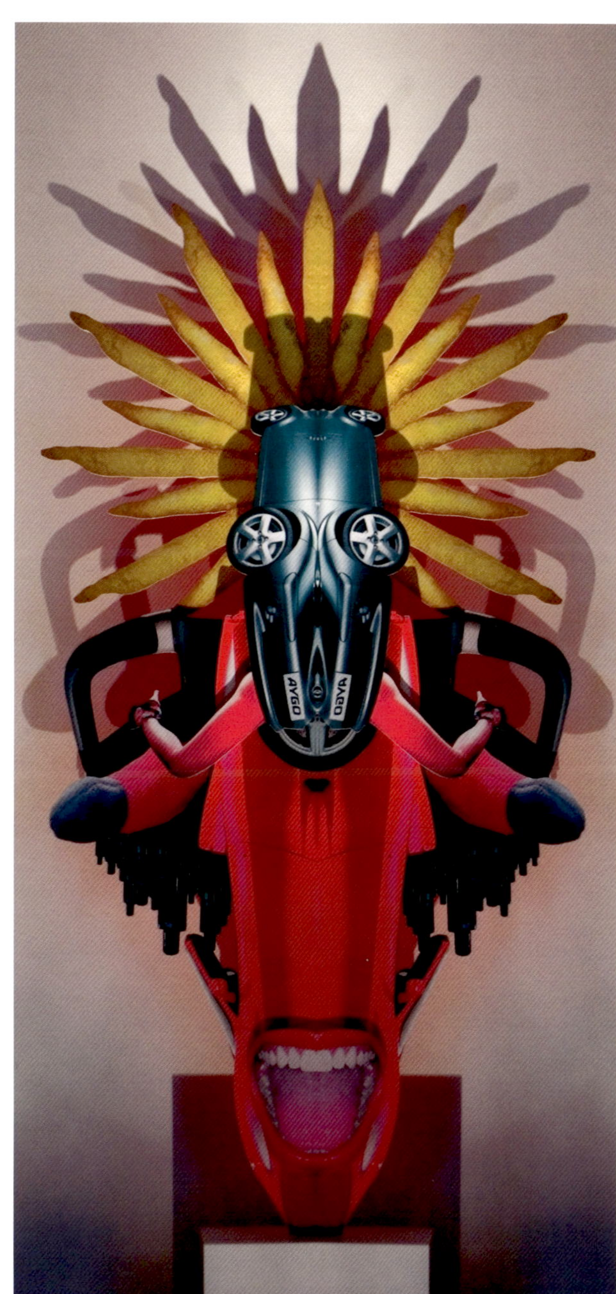

OS GÊMEOS [GUSTAVO & OTAVIO PANDOLFO]

NATIONALITY:	BRAZILIAN
LOCATION:	SAO PAULO & WORLDWIDE
PUBLICATIONS:	ASSUM PRETO, 2008 | ISBN 978-88-95059-05-1
REFERENCES:	YELLOW & RED
EXHIBITIONS:	STREET ART | TATE MODERN – LONDON 2008 THE FLOWERS IN THIS GARDEN WERE PLANTED BY MY GRANDPARENTS | MUSEUM HET DOMEIN – SITTARD NETHERLANDS 2007 ASSUM PRETO | GALLERIA PATRICIA ARMOCIDA – MILAN ITALY 2007 O PEIXE QUE COMIA ESTRELAS CADENTES | GALERIA FORTES VILACA – SAO PAULO 2006 CAVALEIRO MARGINAL | DEITCH PROJECTS – NEW YORK 2005
CONTACT:	WWW.LOST.ART.BR/OSGEMEOS.HTM
TECHNIQUE:	GRAFFITI
BORN:	1974

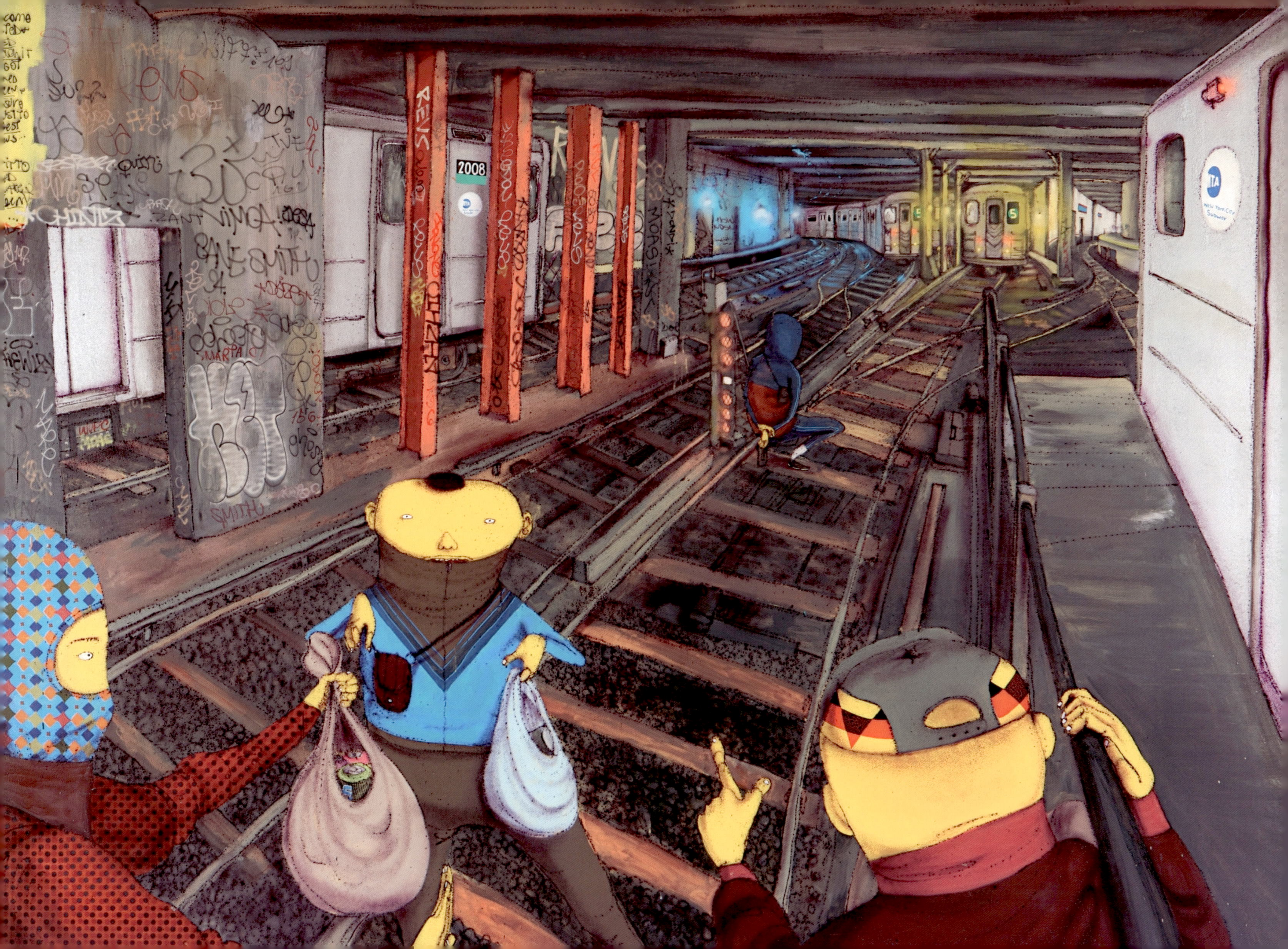
2008
MTA

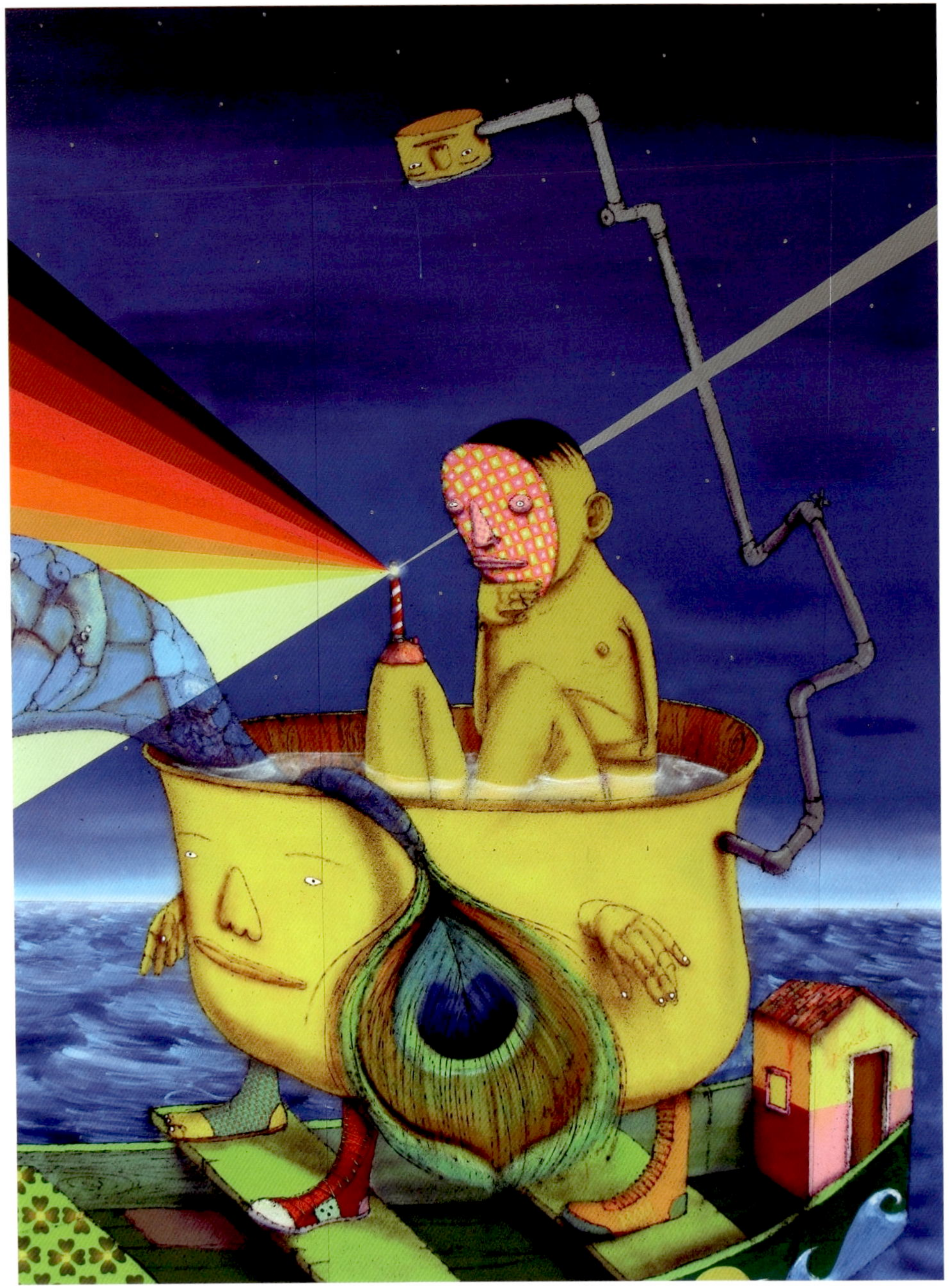

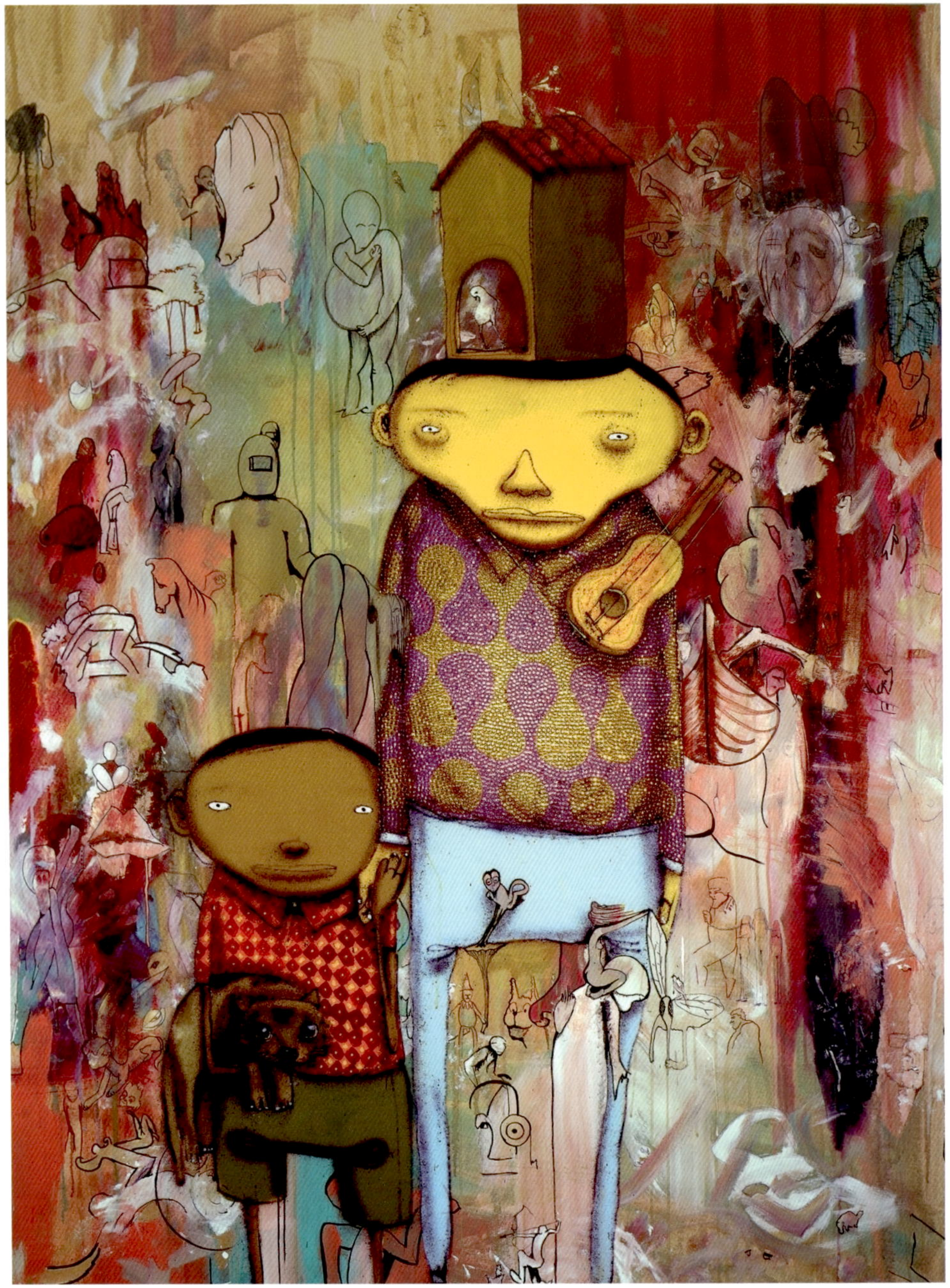

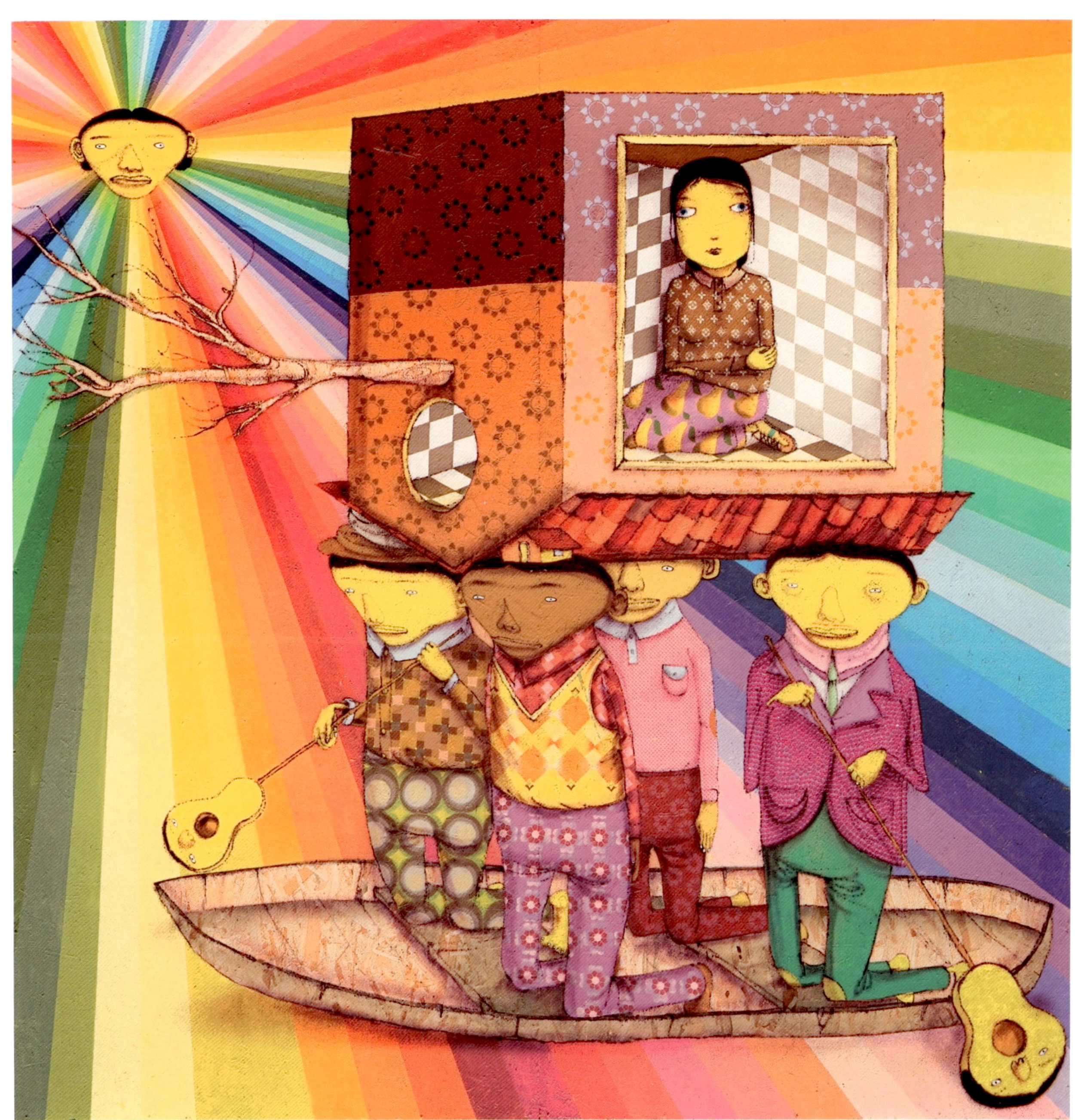

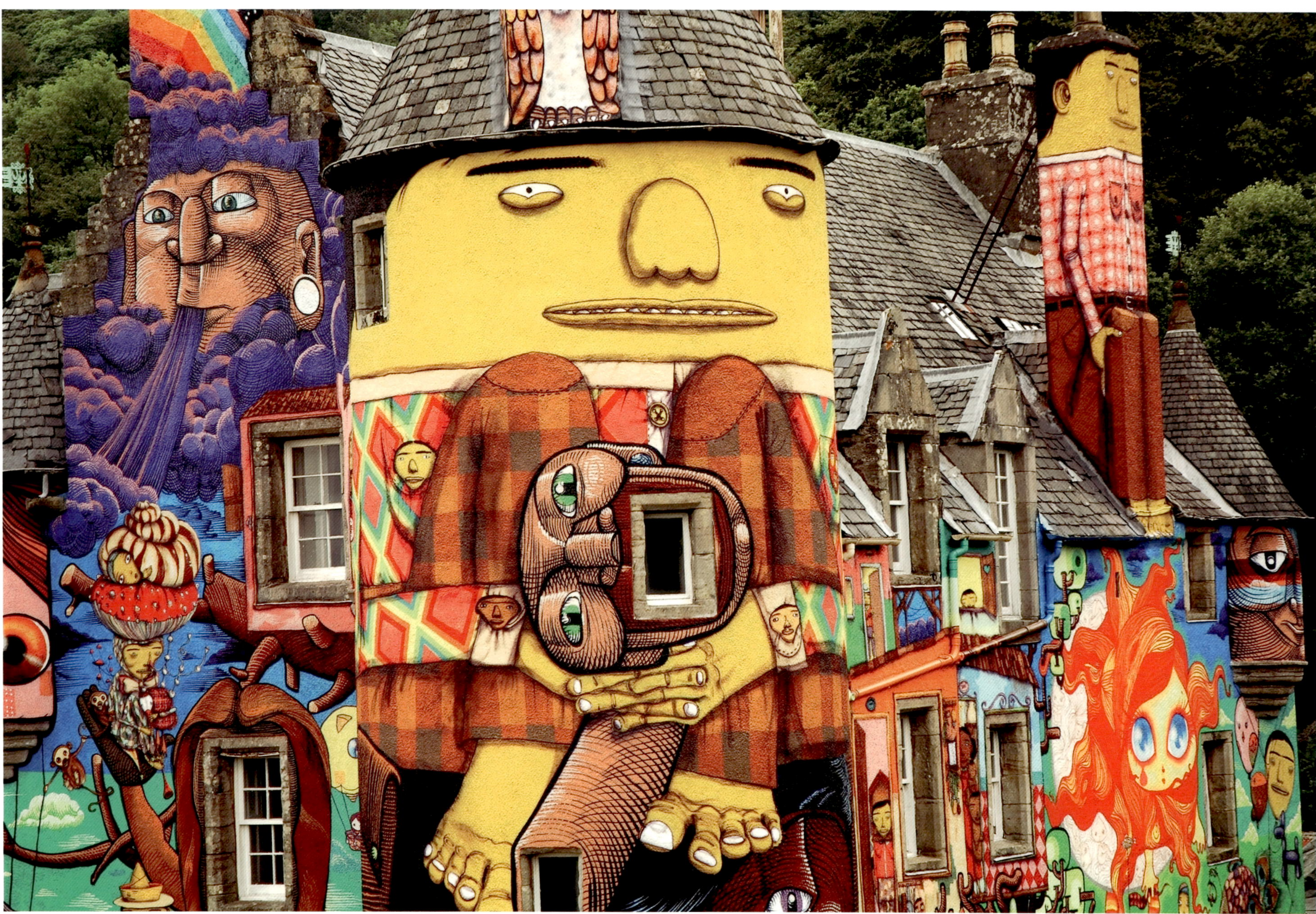

DE Hass und Liebe, der Kampf ums Überleben in unserem Land, wo Kinder in den Straßen betteln, wo du der Regierung scheißegal bist - alles um uns herum beeinflusst uns. Wir können nicht einfach vor dem Fernseher herumsitzen, wenn wir Dinge sehen, die uns zwingen zu reagieren, zu handeln. Die Momente scheinen ewig, wenn wir malen ohne zu denken, in Kleidung voller Farbe auf Leitern steigen und der Polizei lügen auftischen. Regeln sind dazu gemacht, gebrochen zu werden. Für all die Dinge, die wir in uns haben, brauchen wir ein Ventil. Wir wollen lernen, reisen, entdecken, andere Künstler treffen, einfach weiter tun, was uns gut vorkommt, egal was andere davon halten. Brüder sein und alles in der Welt teilen. Alles in diesem spiel ist Teil der Show und wird mitbenutzt – es ist alles eins. Wenn wir etwas tun wollen, ist es schon getan. Die Zeit zum Malen ist uns heilig. Wir wissen nichts. Vielleicht werden wir eines Tages aufwachen und merken, dass alles nur ein Traum war. So navigieren wir im Nebel umher, wie Papierbote im Rinnstein. Aber was ist schon ein normales Leben? Morgen sehen wir weiter – O AMANHA AGENTE VE AMANHA

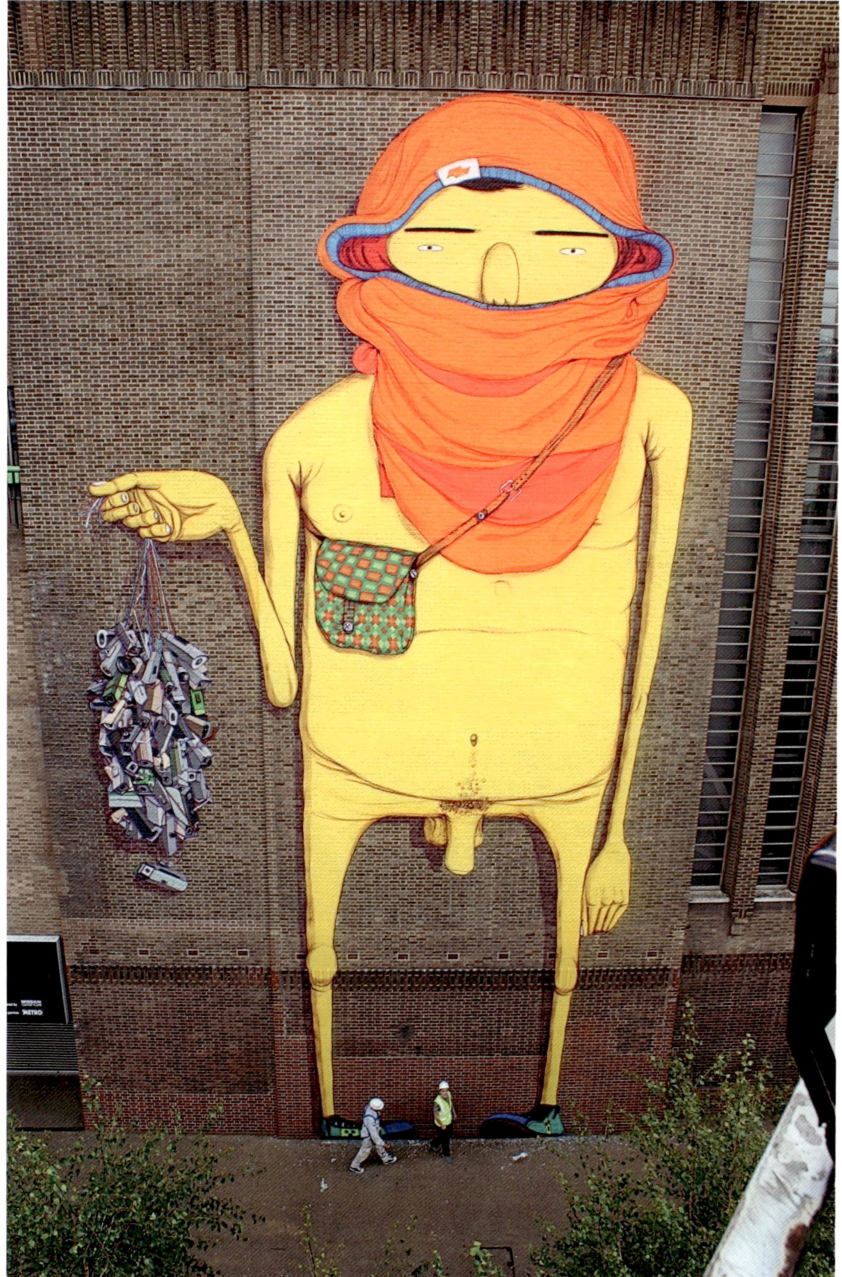

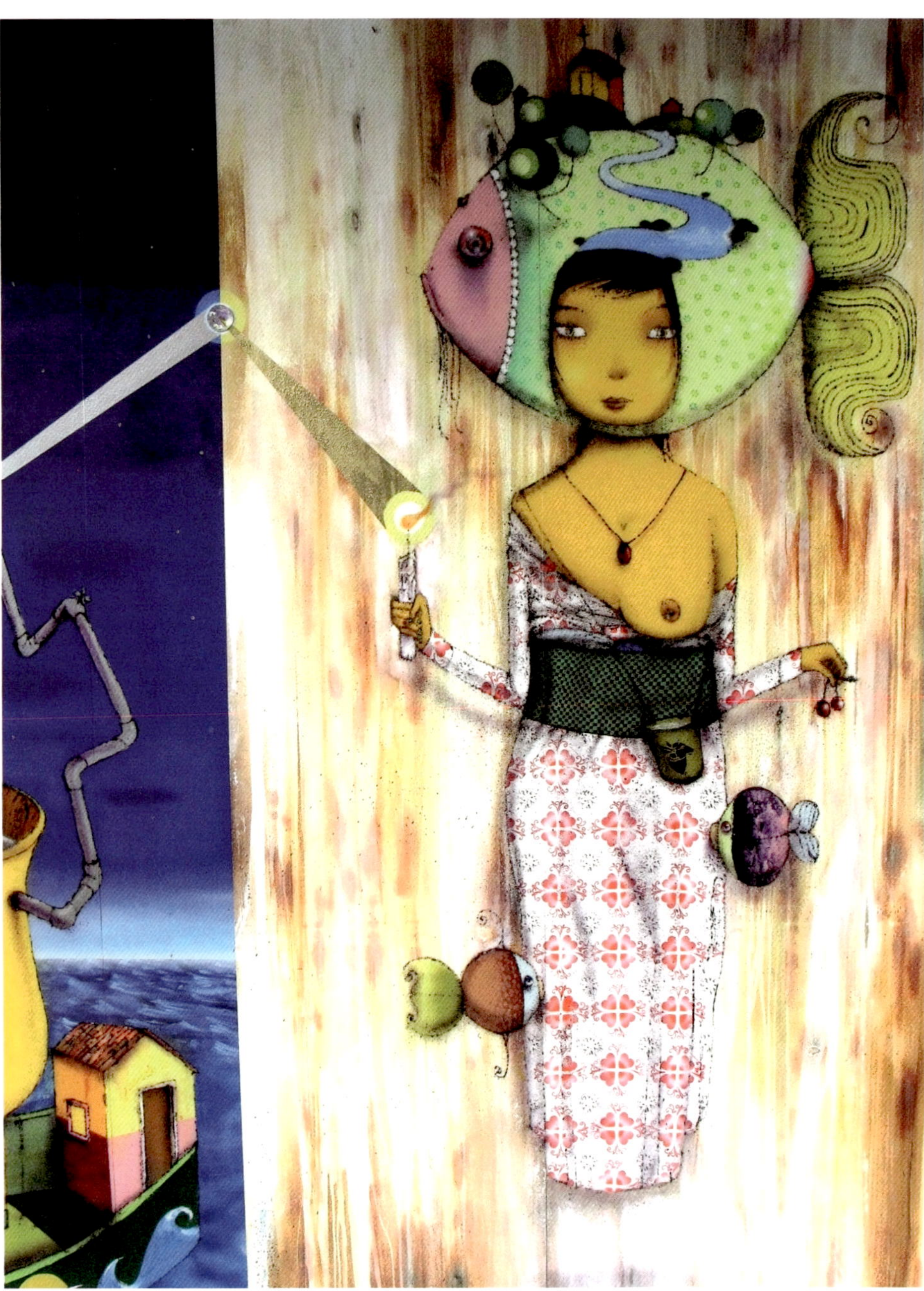

EN Hate and love, the struggle to survive in this country, where children go begging in the streets, where the gouvernment doesn't care about you at all – everything around us is an inspiration for us. We just cannot relax in front of our TV-screen, when we see things that force us to react – to act. The moments seem endless while we're painting without thinking, climbing ladders dressed in clothes full of paint, making jokes of the police. Because rules are meant to be broken. There has to be an outlet for all those things we have inside. We like to learn, travel, explore, meet fellow artists, simply go on doing what feels good, no matter what others might think about it. Being brothers, we share everything this world has to offer. Whatever we come across in this game may be used as part of the show – it's all one. When we feel like doing something, it's already done. Our painting-time feels holy. We don't know a thing. Maybe we're going to wake up one day to realize it was only a dream. So we go on navigating around this misty world, like paper boats on a streamlet. But what's a normal life anyway? Tomorrow we'll see tomorrow – O AMANHA AGENTE VE AMANHA.

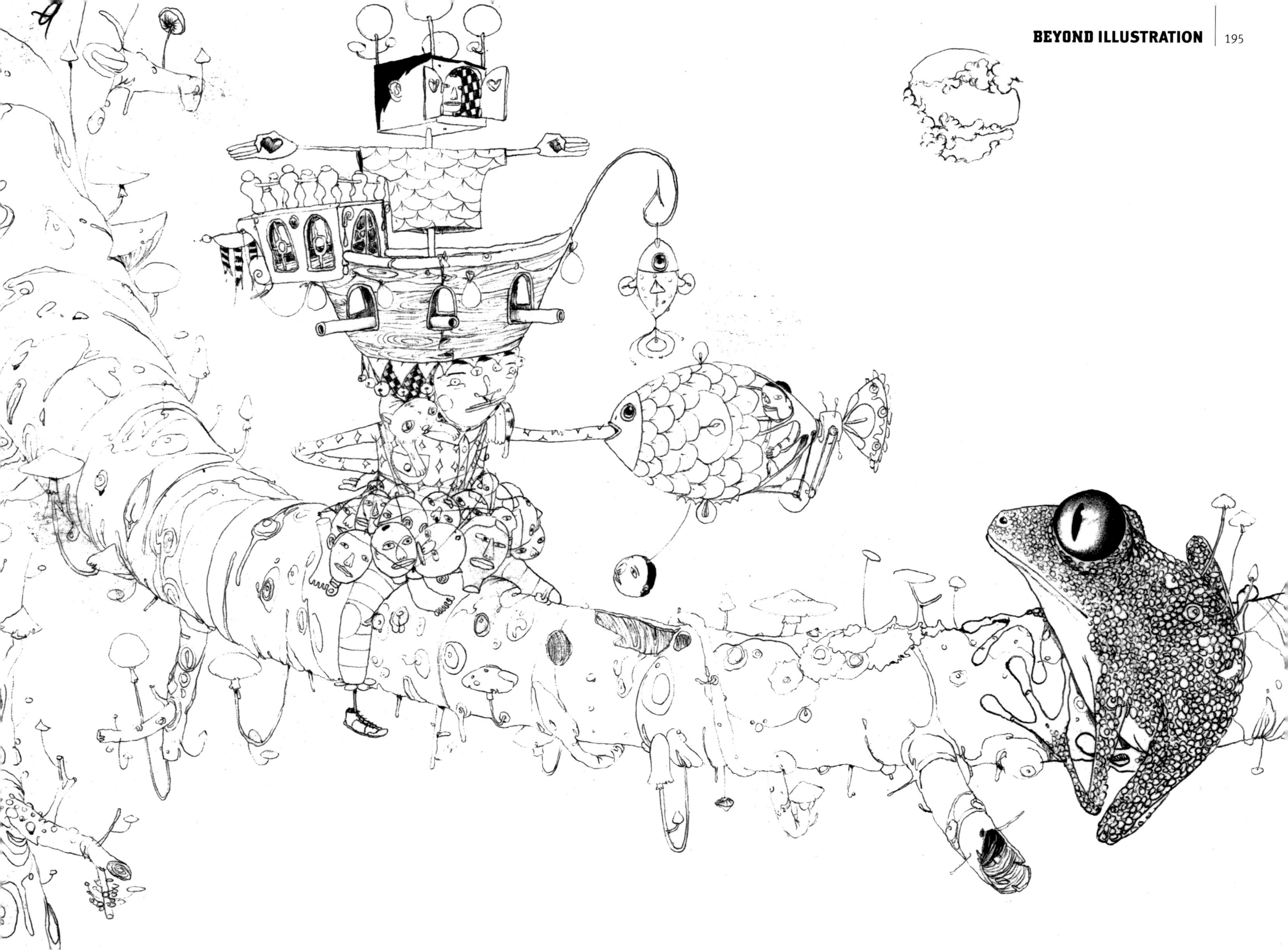

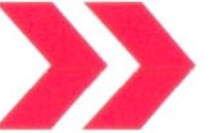 SPECIAL THANKS TO

Marion Appelt | Proofreading
Christophe Fricker | Translation
Fred Kinzel | Translation
Dr. Klaus Balik | Translation
Carmen Tromballa
Christoph Sauter
Kara Walsh
Ray Tischler
Wolf-Dietrich Lorenz
Wolfgang Lehnerer
Sebastian Bühler
Niklas Treugut
Roland Herzog
Martin Nothelfer
Harry Ardeias
Rüdiger Wolf
Jürgen Blümlein
Thomas Ingmire
Andrea Kantioler
Oliver Sommer
Christian Hundertmark
Prof. Mike Loos
Michael Zöbisch
Robert Kaltenhäuser
Markus Christl
Jitter Magazin
Görres10 Gallery

and all contributing artists in over 3 years of "castlemagazine"

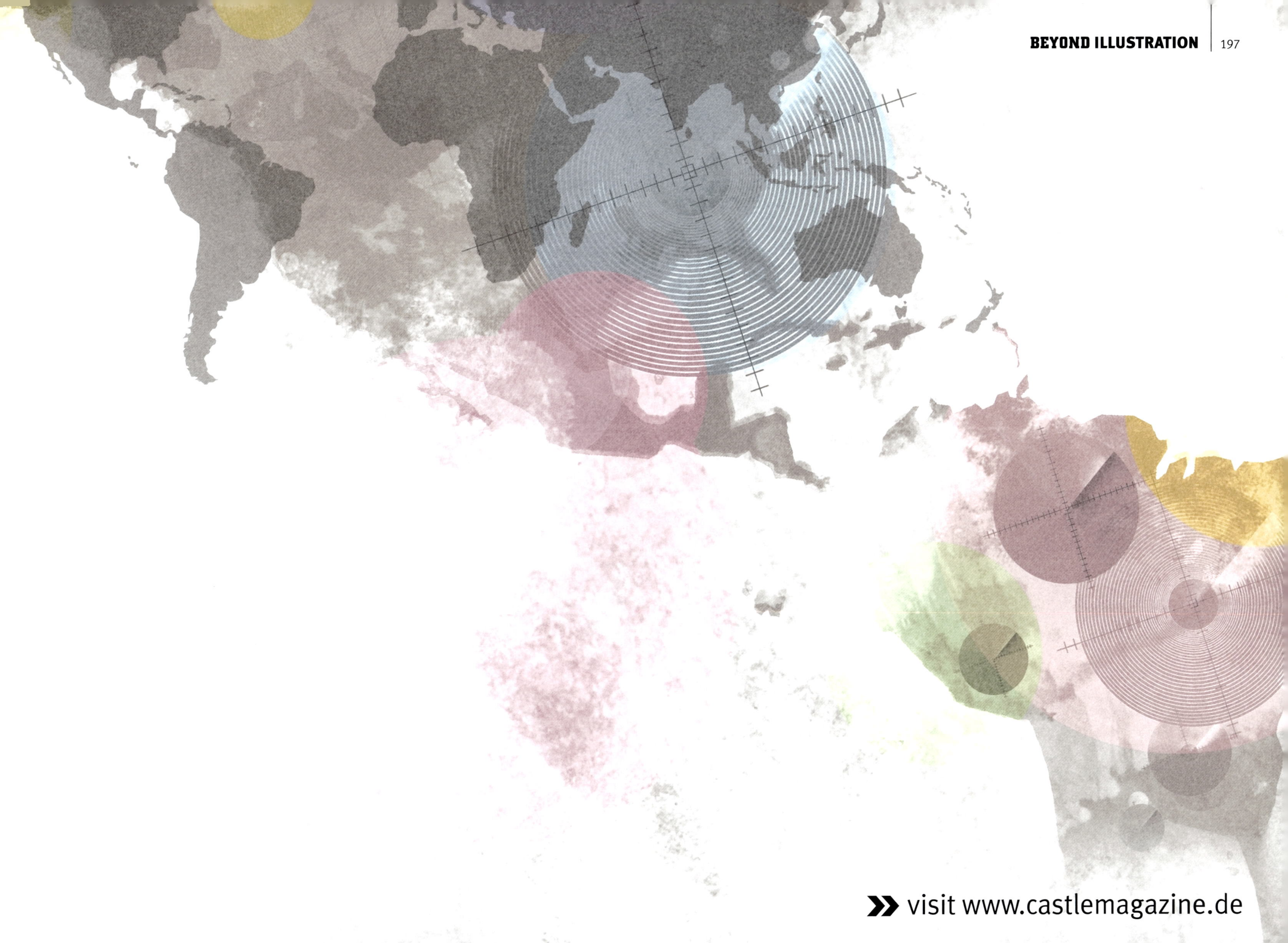

JOYNER ERIC
www.ericjoyner.com
phone 415.305.3992 (U.S.A.)
phone 415.074.0708 (U.S.A.)

OS GÊMEOS
www.lost.art.br/osgemeos.htm

REVOY ANTOINE
www.revoy.net
antoine@revoy.net

SCHIEDON FONS
www.fonztv.nl
office@fonztv.nl
phone +31 6 41555017

SCHÖFFL KONSTANZE
www.konni-s.de
mail@konni-s.de

SCHÜSSLER DANIEL
www.galerielichtpunkt.de
www.danielschuessler.blogspot.com
daniel.schuessler@gmx.de

STARJUMP [ALEXANDER ZÖBISCH]
www.starjumpentertainment.blogspot.com
alex.zoebisch@gmx.de

STYLEFIGHTING [HARTL PATRICK]
www.stylefighting.de
hartl@stylefighting.de

TSUTSUMI DAISUKE
www.simplestroke.com
dice@simplestroke.com

URBAN CLIFFORD
cliffordurban@web.de

VANDATA
phone +49 (0) 176 450 32 907
mickey@vandata.de

VIERFARBRAUM
www.vierfarbraum.de
info@vierfarbraum.de

PUBLISHING PROGRAM

http://www.stylefile.de
http://www.publikat.de

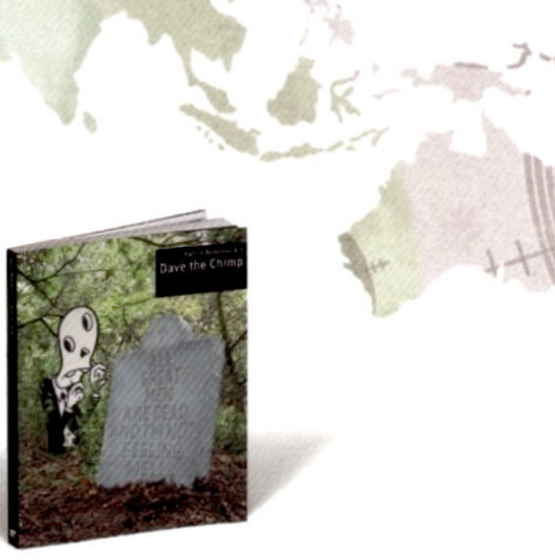

» DAVE THE CHIMP
PART OF REBELLION #2
05.2009
ISBN: 978-3-939566-17-5
C100
PAPERBACK. 15×18,8 CM. 128 PAGES

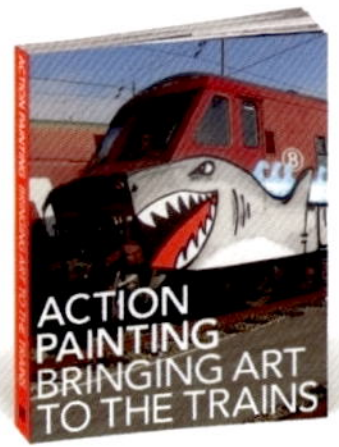

» ACTION PAINTING
BRINGING ART TO THE TRAINS
05.2009
ISBN: 978-3-939566-25-0
KRISTIAN KUTSCHERA
PAPERBACK. 21×26,5 CM. 216 PAGES

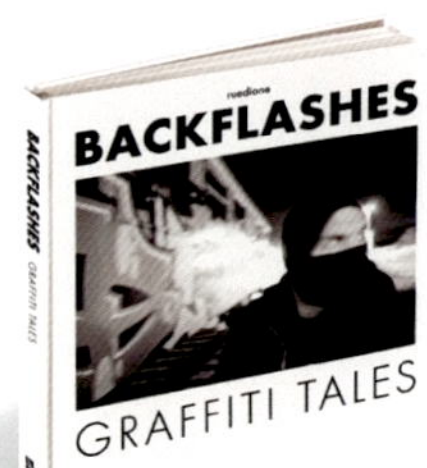

» BACKFLASHES
GRAFFITI TALES
04.2009
ISBN: 978-3-939566-21-2
RUEDIONE
HARDCOVER. 28×28 CM. 228 PAGES

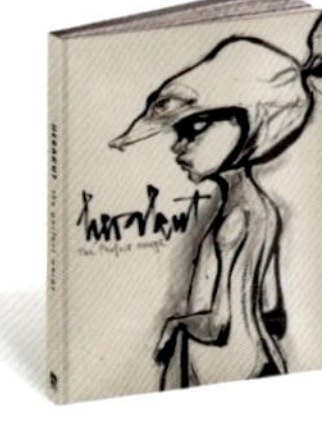

» HERAKUT
THE PERFECT MERGE
04.2009
ISBN: 978-3-939566-24-3
JASMIN SIDDIQUI, FALK LEHMANN
FLEXCOVER. 21×26 CM. 208 PAGES

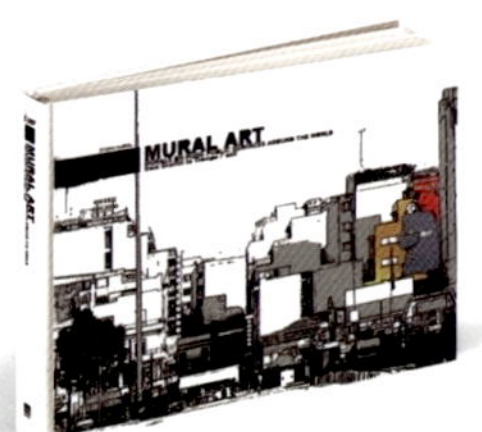

» MURAL ART
MURALS ON HUGE PUBLIC SURFACES AROUND THE WORLD
11.2008
ISBN: 978-3-939566-22-9
KIRIAKOS IOSIFIDIS
HARDCOVER. 30×21 CM. 288 PAGES

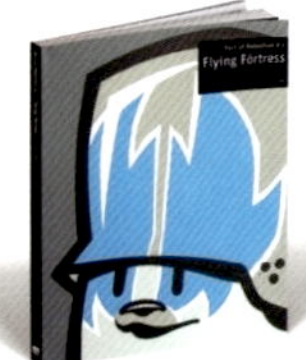

» FLYING FÖRTRESS
PART OF REBELLION #1
11.2008
ISBN: 978-3-939566-16-8
C100
PAPERBACK. 15×18,8 CM. 128 PAGES

» BEST OF STYLEFILE #2
THE BEST OF ISSUE 11-20
10.2008
ISBN: 978-3-939566-13-7
OLE ZIMMERMANN, MARKUS CHRISTL
PAPERBACK. 23×16 CM. 256 PAGES

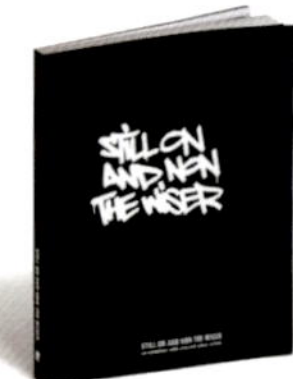

» STILL ON AND NON THE WISER
AN EXIBITION WITH SELECTED URBAN ARTISTS
07.2008
ISBN: 978-3-939566-20-5
RIK REINKING
PAPERBACK. 16,5×23,5CM. 144 PAGES

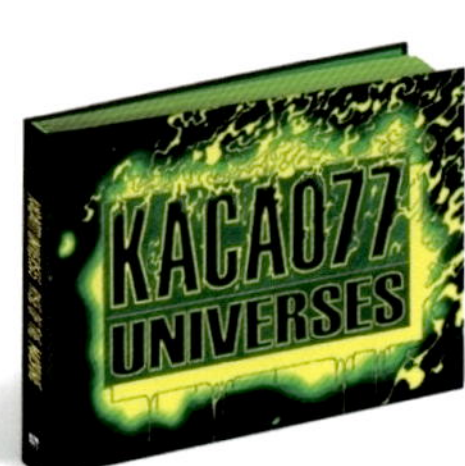

» KACA077 UNIVERSES
RISE OF THE MACHINE
04.2008
ISBN: 978-3-9809909-8-1
MARKUS CHRISTL
HARDCOVER. 29×21 CM. 192 PAGES

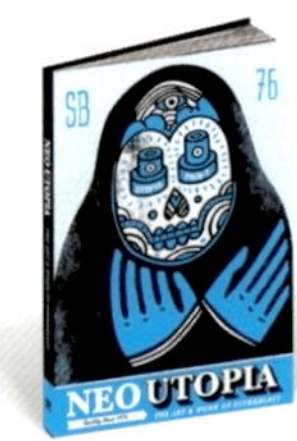

» NEO UTOPIA
THE ART AND WORK OF SUPERBLAST
04.2008
ISBN: 978-3-939566-11-3
MANUEL OSTERHOLT
FLEXCOVER. 18,5×27 CM. 160 PAGES

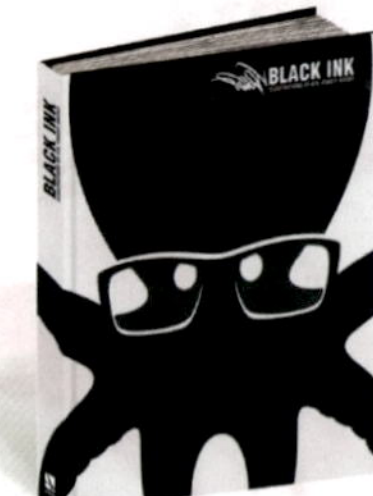

» BLACK INK
ILLUSTRATIONS OF ATA TOAST BOZACI
10.2007
ISBN: 978-3-939566-06-9
ATA BOZACI
HARDCOVER. 24×28 CM. 240 PAGES

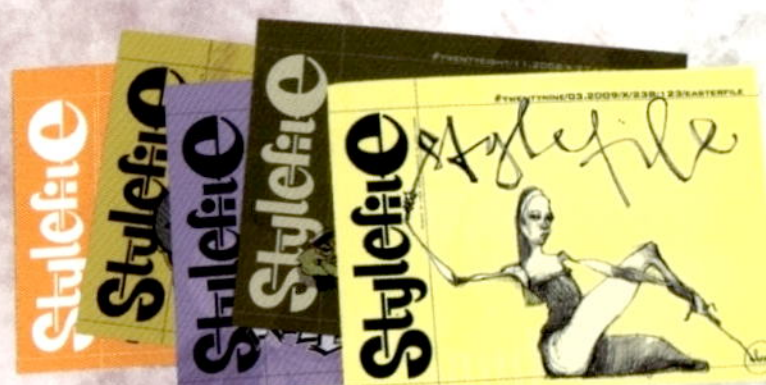

» STYLEFILE
GRAFFITI MAGAZINE
out every march, july and november.
documenting in high quality the graffiti movement all over the planet.
for details and further information check
http://www.stylefile.de